Kanra: Not that much, really!
Oh, how about this?
There's this old urban legend,
see...

Setton: Oh, I know what you're
talking about.
But that's not an urban legend
or anything...

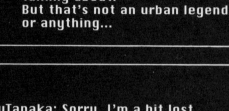

TarouTanaka: Sorry, I'm a bit lost...

Kanra: You've never heard of this,
TarouTanaka-san?

TarouTanaka: ??

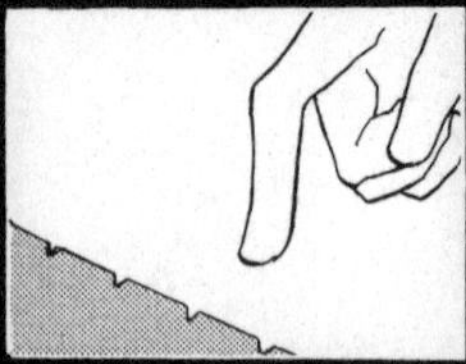

ABOUT THE BLACK RIDER.

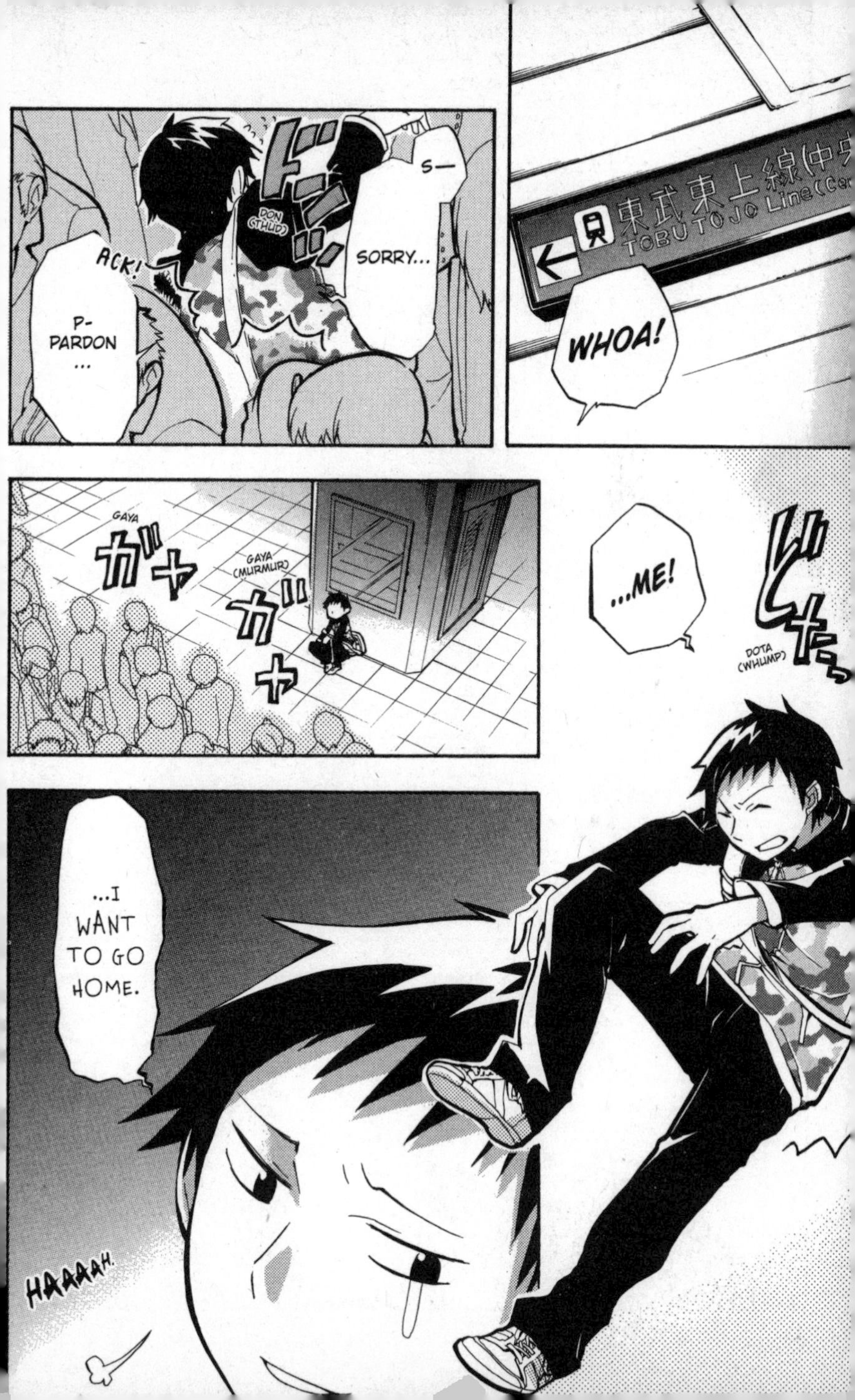
東武東上線
TOBU TOJO Line
WHOA!
S—
SORRY...
DON (THUD)
ACK!
P-PARDON ...
...ME!
DOTA (WHUMP)
GAYA
GAYA (MURMUR)
...I WANT TO GO HOME.
HAAAAH.

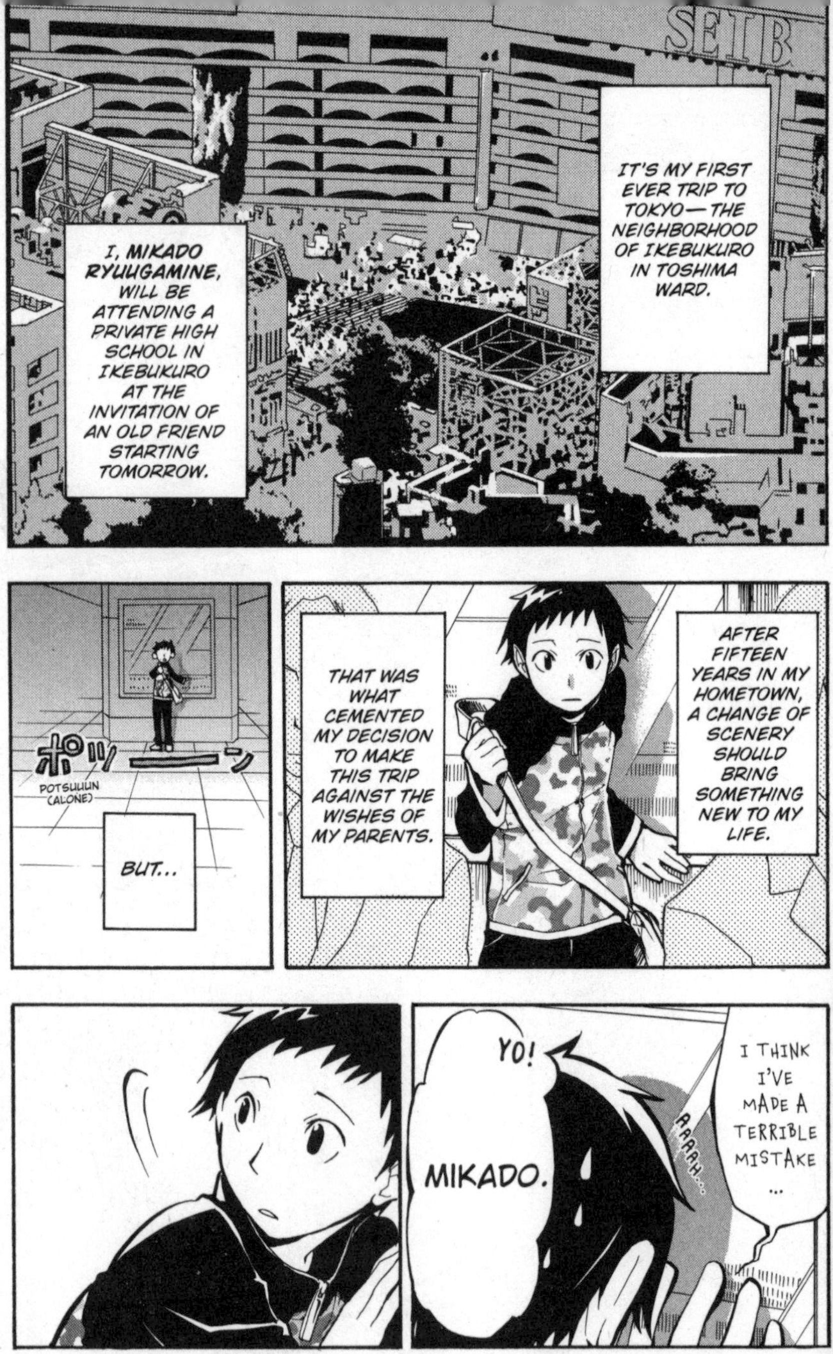
SEIB
IT'S MY FIRST EVER TRIP TO TOKYO—THE NEIGHBORHOOD OF IKEBUKURO IN TOSHIMA WARD.
I, MIKADO RYUUGAMINE, WILL BE ATTENDING A PRIVATE HIGH SCHOOL IN IKEBUKURO AT THE INVITATION OF AN OLD FRIEND STARTING TOMORROW.
AFTER FIFTEEN YEARS IN MY HOMETOWN, A CHANGE OF SCENERY SHOULD BRING SOMETHING NEW TO MY LIFE.
THAT WAS WHAT CEMENTED MY DECISION TO MAKE THIS TRIP AGAINST THE WISHES OF MY PARENTS.
ポツーン
POTSUUUN (ALONE)
BUT...
I THINK I'VE MADE A TERRIBLE MISTAKE ...
AAAAH...
YO!
MIKADO.

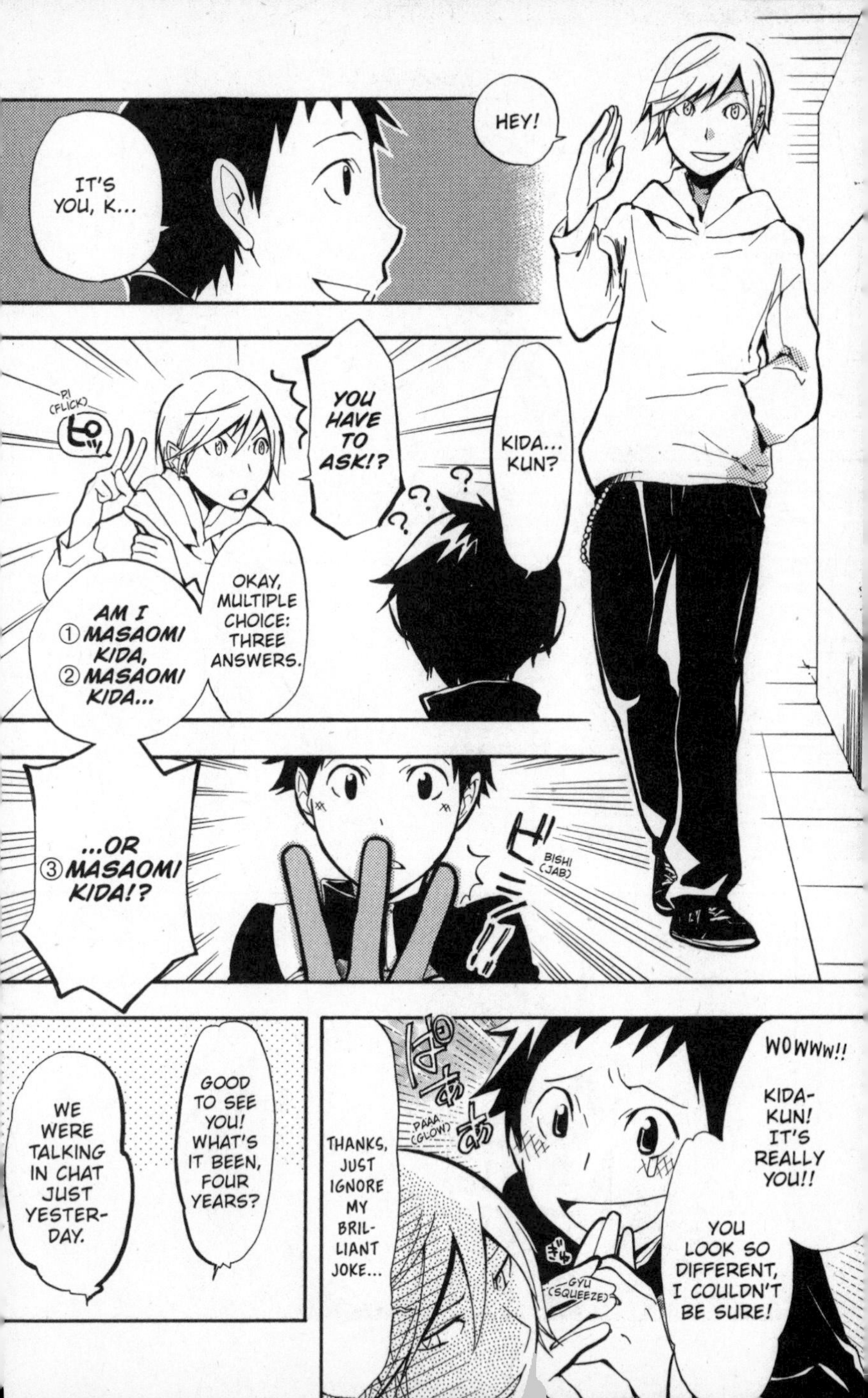

HEY!
IT'S YOU, K...
KIDA... KUN?
YOU HAVE TO ASK!?
PI (FLICK)
OKAY, MULTIPLE CHOICE: THREE ANSWERS.
AM I ① MASAOMI KIDA, ② MASAOMI KIDA...
...OR ③ MASAOMI KIDA!?
BISHI (JAB)
WOWWW!!
KIDA-KUN! IT'S REALLY YOU!!
PAAA (GLOW)
YOU LOOK SO DIFFERENT, I COULDN'T BE SURE!
GYU (SQUEEZE)
THANKS, JUST IGNORE MY BRIL-LIANT JOKE...
GOOD TO SEE YOU! WHAT'S IT BEEN, FOUR YEARS?
WE WERE TALKING IN CHAT JUST YESTER-DAY.

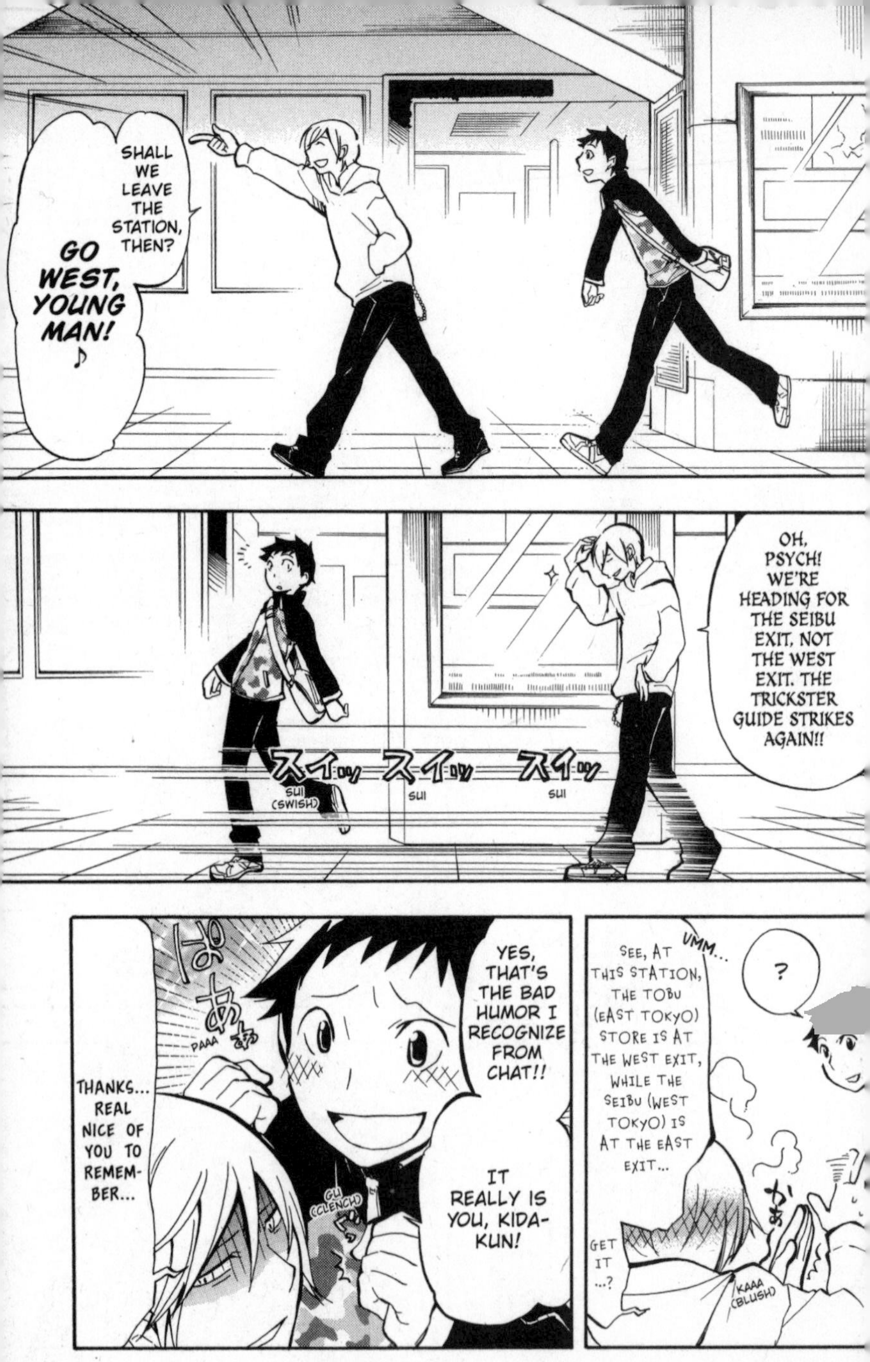
SHALL WE LEAVE THE STATION, THEN?
GO WEST, YOUNG MAN! ♪
OH, PSYCH! WE'RE HEADING FOR THE SEIBU EXIT, NOT THE WEST EXIT. THE TRICKSTER GUIDE STRIKES AGAIN!!
スイッ
SUI
スイッ
SUI
スイッ
SUI (SWISH)
?
UMM...
SEE, AT THIS STATION, THE TOBU (EAST TOKYO) STORE IS AT THE WEST EXIT, WHILE THE SEIBU (WEST TOKYO) IS AT THE EAST EXIT...
KAAA (BLUSH)
GET IT ...?
YES, THAT'S THE BAD HUMOR I RECOGNIZE FROM CHAT!!
IT REALLY IS YOU, KIDA-KUN!
PAAA
THANKS... REAL NICE OF YOU TO REMEMBER...
GU (CLENCH)

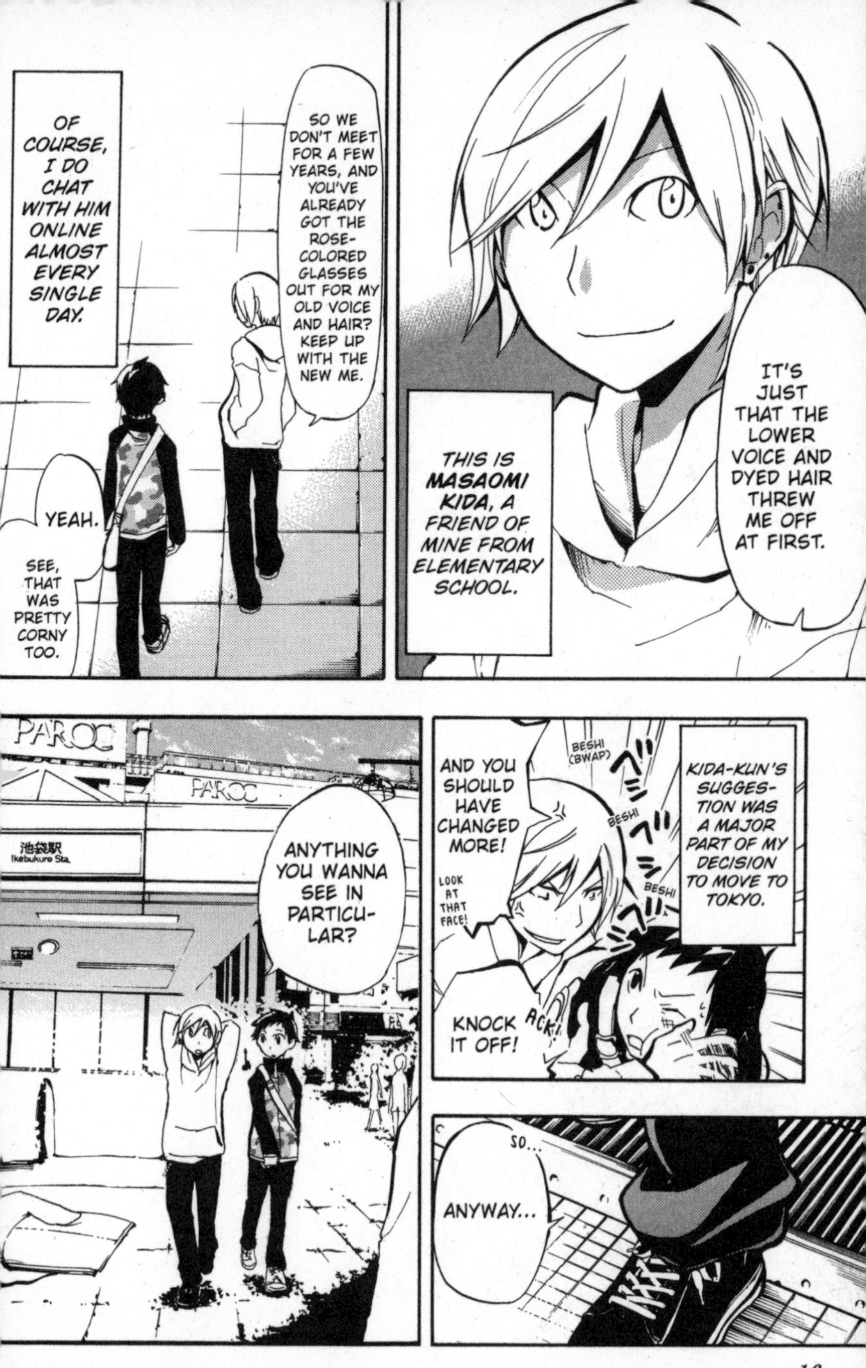
IT'S JUST THAT THE LOWER VOICE AND DYED HAIR THREW ME OFF AT FIRST.
THIS IS MASAOMI KIDA, A FRIEND OF MINE FROM ELEMENTARY SCHOOL.
SO WE DON'T MEET FOR A FEW YEARS, AND YOU'VE ALREADY GOT THE ROSE-COLORED GLASSES OUT FOR MY OLD VOICE AND HAIR? KEEP UP WITH THE NEW ME.
OF COURSE, I DO CHAT WITH HIM ONLINE ALMOST EVERY SINGLE DAY.
YEAH.
SEE, THAT WAS PRETTY CORNY TOO.
KIDA-KUN'S SUGGESTION WAS A MAJOR PART OF MY DECISION TO MOVE TO TOKYO.
BESHI (BWAP)
AND YOU SHOULD HAVE CHANGED MORE!
BESHI
BESHI
LOOK AT THAT FACE!
ACK!
KNOCK IT OFF!
SO...
ANYWAY...
PARCO
PARCO
池袋駅
Ikebukuro Sta.
ANYTHING YOU WANNA SEE IN PARTICULAR?

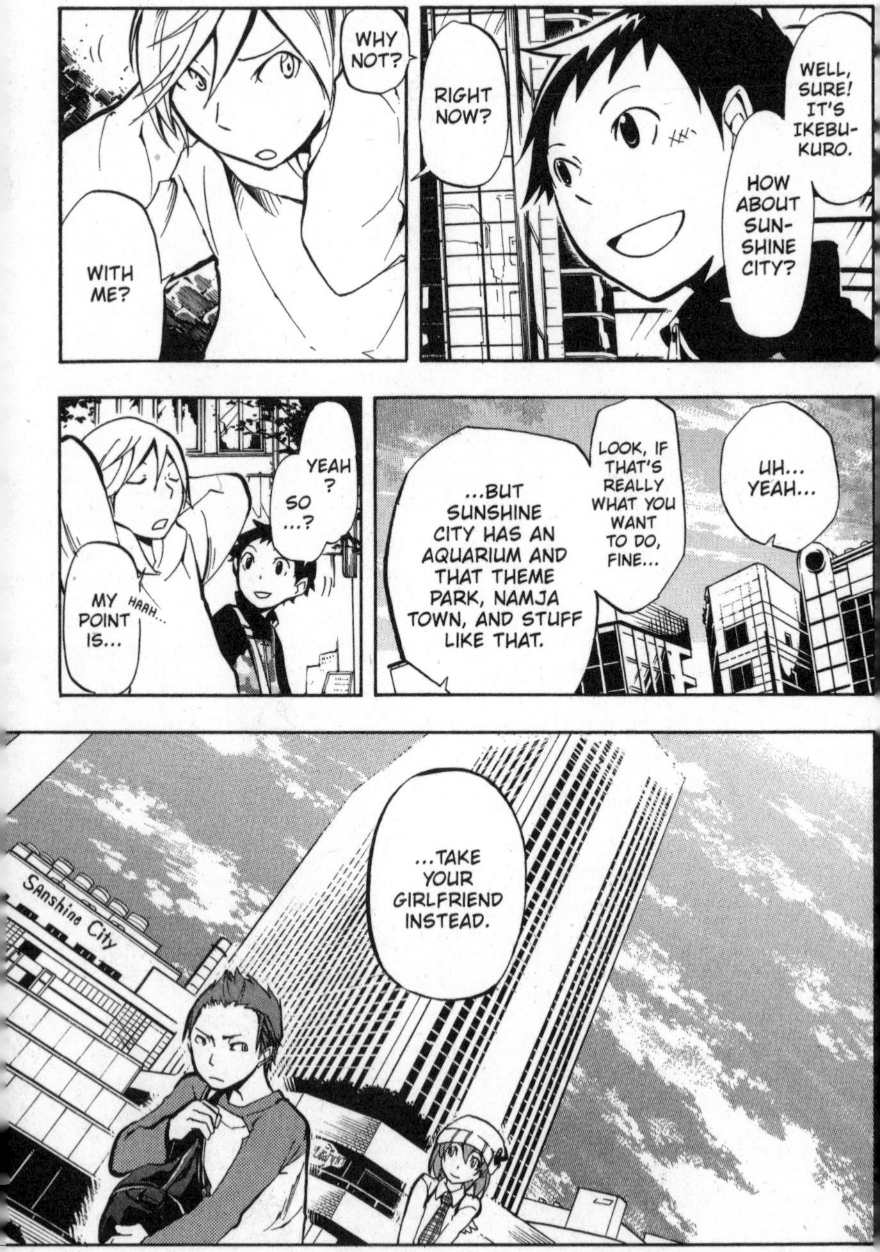
WELL, SURE! IT'S IKEBUKURO.
HOW ABOUT SUNSHINE CITY?
RIGHT NOW?
WHY NOT?
WITH ME?
UH... YEAH...
LOOK, IF THAT'S REALLY WHAT YOU WANT TO DO, FINE...
...BUT SUNSHINE CITY HAS AN AQUARIUM AND THAT THEME PARK, NAMJA TOWN, AND STUFF LIKE THAT.
YEAH? SO ...?
HAAH...
MY POINT IS...
...TAKE YOUR GIRLFRIEND INSTEAD.
Sanshine City

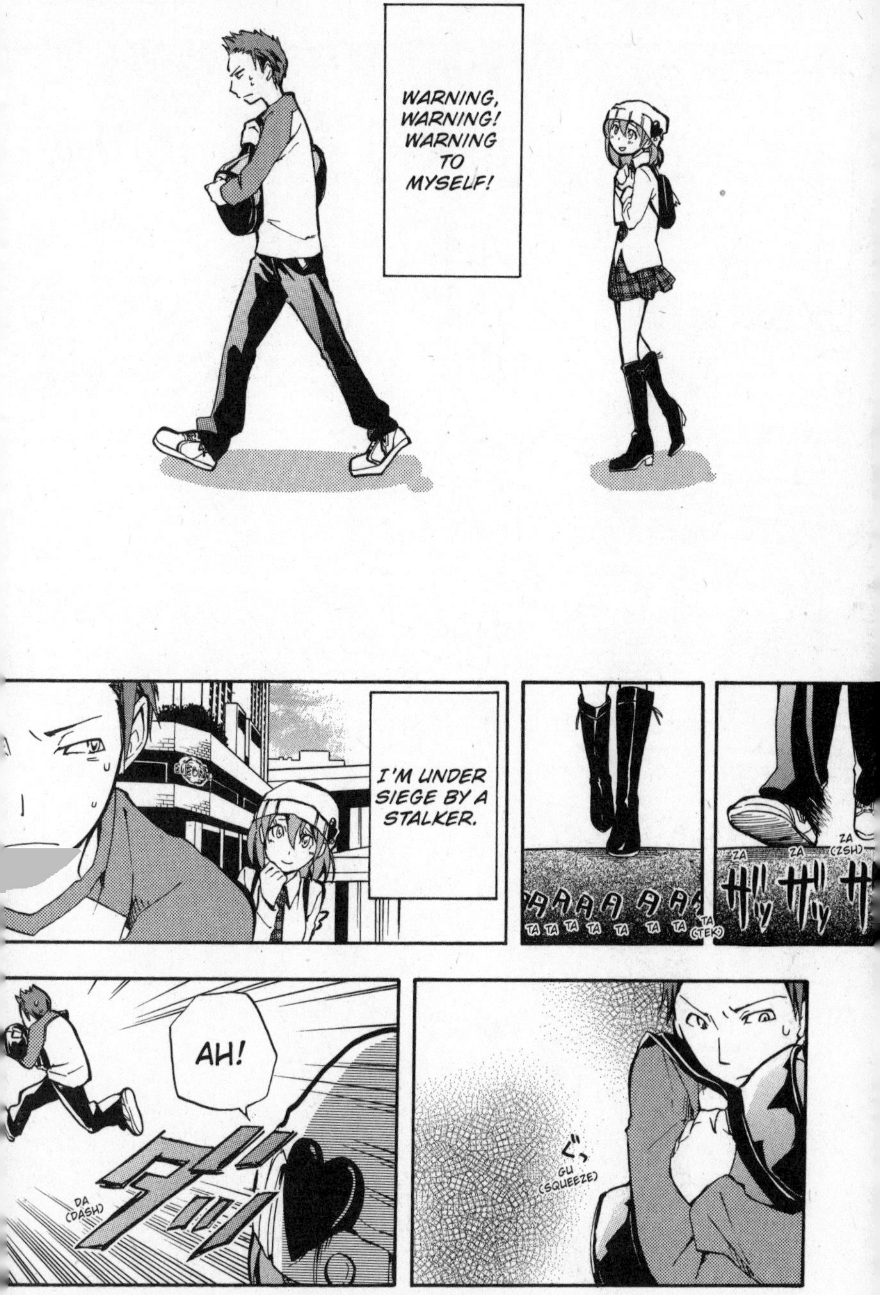

WARNING, WARNING! WARNING TO MYSELF!
ZA ZA ZA (ZSH)
TA TA TA TA TA TA TA TA (TEK)
I'M UNDER SIEGE BY A STALKER.
ぐっ
GU (SQUEEZE)
AH!
DA (DASH)

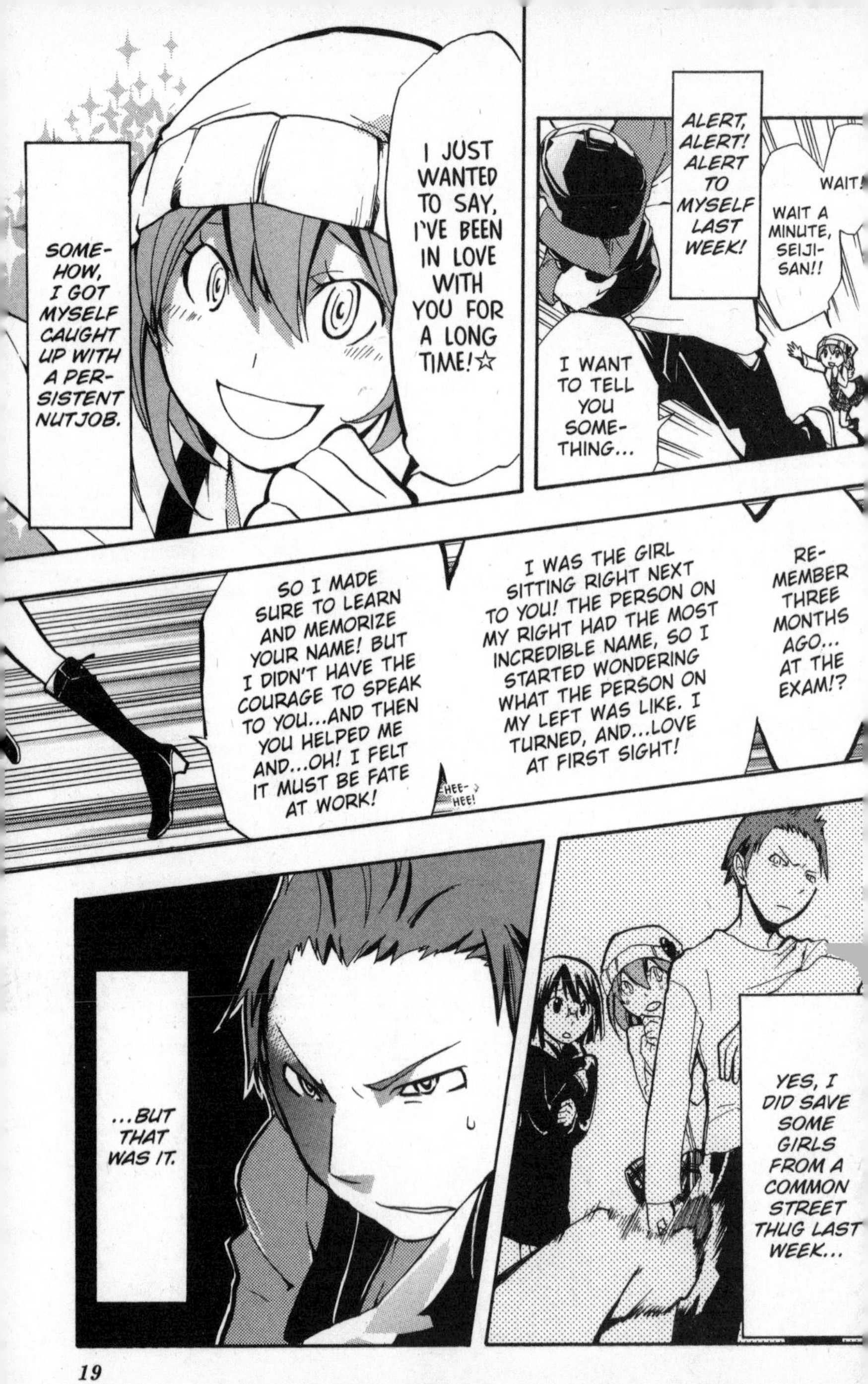
WAIT!
WAIT A MINUTE, SEIJI-SAN!!
ALERT, ALERT! ALERT TO MYSELF LAST WEEK!
I WANT TO TELL YOU SOMETHING...
I JUST WANTED TO SAY, I'VE BEEN IN LOVE WITH YOU FOR A LONG TIME!☆
SOMEHOW, I GOT MYSELF CAUGHT UP WITH A PERSISTENT NUTJOB.
REMEMBER THREE MONTHS AGO... AT THE EXAM!?
I WAS THE GIRL SITTING RIGHT NEXT TO YOU! THE PERSON ON MY RIGHT HAD THE MOST INCREDIBLE NAME, SO I STARTED WONDERING WHAT THE PERSON ON MY LEFT WAS LIKE. I TURNED, AND...LOVE AT FIRST SIGHT!
HEE-HEE!
SO I MADE SURE TO LEARN AND MEMORIZE YOUR NAME! BUT I DIDN'T HAVE THE COURAGE TO SPEAK TO YOU...AND THEN YOU HELPED ME AND...OH! I FELT IT MUST BE FATE AT WORK!
YES, I DID SAVE SOME GIRLS FROM A COMMON STREET THUG LAST WEEK...
...BUT THAT WAS IT.

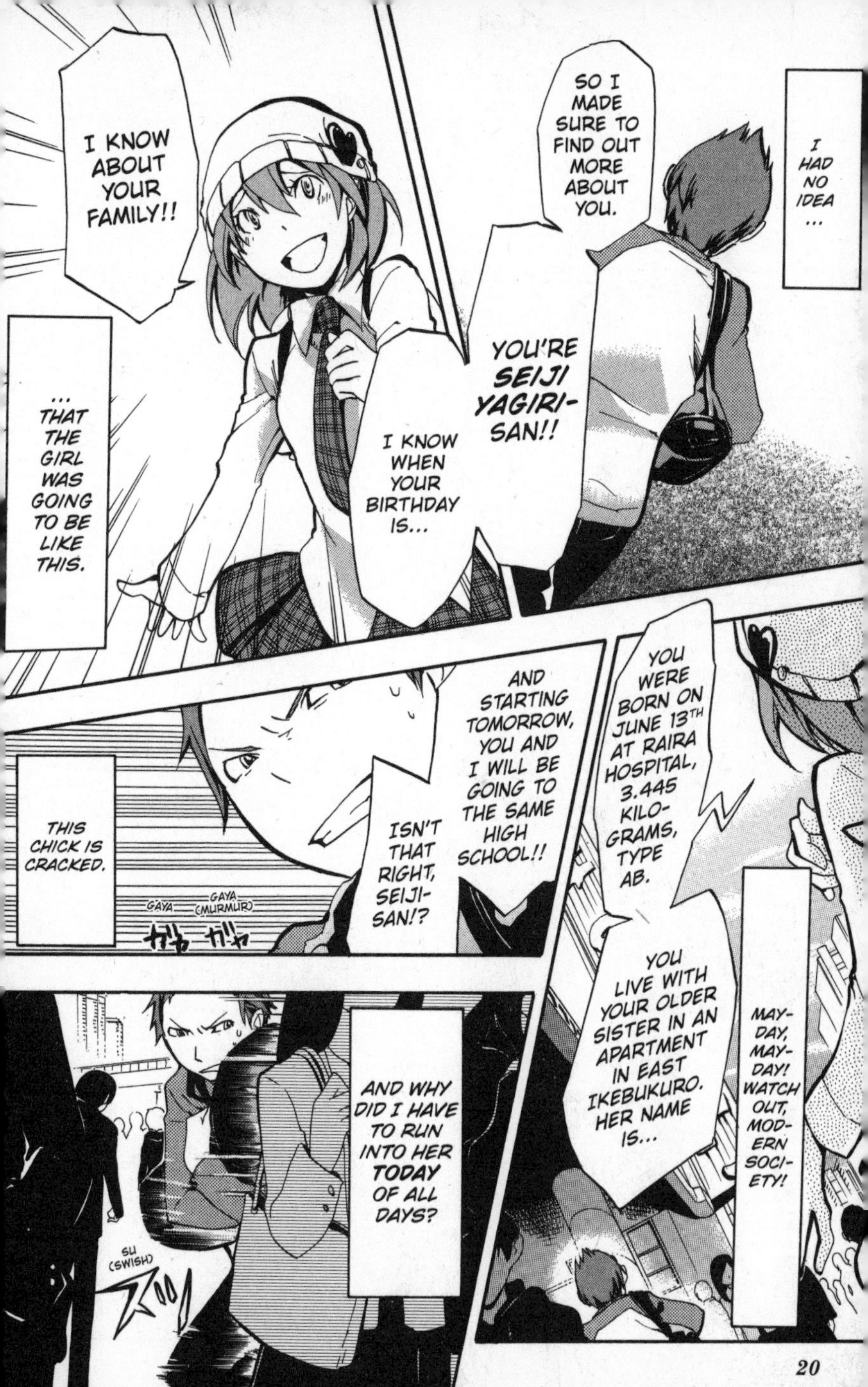
I HAD NO IDEA...
SO I MADE SURE TO FIND OUT MORE ABOUT YOU.
I KNOW ABOUT YOUR FAMILY!!
YOU'RE SEIJI YAGIRI-SAN!!
I KNOW WHEN YOUR BIRTHDAY IS...
...THAT THE GIRL WAS GOING TO BE LIKE THIS.
YOU WERE BORN ON JUNE 13TH AT RAIRA HOSPITAL, 3.445 KILOGRAMS, TYPE AB.
YOU LIVE WITH YOUR OLDER SISTER IN AN APARTMENT IN EAST IKEBUKURO. HER NAME IS...
MAY-DAY, MAY-DAY! WATCH OUT, MODERN SOCIETY!
AND STARTING TOMORROW, YOU AND I WILL BE GOING TO THE SAME HIGH SCHOOL!!
ISN'T THAT RIGHT, SEIJI-SAN!?
THIS CHICK IS CRACKED.
GAYA GAYA (MURMUR)
AND WHY DID I HAVE TO RUN INTO HER TODAY OF ALL DAYS?
SU (SWISH)

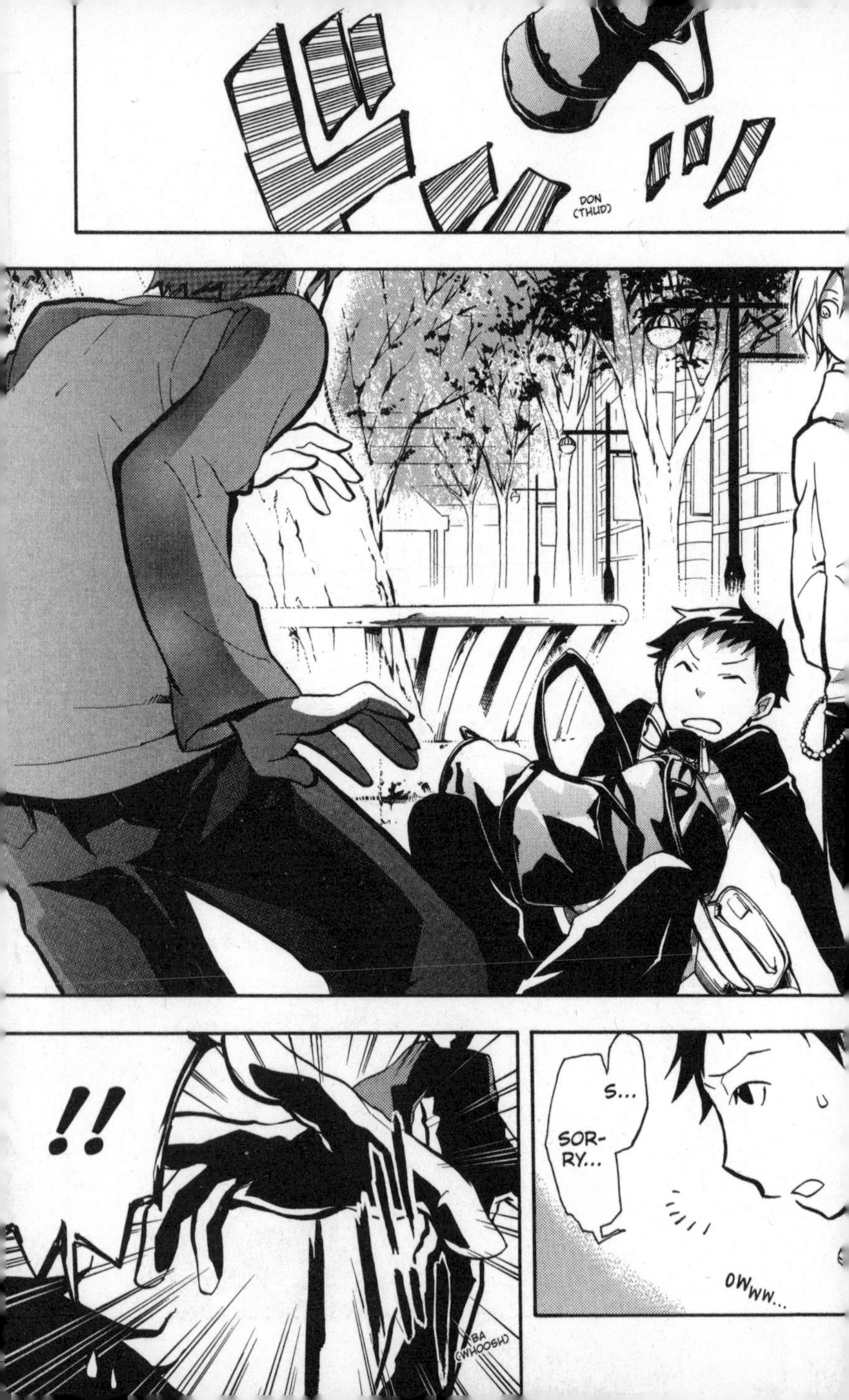
DON
(THUD)
S...
SOR-
RY...
OWWW...
!!
BA
(WHOOSH)

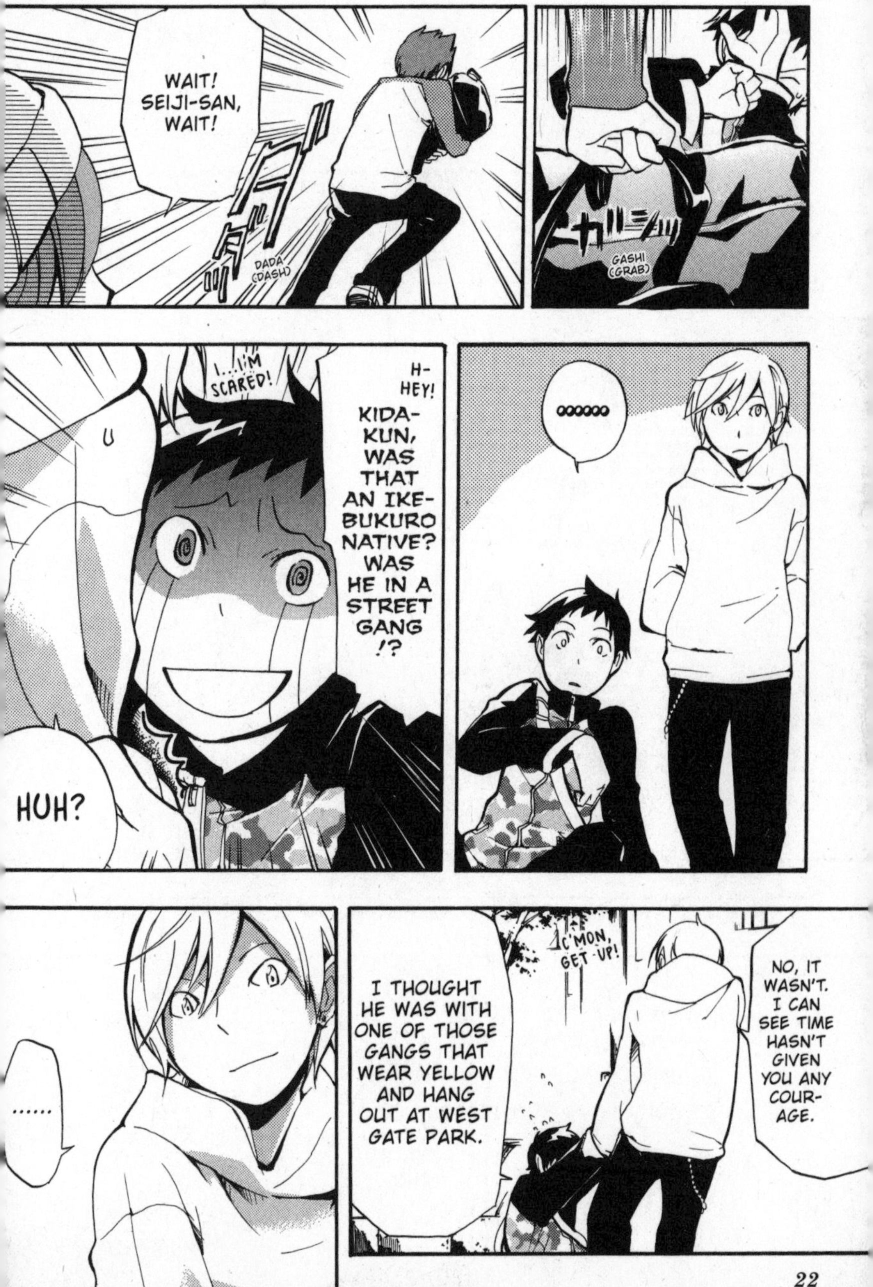
GASHI (GRAB)
WAIT! SEIJI-SAN, WAIT!
DADA (DASH)
......
H-HEY! KIDA-KUN, WAS THAT AN IKEBUKURO NATIVE? WAS HE IN A STREET GANG!?
I...I'M SCARED!
HUH?
NO, IT WASN'T. I CAN SEE TIME HASN'T GIVEN YOU ANY COURAGE.
C'MON, GET UP!
I THOUGHT HE WAS WITH ONE OF THOSE GANGS THAT WEAR YELLOW AND HANG OUT AT WEST GATE PARK.
......

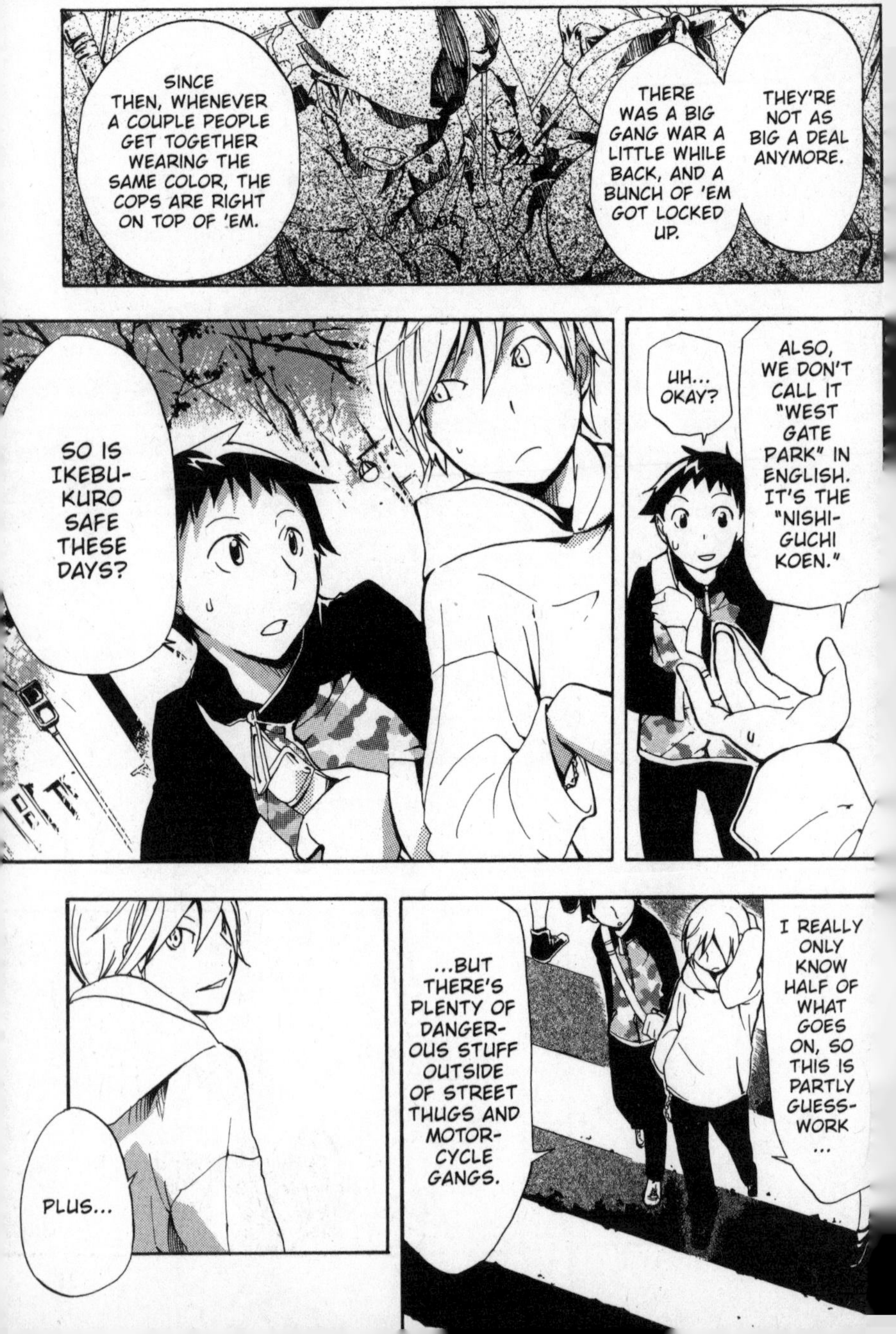
THEY'RE NOT AS BIG A DEAL ANYMORE.
THERE WAS A BIG GANG WAR A LITTLE WHILE BACK, AND A BUNCH OF 'EM GOT LOCKED UP.
SINCE THEN, WHENEVER A COUPLE PEOPLE GET TOGETHER WEARING THE SAME COLOR, THE COPS ARE RIGHT ON TOP OF 'EM.
ALSO, WE DON'T CALL IT "WEST GATE PARK" IN ENGLISH. IT'S THE "NISHI-GUCHI KOEN."
UH... OKAY?
SO IS IKEBU-KURO SAFE THESE DAYS?
I REALLY ONLY KNOW HALF OF WHAT GOES ON, SO THIS IS PARTLY GUESS-WORK...
...BUT THERE'S PLENTY OF DANGER-OUS STUFF OUTSIDE OF STREET THUGS AND MOTOR-CYCLE GANGS.
PLUS...

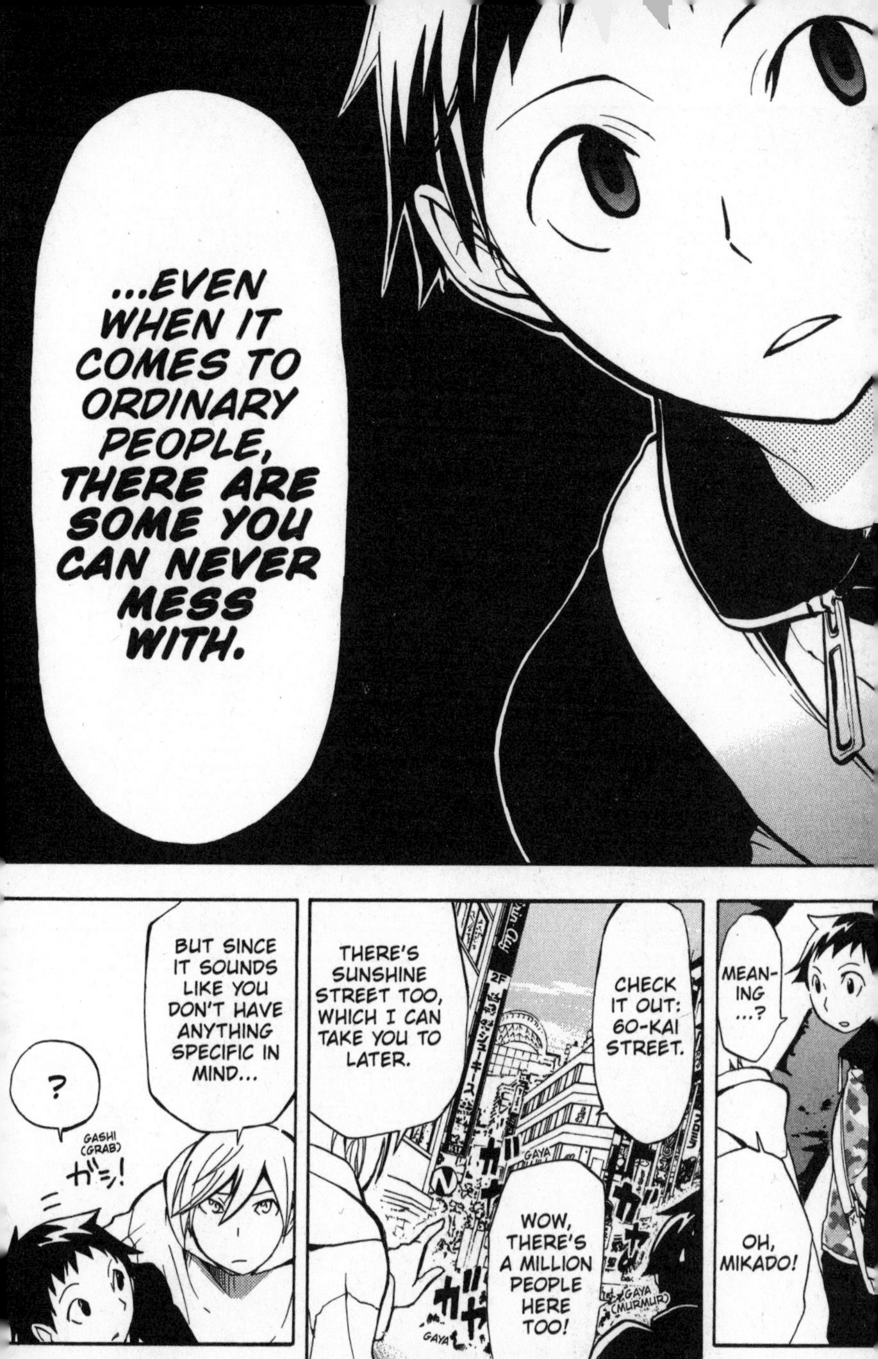
...EVEN WHEN IT COMES TO ORDINARY PEOPLE, THERE ARE SOME YOU CAN NEVER MESS WITH.
MEAN-ING...?
OH, MIKADO!
CHECK IT OUT: 60-KAI STREET.
THERE'S SUNSHINE STREET TOO, WHICH I CAN TAKE YOU TO LATER.
WOW, THERE'S A MILLION PEOPLE HERE TOO!
GAYA
GAYA (MURMUR)
GAYA
BUT SINCE IT SOUNDS LIKE YOU DON'T HAVE ANYTHING SPECIFIC IN MIND...
?
GASHI (GRAB)

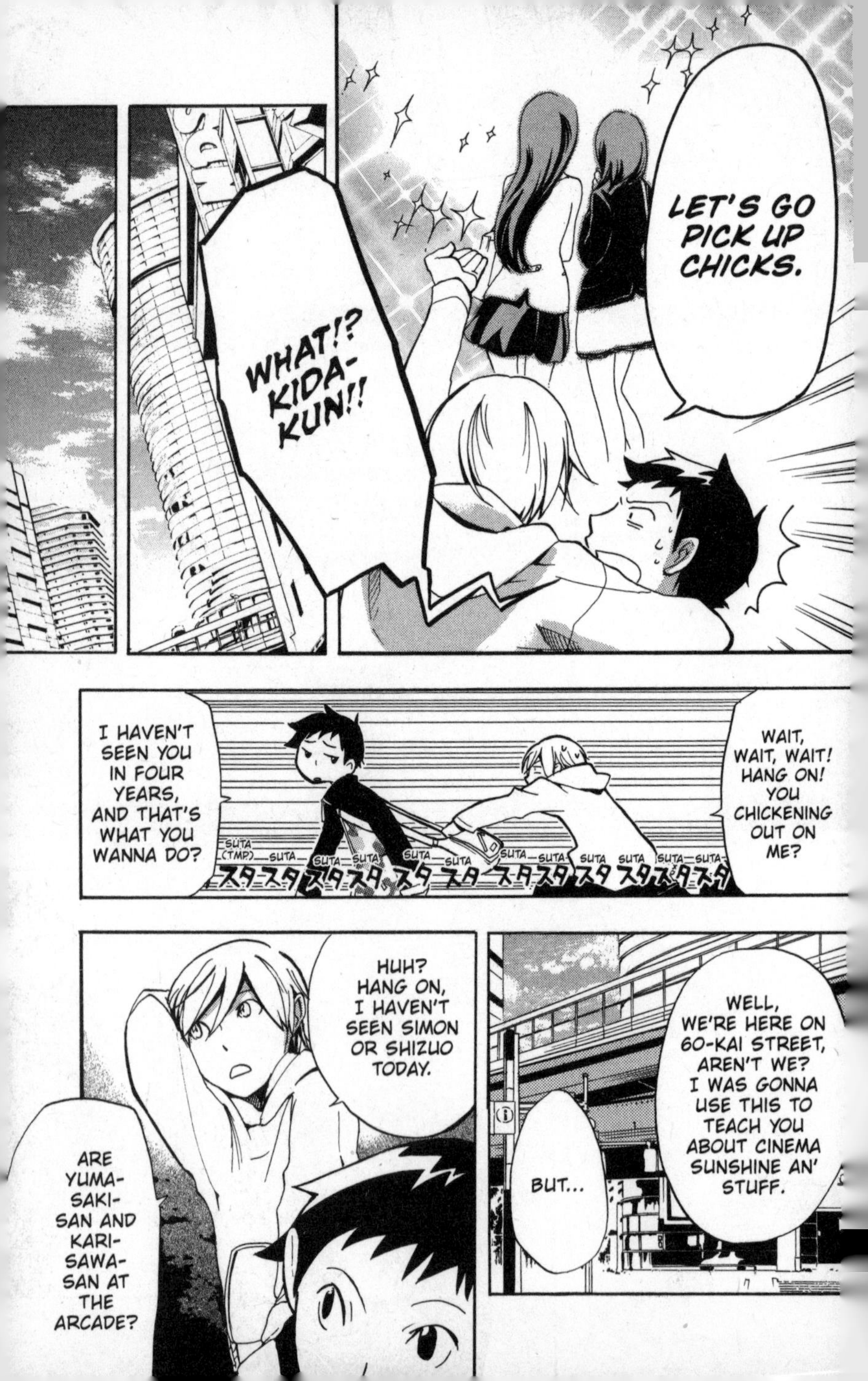
LET'S GO PICK UP CHICKS.
WHAT!? KIDA-KUN!!
WAIT, WAIT, WAIT! HANG ON! YOU CHICKENING OUT ON ME?
SUTA SUTA SUTA SUTA SUTA SUTA SUTA SUTA SUTA SUTA SUTA SUTA
SUTA (TMP)
スタスタスタスタスタスタスタスタスタスタスタスタ
I HAVEN'T SEEN YOU IN FOUR YEARS, AND THAT'S WHAT YOU WANNA DO?
WELL, WE'RE HERE ON 60-KAI STREET, AREN'T WE? I WAS GONNA USE THIS TO TEACH YOU ABOUT CINEMA SUNSHINE AN' STUFF.
BUT...
HUH? HANG ON, I HAVEN'T SEEN SIMON OR SHIZUO TODAY.
ARE YUMA-SAKI-SAN AND KARI-SAWA-SAN AT THE ARCADE?

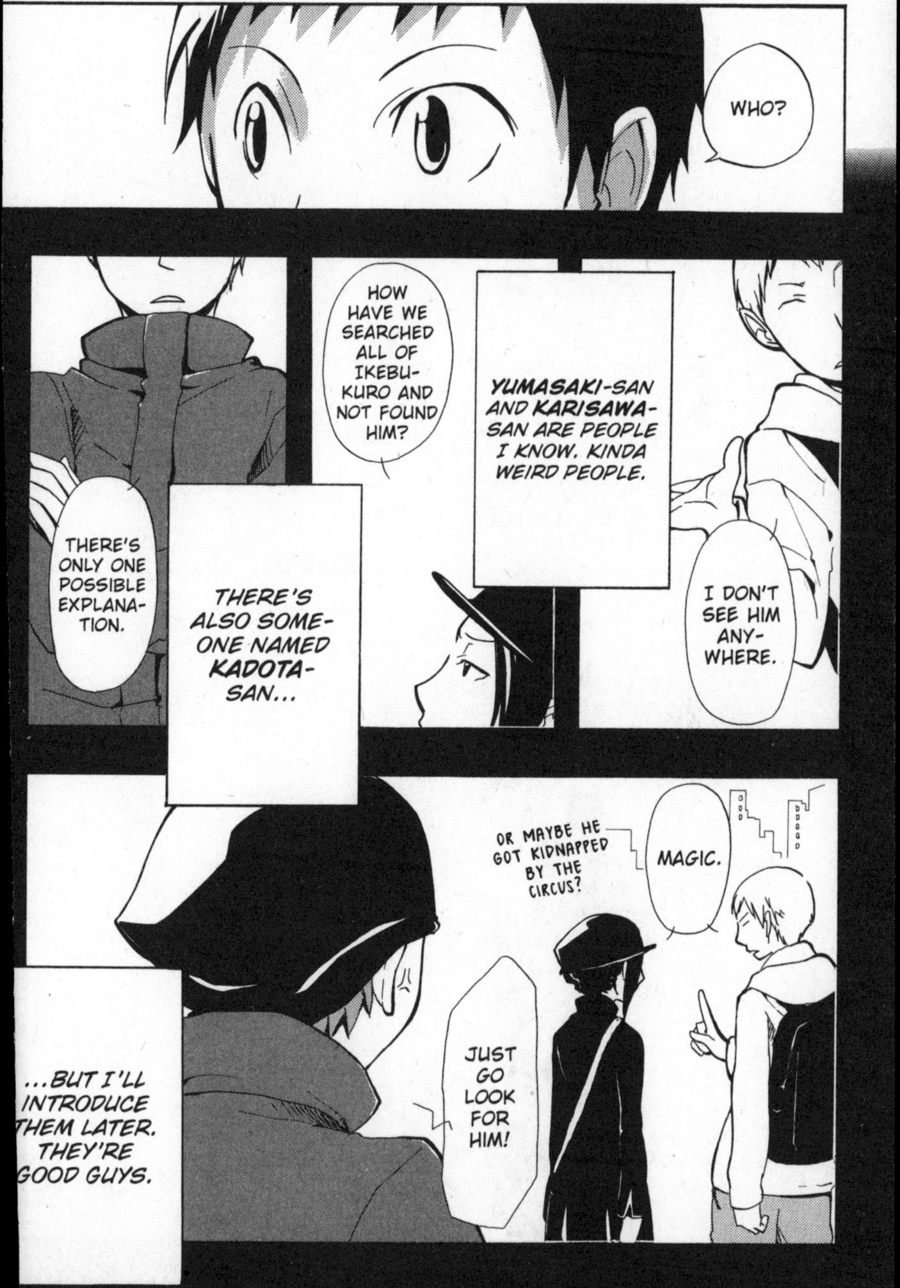
WHO?
I DON'T SEE HIM ANYWHERE.
YUMASAKI-SAN AND KARISAWA-SAN ARE PEOPLE I KNOW. KINDA WEIRD PEOPLE.
HOW HAVE WE SEARCHED ALL OF IKEBUKURO AND NOT FOUND HIM?
THERE'S ONLY ONE POSSIBLE EXPLANATION.
THERE'S ALSO SOMEONE NAMED KADOTA-SAN...
MAGIC.
OR MAYBE HE GOT KIDNAPPED BY THE CIRCUS?
JUST GO LOOK FOR HIM!
...BUT I'LL INTRODUCE THEM LATER. THEY'RE GOOD GUYS.

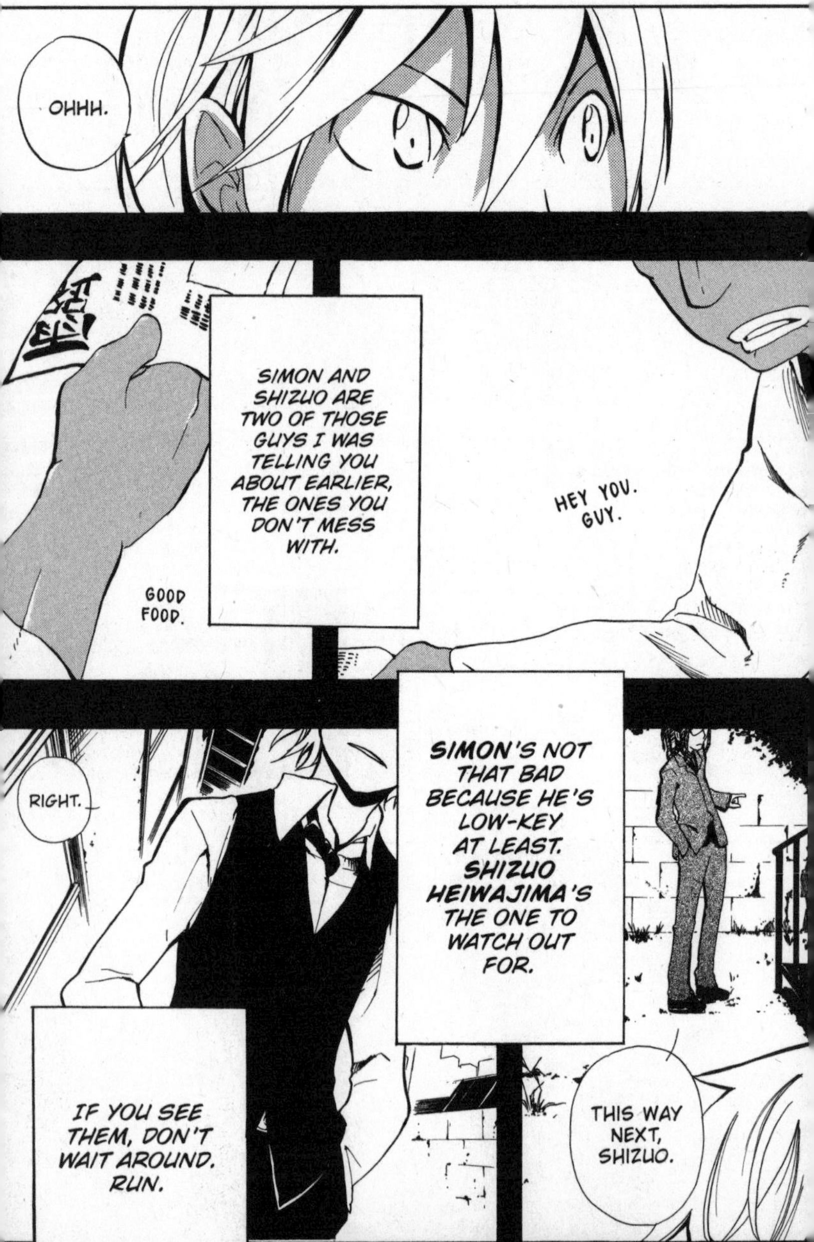

OHHH.
HEY YOU. GUY.
SIMON AND SHIZUO ARE TWO OF THOSE GUYS I WAS TELLING YOU ABOUT EARLIER, THE ONES YOU DON'T MESS WITH.
GOOD FOOD.
SIMON'S NOT THAT BAD BECAUSE HE'S LOW-KEY AT LEAST. SHIZUO HEIWAJIMA'S THE ONE TO WATCH OUT FOR.
THIS WAY NEXT, SHIZUO.
RIGHT.
IF YOU SEE THEM, DON'T WAIT AROUND. RUN.

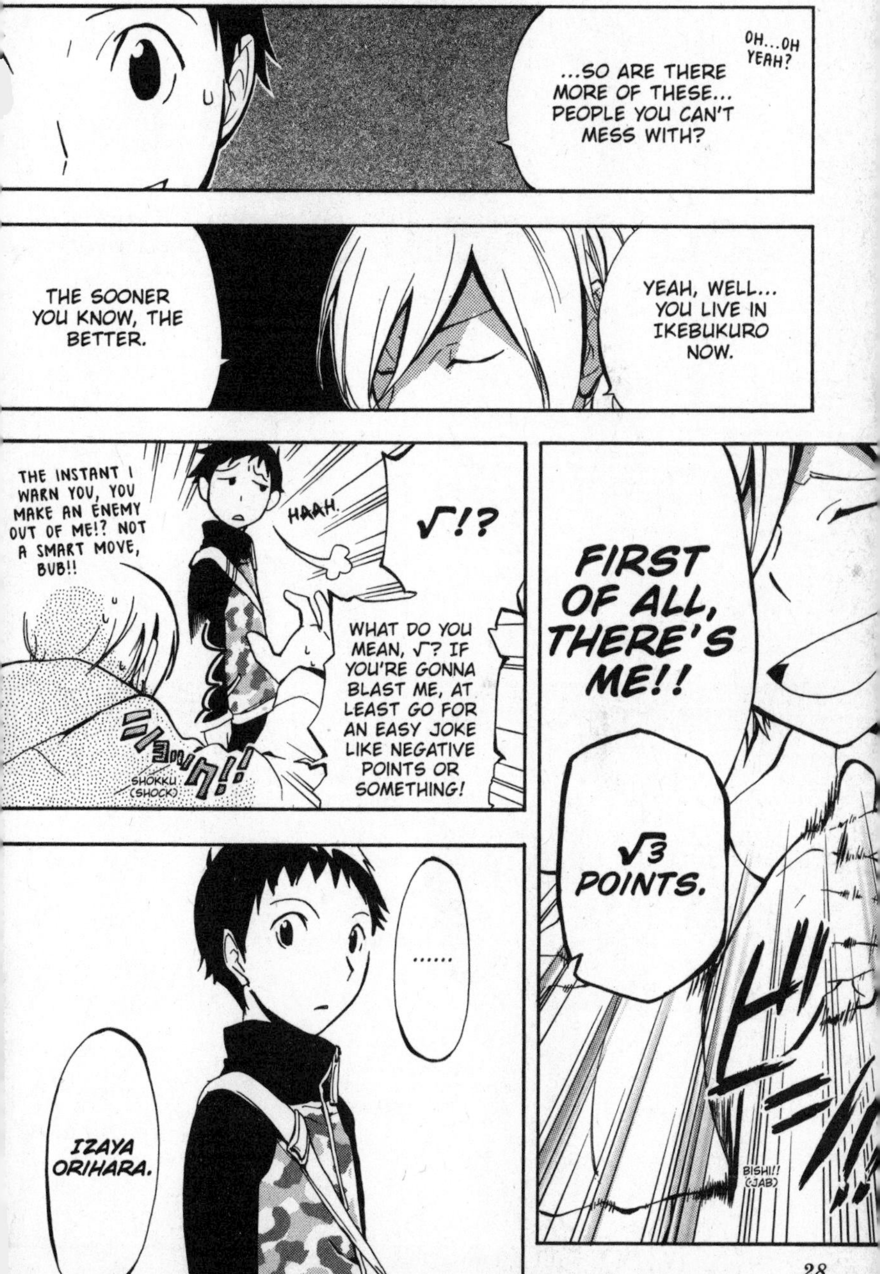
OH...OH YEAH?
...SO ARE THERE MORE OF THESE... PEOPLE YOU CAN'T MESS WITH?
YEAH, WELL... YOU LIVE IN IKEBUKURO NOW.
THE SOONER YOU KNOW, THE BETTER.
FIRST OF ALL, THERE'S ME!!
$\sqrt{3}$ POINTS.
BISHI!! (JAB)
√!?
HAAH.
THE INSTANT I WARN YOU, YOU MAKE AN ENEMY OUT OF ME!? NOT A SMART MOVE, BUB!!
WHAT DO YOU MEAN, √? IF YOU'RE GONNA BLAST ME, AT LEAST GO FOR AN EASY JOKE LIKE NEGATIVE POINTS OR SOMETHING!
SHOKKU (SHOCK)
......
IZAYA ORIHARA.

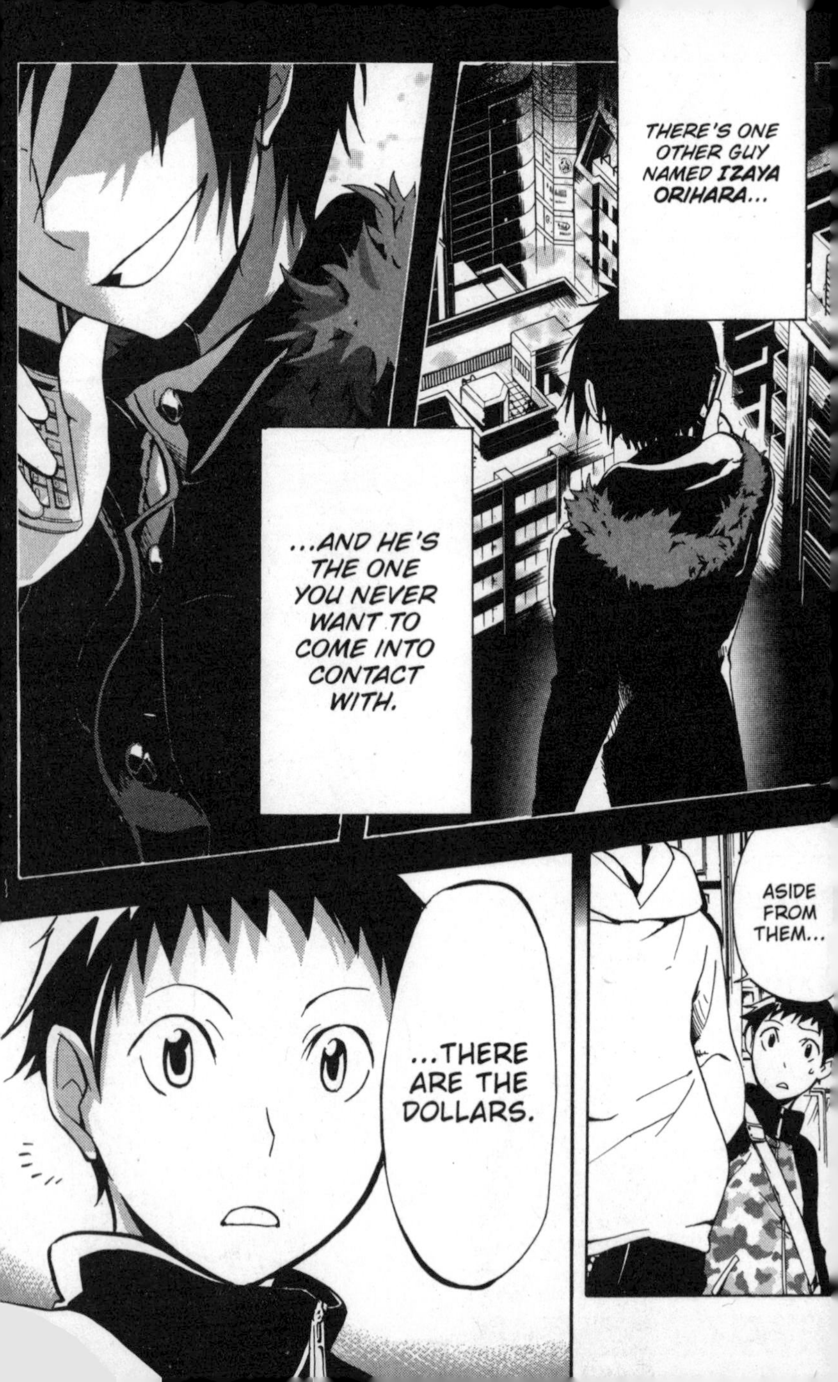
THERE'S ONE OTHER GUY NAMED IZAYA ORIHARA...
...AND HE'S THE ONE YOU NEVER WANT TO COME INTO CONTACT WITH.
ASIDE FROM THEM...
...THERE ARE THE DOLLARS.

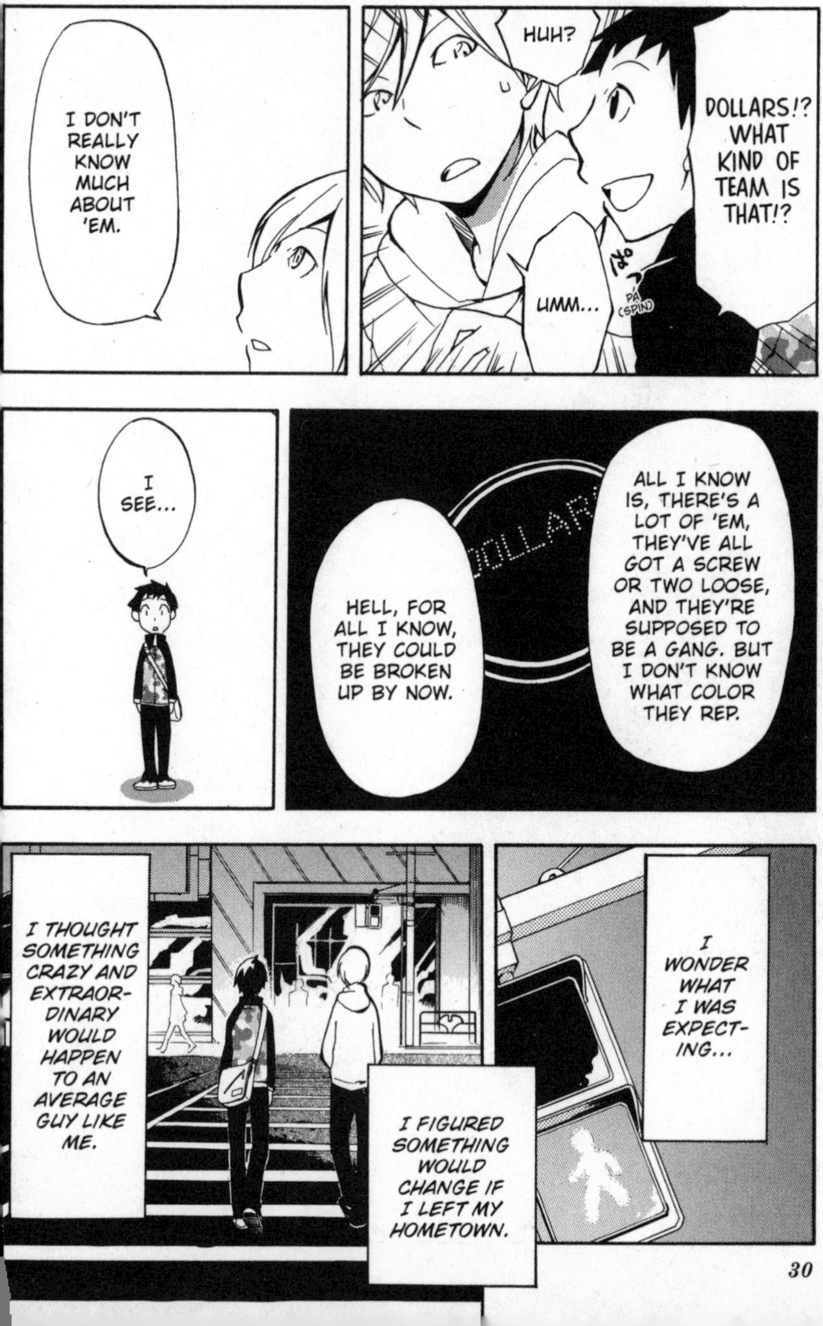
HUH?
DOLLARS!? WHAT KIND OF TEAM IS THAT!?
UMM...
PA (SPIN)
I DON'T REALLY KNOW MUCH ABOUT 'EM.
DOLLARS
ALL I KNOW IS, THERE'S A LOT OF 'EM, THEY'VE ALL GOT A SCREW OR TWO LOOSE, AND THEY'RE SUPPOSED TO BE A GANG. BUT I DON'T KNOW WHAT COLOR THEY REP.
HELL, FOR ALL I KNOW, THEY COULD BE BROKEN UP BY NOW.
I SEE...
I WONDER WHAT I WAS EXPECTING...
I THOUGHT SOMETHING CRAZY AND EXTRAORDINARY WOULD HAPPEN TO AN AVERAGE GUY LIKE ME.
I FIGURED SOMETHING WOULD CHANGE IF I LEFT MY HOMETOWN.

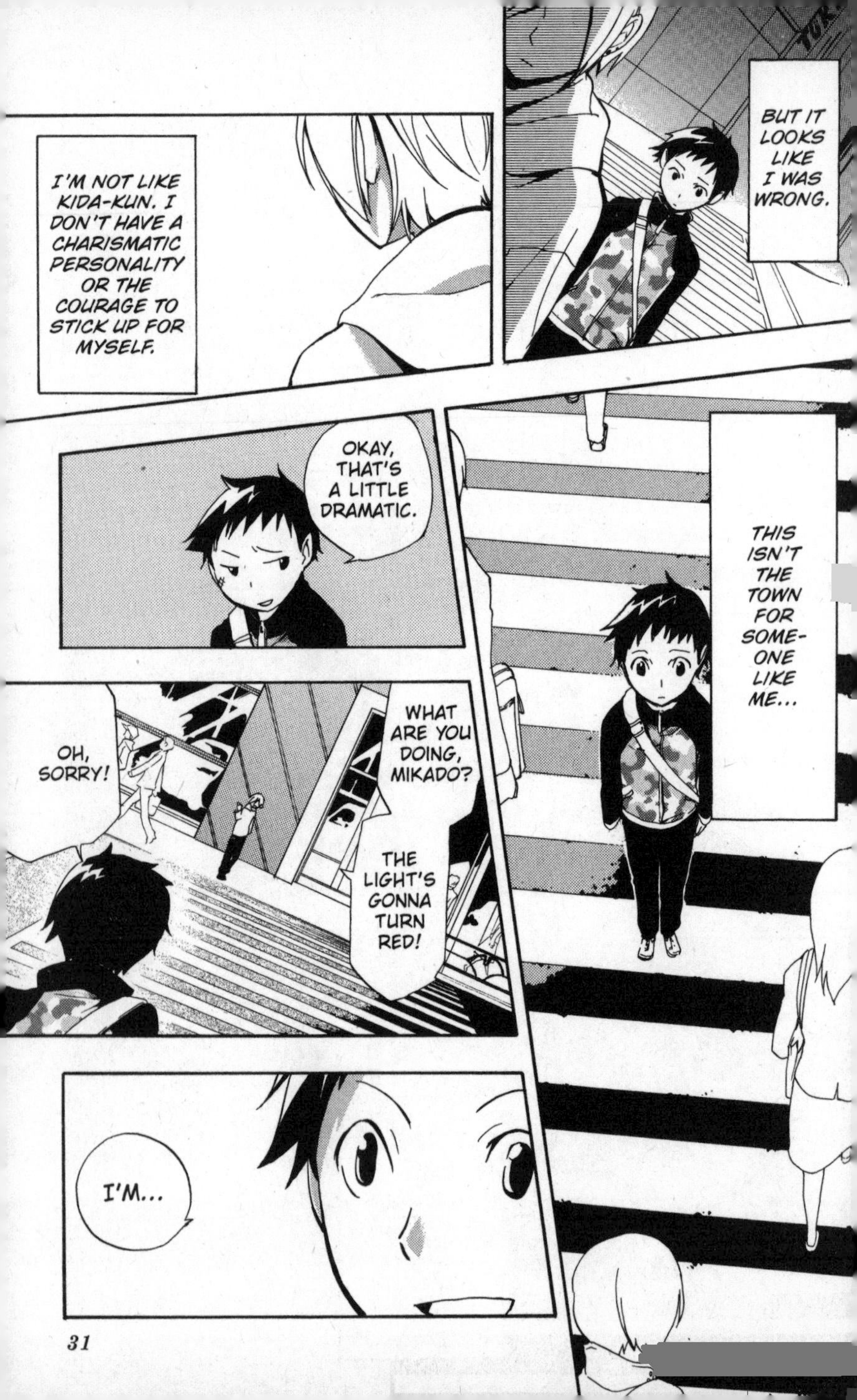
BUT IT LOOKS LIKE I WAS WRONG.
I'M NOT LIKE KIDA-KUN. I DON'T HAVE A CHARISMATIC PERSONALITY OR THE COURAGE TO STICK UP FOR MYSELF.
THIS ISN'T THE TOWN FOR SOME-ONE LIKE ME...
OKAY, THAT'S A LITTLE DRAMATIC.
WHAT ARE YOU DOING, MIKADO?
THE LIGHT'S GONNA TURN RED!
OH, SORRY!
I'M...

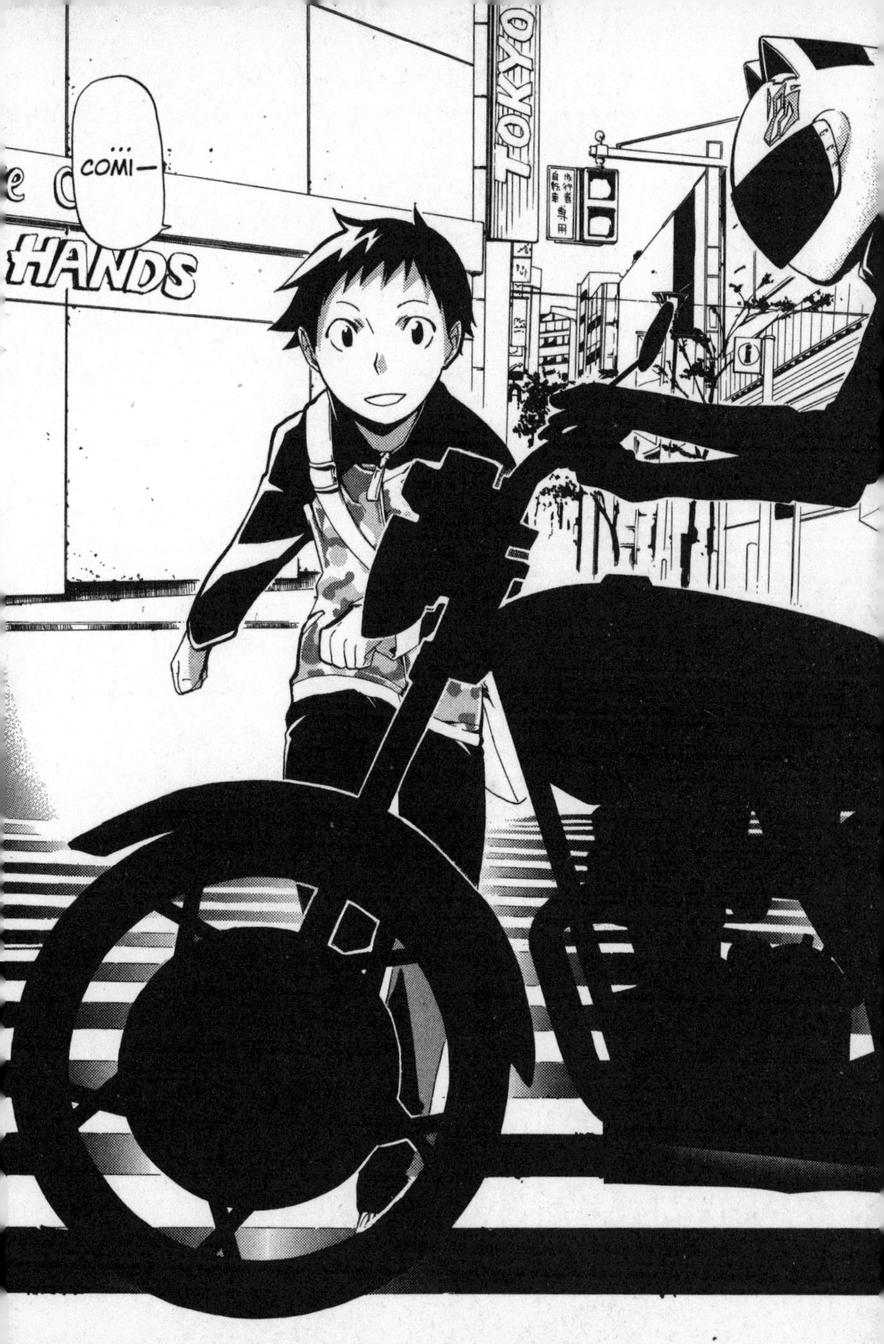
...COMI—
HANDS
TOKYO
歩行者自転車専用

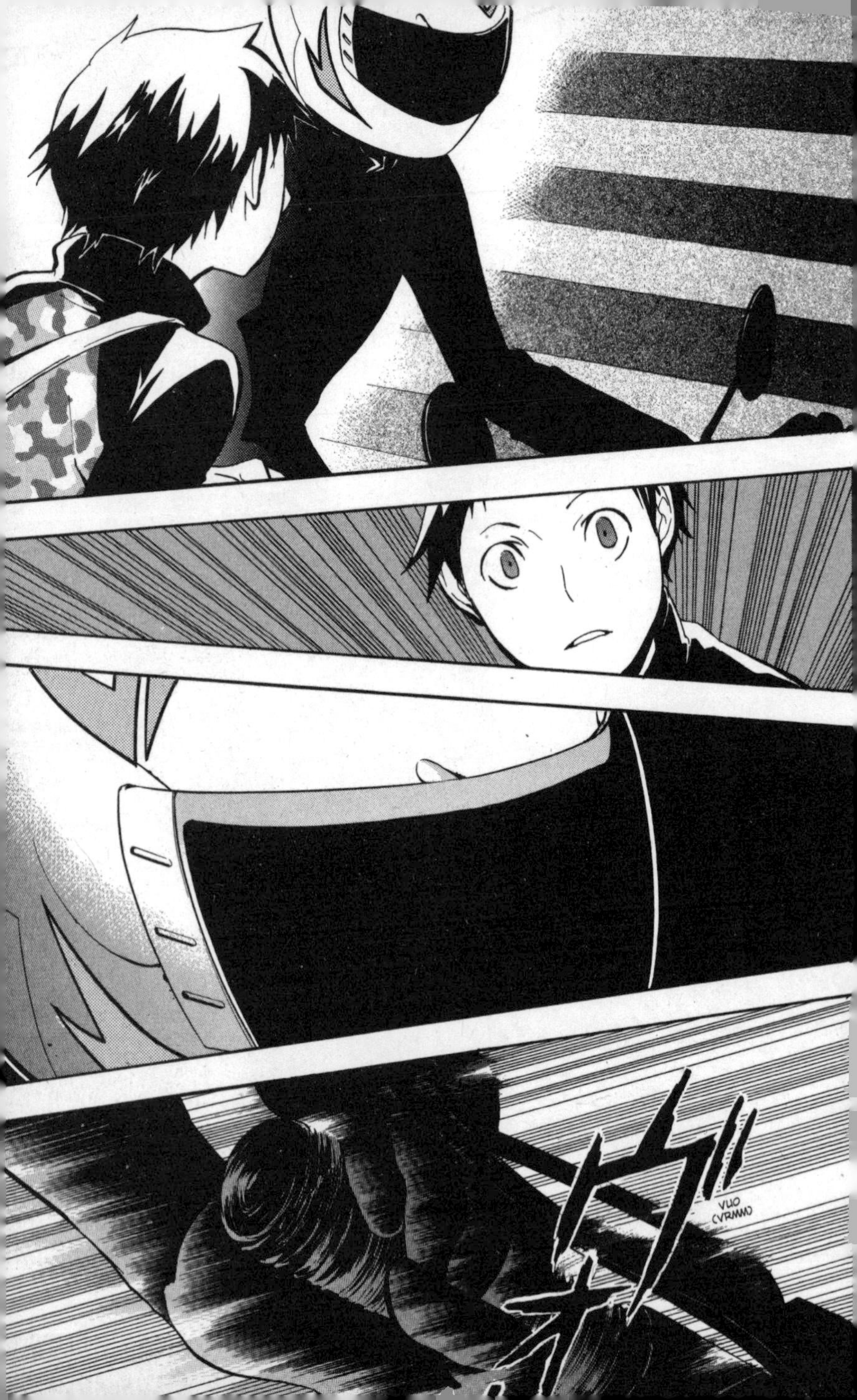
VUO
(VRMM)

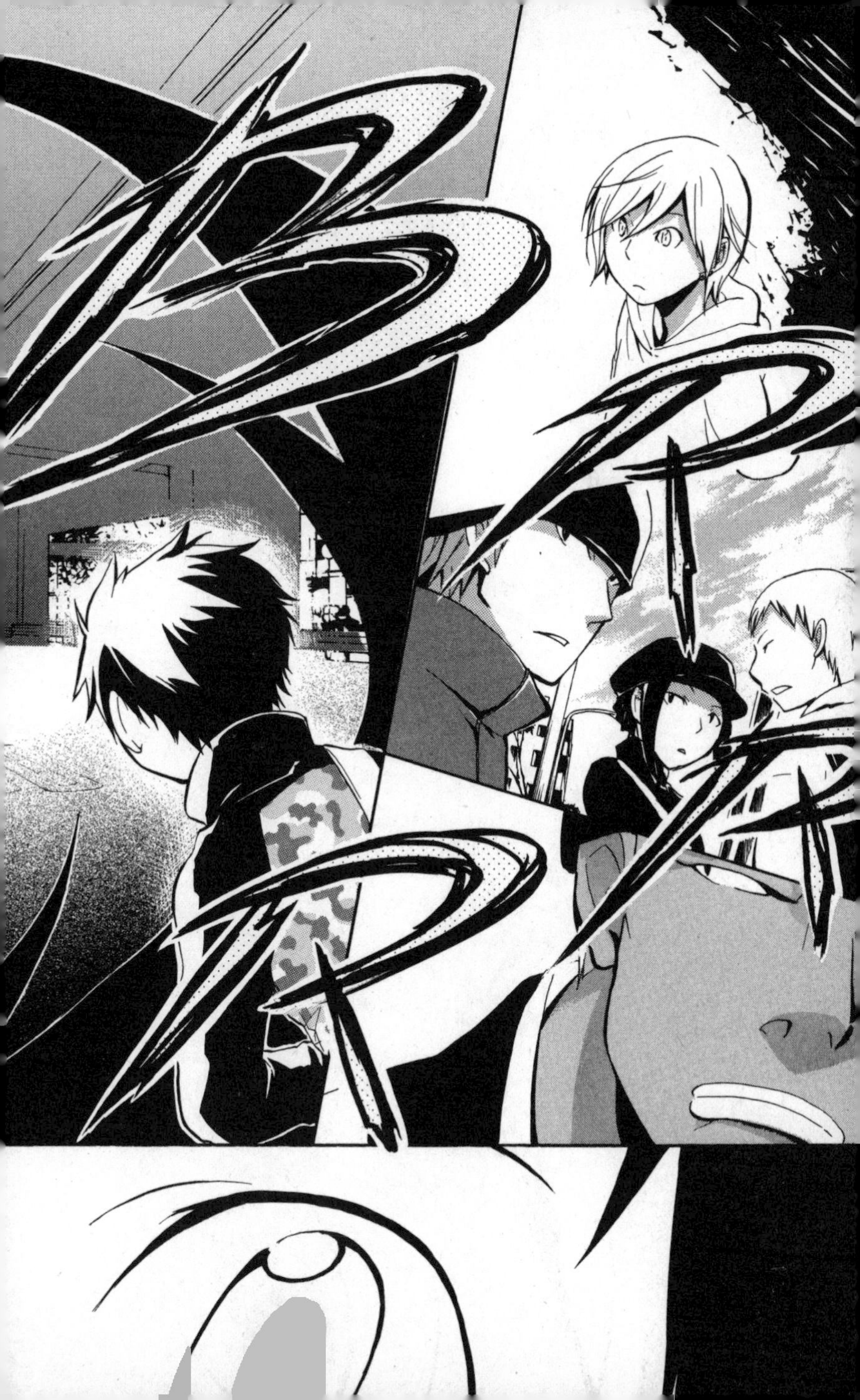

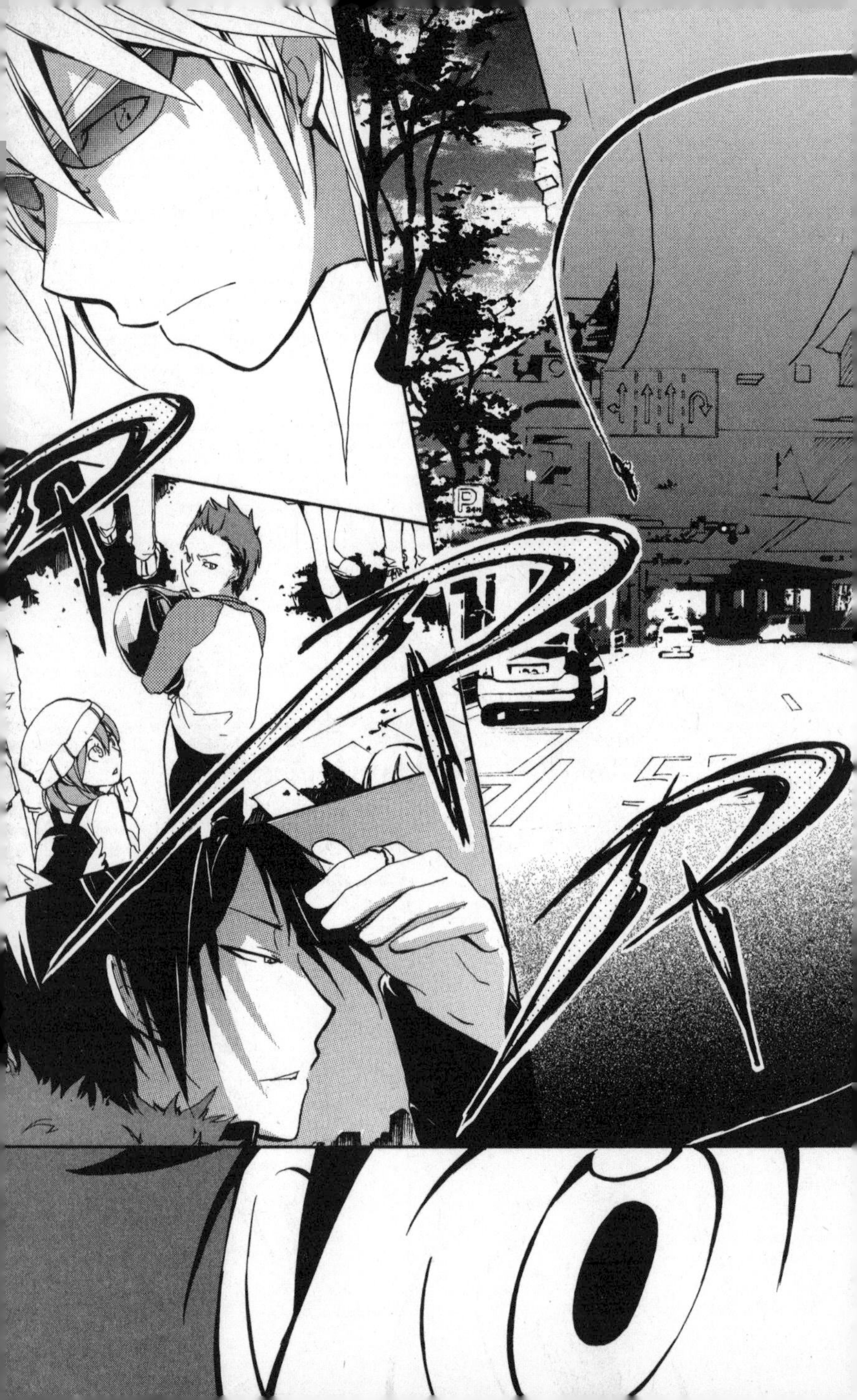

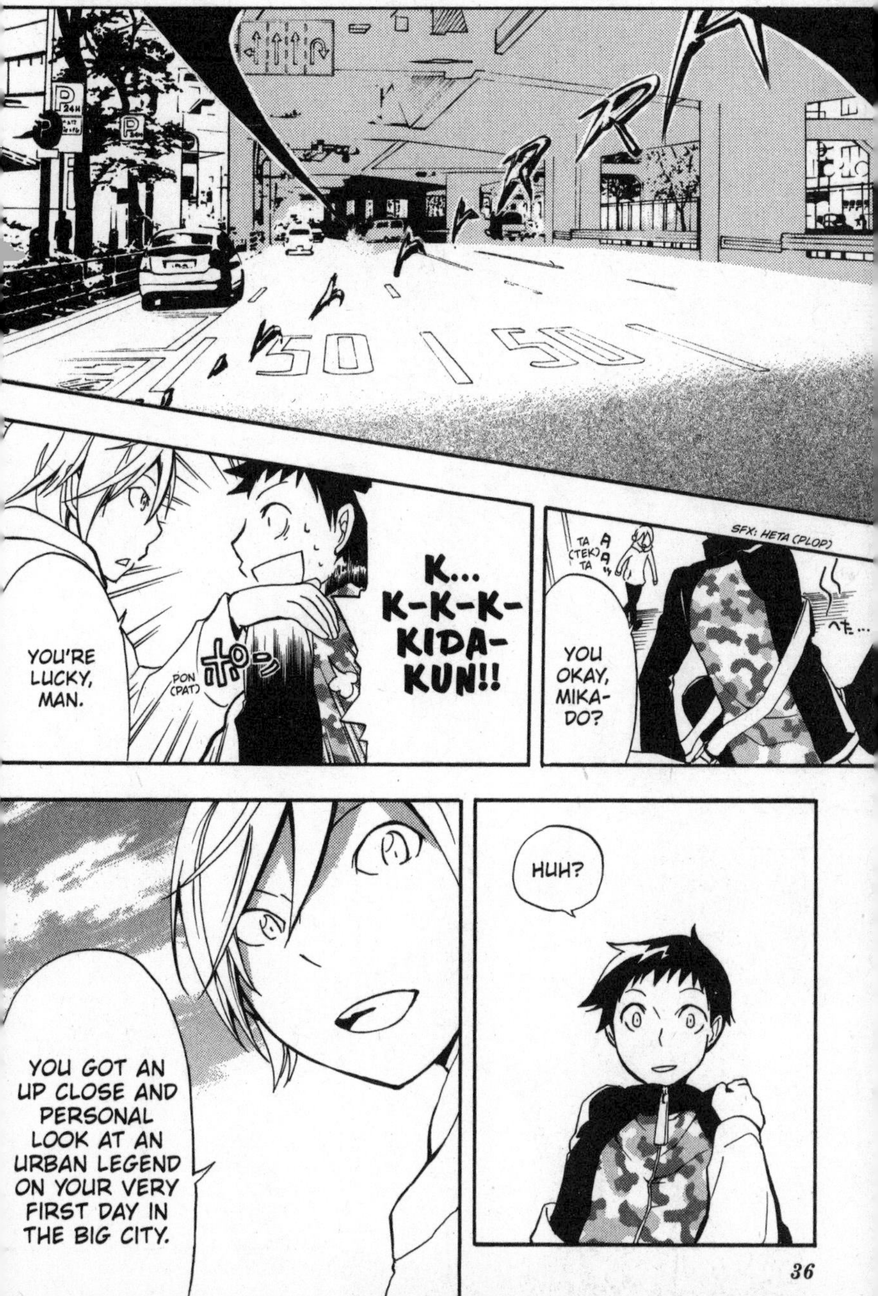
SFX: HETA (PLOP)
TA (TEK) TA
YOU OKAY, MIKA-DO?
K... K-K-K-KIDA-KUN!!
PON (PAT)
YOU'RE LUCKY, MAN.
HUH?
YOU GOT AN UP CLOSE AND PERSONAL LOOK AT AN URBAN LEGEND ON YOUR VERY FIRST DAY IN THE BIG CITY.

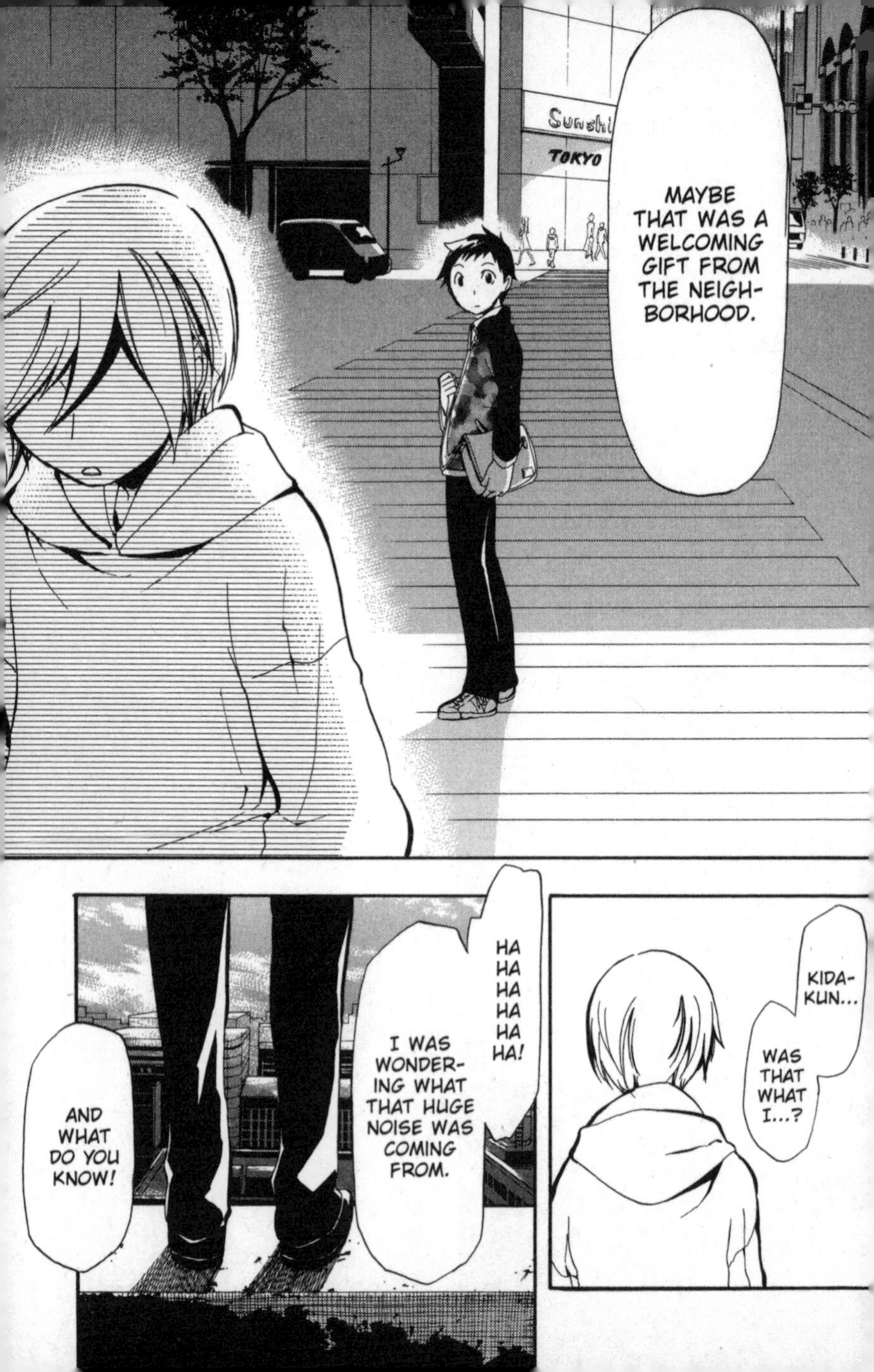
TOKYO
MAYBE THAT WAS A WELCOMING GIFT FROM THE NEIGH-BORHOOD.
KIDA-KUN...
WAS THAT WHAT I...?
HA HA HA HA HA HA!
I WAS WONDER-ING WHAT THAT HUGE NOISE WAS COMING FROM.
AND WHAT DO YOU KNOW!

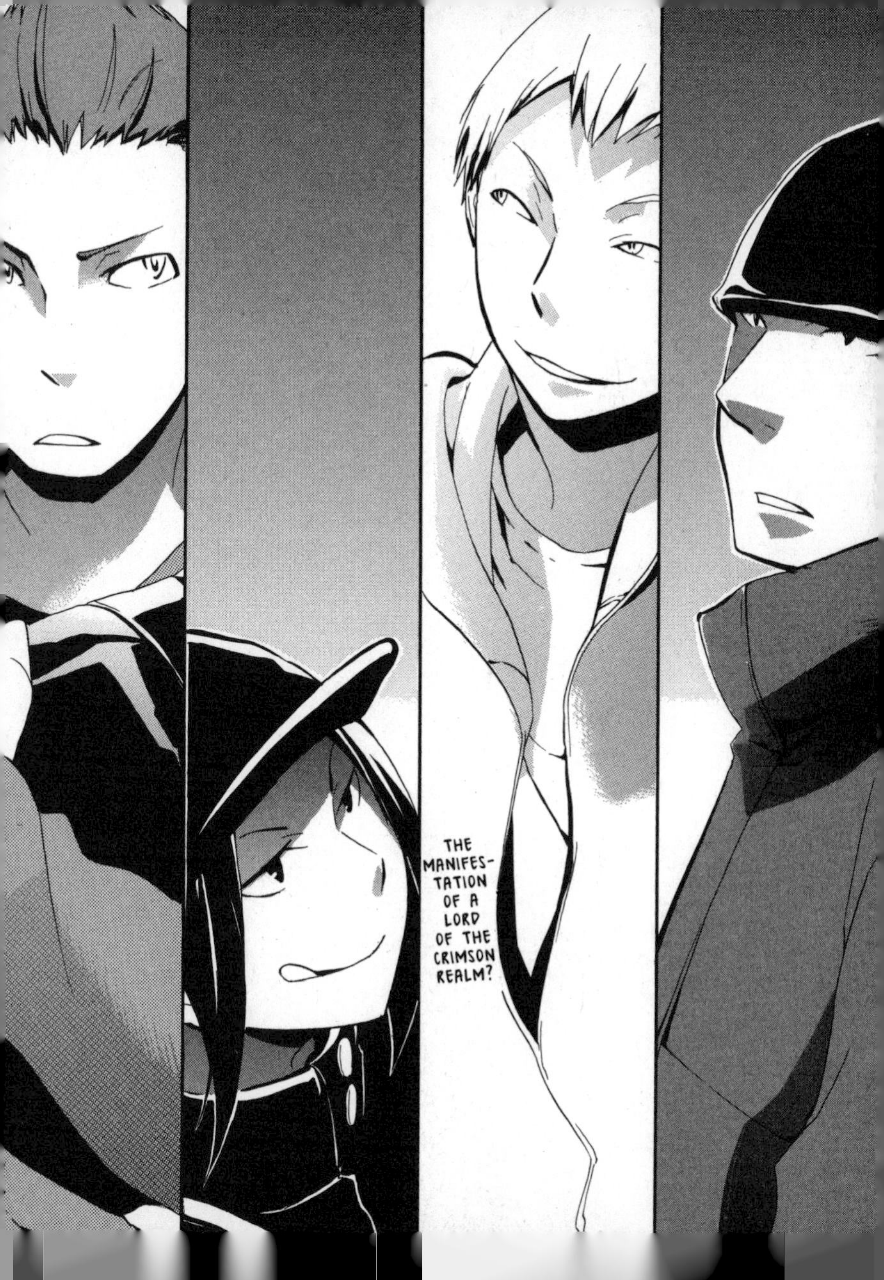
THE MANIFESTATION OF A LORD OF THE CRIMSON REALM?

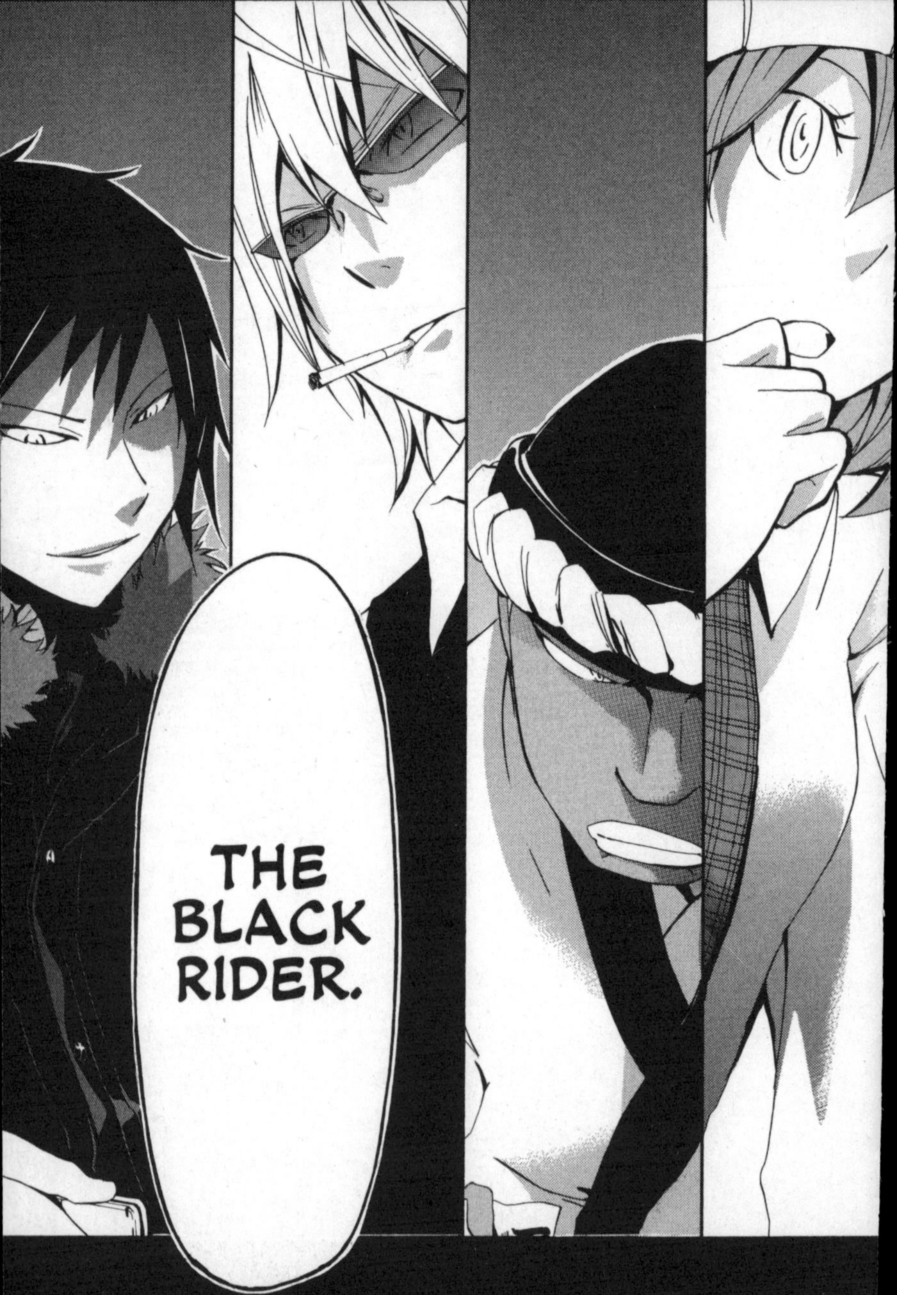
THE BLACK RIDER.

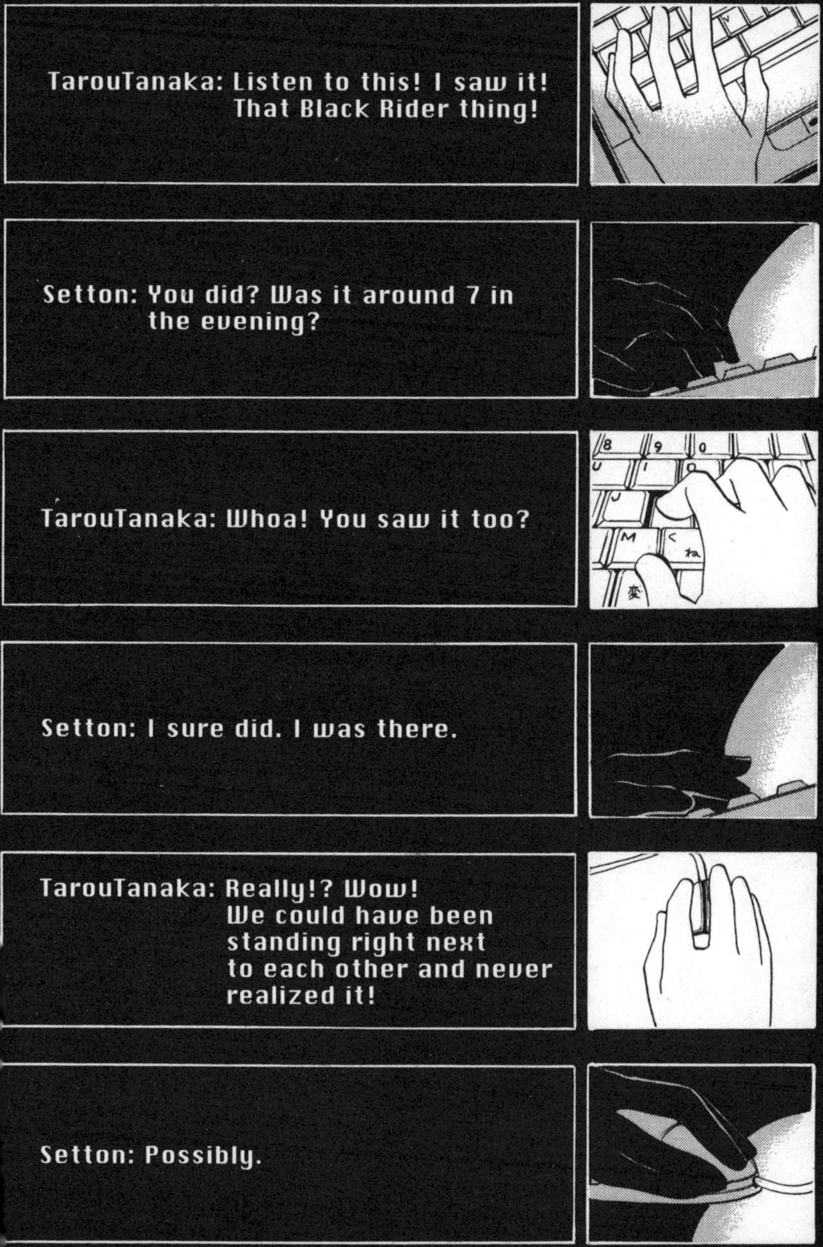

TarouTanaka: Listen to this! I saw it!
That Black Rider thing!

Setton: You did? Was it around 7 in
the evening?

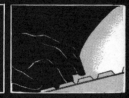

TarouTanaka: Whoa! You saw it too?

Setton: I sure did. I was there.

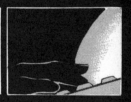

TarouTanaka: Really!? Wow!
We could have been
standing right next
to each other and never
realized it!

Setton: Possibly.

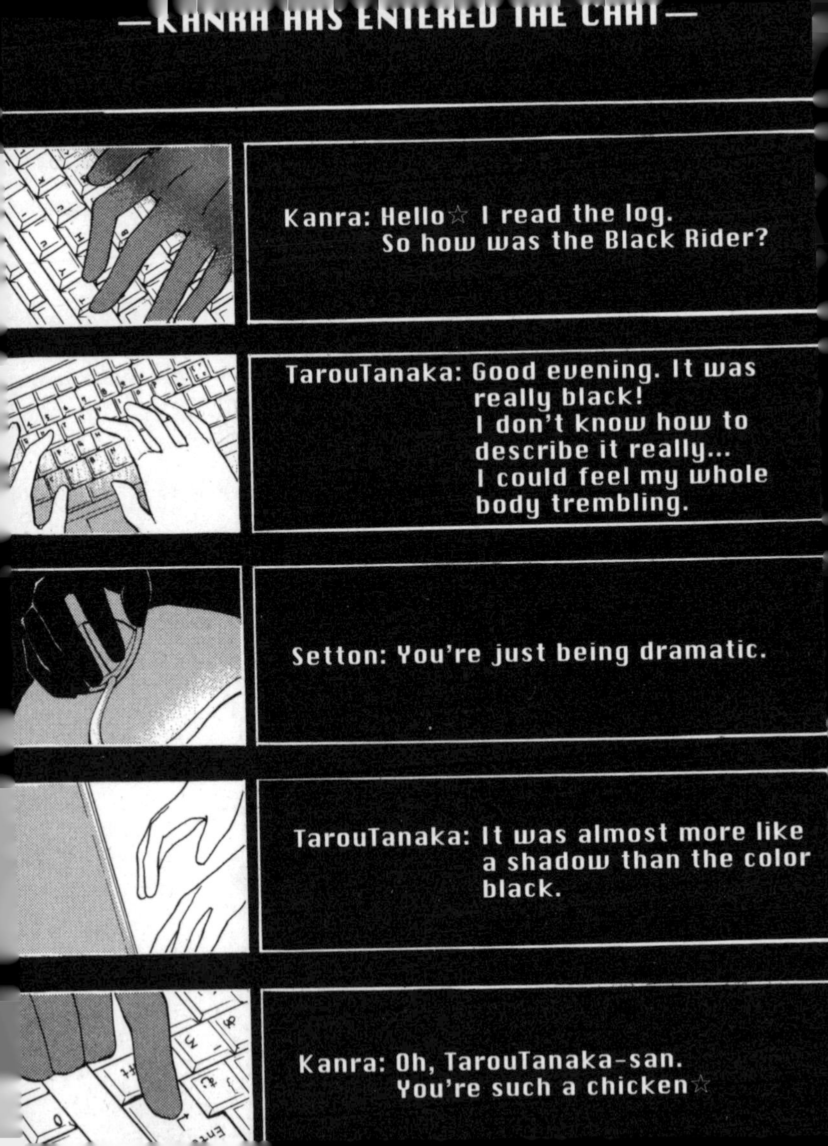
—KANRA HAS ENTERED THE CHAT—
Kanra: Hello☆ I read the log. So how was the Black Rider?
TarouTanaka: Good evening. It was really black! I don't know how to describe it really... I could feel my whole body trembling.
Setton: You're just being dramatic.
TarouTanaka: It was almost more like a shadow than the color black.
Kanra: Oh, TarouTanaka-san. You're such a chicken☆

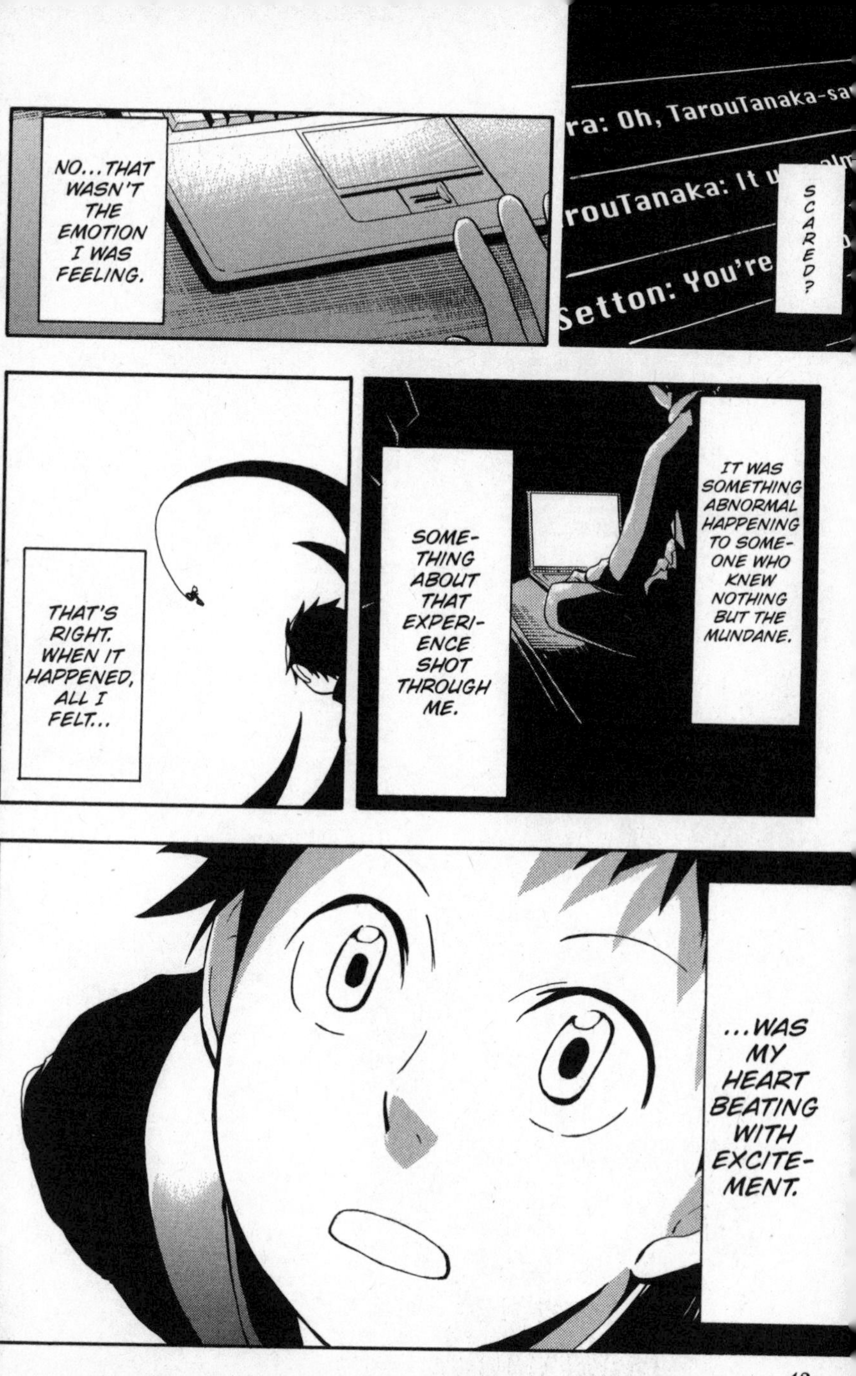
ra: Oh, TarouTanaka-sa
rouTanaka: It w
Setton: You're
SCARED?
NO...THAT WASN'T THE EMOTION I WAS FEELING.
IT WAS SOMETHING ABNORMAL HAPPENING TO SOME-ONE WHO KNEW NOTHING BUT THE MUNDANE.
SOME-THING ABOUT THAT EXPERI-ENCE SHOT THROUGH ME.
THAT'S RIGHT. WHEN IT HAPPENED, ALL I FELT...
...WAS MY HEART BEATING WITH EXCITE-MENT.

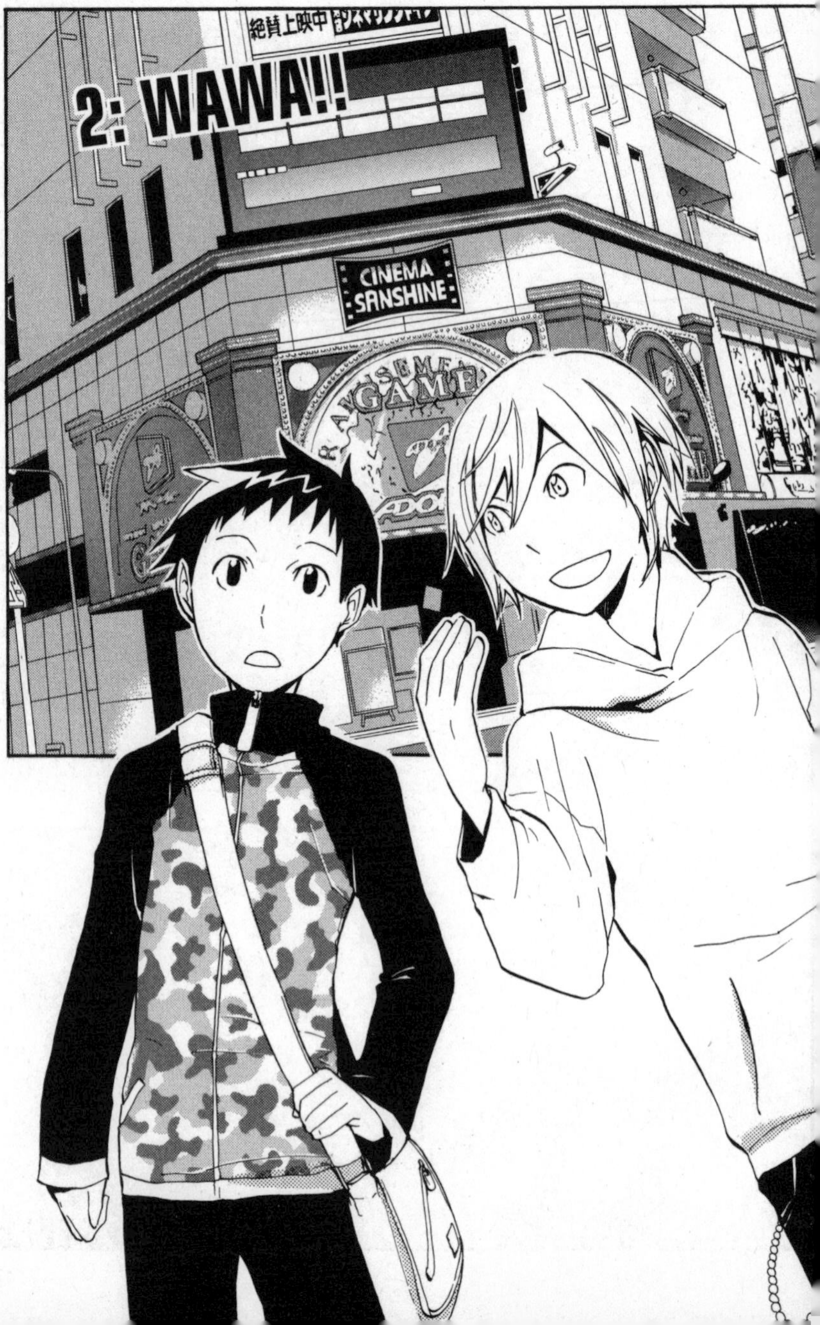
絶賛上映中
2: WAWA!!
CINEMA SANSHINE
GAME

BOXES: MOVING CENTER

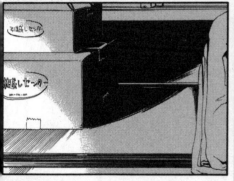

KACHI
(CLICK)

カチッ

カチカチ

KACHI

KACHI

LET'S
SEE...

BLACK
RIDER
...

FIRST
SPOTTED
IN THE CITY
AROUND
TWENTY
YEARS
AGO.

GAINED
NOTORIETY
LAST YEAR
WHEN THE
RIDER SHOWED
UP ON FILM
DURING THE
NEWS PROGRAM
CAUGHT ON
TAPE! TWENTY-
FOUR HOURS IN
IKEBUKURO...

KACHI

KACHI

44

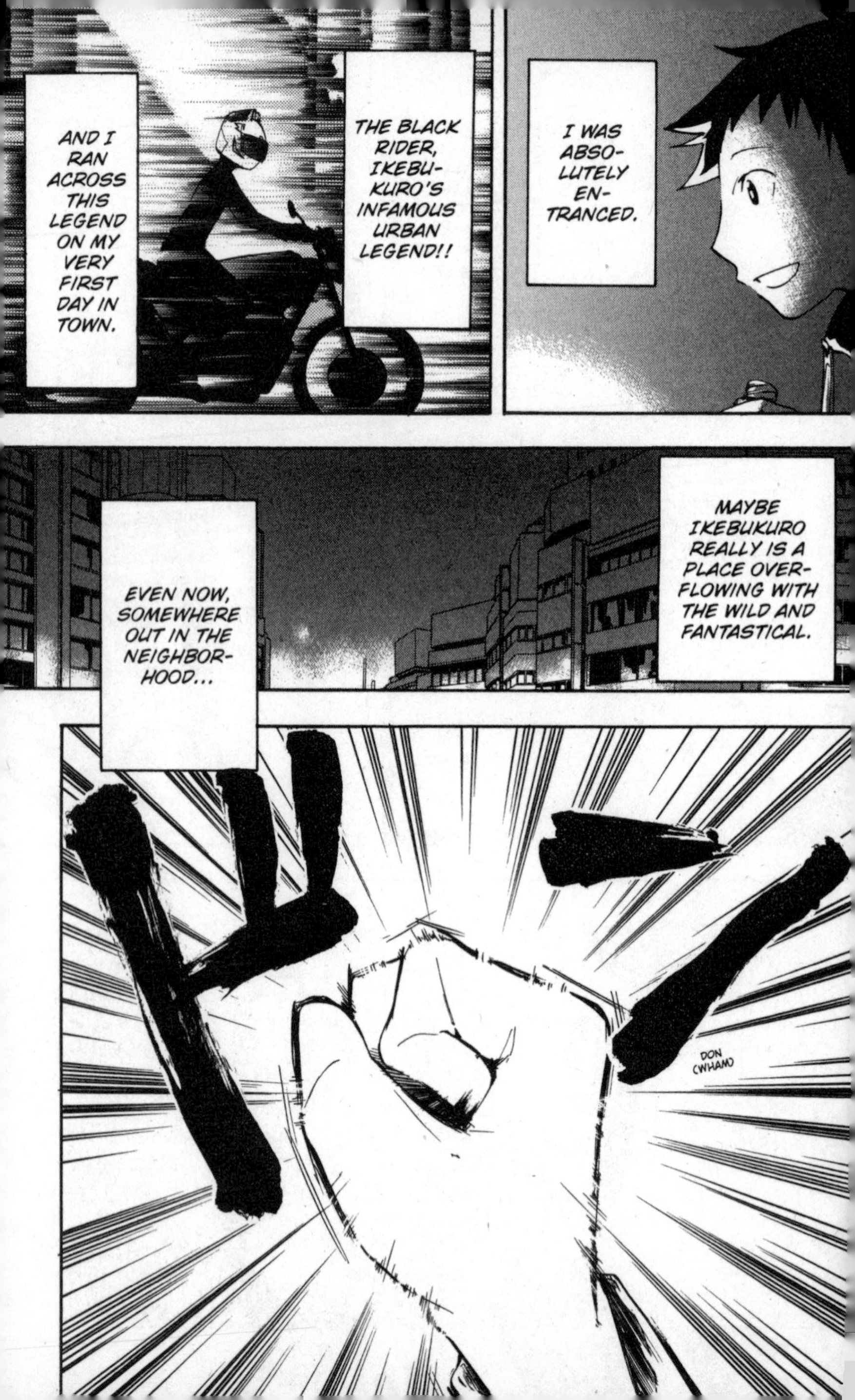
I WAS ABSO-LUTELY EN-TRANCED.
THE BLACK RIDER, IKEBU-KURO'S INFAMOUS URBAN LEGEND!!
AND I RAN ACROSS THIS LEGEND ON MY VERY FIRST DAY IN TOWN.
MAYBE IKEBUKURO REALLY IS A PLACE OVER-FLOWING WITH THE WILD AND FANTASTICAL.
EVEN NOW, SOMEWHERE OUT IN THE NEIGHBOR-HOOD...
DON (WHAM)

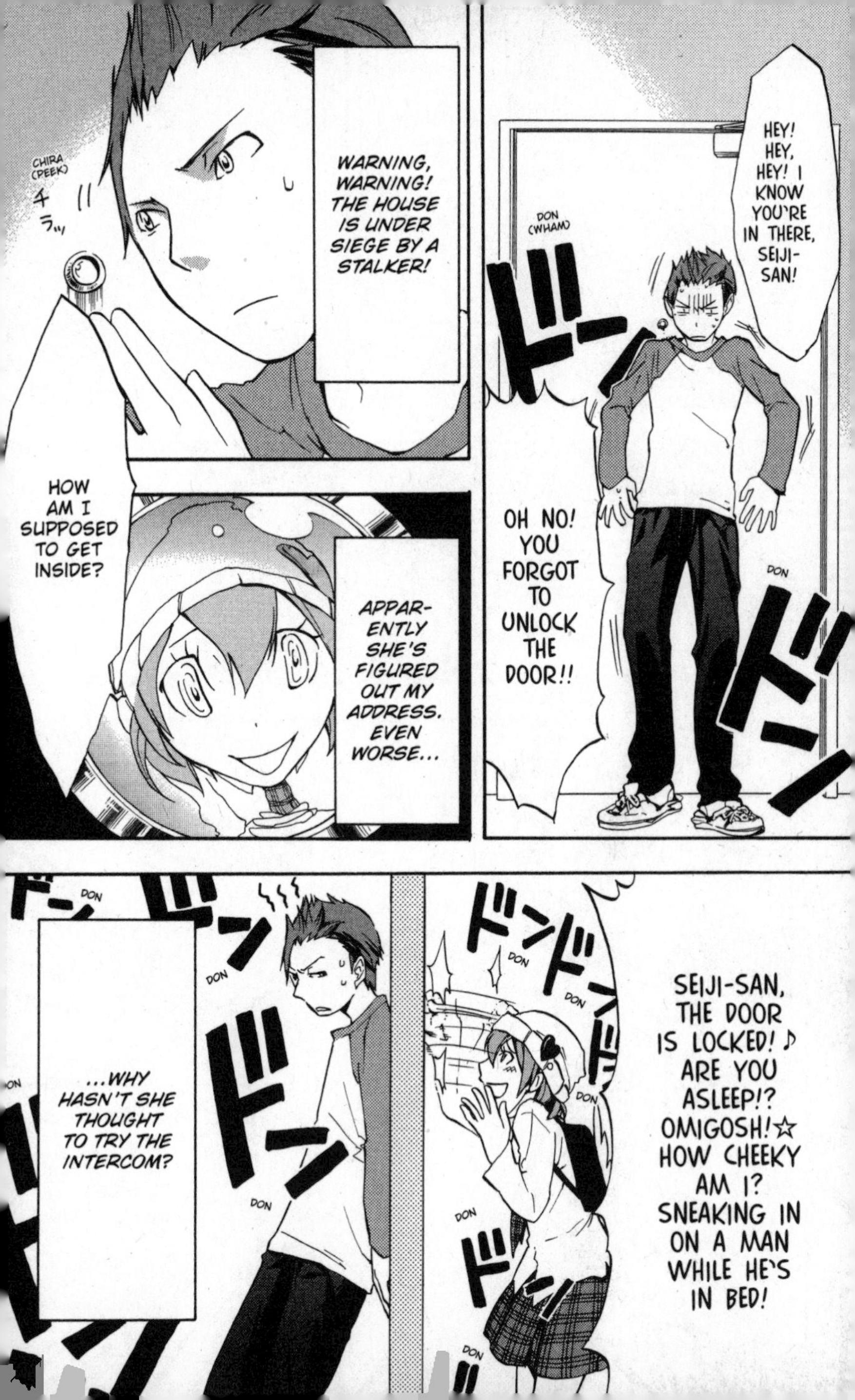

HEY! HEY, HEY! I KNOW YOU'RE IN THERE, SEIJI-SAN!
DON (WHAM)
OH NO! YOU FORGOT TO UNLOCK THE DOOR!!
DON
WARNING, WARNING! THE HOUSE IS UNDER SIEGE BY A STALKER!
CHIRA (PEEK)
APPARENTLY SHE'S FIGURED OUT MY ADDRESS. EVEN WORSE...
HOW AM I SUPPOSED TO GET INSIDE?
SEIJI-SAN, THE DOOR IS LOCKED! ♪ ARE YOU ASLEEP!? OMIGOSH! ☆ HOW CHEEKY AM I? SNEAKING IN ON A MAN WHILE HE'S IN BED!
DON
DON
DON
DON
DON
DON
...WHY HASN'T SHE THOUGHT TO TRY THE INTERCOM?
DON
DON

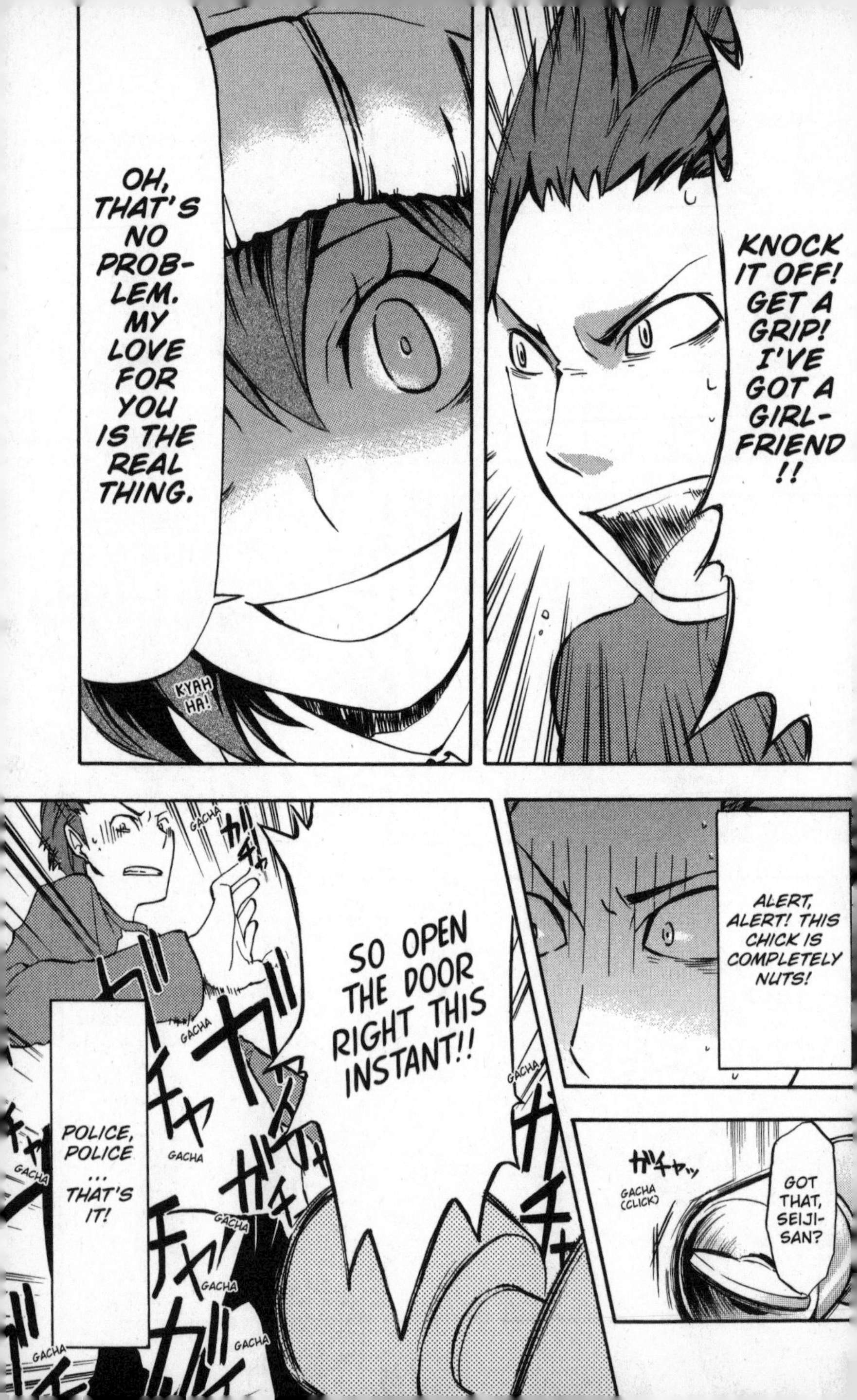
KNOCK IT OFF! GET A GRIP! I'VE GOT A GIRL-FRIEND!!
OH, THAT'S NO PROB-LEM. MY LOVE FOR YOU IS THE REAL THING.
KYAH HA!
ALERT, ALERT! THIS CHICK IS COMPLETELY NUTS!
ガチャッ
GACHA (CLICK)
GOT THAT, SEIJI-SAN?
SO OPEN THE DOOR RIGHT THIS INSTANT!!
GACHA
POLICE, POLICE ... THAT'S IT!
GACHA
GACHA
GACHA
GACHA
GACHA
GACHA
GACHA

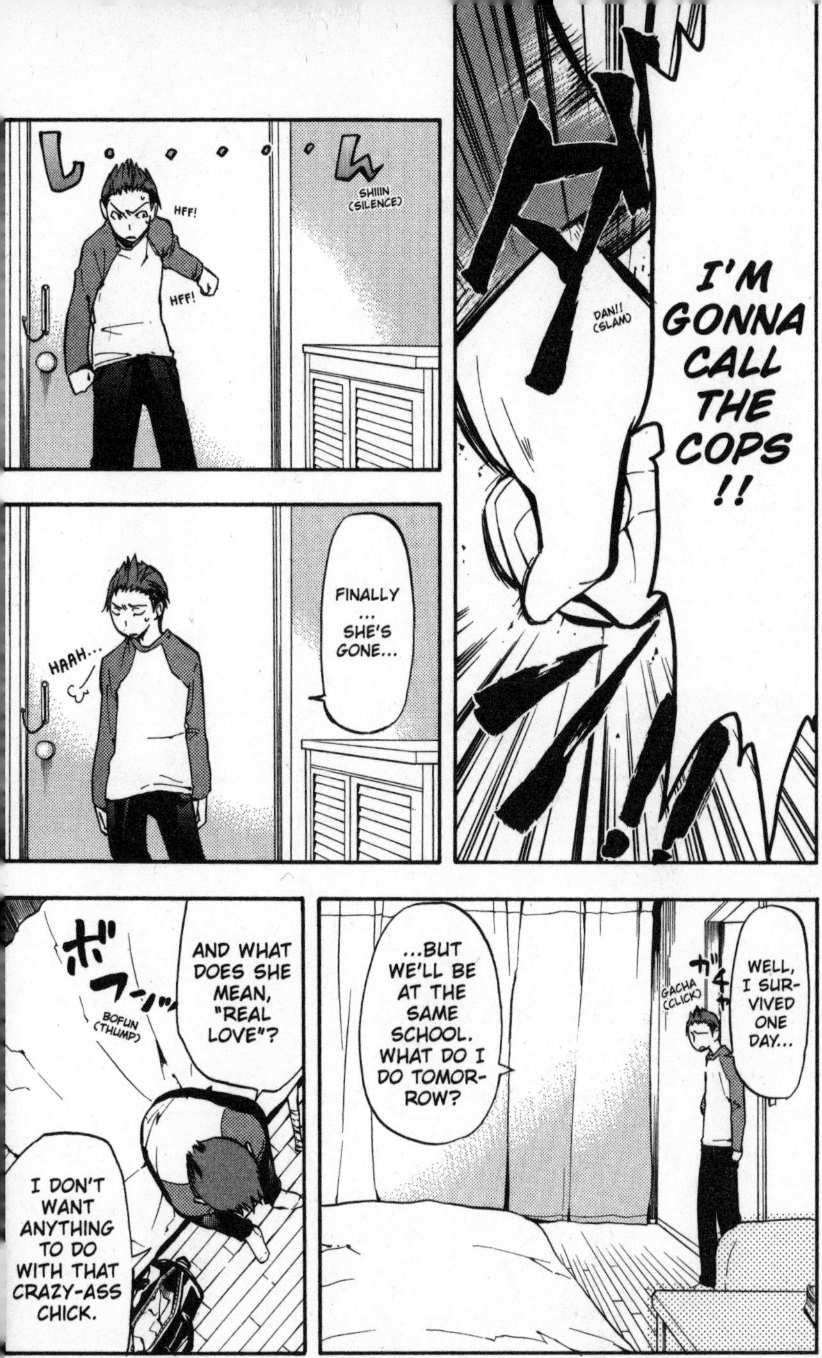
I'M GONNA CALL THE COPS!!
DAN!! (SLAM)
SHIIIN (SILENCE)
HFF!
HFF!
FINALLY... SHE'S GONE...
HAAH...
WELL, I SURVIVED ONE DAY...
GACHA (CLICK)
...BUT WE'LL BE AT THE SAME SCHOOL. WHAT DO I DO TOMORROW?
AND WHAT DOES SHE MEAN, "REAL LOVE"?
BOFUN (THUMP)
I DON'T WANT ANYTHING TO DO WITH THAT CRAZY-ASS CHICK.

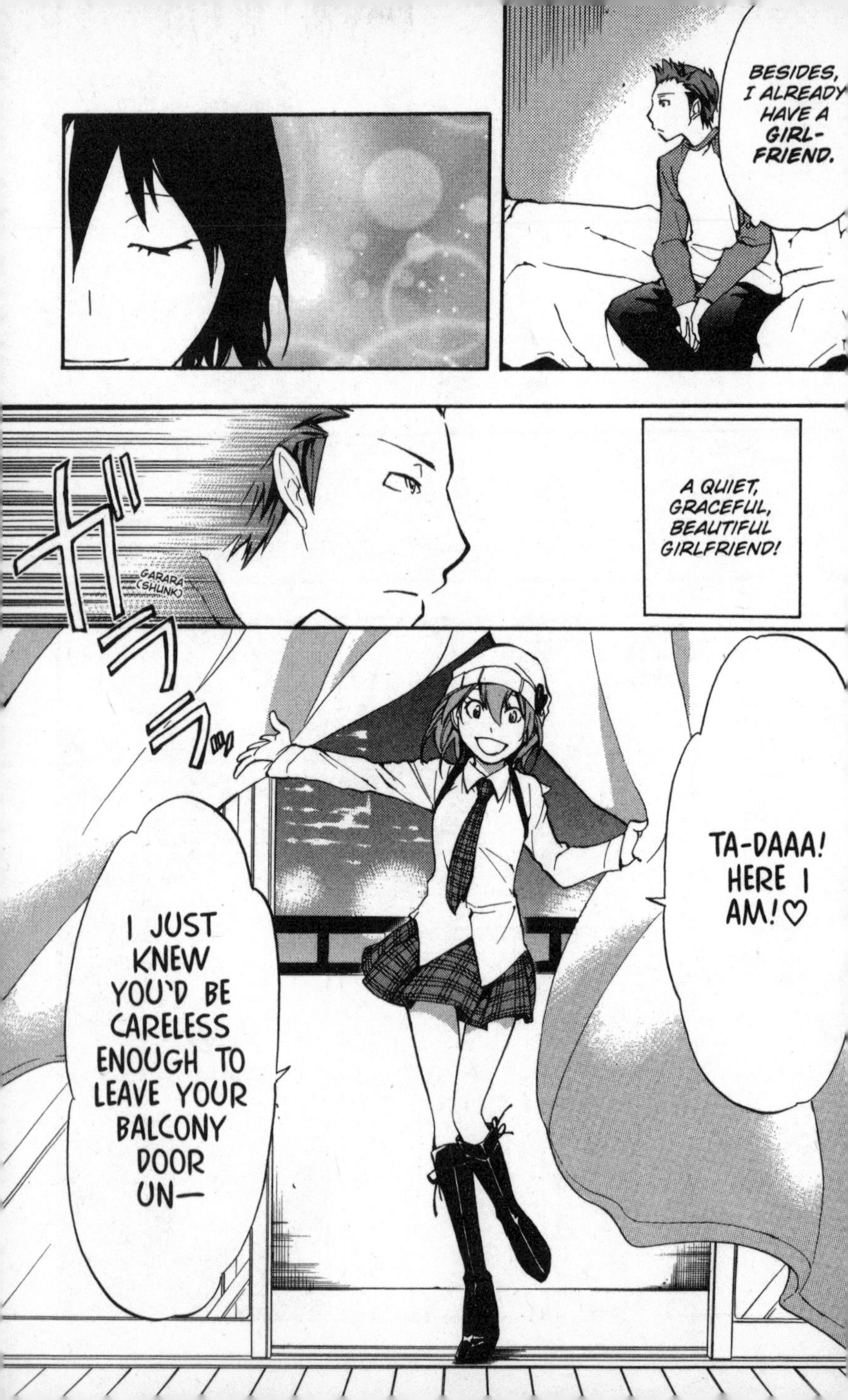
BESIDES, I ALREADY HAVE A GIRL-FRIEND.
A QUIET, GRACEFUL, BEAUTIFUL GIRLFRIEND!
GARARA (SHUNK)
TA-DAAA! HERE I AM!♡
I JUST KNEW YOU'D BE CARELESS ENOUGH TO LEAVE YOUR BALCONY DOOR UN—

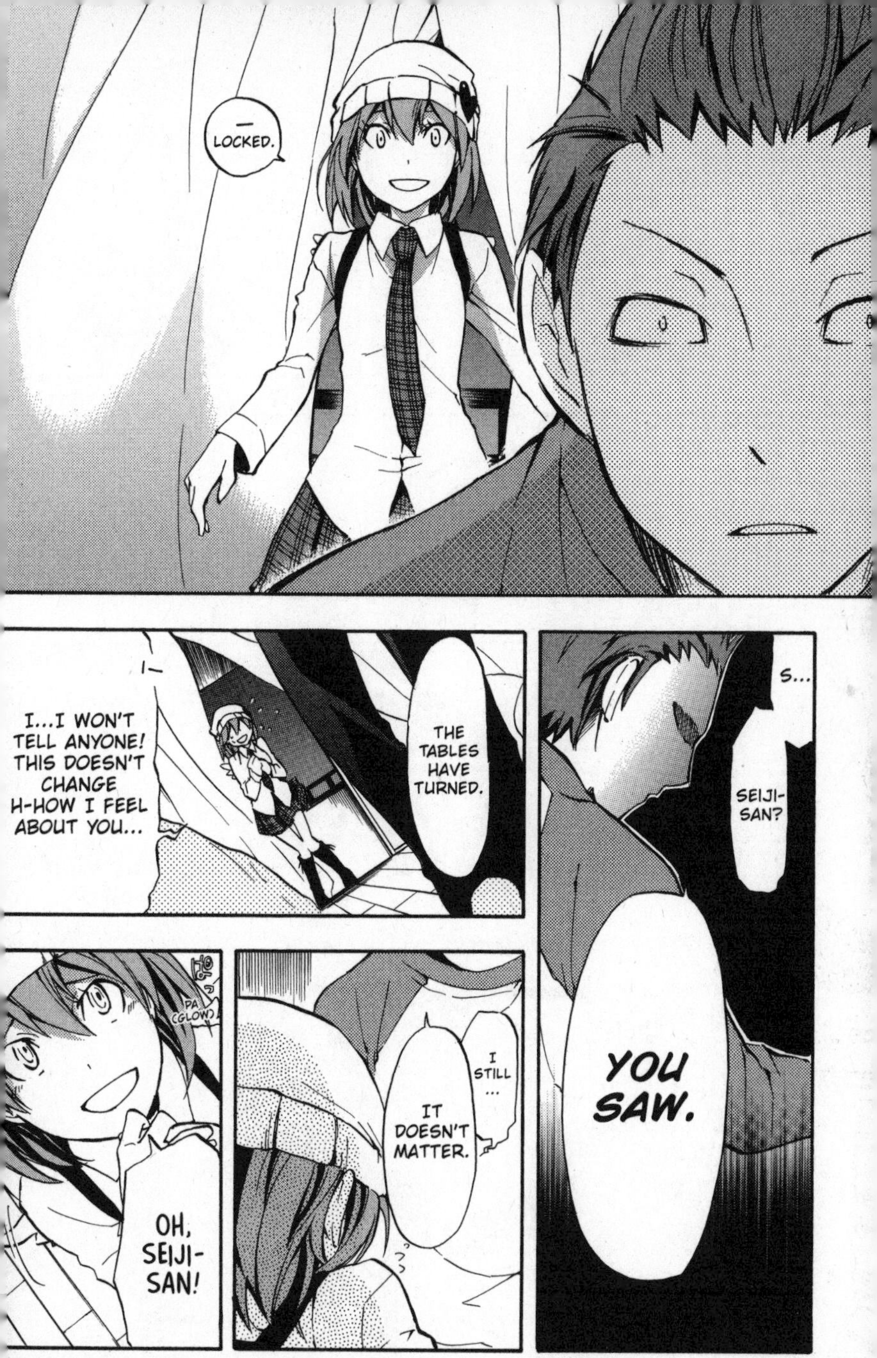
—LOCKED.
S...
SEIJI-SAN?
YOU SAW.
THE TABLES HAVE TURNED.
I—
I...I WON'T TELL ANYONE! THIS DOESN'T CHANGE H-HOW I FEEL ABOUT YOU...
I STILL ...
IT DOESN'T MATTER.
PA (GLOW)
OH, SEIJI-SAN!

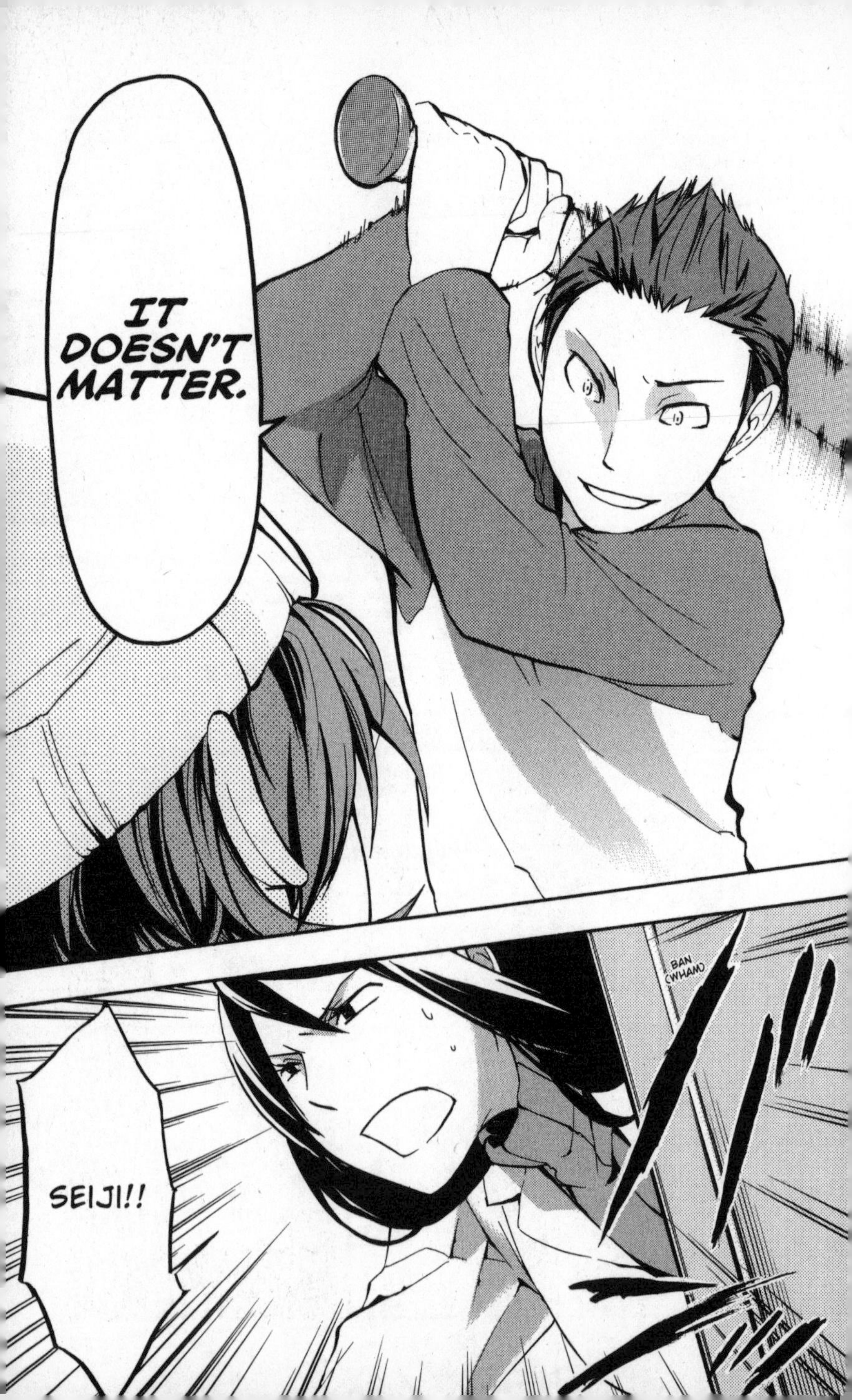
IT DOESN'T MATTER.
BAN (WHAM)
SEIJI!!

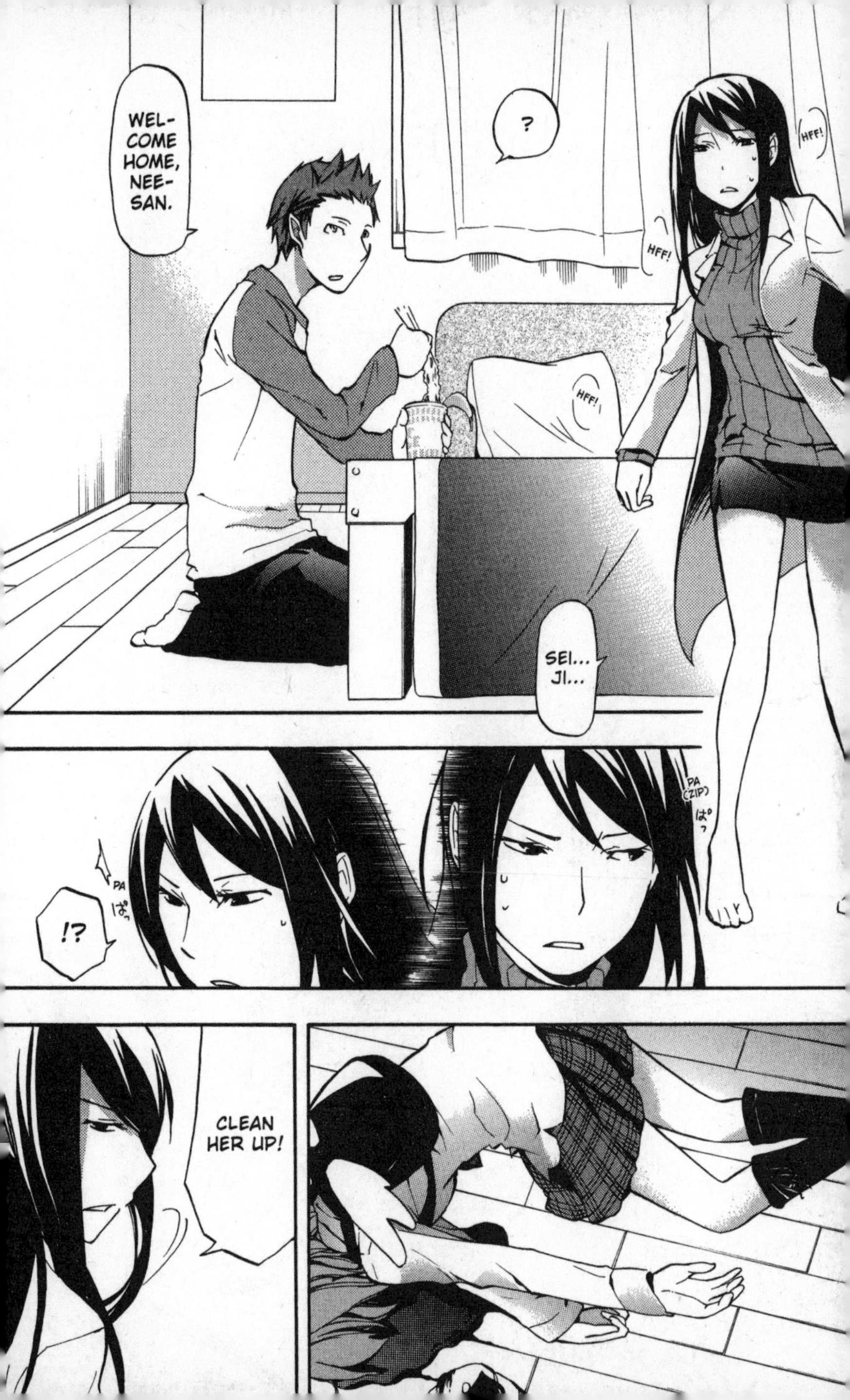
HFF!
?
HFF!
WEL-COME HOME, NEE-SAN.
HFF!
SEI... JI...
PA (ZIP) ぱっ
PA ぱっ
!?
CLEAN HER UP!

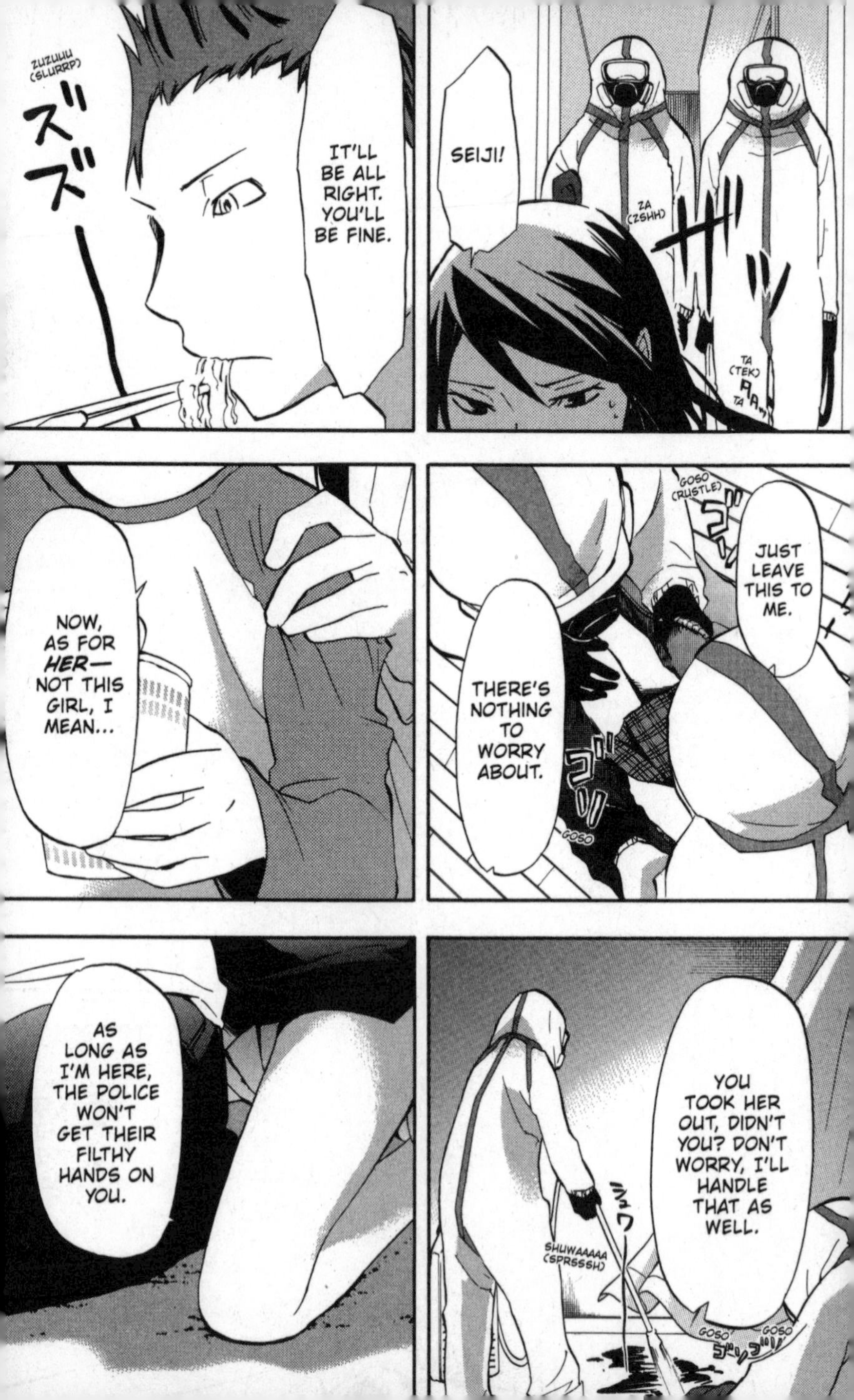
SEIJI!
ZA (ZSHH)
TA (TEK)
IT'LL BE ALL RIGHT. YOU'LL BE FINE.
ZUZUUU (SLURRP)
GOSO (RUSTLE)
JUST LEAVE THIS TO ME.
THERE'S NOTHING TO WORRY ABOUT.
GOSO
NOW, AS FOR *HER*—NOT THIS GIRL, I MEAN...
YOU TOOK HER OUT, DIDN'T YOU? DON'T WORRY, I'LL HANDLE THAT AS WELL.
SHUWAAAAA (SPRSSSH)
GOSO GOSO
AS LONG AS I'M HERE, THE POLICE WON'T GET THEIR FILTHY HANDS ON YOU.

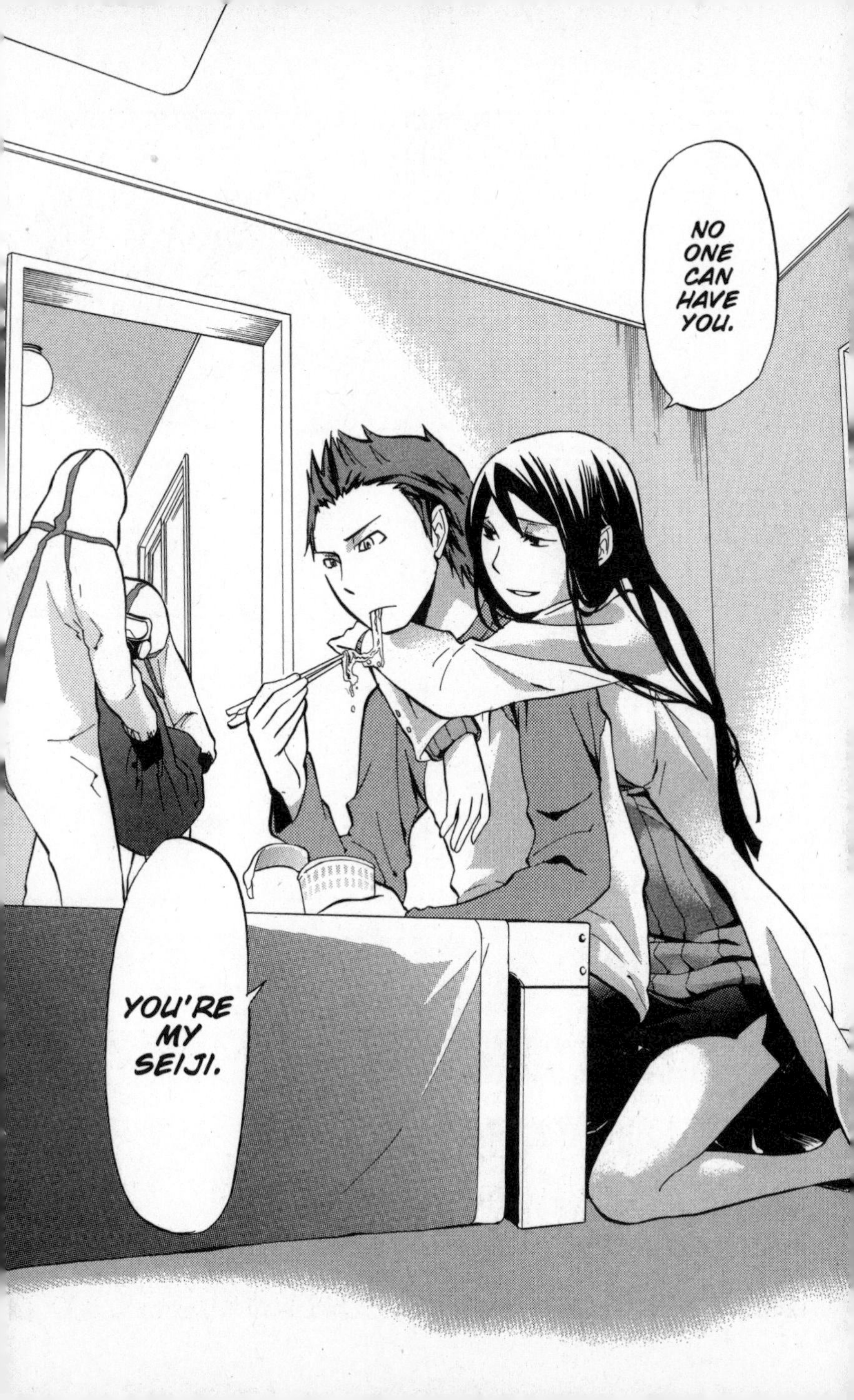
NO ONE CAN HAVE YOU.
YOU'RE MY SEIJI.

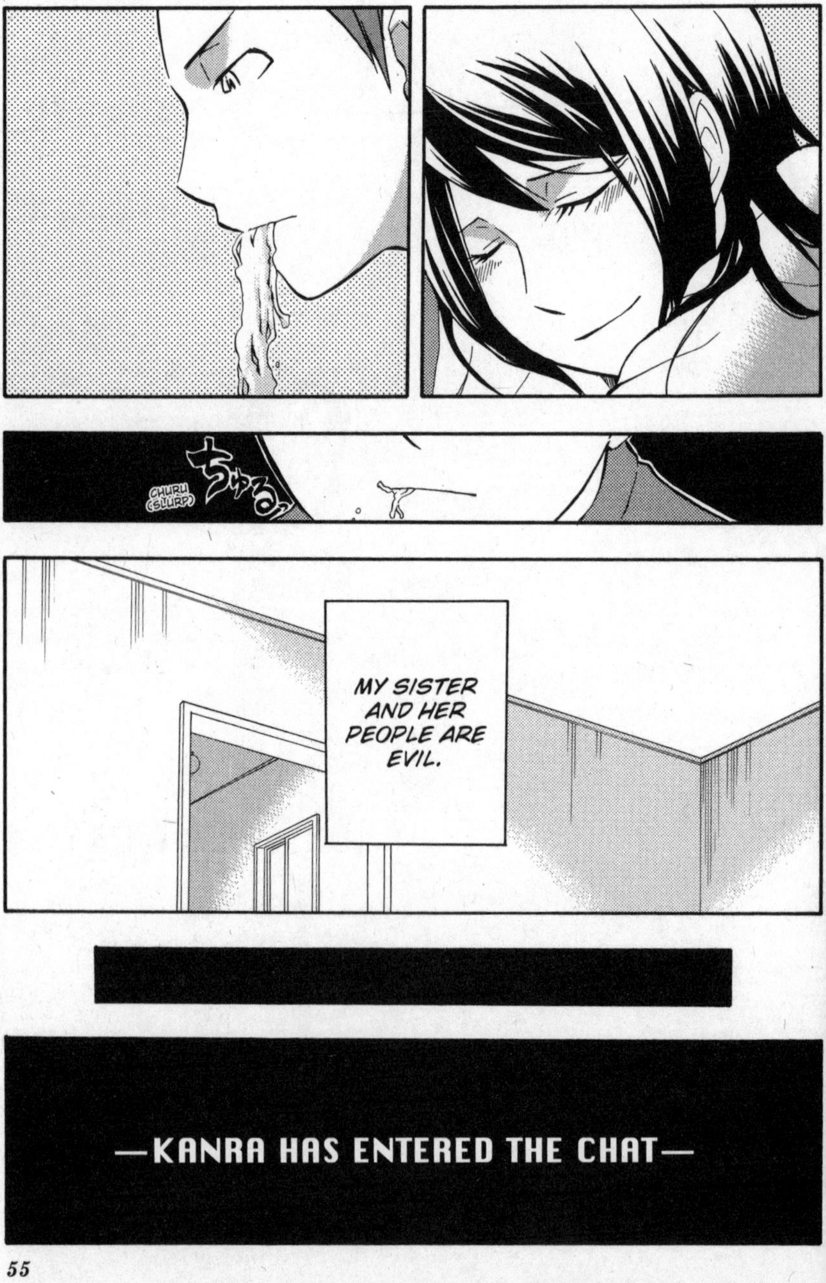
CHURU (SLURP)
MY SISTER AND HER PEOPLE ARE EVIL.
—KANRA HAS ENTERED THE CHAT—

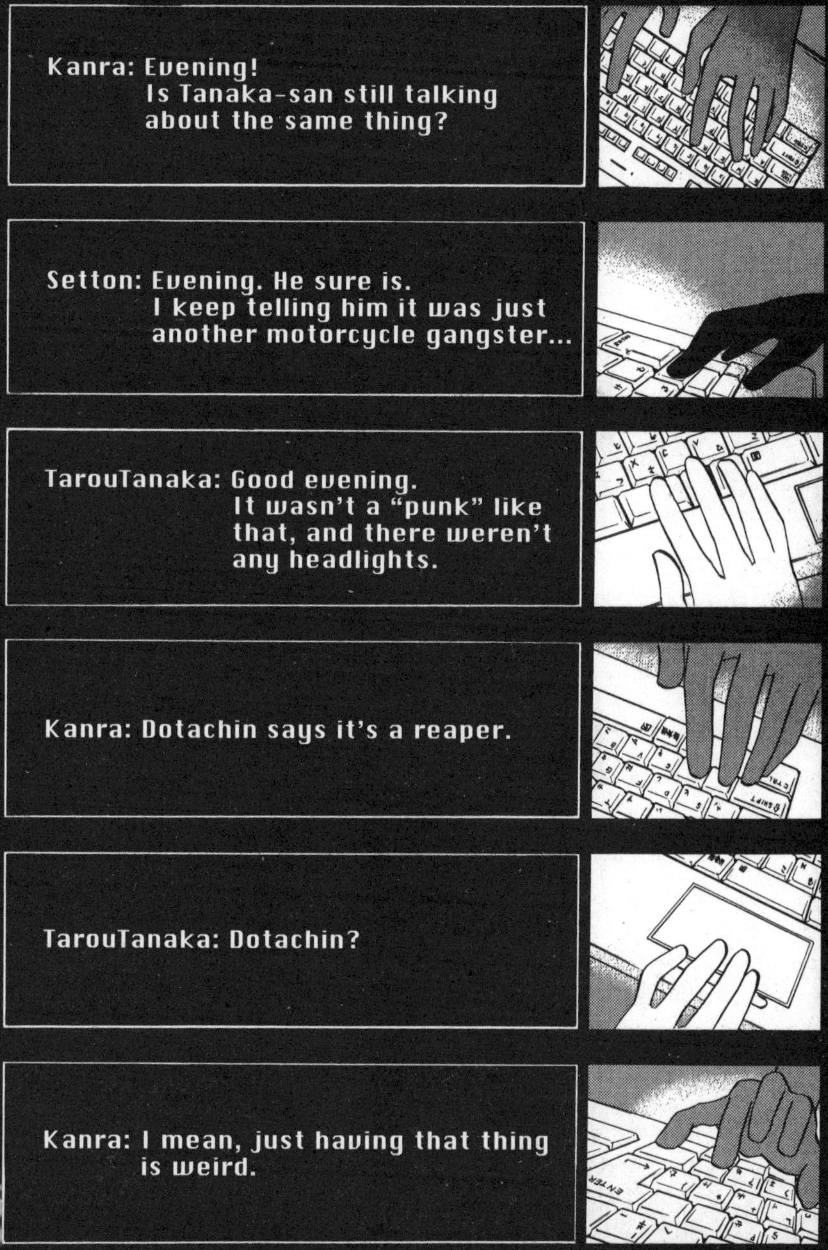
Kanra: Evening!
Is Tanaka-san still talking about the same thing?
Setton: Evening. He sure is.
I keep telling him it was just another motorcycle gangster...
TarouTanaka: Good evening.
It wasn't a "punk" like that, and there weren't any headlights.
Kanra: Dotachin says it's a reaper.
TarouTanaka: Dotachin?
Kanra: I mean, just having that thing is weird.

TarouTanaka: Gonna leave me hanging?
Who's Dotachin?

Setton: I'm sorry.
I've got to log off for the night, got business to attend to...

TarouTanaka: Aww, look at the time!
Dang...I want to hear more details, but I've got an early morning tomorrow.

Kanra: Well, talk to you later.
Heh-heh, wait, one last thing...

TarouTanaka: ?

Kanra: The guy riding the black motorcycle—

C-CAN IT BE...!?

—THERE ARE CURRENTLY NO USERS IN THE CHAT ROOM—

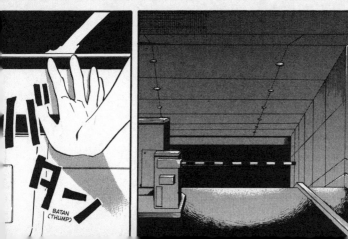

BATAN
(THUMP)

P
← 24H

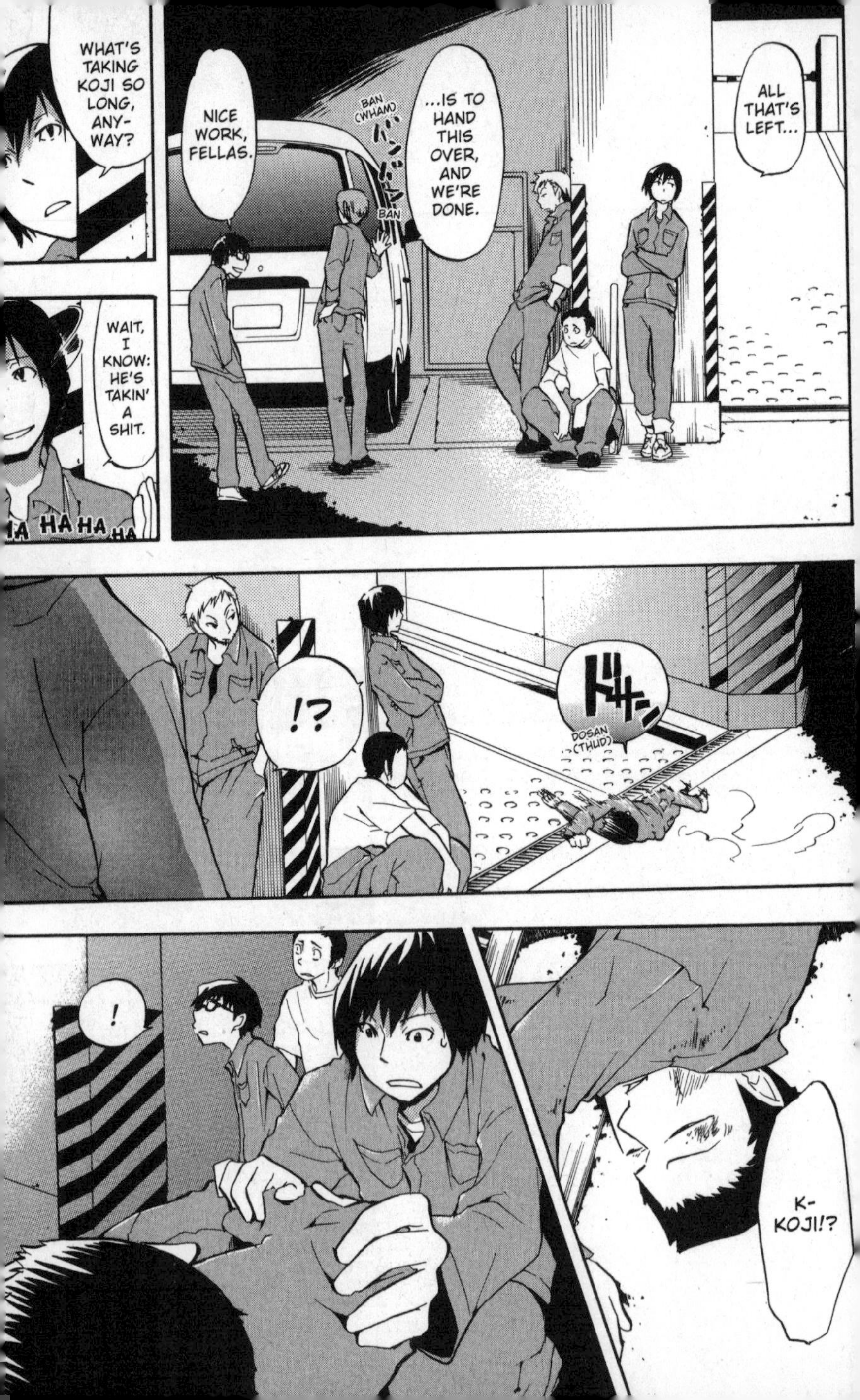
ALL THAT'S LEFT...
...IS TO HAND THIS OVER, AND WE'RE DONE.
BAN (WHAM)
BAN
NICE WORK, FELLAS.
WHAT'S TAKING KOJI SO LONG, ANY-WAY?
WAIT, I KNOW: HE'S TAKIN' A SHIT.
HA HA HA
DOSAN (THUD)
!?
K-KOJI!?
!

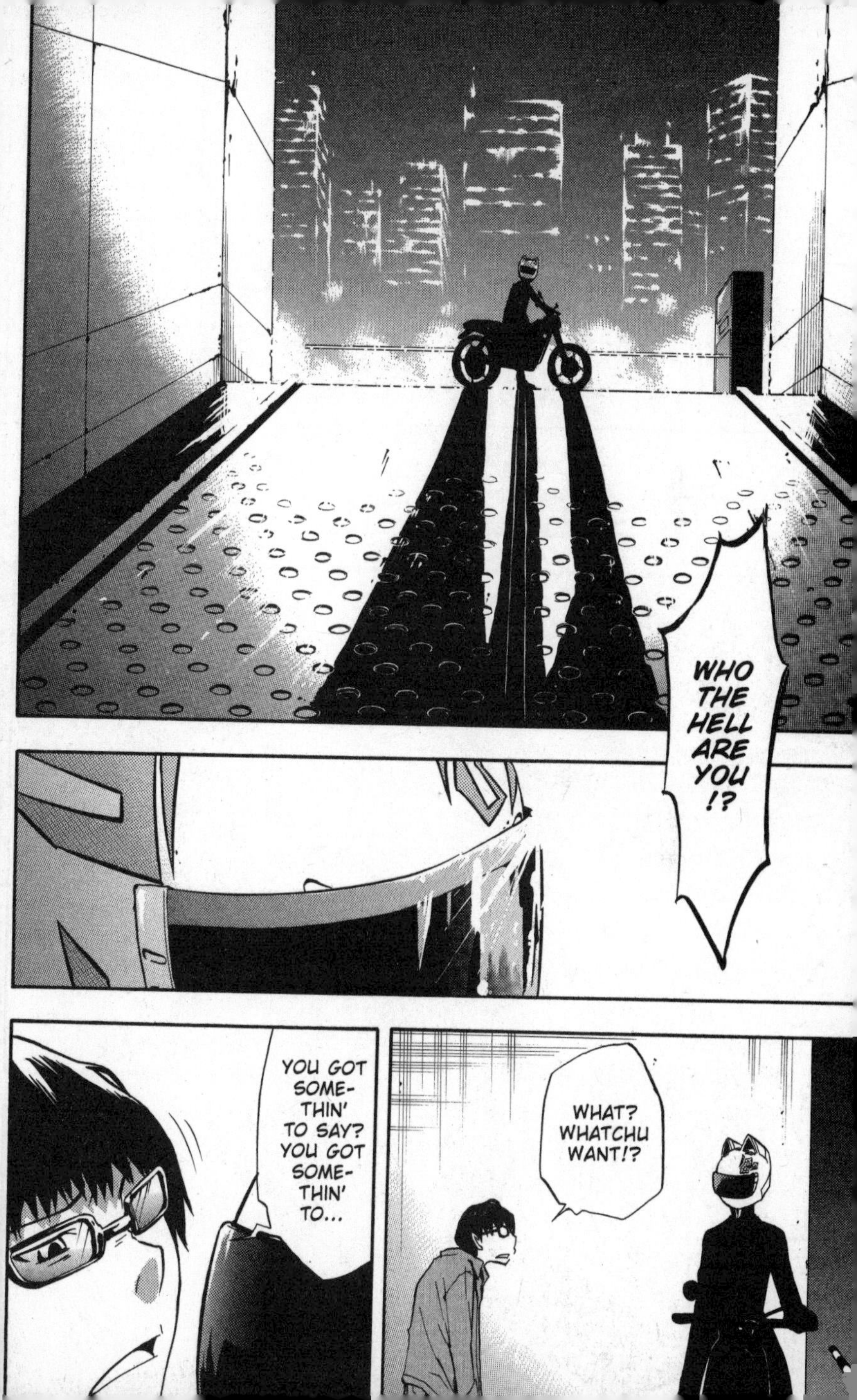
WHO THE HELL ARE YOU!?
WHAT? WHATCHU WANT!?
YOU GOT SOME-THIN' TO SAY? YOU GOT SOME-THIN' TO...

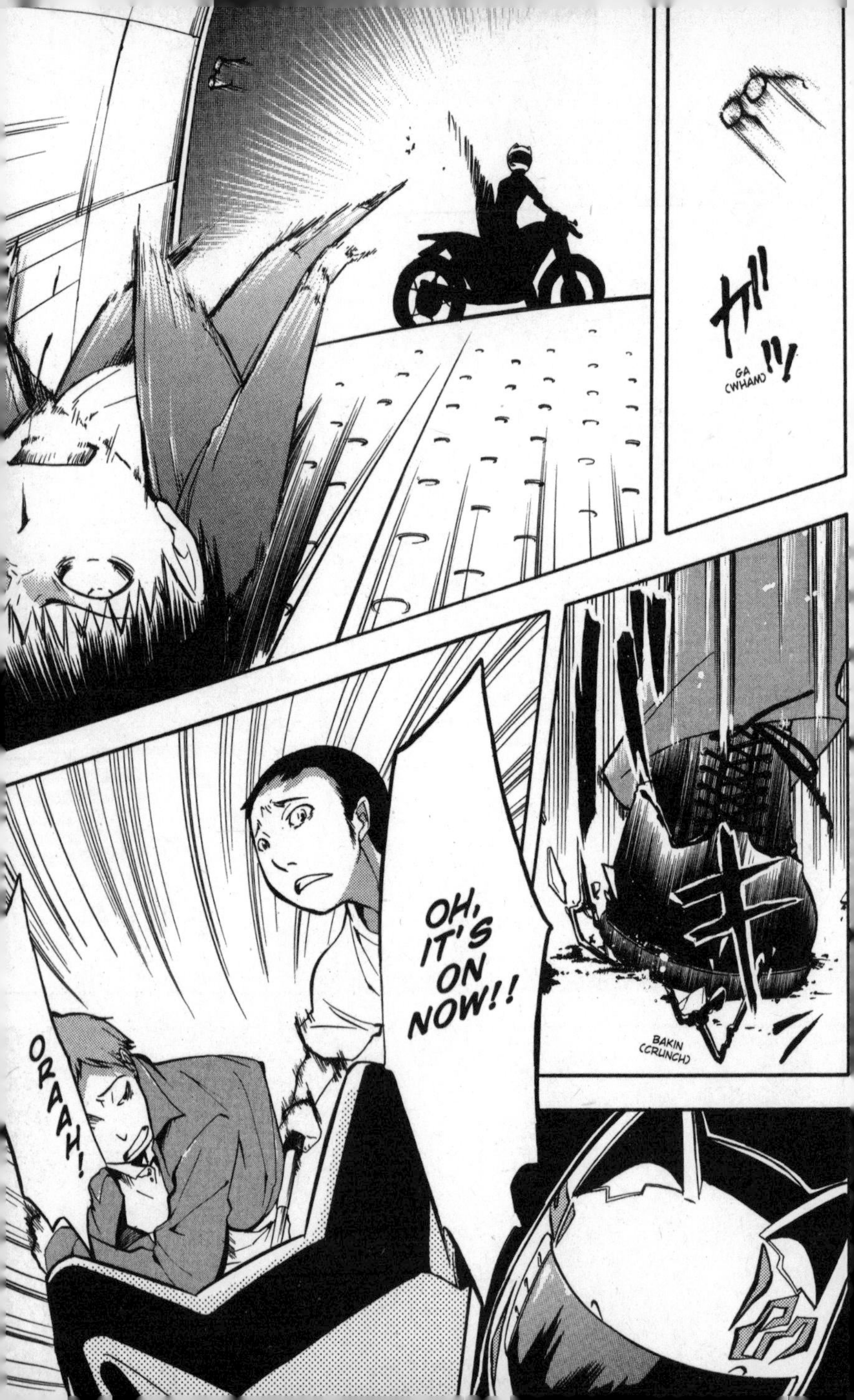

GA (WHAM)!!
BAKIN (CRUNCH)
OH, IT'S ON NOW!!
ORAAAH!

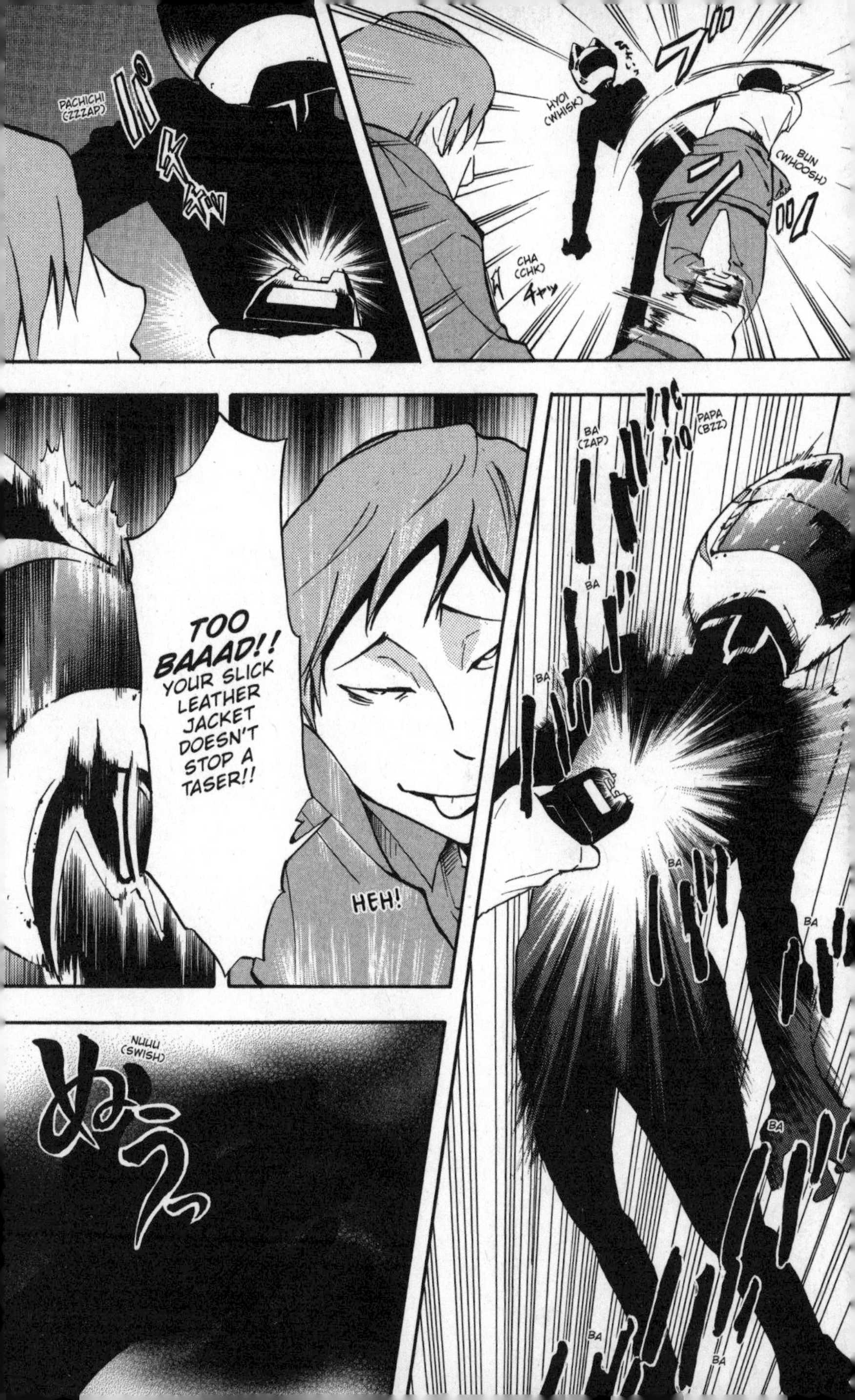
HYOI (WHISK)
BUN (WHOOSH)
CHA (CHK)
PACHICHI (ZZZAP)
PAPA (BZZ)
BA (ZAP)
BA
BA
BA
BA
BA
BA
BA
TOO BAAAD!! YOUR SLICK LEATHER JACKET DOESN'T STOP A TASER!!
HEH!
NUUU (SWISH)

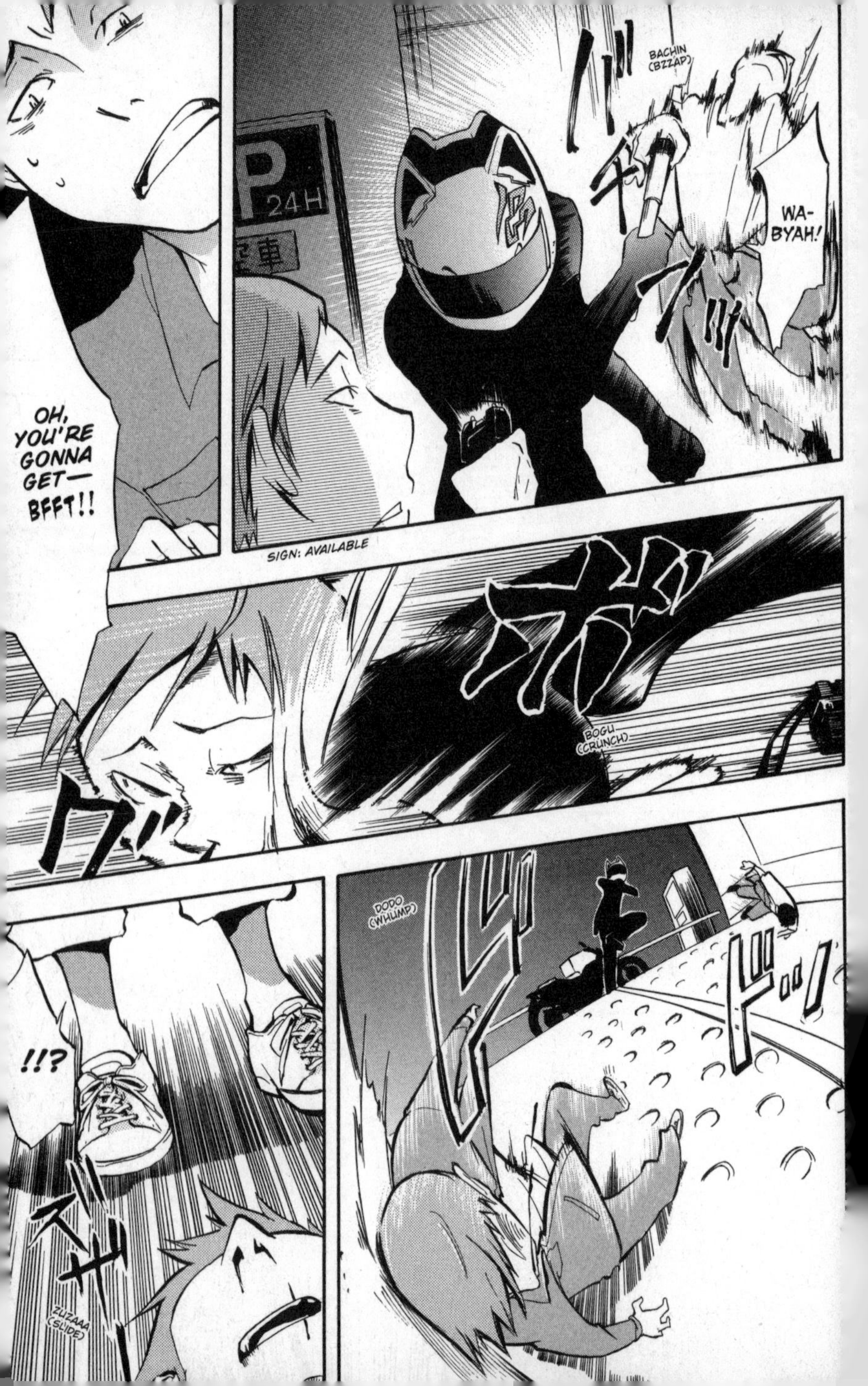
BACHIN (BZZAP)
WA-BYAH!
SIGN: AVAILABLE
OH, YOU'RE GONNA GET—BFFT!!
BOGU (CRUNCH)
DODO (WHUMP)
!!?
ZUZAAA (SLIDE)

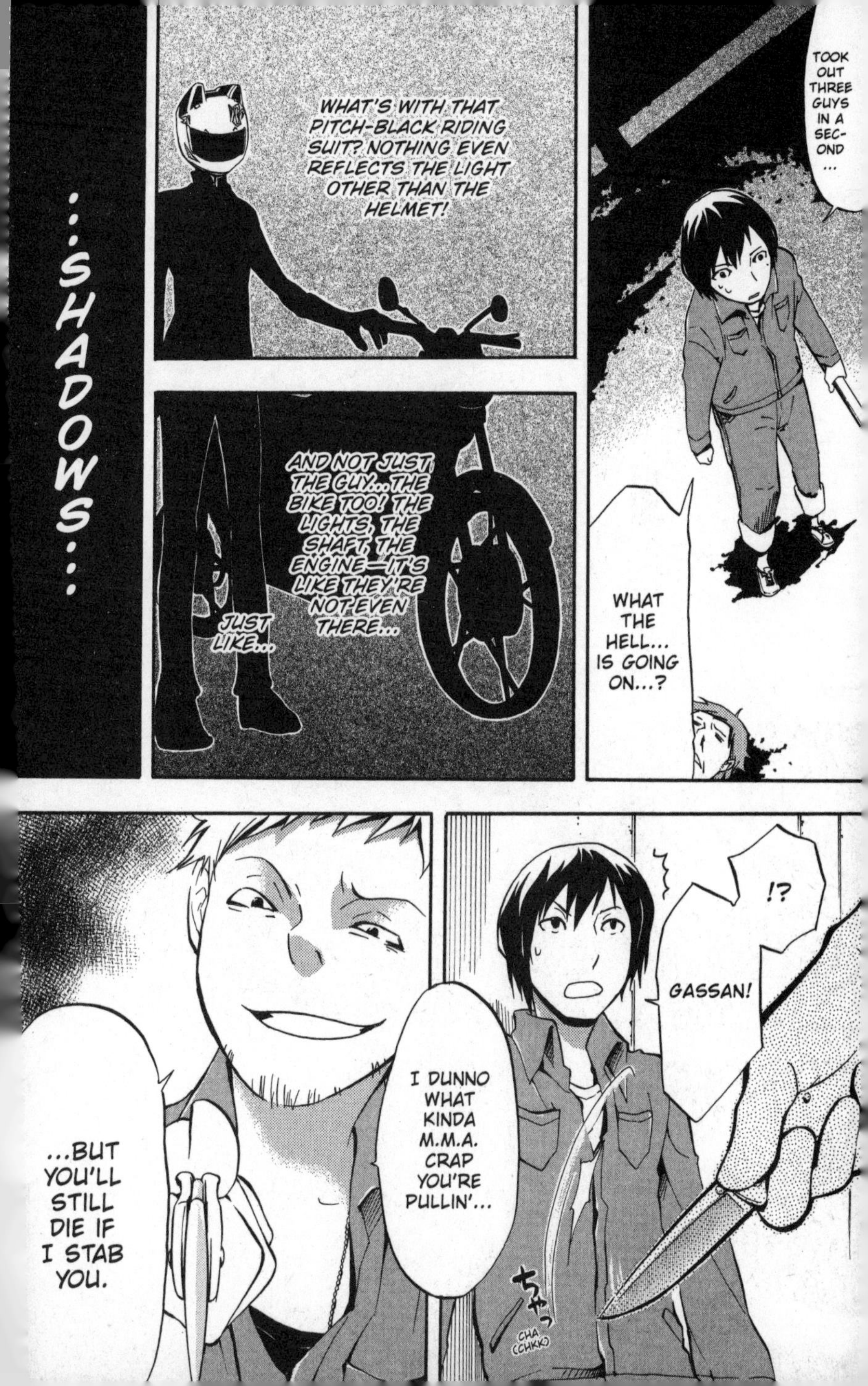
TOOK OUT THREE GUYS IN A SEC-OND...
WHAT THE HELL... IS GOING ON...?
WHAT'S WITH THAT PITCH-BLACK RIDING SUIT? NOTHING EVEN REFLECTS THE LIGHT OTHER THAN THE HELMET!
AND NOT JUST THE GUY... THE BIKE TOO! THE LIGHTS, THE SHAFT, THE ENGINE—IT'S LIKE THEY'RE NOT EVEN THERE...
JUST LIKE...
...SHADOWS...
!?
GASSAN!
ちゃっ
CHA (CHKK)
I DUNNO WHAT KINDA M.M.A. CRAP YOU'RE PULLIN'...
...BUT YOU'LL STILL DIE IF I STAB YOU.

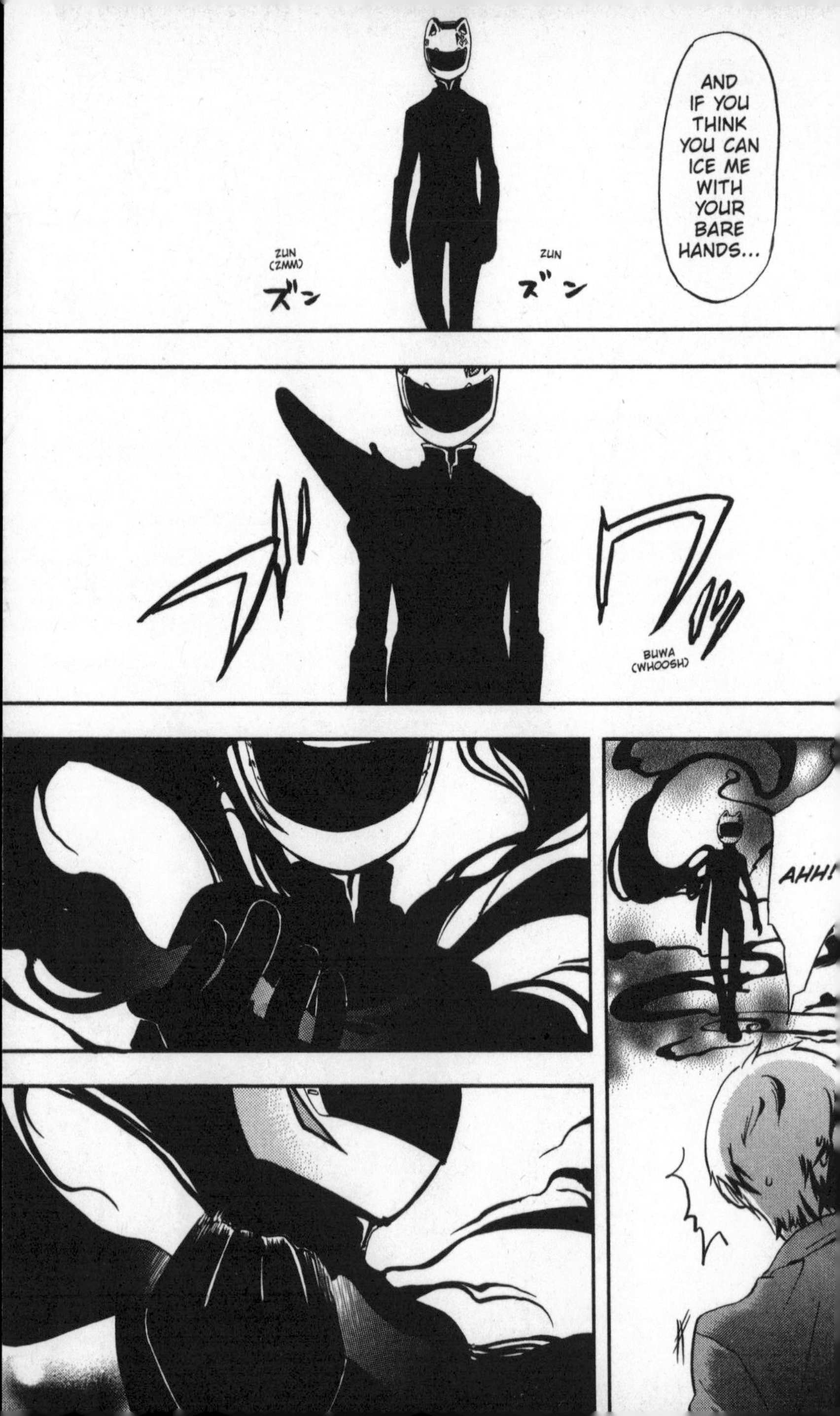
AND IF YOU THINK YOU CAN ICE ME WITH YOUR BARE HANDS...
ZUN
ズン
ZUN (ZMM)
ズン
ブワッ
BUWA (WHOOSH)
AHH!

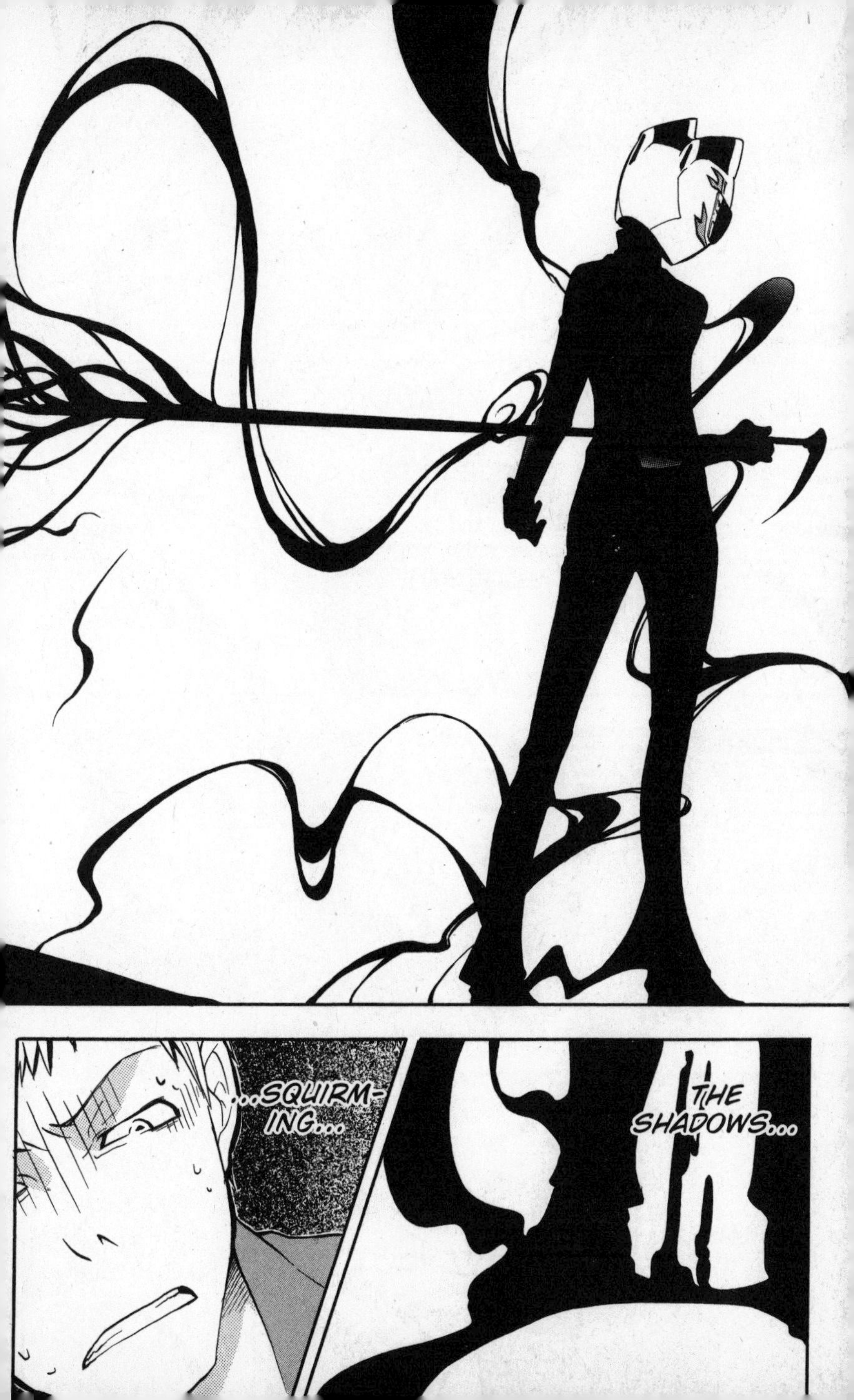
THE SHADOWS...
...SQUIRM-
ING...

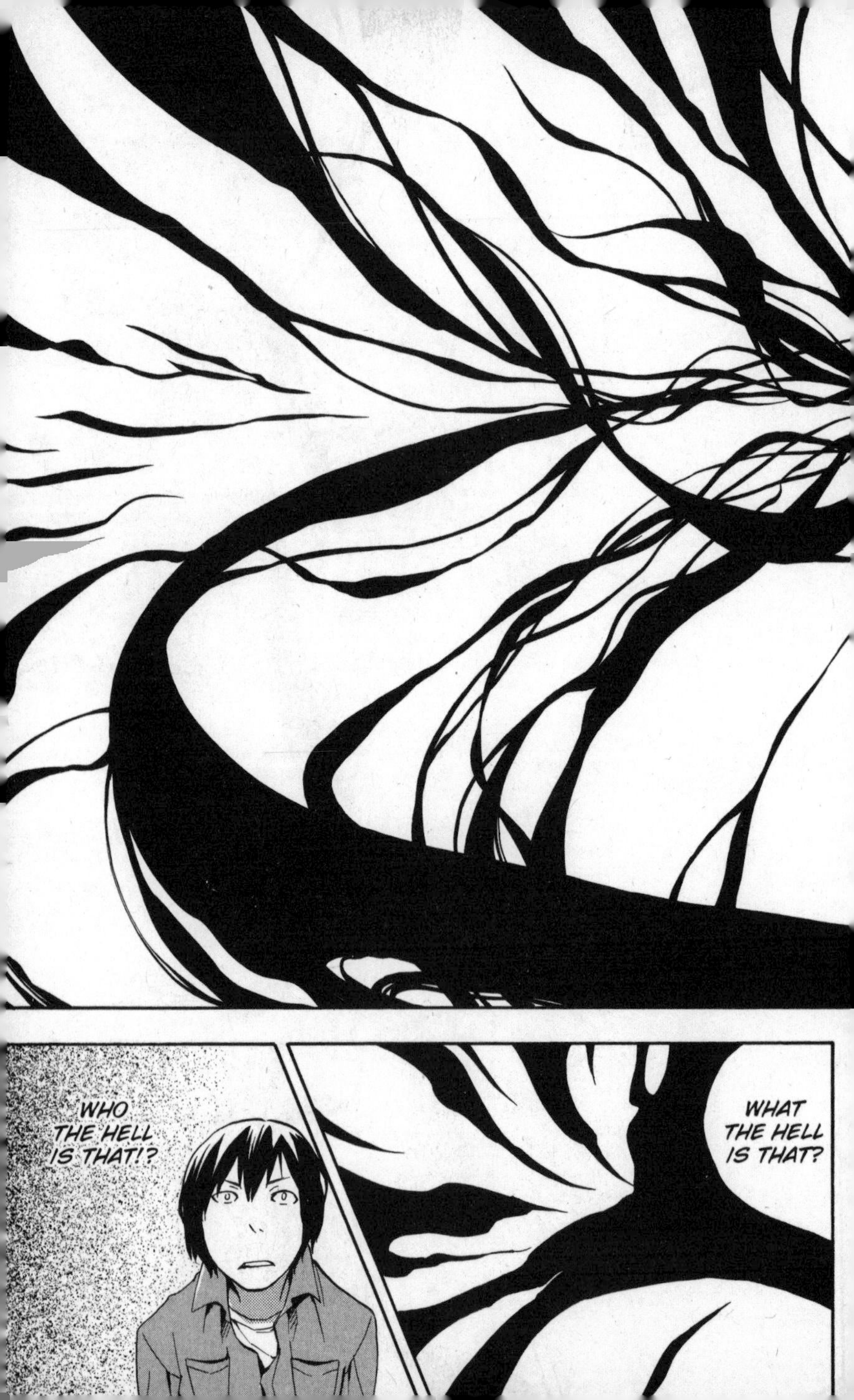
WHAT THE HELL IS THAT?
WHO THE HELL IS THAT!?

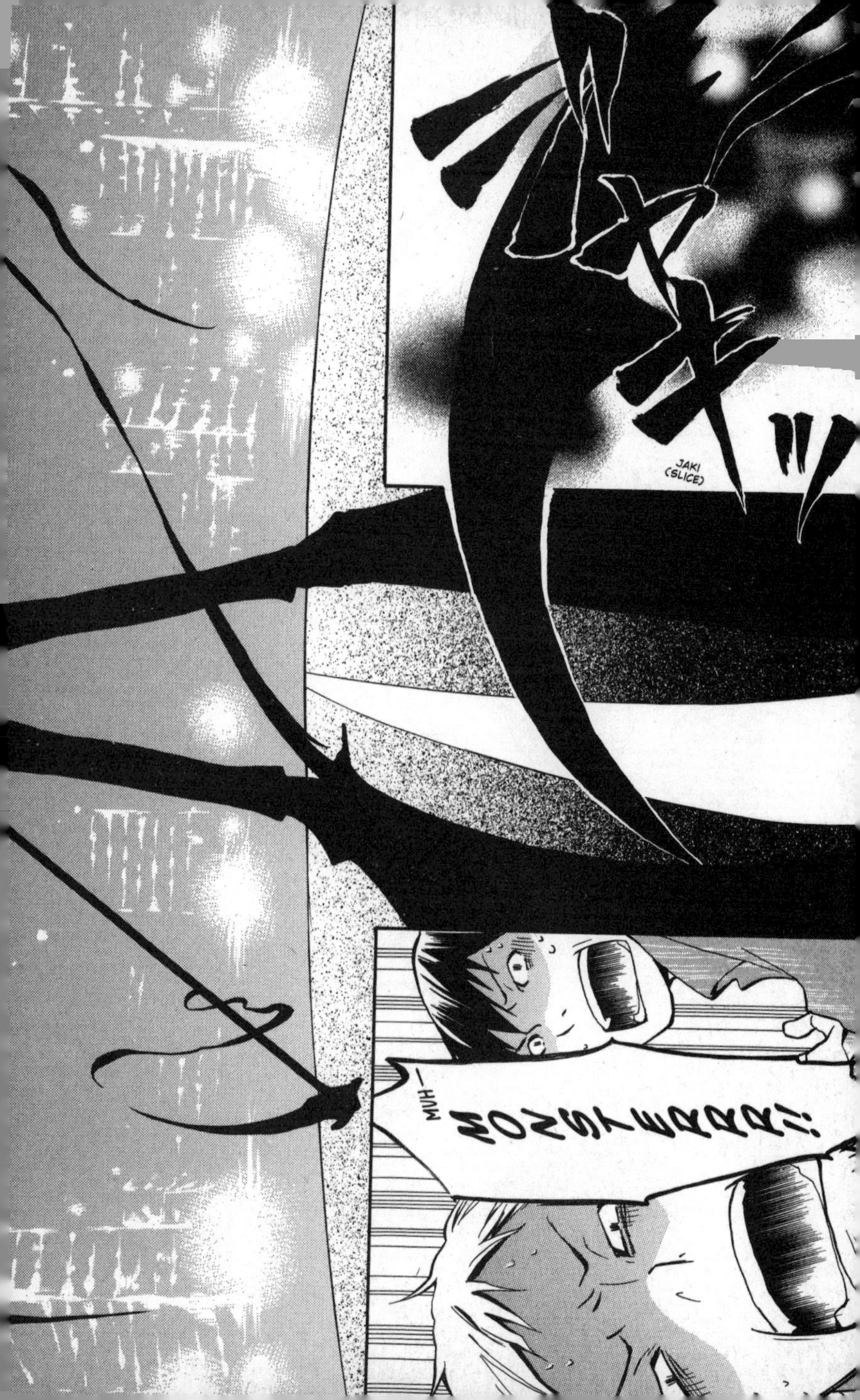
JAKI (SLICE)
MUH—
MONSTERRR!!

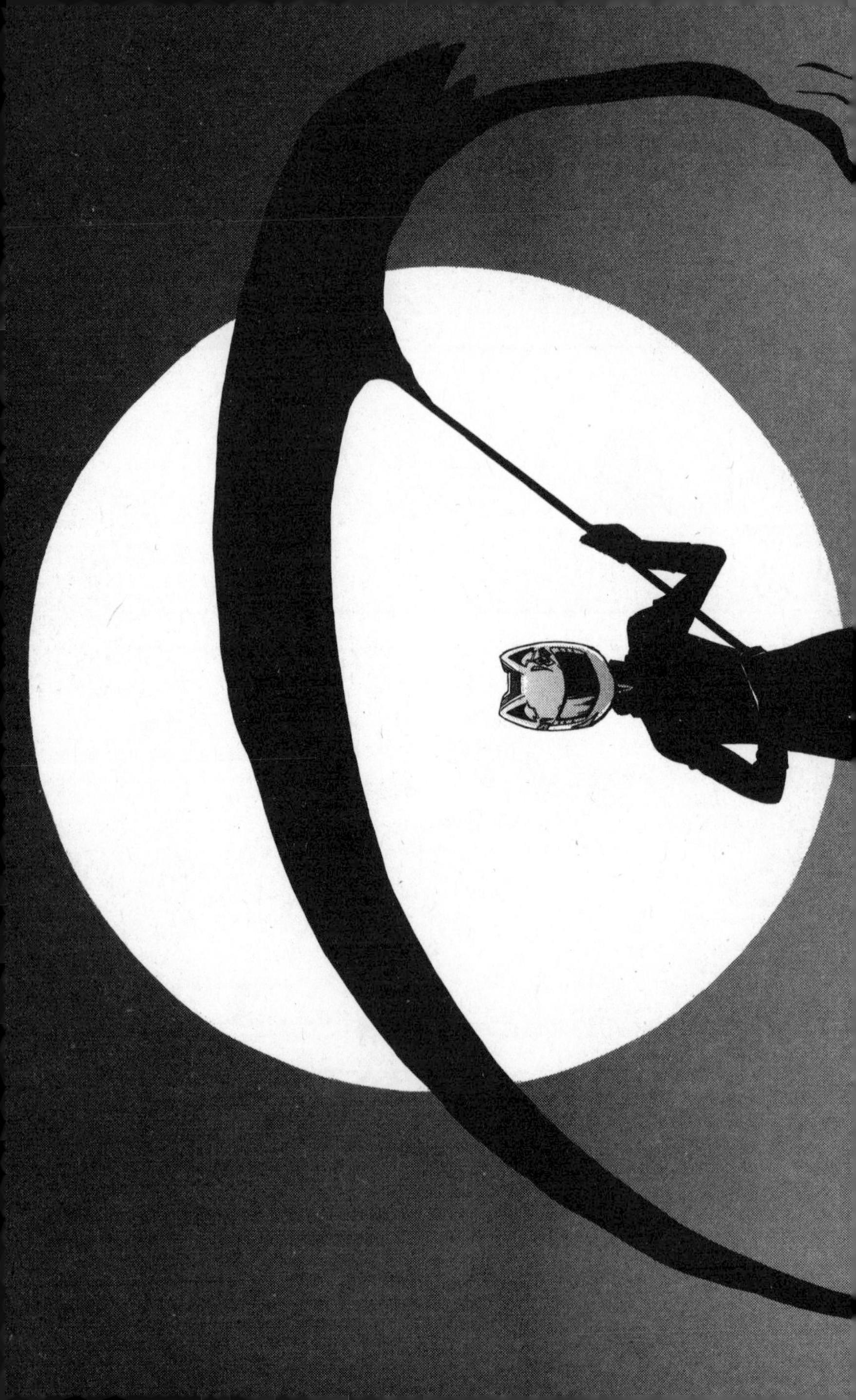

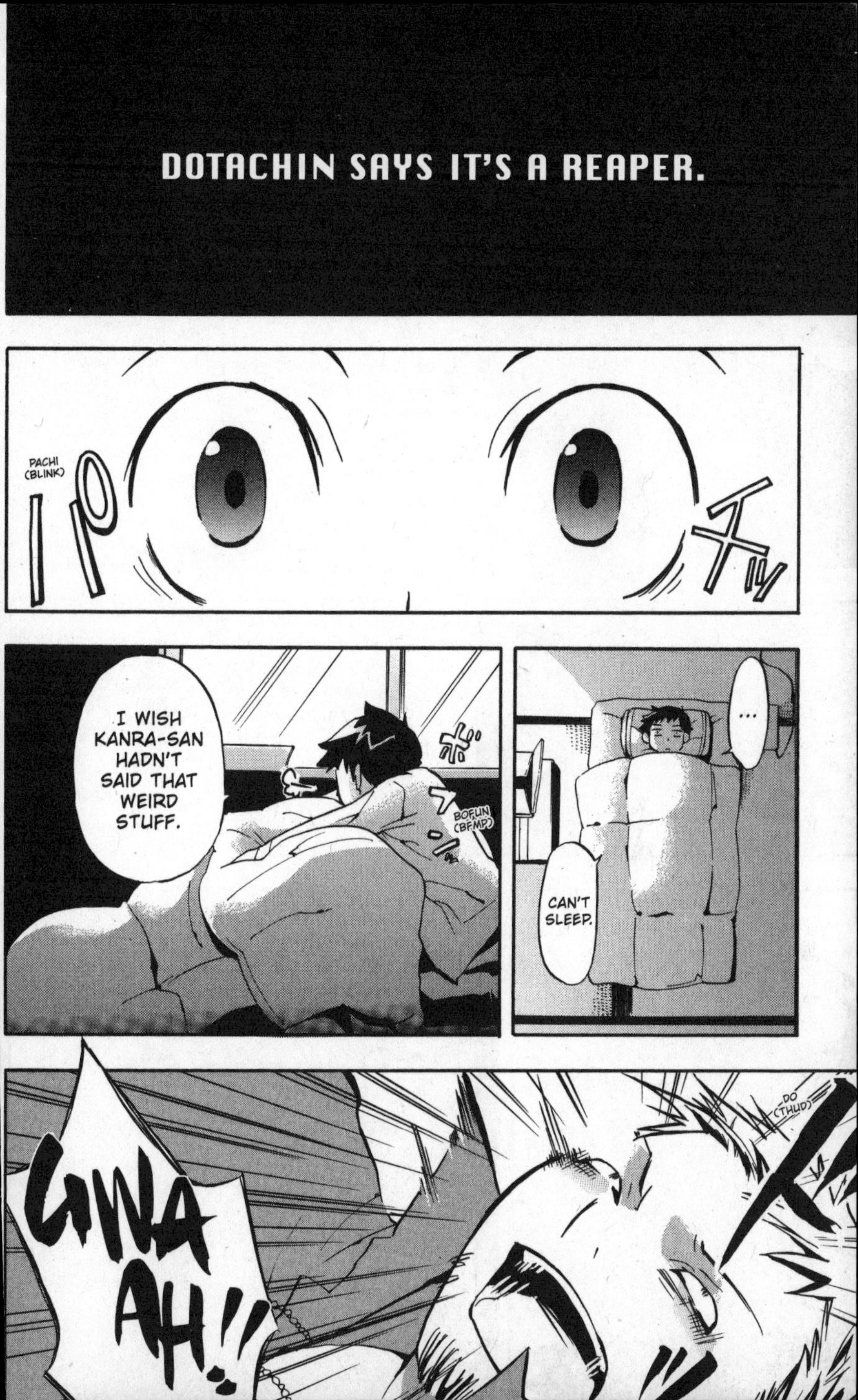
DOTACHIN SAYS IT'S A REAPER.
PACHI (BLINK)
...
CAN'T SLEEP.
BOFUN (BFMP)
I WISH KANRA-SAN HADN'T SAID THAT WEIRD STUFF.
DO (THUD)
GWA AH!!

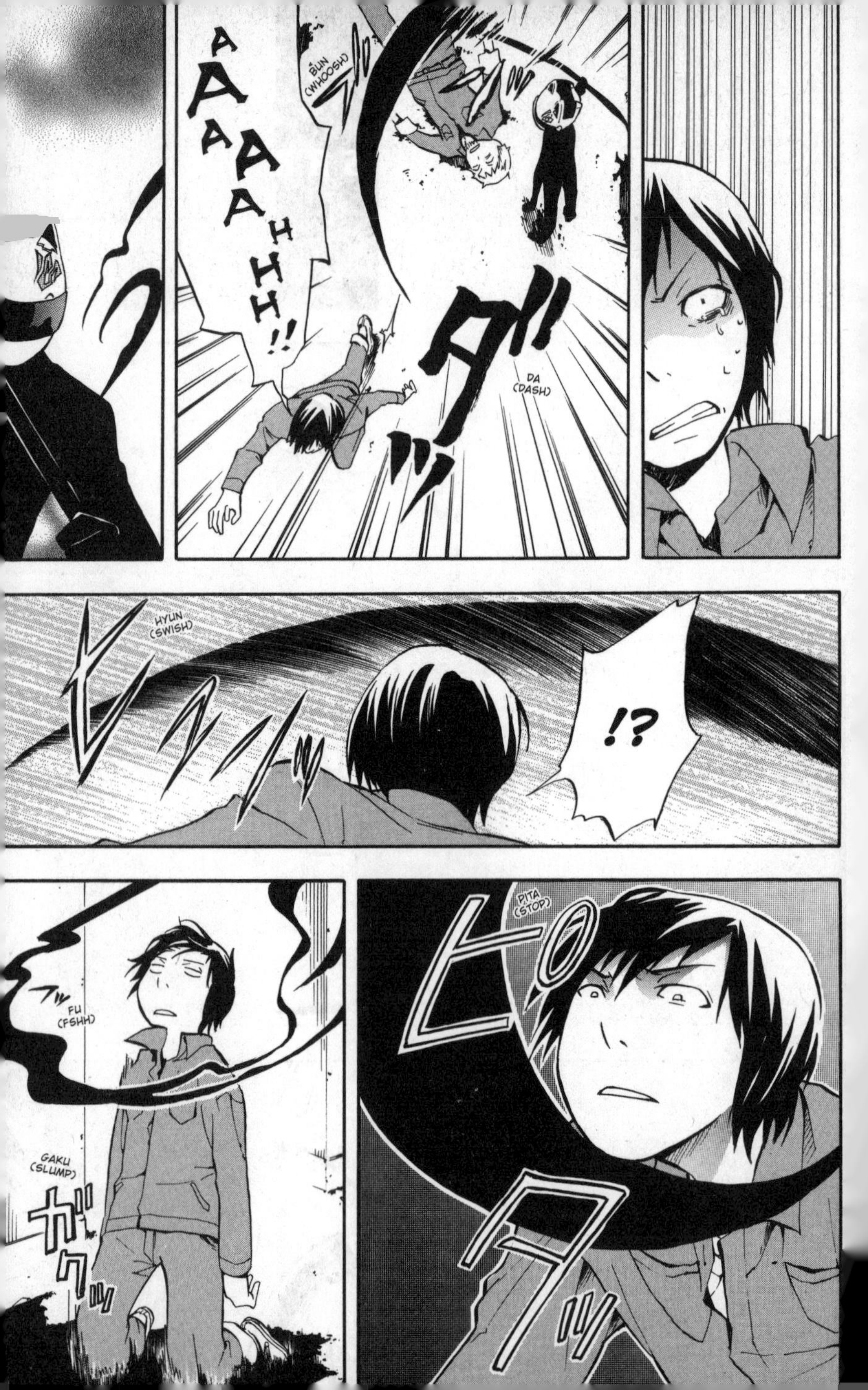
BUN (WHOOSH)
AAAAAHHH!!
DA (DASH)
HYUN (SWISH)
!?
PITA (STOP)
FU (FSHH)
GAKU (SLUMP)

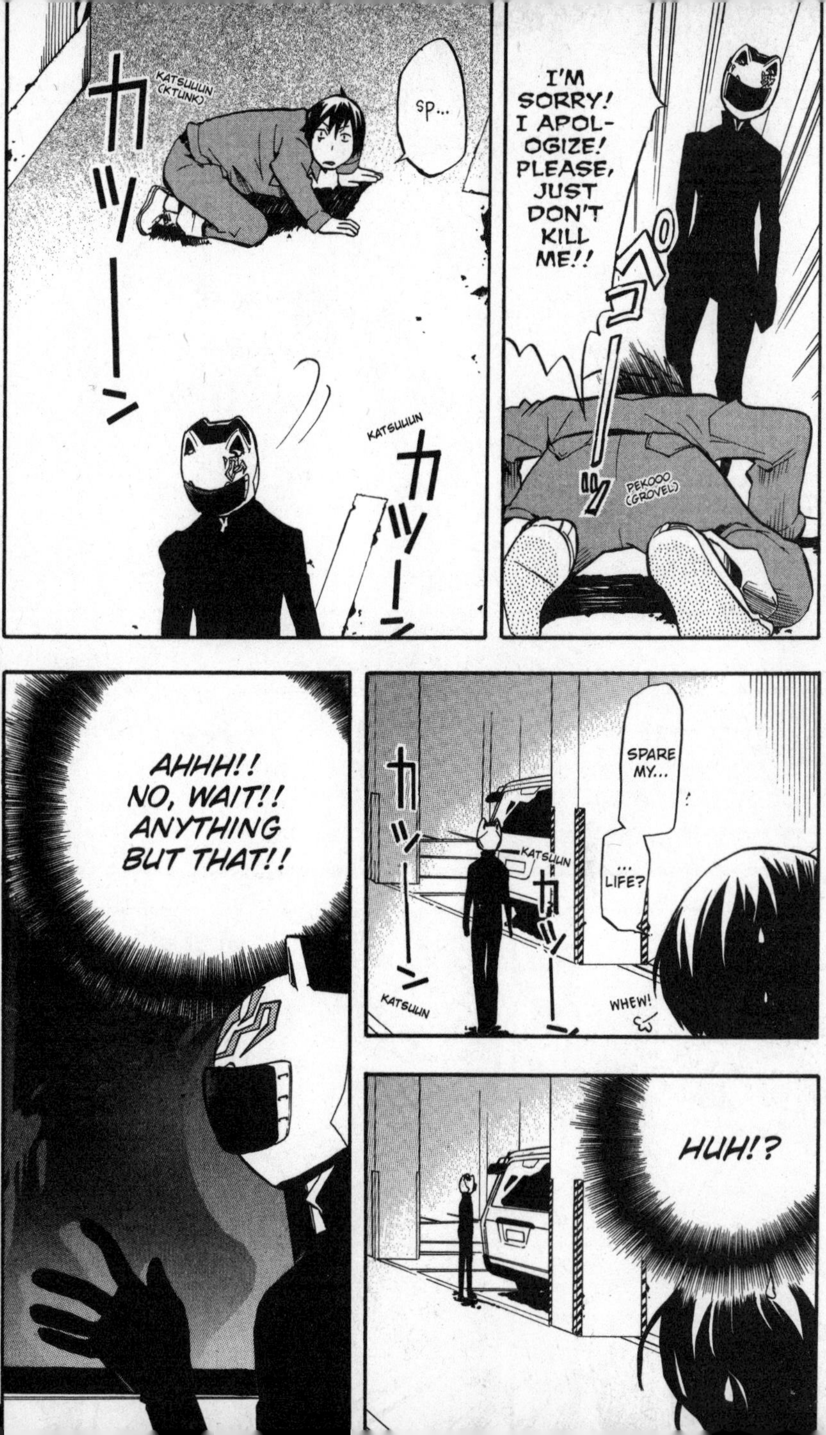
I'M SORRY! I APOLOGIZE! PLEASE, JUST DON'T KILL ME!!
PEKOOO (GROVEL)
sp...
KATSUUUN (KTUNK)
KATSUUUN
SPARE MY...
... LIFE?
KATSUUN
KATSUUN
WHEW!
HUH!?
AHHH!! NO, WAIT!! ANYTHING BUT THAT!!

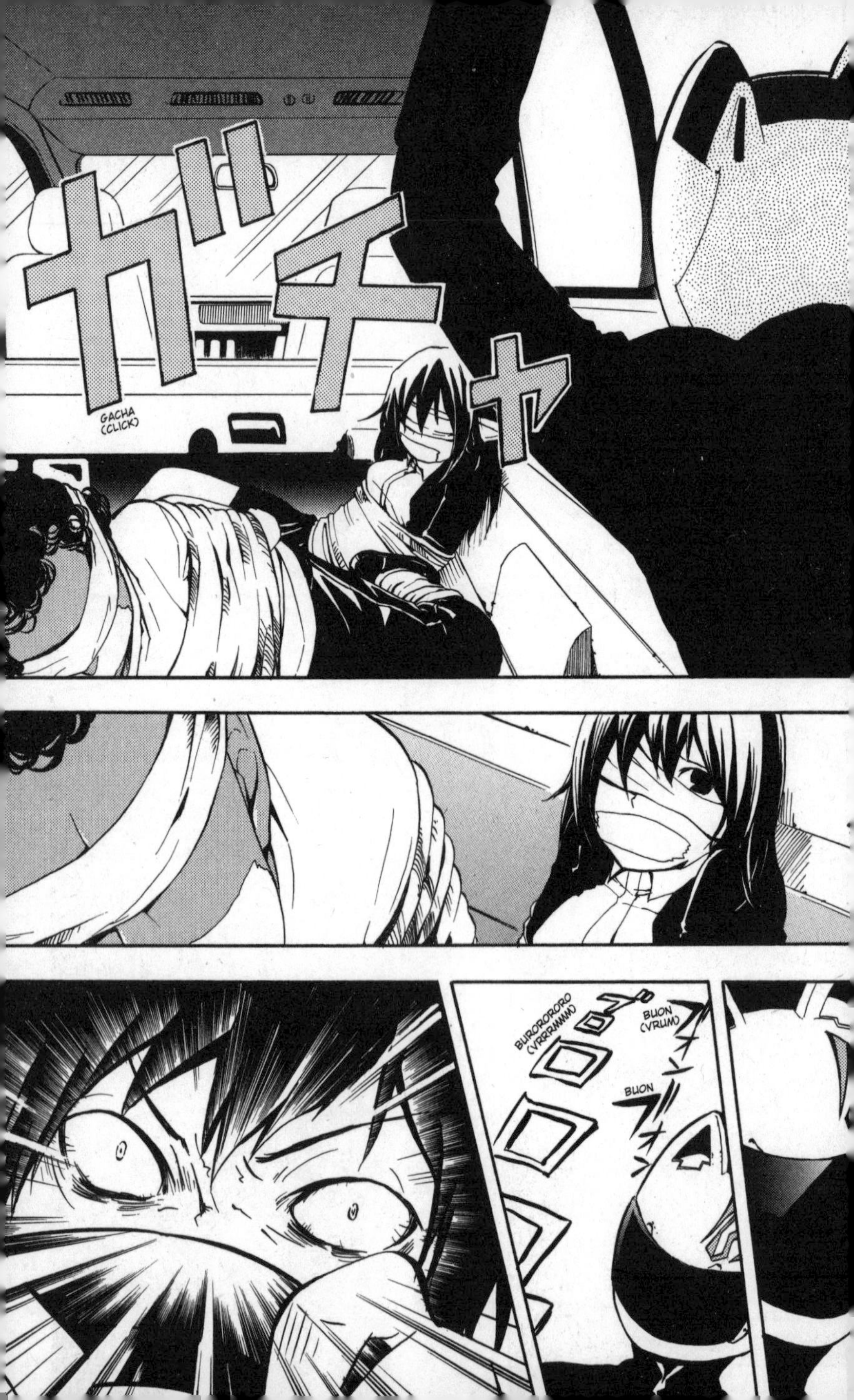
ガチャ
GACHA (CLICK)
BUON (VRUM)
BUON
BURORORO (VRRRMMM)

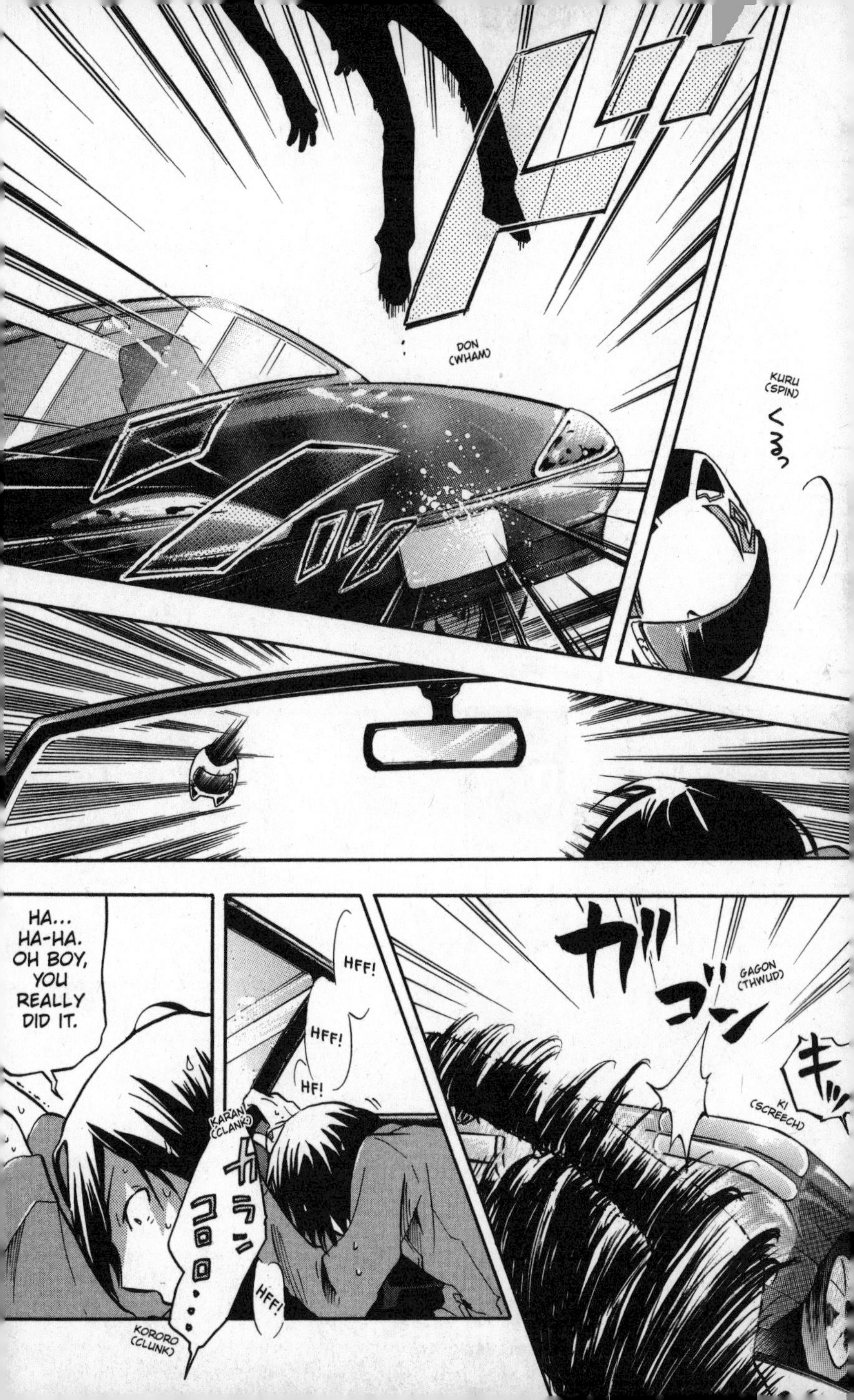
KURU (SPIN)
くるっ
DON (WHAM)
ガゴン
GAGON (THWUD)
キッ
KI (SCREECH)
HFF!
HFF!
HF!
HA... HA-HA. OH BOY, YOU REALLY DID IT.
カラン
KARAN (CLANK)
コロロ...
KORORO (CLUNK)
HFF!

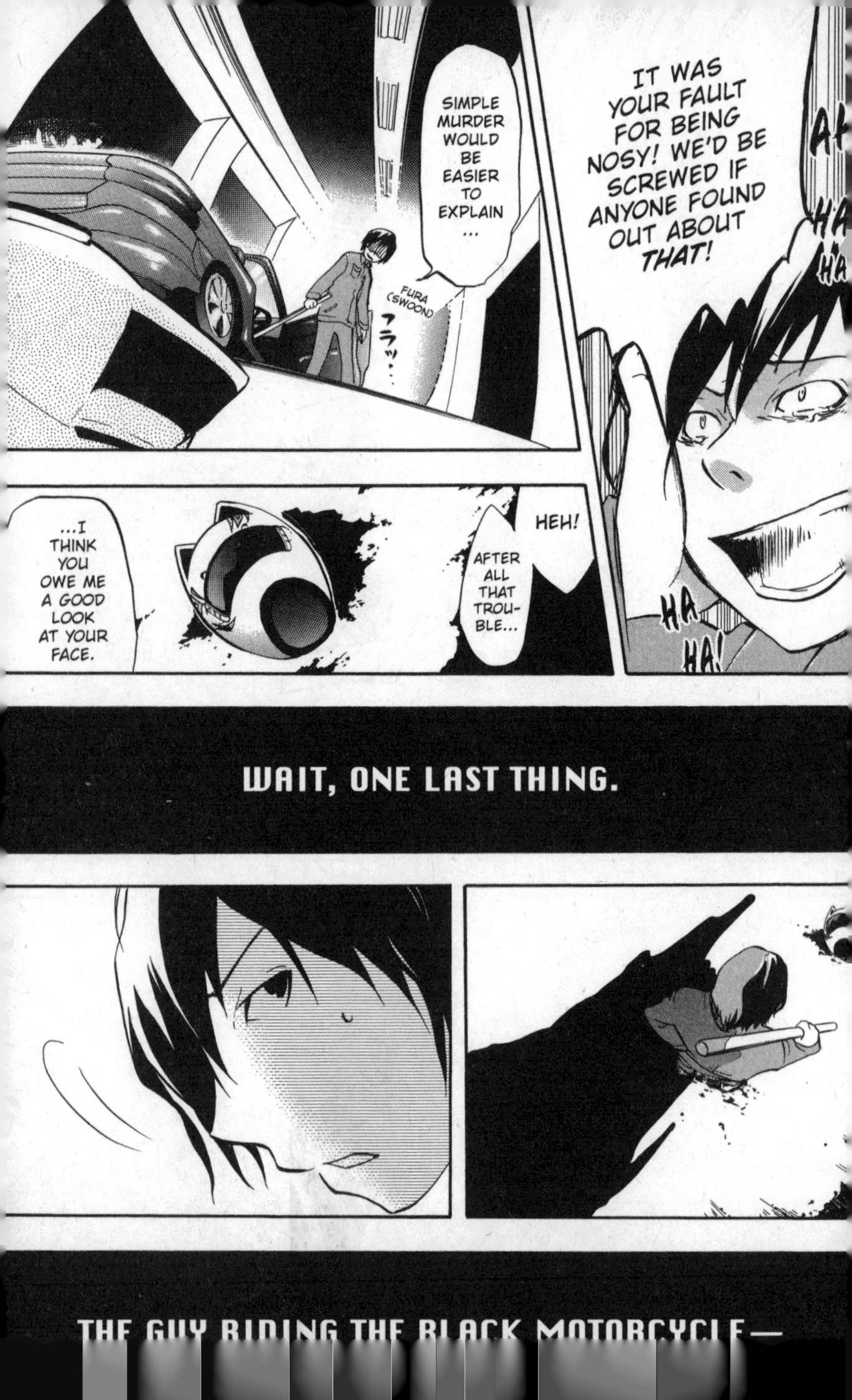
IT WAS YOUR FAULT FOR BEING NOSY! WE'D BE SCREWED IF ANYONE FOUND OUT ABOUT THAT!
HA HA!
SIMPLE MURDER WOULD BE EASIER TO EXPLAIN...
FURA (SWOON)
フラッ…
HEH!
AFTER ALL THAT TROUBLE...
...I THINK YOU OWE ME A GOOD LOOK AT YOUR FACE.
WAIT, ONE LAST THING.
THE GUY RIDING THE BLACK MOTORCYCLE—

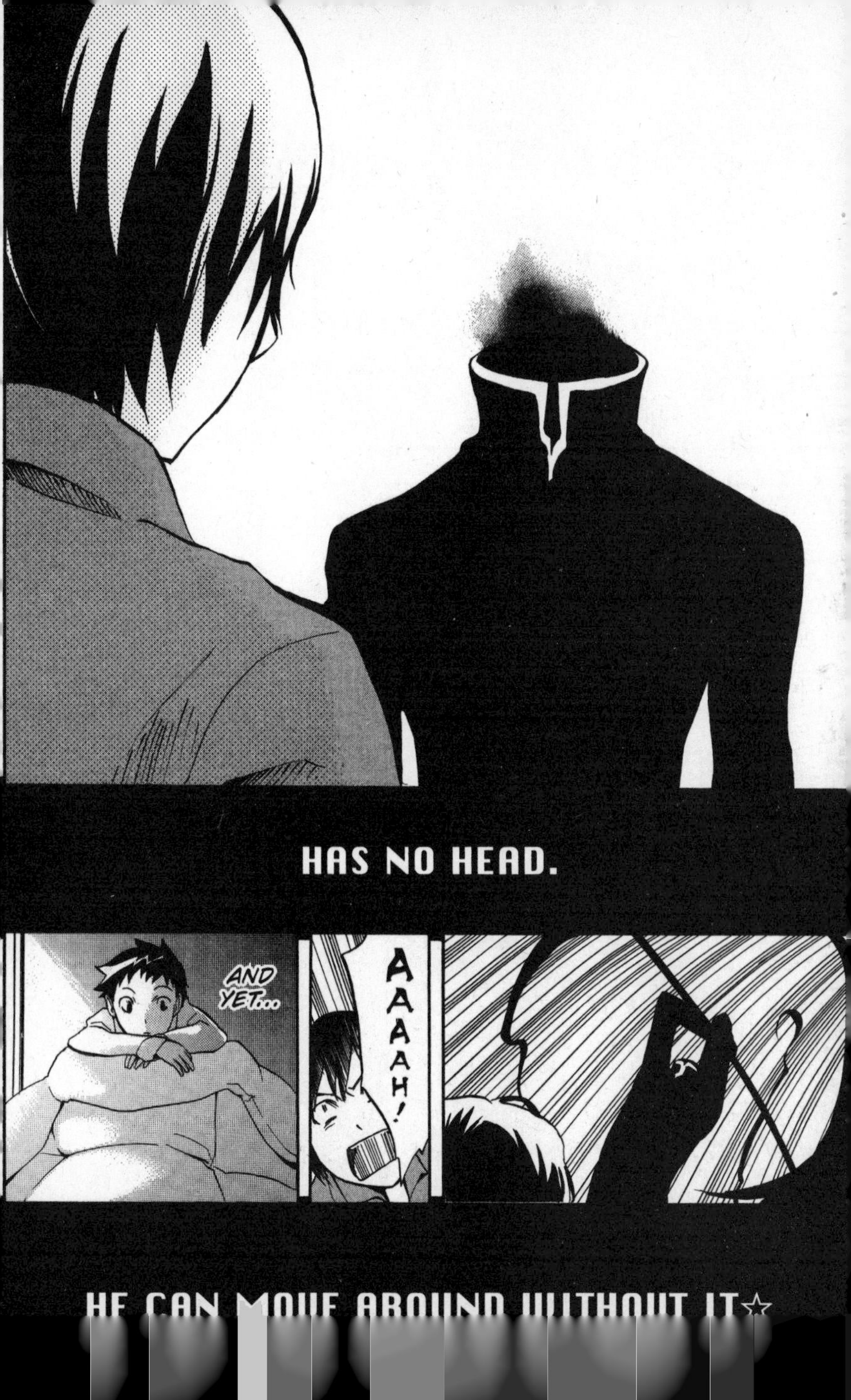
HAS NO HEAD.
AAAAH!
AND YET...
HE CAN MOVE AROUND WITHOUT IT☆

3: WAWAWA!!

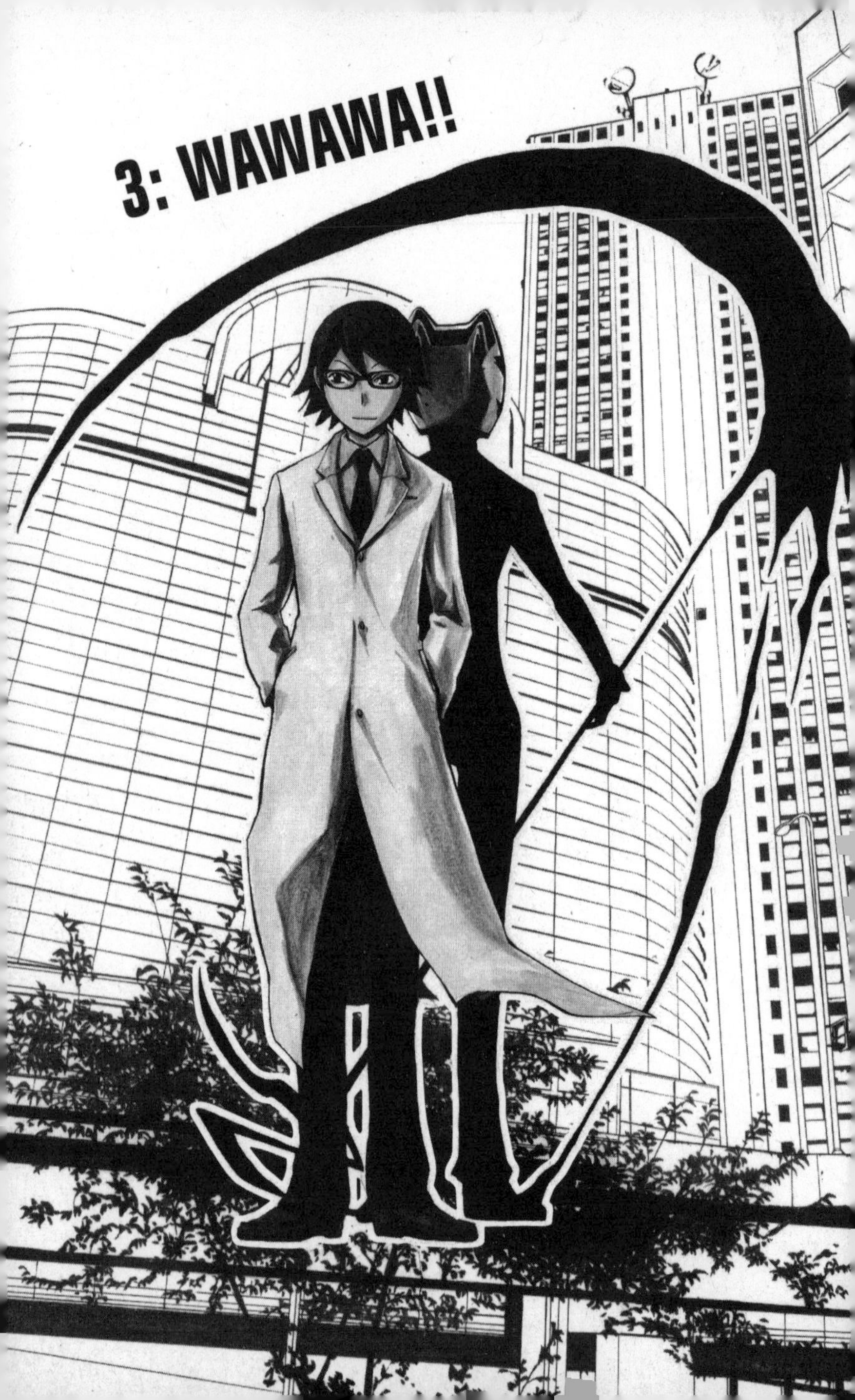

DRRR!!

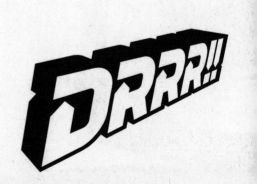

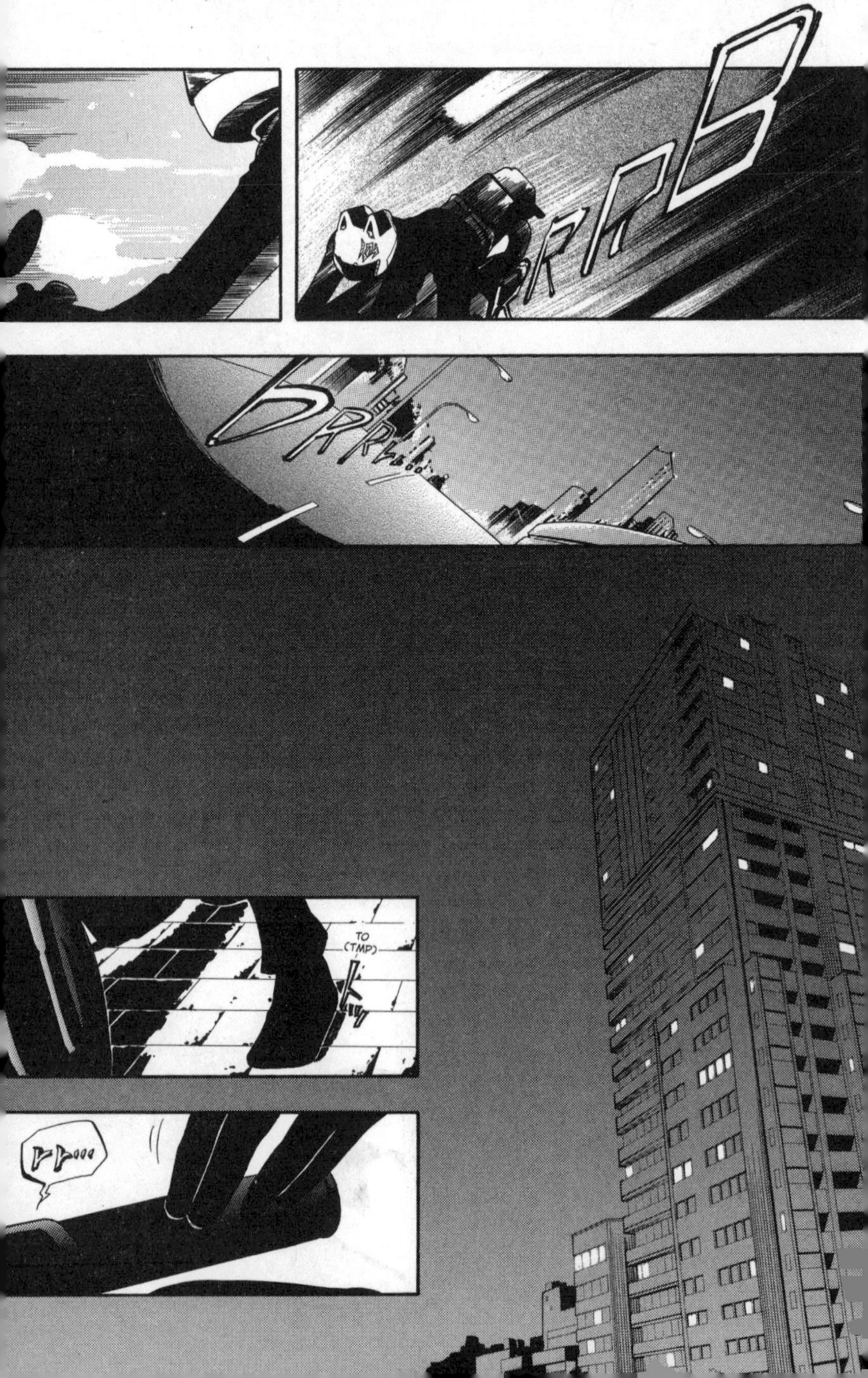
TO
(TMP)

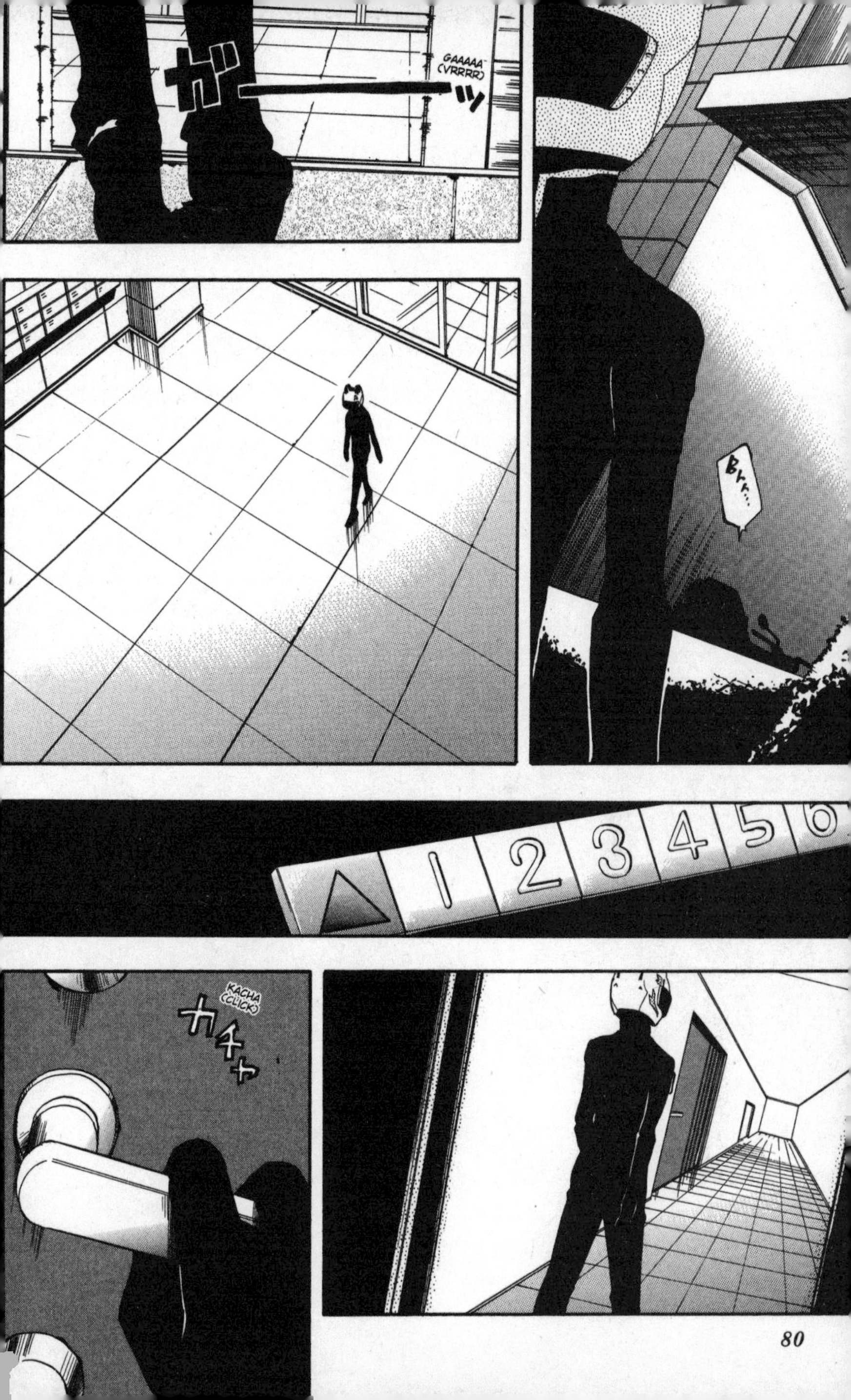
GAAAAA (VRRRR)
KACHA (CLICK)

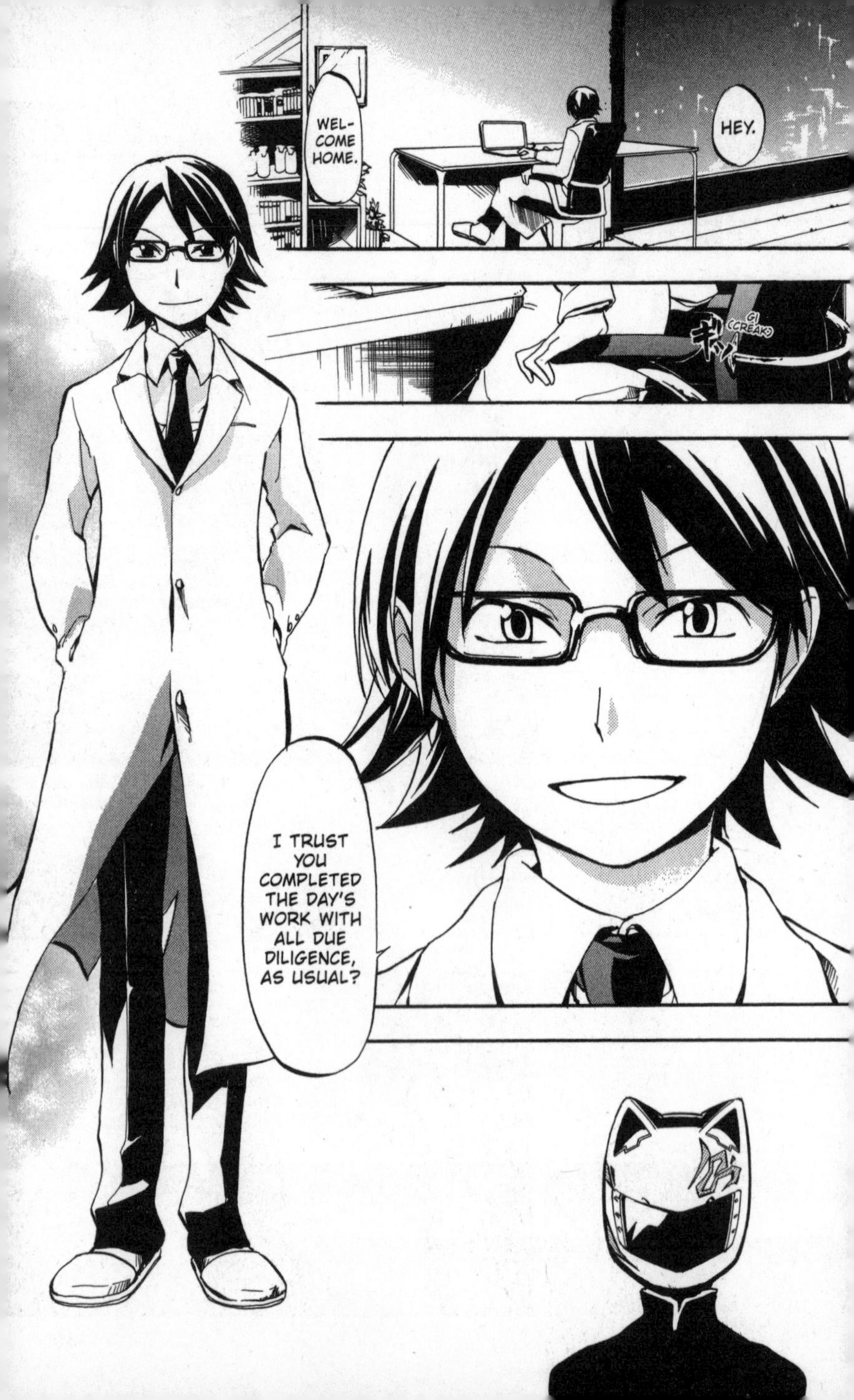
HEY.
WEL-COME HOME.
ギッ
GI (CREAK)
I TRUST YOU COMPLETED THE DAY'S WORK WITH ALL DUE DILIGENCE, AS USUAL?

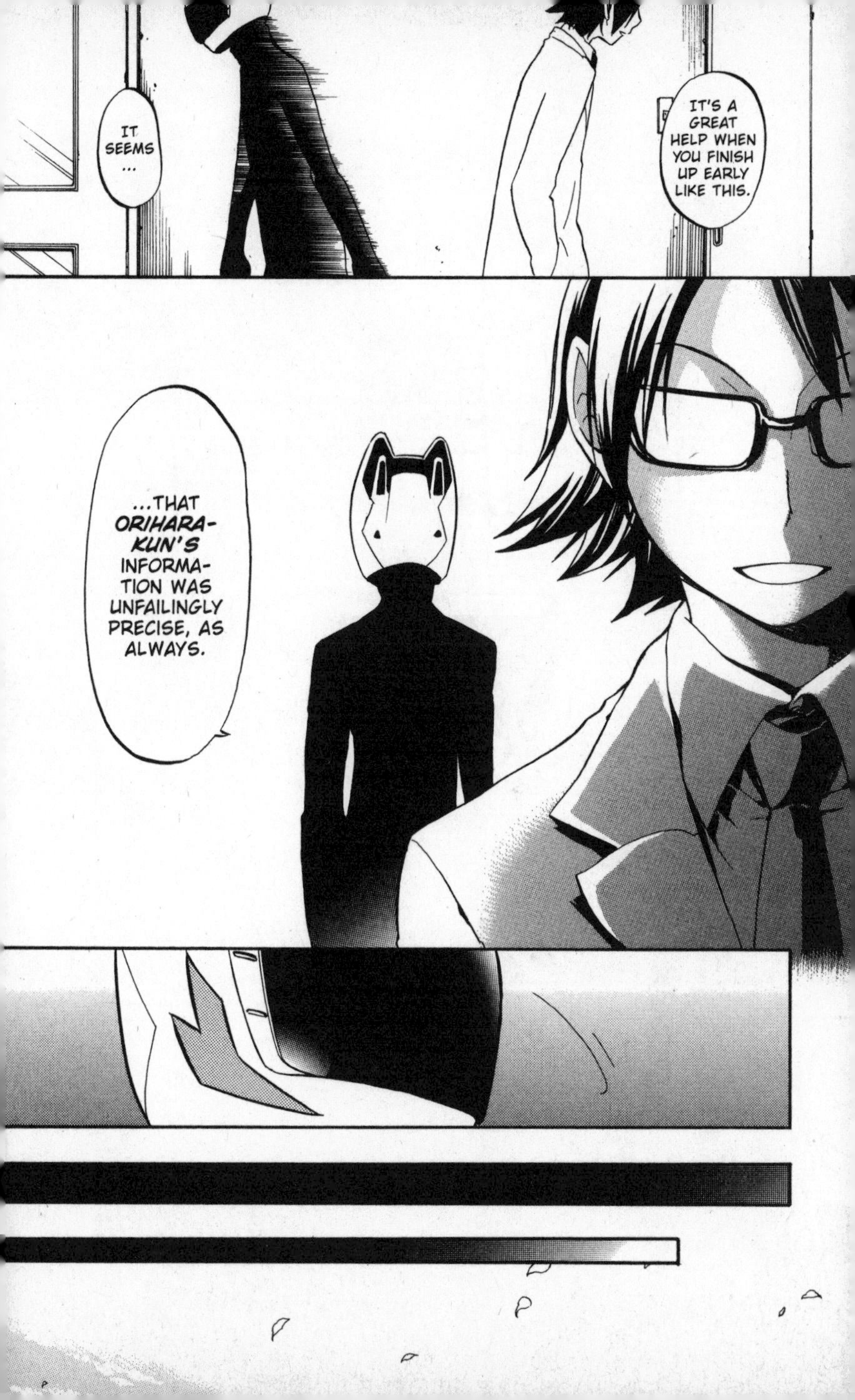
IT'S A GREAT HELP WHEN YOU FINISH UP EARLY LIKE THIS.
IT SEEMS ...
...THAT *ORIHARA-KUN'S* INFORMATION WAS UNFAILINGLY PRECISE, AS ALWAYS.

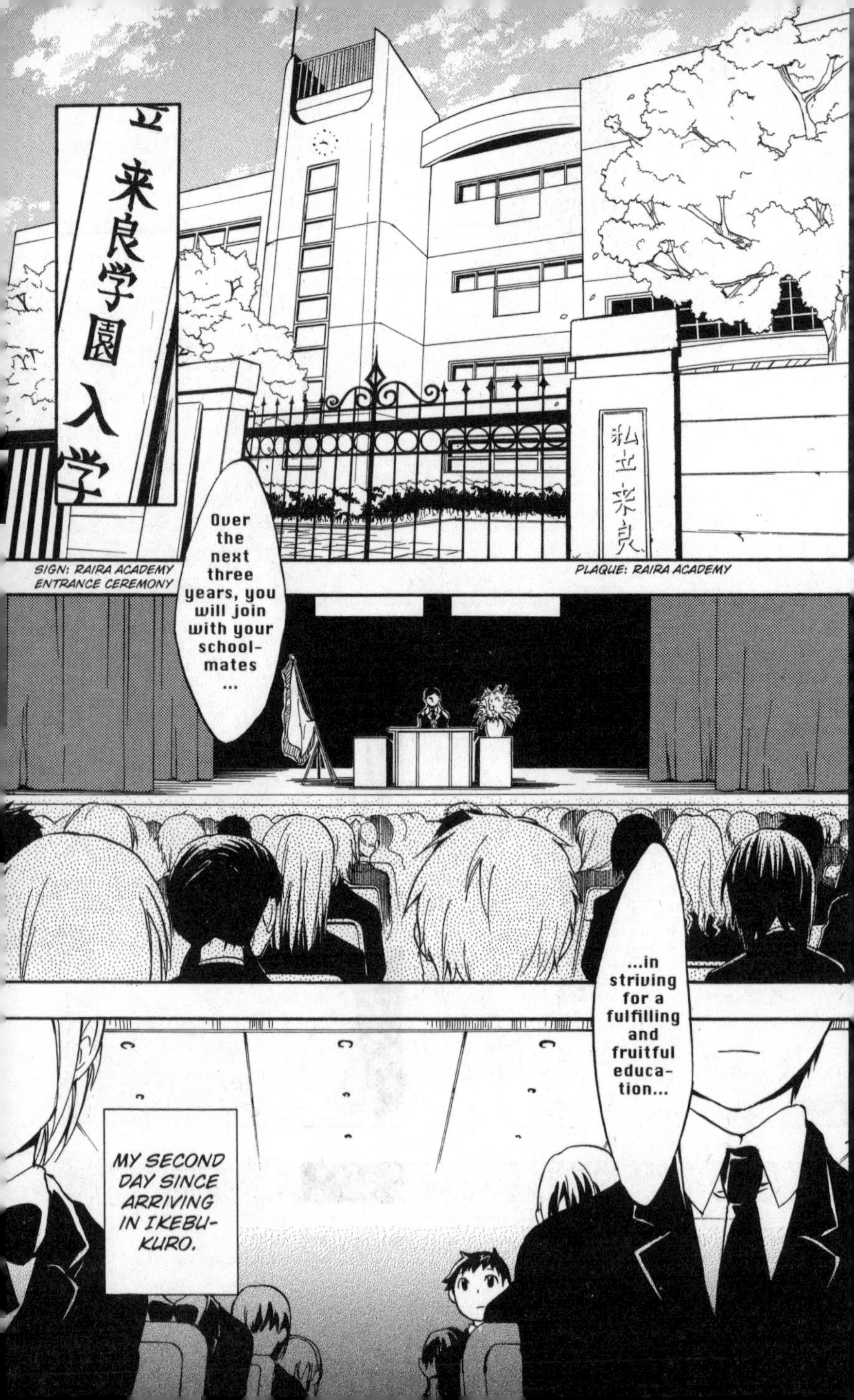
私立来良
立来良学園入学
Over the next three years, you will join with your school-mates...
SIGN: RAIRA ACADEMY ENTRANCE CEREMONY
PLAQUE: RAIRA ACADEMY
...in striving for a fulfilling and fruitful educa-tion...
MY SECOND DAY SINCE ARRIVING IN IKEBU-KURO.

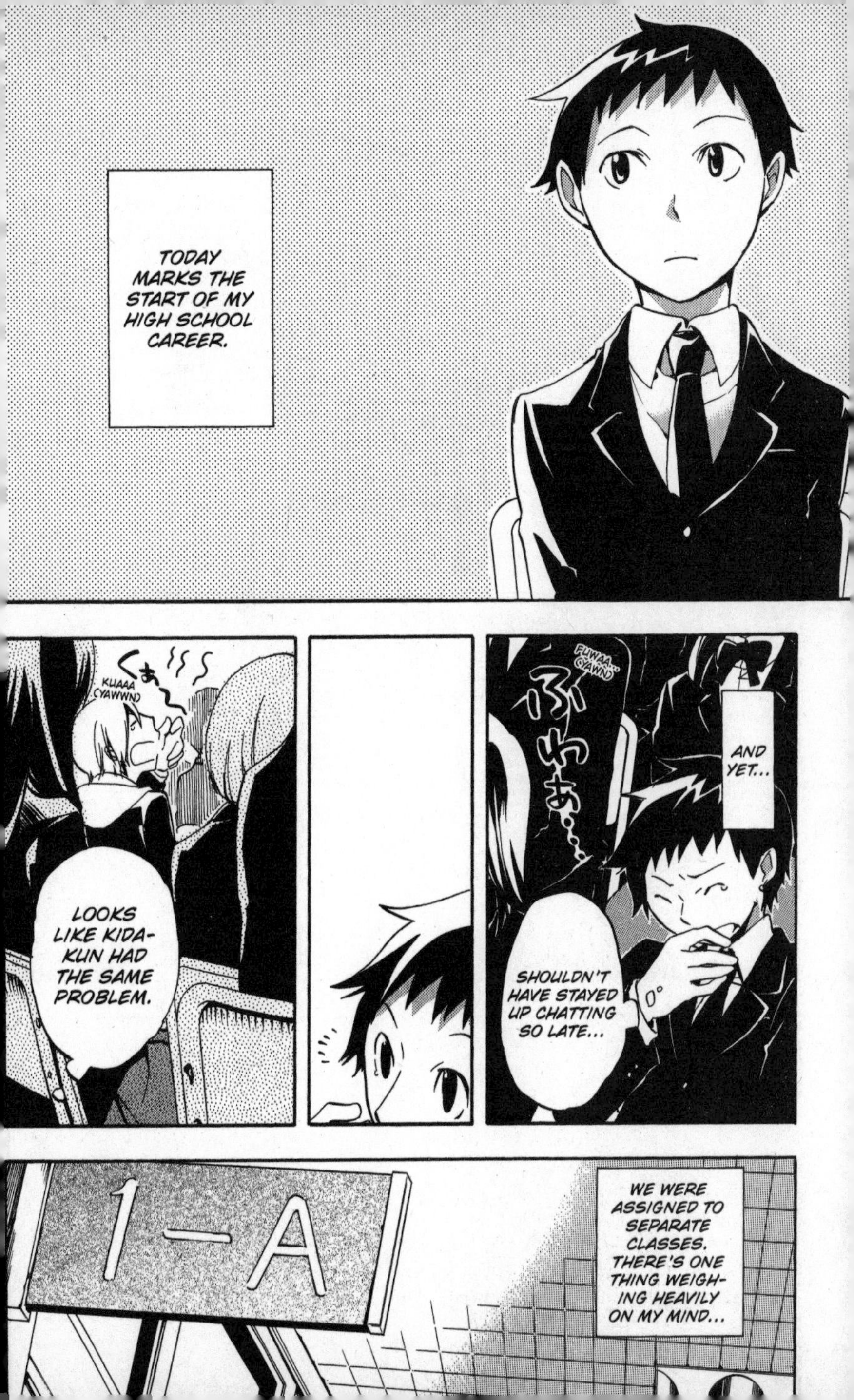
TODAY MARKS THE START OF MY HIGH SCHOOL CAREER.
AND YET...
ふわぁ…
FUWAA... (YAWN)
SHOULDN'T HAVE STAYED UP CHATTING SO LATE...
くぁ~
KUAAA (YAWWN)
LOOKS LIKE KIDA-KUN HAD THE SAME PROBLEM.
WE WERE ASSIGNED TO SEPARATE CLASSES. THERE'S ONE THING WEIGHING HEAVILY ON MY MIND...
1-A

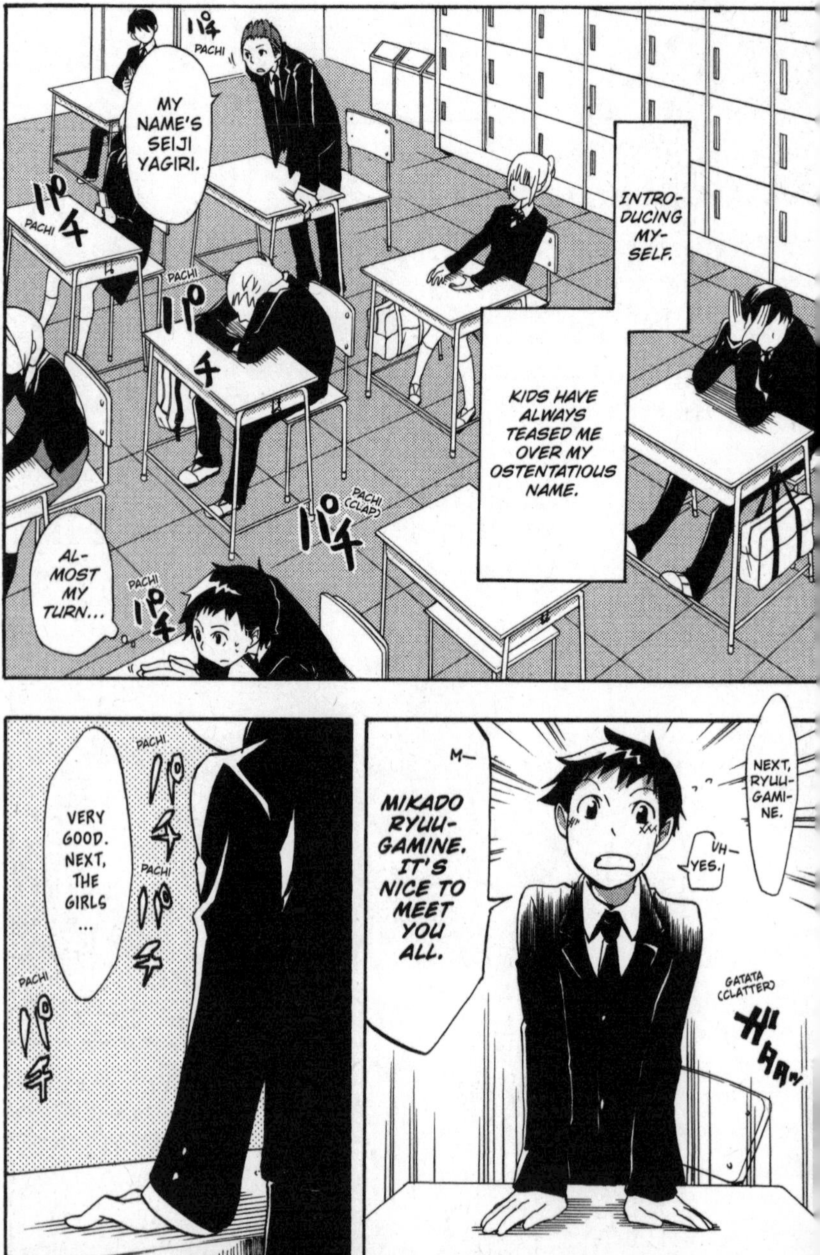
INTRODUCING MYSELF.
KIDS HAVE ALWAYS TEASED ME OVER MY OSTENTATIOUS NAME.
PACHI
MY NAME'S SEIJI YAGIRI.
PACHI
PACHI
PACHI (CLAP)
ALMOST MY TURN...
PACHI
NEXT, RYUUGAMINE.
UH— YES.
M—
GATATA (CLATTER)
MIKADO RYUUGAMINE. IT'S NICE TO MEET YOU ALL.
PACHI
PACHI
VERY GOOD. NEXT, THE GIRLS...
PACHI

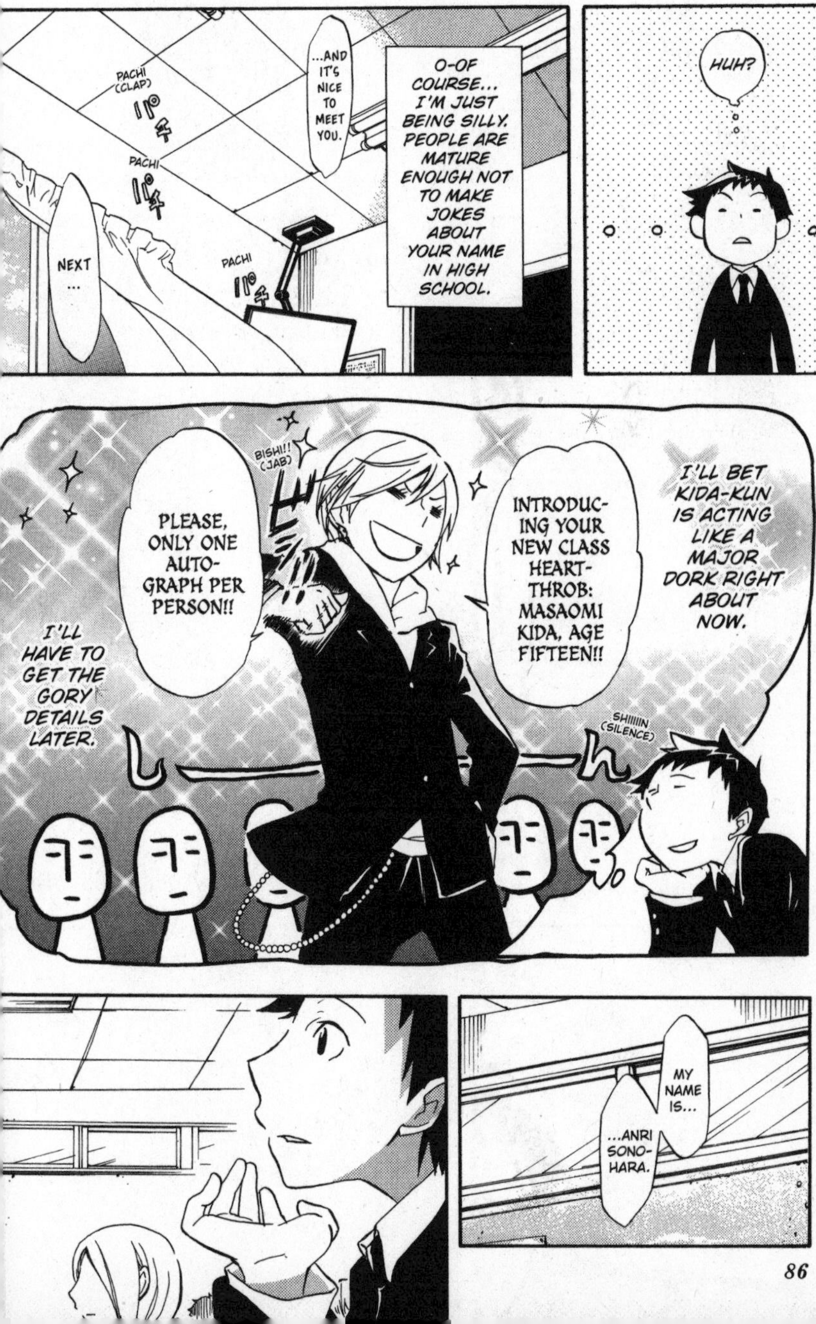
HUH?
O-OF COURSE... I'M JUST BEING SILLY. PEOPLE ARE MATURE ENOUGH NOT TO MAKE JOKES ABOUT YOUR NAME IN HIGH SCHOOL.
...AND IT'S NICE TO MEET YOU.
PACHI (CLAP)
PACHI
PACHI
NEXT...
I'LL BET KIDA-KUN IS ACTING LIKE A MAJOR DORK RIGHT ABOUT NOW.
INTRODUCING YOUR NEW CLASS HEART-THROB: MASAOMI KIDA, AGE FIFTEEN!!
BISHI!! (JAB)
PLEASE, ONLY ONE AUTO-GRAPH PER PERSON!!
SHIIIIIN (SILENCE)
I'LL HAVE TO GET THE GORY DETAILS LATER.
MY NAME IS...
...ANRI SONO-HARA.

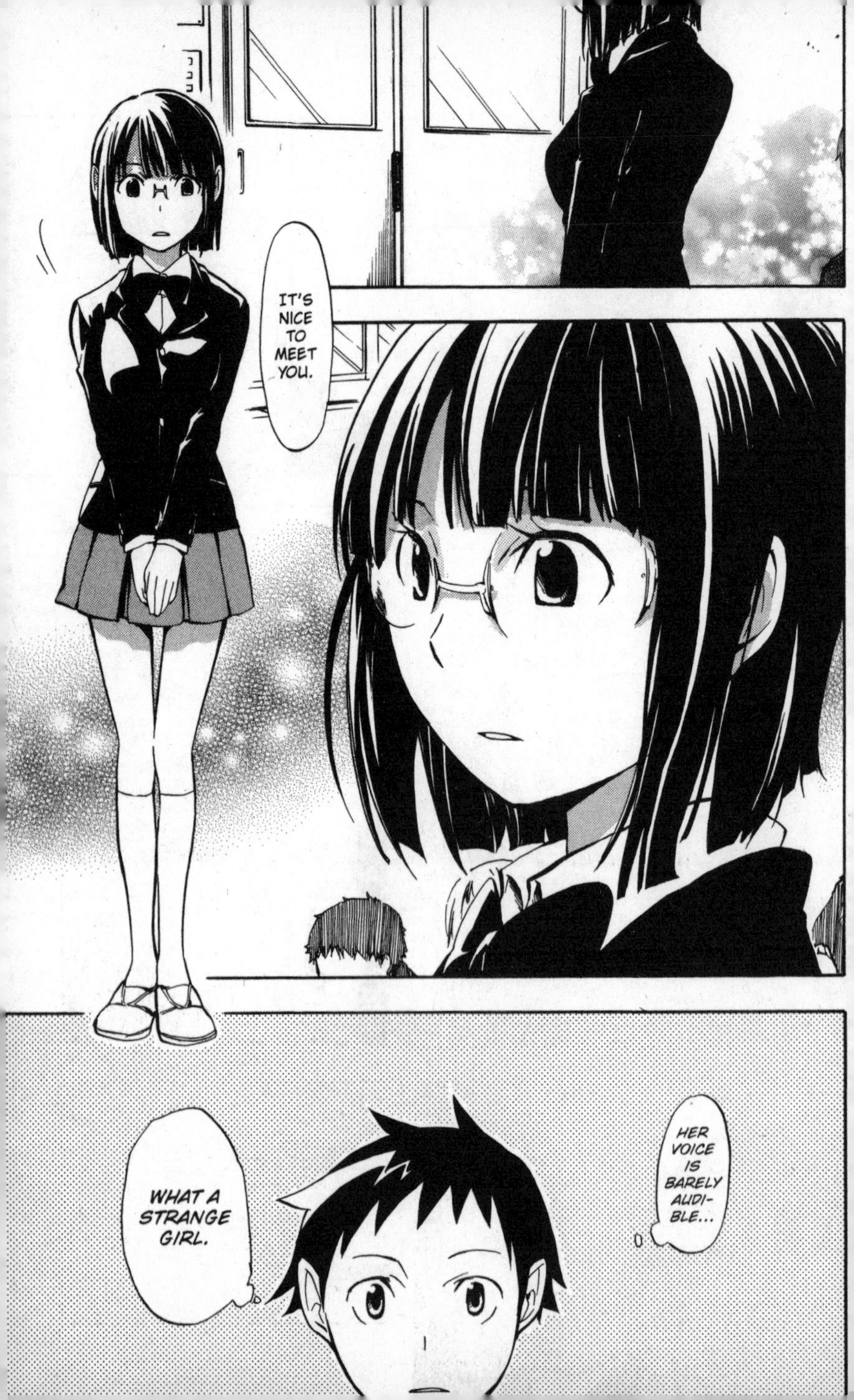
IT'S NICE TO MEET YOU.
HER VOICE IS BARELY AUDI-BLE...
WHAT A STRANGE GIRL.

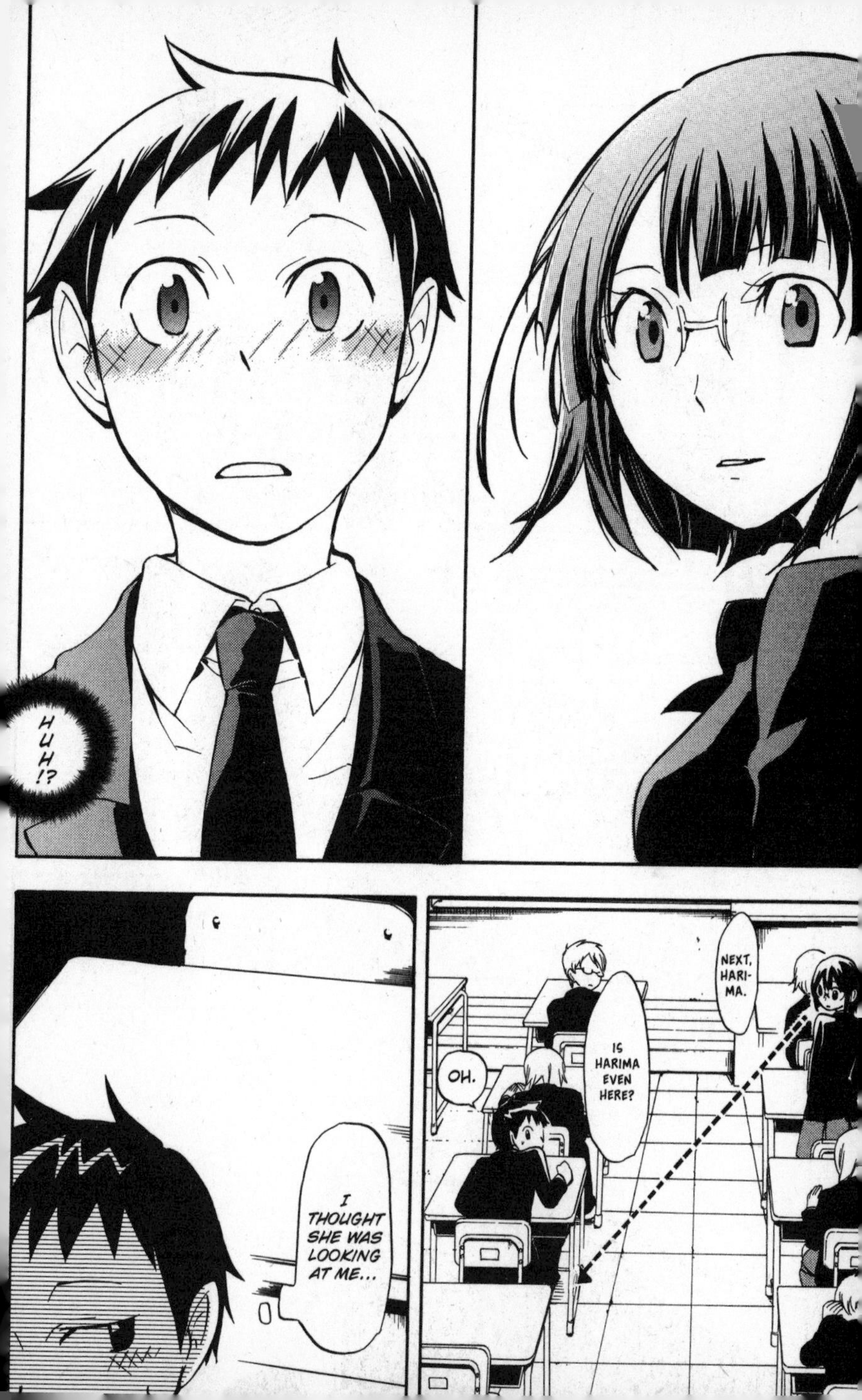
HUH!?
NEXT, HARIMA.
IS HARIMA EVEN HERE?
OH.
I THOUGHT SHE WAS LOOKING AT ME...

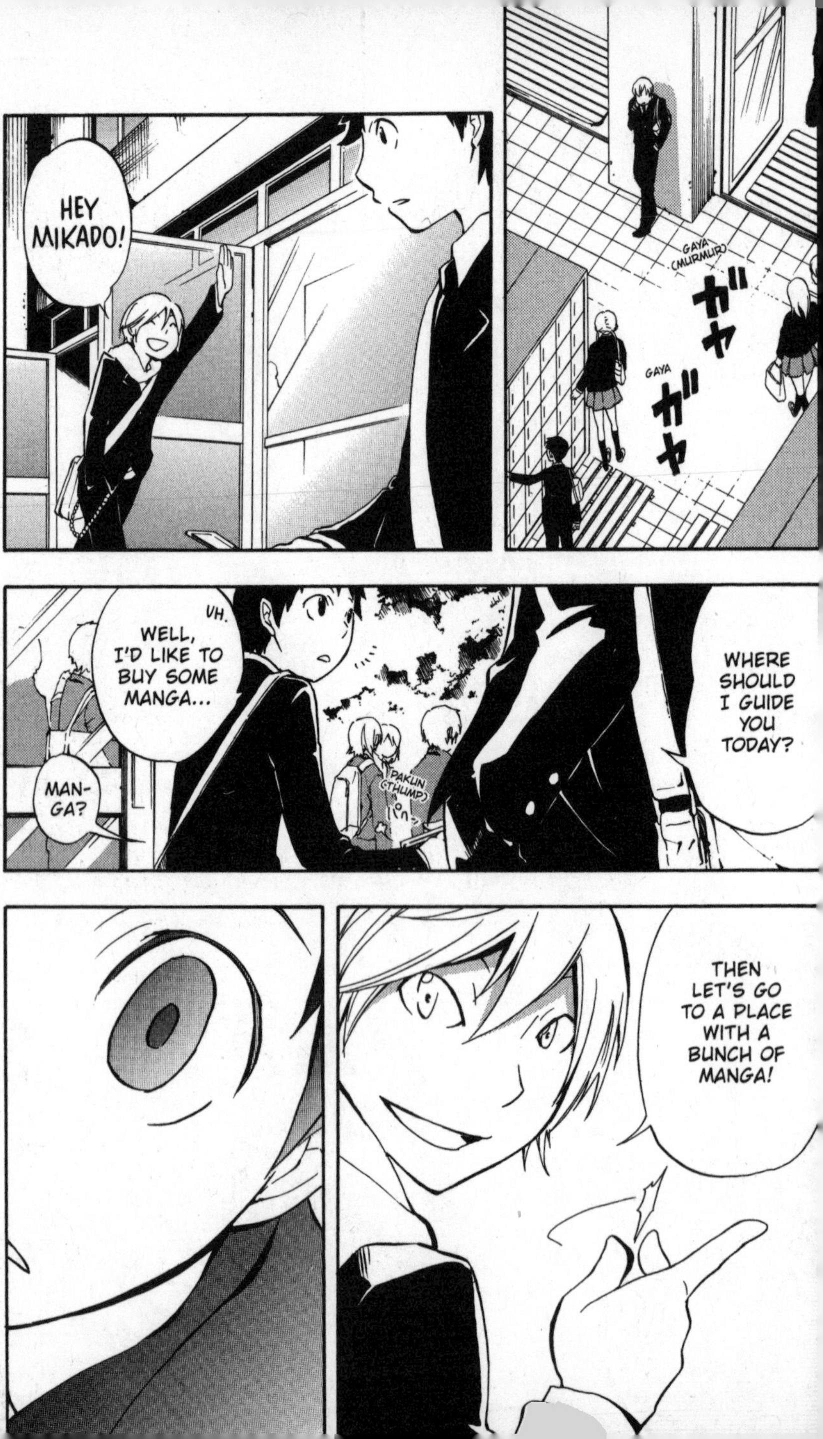
GAYA (MURMUR)
ガヤ
GAYA
ガヤ
HEY MIKADO!
WHERE SHOULD I GUIDE YOU TODAY?
UH.
WELL, I'D LIKE TO BUY SOME MANGA...
PAKUN (THUMP)
パクン
MAN-GA?
THEN LET'S GO TO A PLACE WITH A BUNCH OF MANGA!

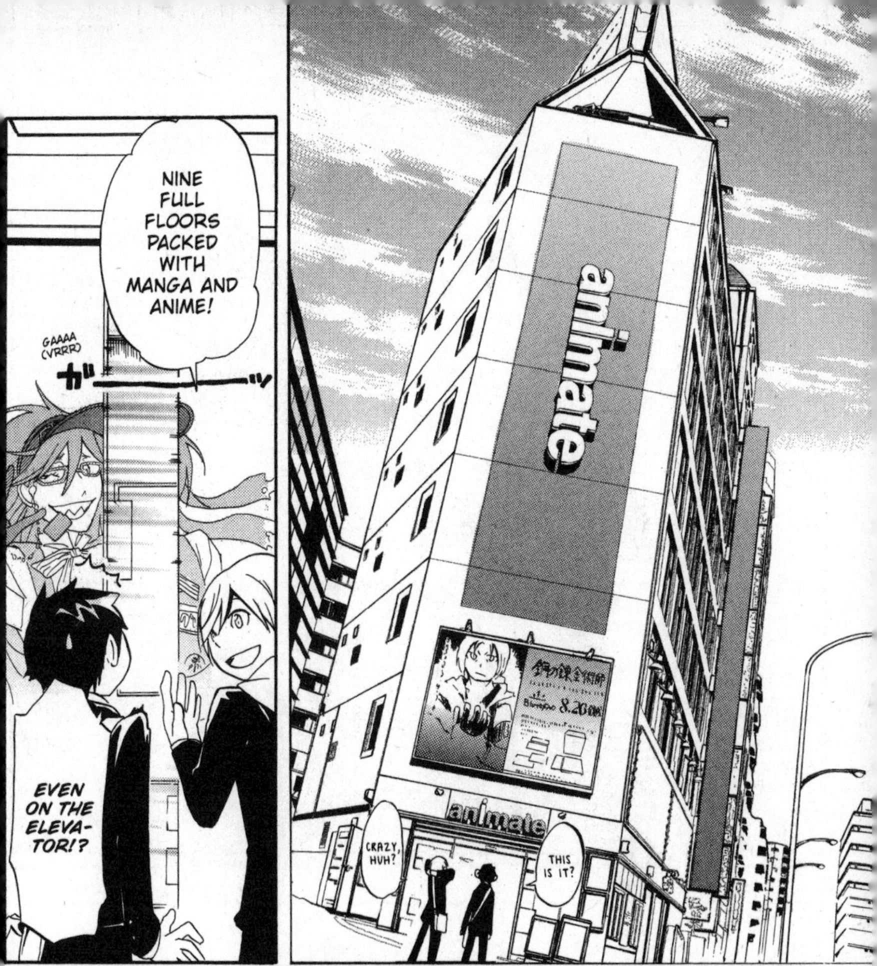
animate
animate
THIS IS IT?
CRAZY, HUH?
NINE FULL FLOORS PACKED WITH MANGA AND ANIME!
GAAAA (VRRR)
EVEN ON THE ELEVATOR!?

*SPECIAL THANKS TO THE ANIMATE IKEBUKURO STORE FOR THEIR COOPERATION
SIGN: FULLMETAL ALCHEMIST

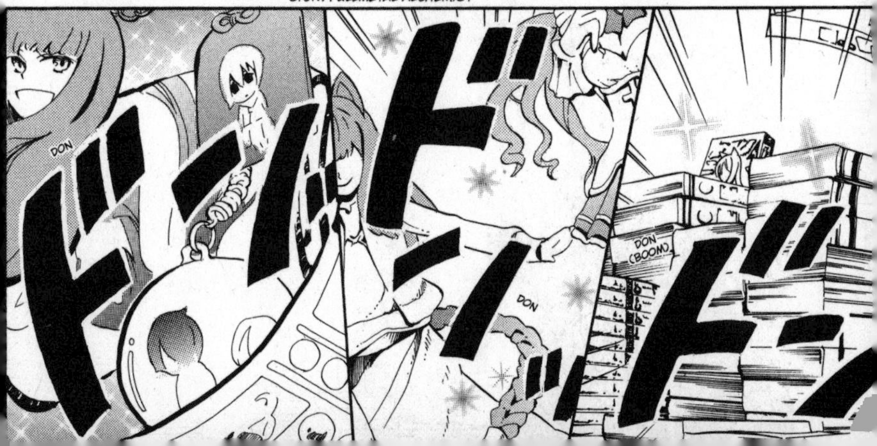
DON (BOOM)
DON
DON

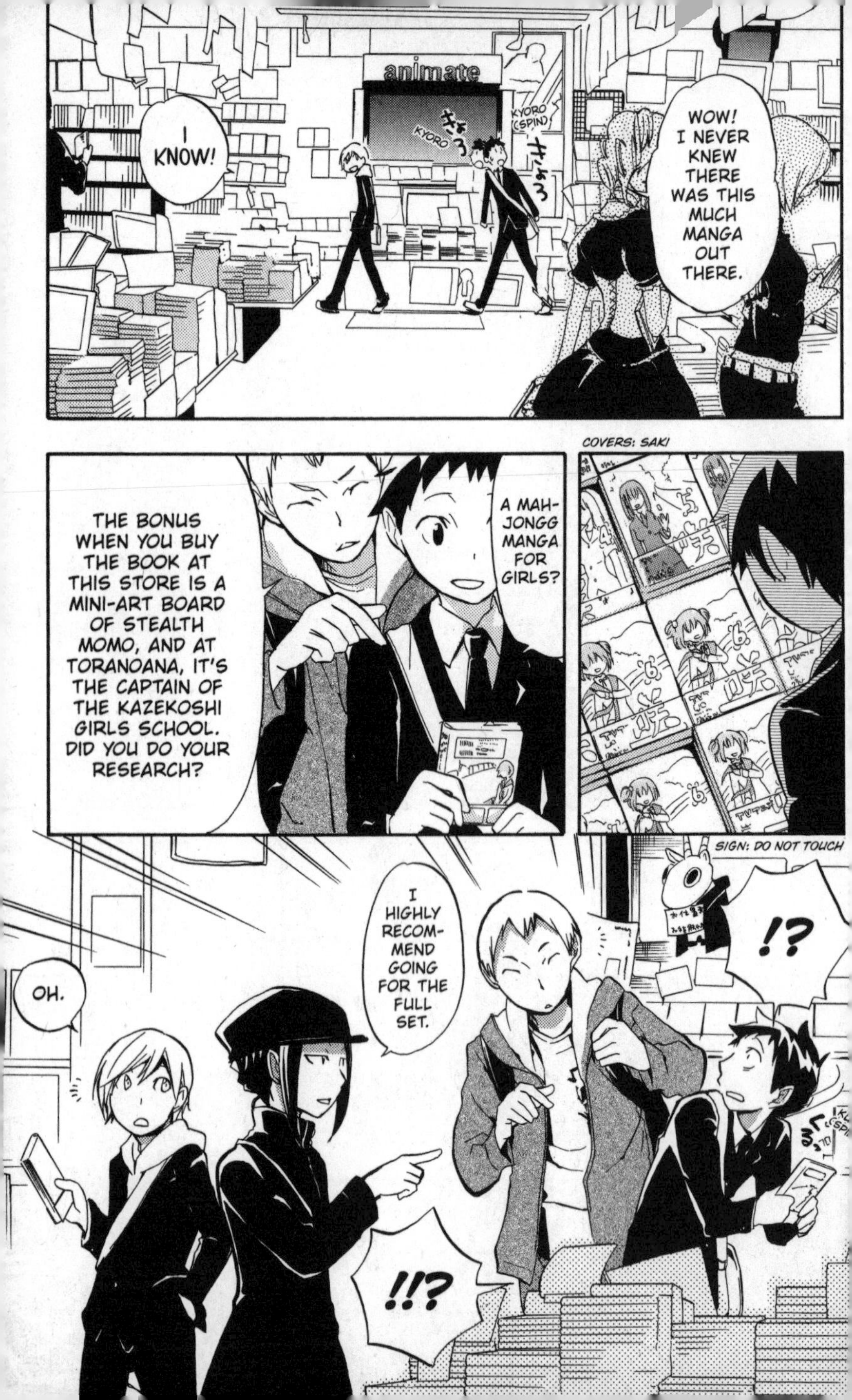
animate
WOW! I NEVER KNEW THERE WAS THIS MUCH MANGA OUT THERE.
KYORO (SPIN)
KYORO
I KNOW!
COVERS: SAKI
A MAH-JONGG MANGA FOR GIRLS?
THE BONUS WHEN YOU BUY THE BOOK AT THIS STORE IS A MINI-ART BOARD OF STEALTH MOMO, AND AT TORANOANA, IT'S THE CAPTAIN OF THE KAZEKOSHI GIRLS SCHOOL. DID YOU DO YOUR RESEARCH?
SIGN: DO NOT TOUCH
!?
I HIGHLY RECOM-MEND GOING FOR THE FULL SET.
OH.
!!?

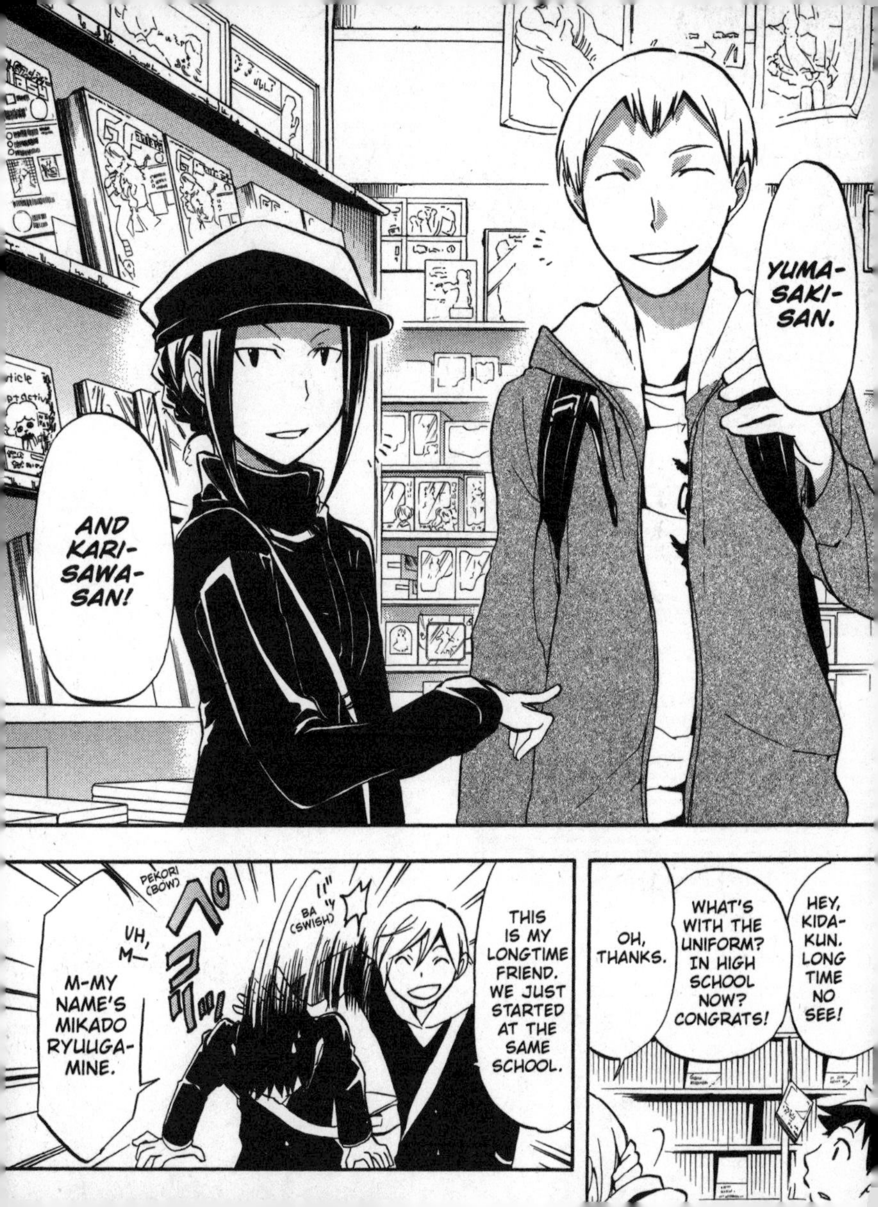
YUMA-SAKI-SAN.
AND KARI-SAWA-SAN!
HEY, KIDA-KUN. LONG TIME NO SEE!
WHAT'S WITH THE UNIFORM? IN HIGH SCHOOL NOW? CONGRATS!
OH, THANKS.
THIS IS MY LONGTIME FRIEND. WE JUST STARTED AT THE SAME SCHOOL.
BA (SWISH)
PEKORI (BOW)
UH, M—
M-MY NAME'S MIKADO RYUUGA-MINE.

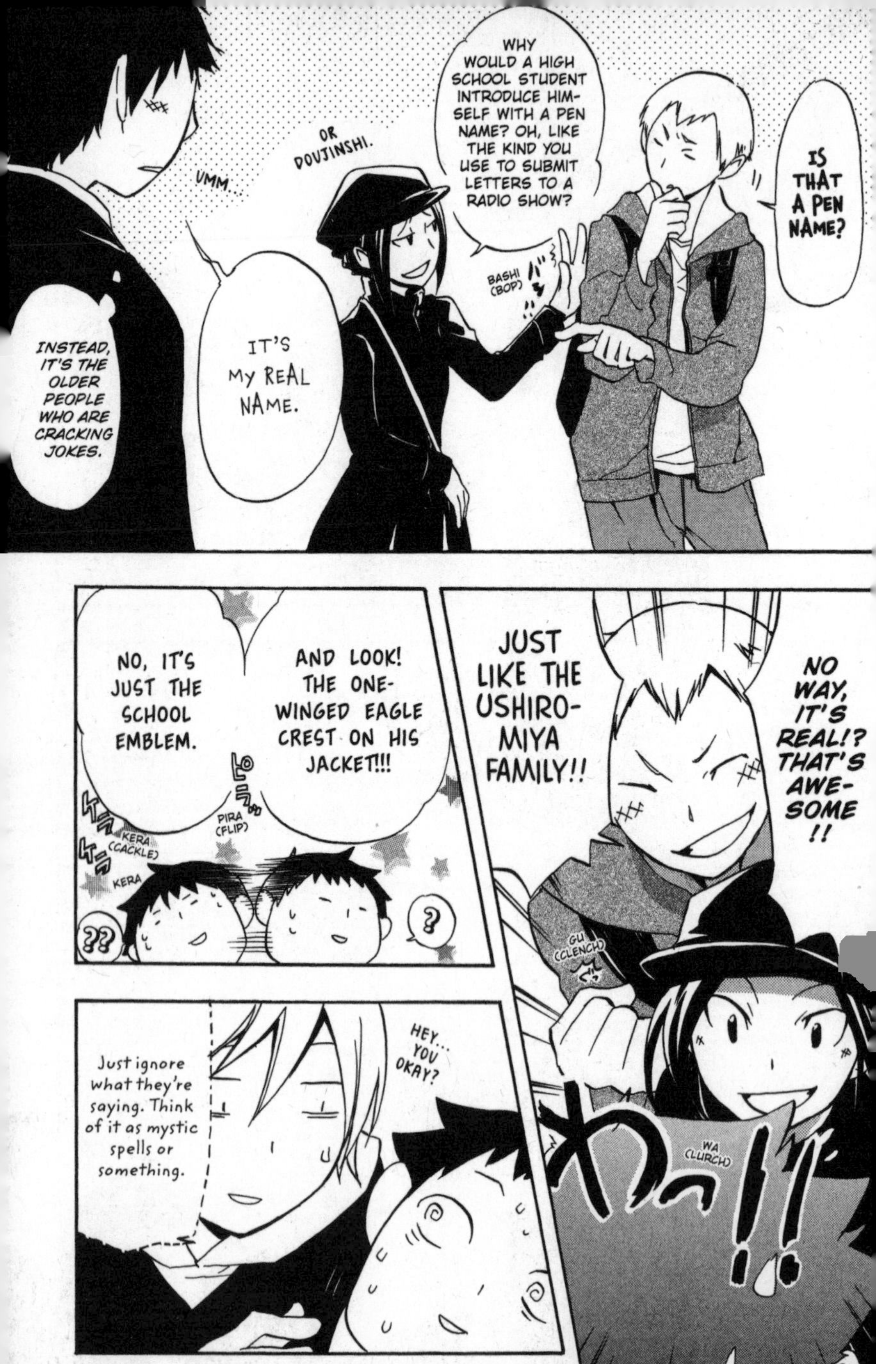

IS THAT A PEN NAME?
WHY WOULD A HIGH SCHOOL STUDENT INTRODUCE HIMSELF WITH A PEN NAME? OH, LIKE THE KIND YOU USE TO SUBMIT LETTERS TO A RADIO SHOW?
OR DOUJINSHI.
BASHI (BOP)
UMM...
IT'S MY REAL NAME.
INSTEAD, IT'S THE OLDER PEOPLE WHO ARE CRACKING JOKES.
NO WAY, IT'S REAL!? THAT'S AWESOME!!
JUST LIKE THE USHIROMIYA FAMILY!!
GU (CLENCH)
WA (LURCH)
AND LOOK! THE ONE-WINGED EAGLE CREST ON HIS JACKET!!!
NO, IT'S JUST THE SCHOOL EMBLEM.
PIRA (FLIP)
KERA (CACKLE)
KERA
?
??
HEY... YOU OKAY?
Just ignore what they're saying. Think of it as mystic spells or something.

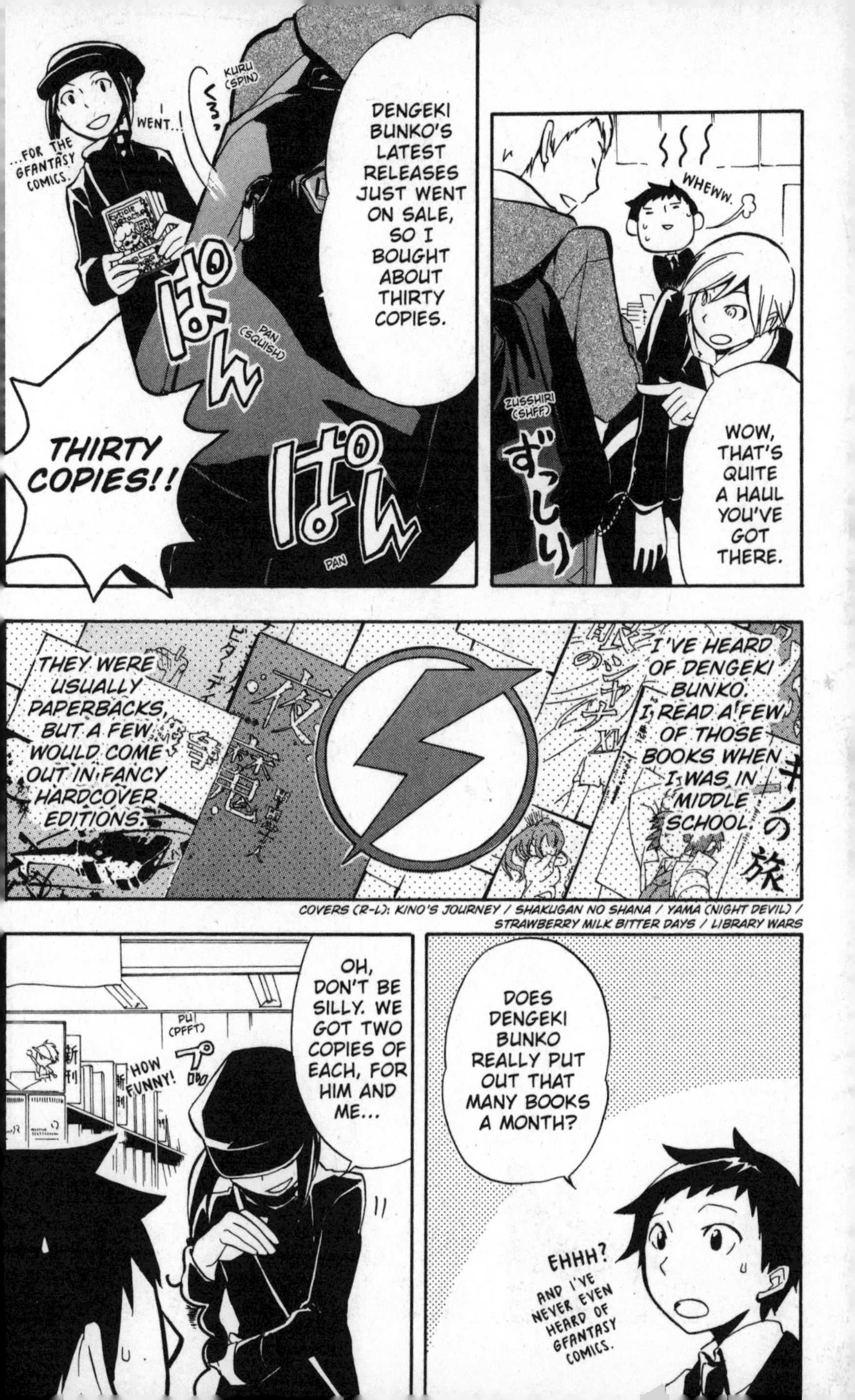
WHEWW.
ZUSSHIRI (SHFF)
WOW, THAT'S QUITE A HAUL YOU'VE GOT THERE.
DENGEKI BUNKO'S LATEST RELEASES JUST WENT ON SALE, SO I BOUGHT ABOUT THIRTY COPIES.
KURU (SPIN)
I WENT...!
...FOR THE GFANTASY COMICS.
PAN (SQUISH)
THIRTY COPIES!!
PAN
I'VE HEARD OF DENGEKI BUNKO. I READ A FEW OF THOSE BOOKS WHEN I WAS IN MIDDLE SCHOOL.
THEY WERE USUALLY PAPERBACKS, BUT A FEW WOULD COME OUT IN FANCY HARDCOVER EDITIONS.
COVERS (R-L): KINO'S JOURNEY / SHAKUGAN NO SHANA / YAMA (NIGHT DEVIL) / STRAWBERRY MILK BITTER DAYS / LIBRARY WARS
DOES DENGEKI BUNKO REALLY PUT OUT THAT MANY BOOKS A MONTH?
EHHH?
AND I'VE NEVER EVEN HEARD OF GFANTASY COMICS.
OH, DON'T BE SILLY. WE GOT TWO COPIES OF EACH, FOR HIM AND ME...
PU (PFFT)
HOW FUNNY!

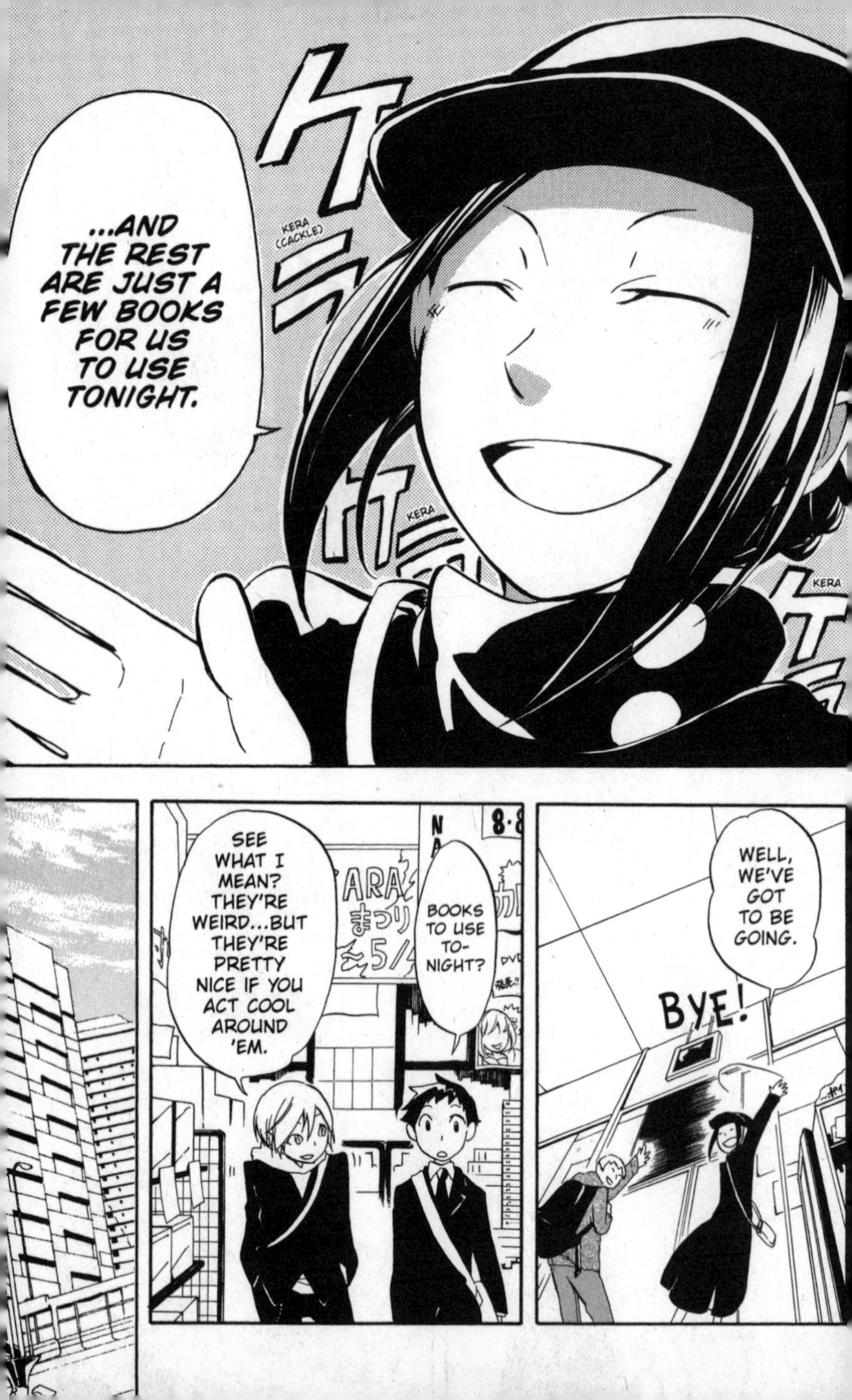
...AND THE REST ARE JUST A FEW BOOKS FOR US TO USE TONIGHT.
KERA (CACKLE)
KERA
KERA
WELL, WE'VE GOT TO BE GOING.
BYE!
BOOKS TO USE TO-NIGHT?
SEE WHAT I MEAN? THEY'RE WEIRD...BUT THEY'RE PRETTY NICE IF YOU ACT COOL AROUND 'EM.

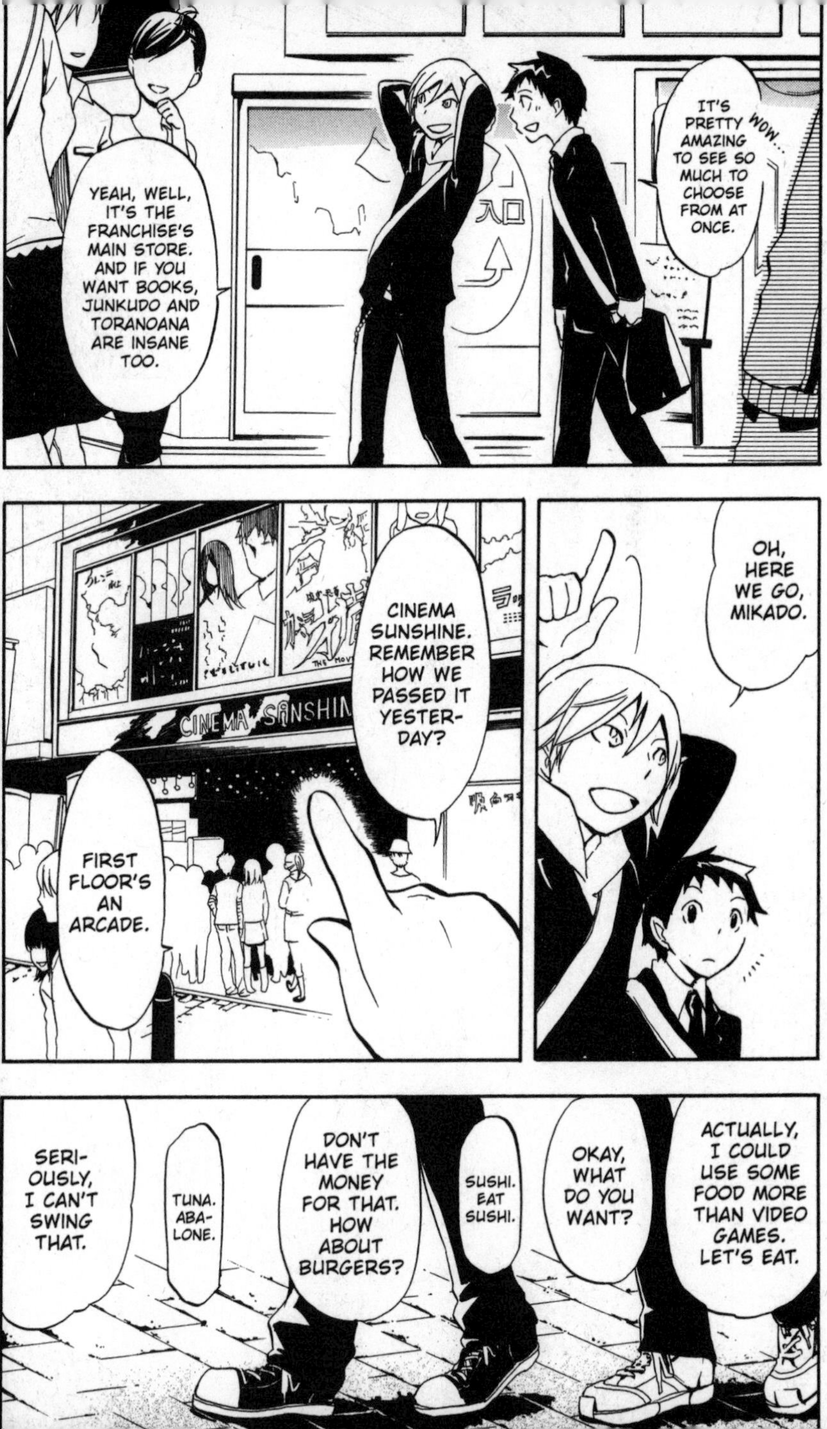
WOW...
IT'S PRETTY AMAZING TO SEE SO MUCH TO CHOOSE FROM AT ONCE.
YEAH, WELL, IT'S THE FRANCHISE'S MAIN STORE. AND IF YOU WANT BOOKS, JUNKUDO AND TORANOANA ARE INSANE TOO.
OH, HERE WE GO, MIKADO.
CINEMA SUNSHINE. REMEMBER HOW WE PASSED IT YESTER-DAY?
FIRST FLOOR'S AN ARCADE.
ACTUALLY, I COULD USE SOME FOOD MORE THAN VIDEO GAMES. LET'S EAT.
OKAY, WHAT DO YOU WANT?
SUSHI. EAT SUSHI.
DON'T HAVE THE MONEY FOR THAT. HOW ABOUT BURGERS?
TUNA. ABA-LONE.
SERI-OUSLY, I CAN'T SWING THAT.

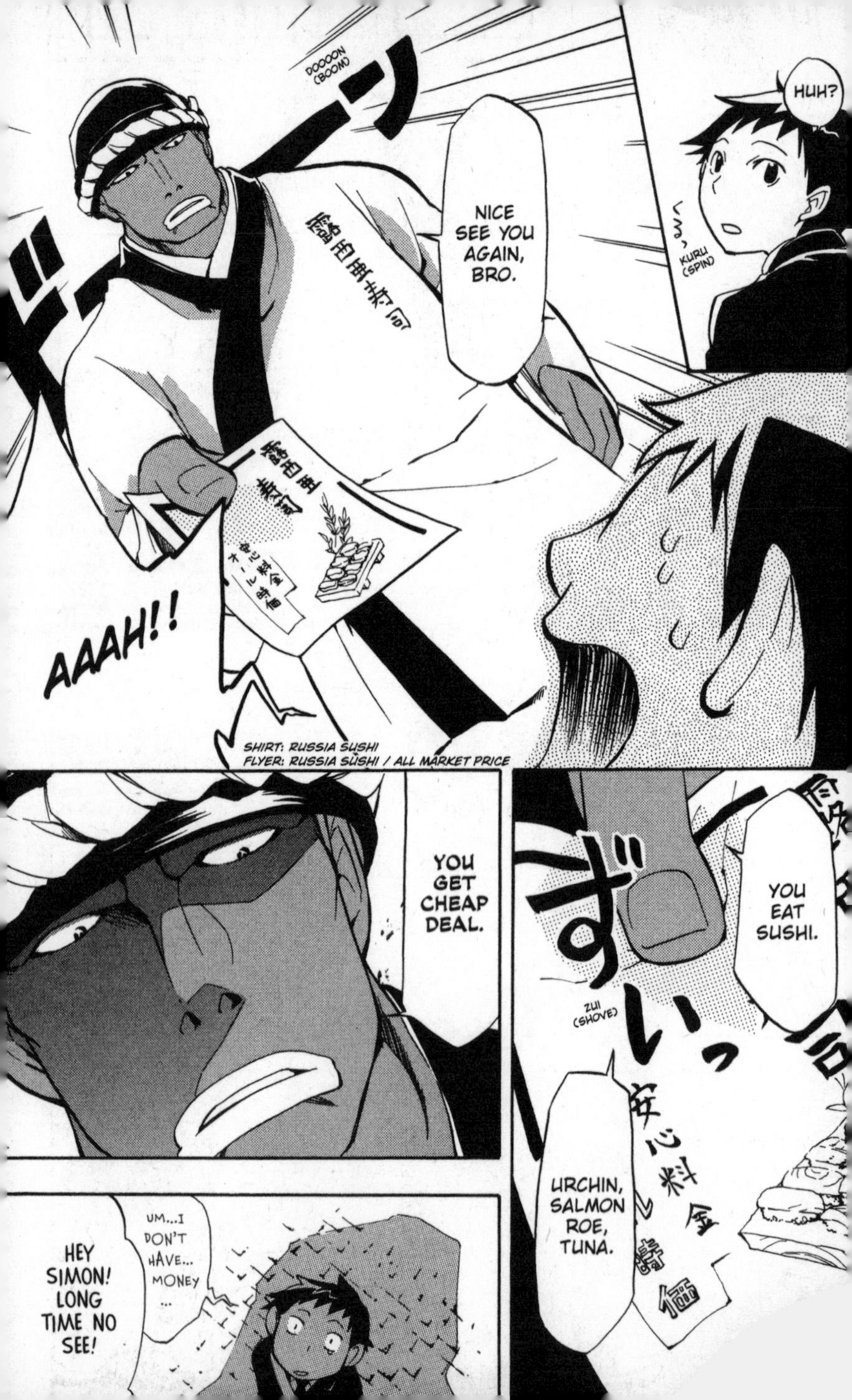
HUH?
KURU (SPIN)
NICE SEE YOU AGAIN, BRO.
DOOOON (BOOM)
AAAH!!
SHIRT: RUSSIA SUSHI
FLYER: RUSSIA SUSHI / ALL MARKET PRICE
YOU EAT SUSHI.
ZUI (SHOVE)
URCHIN, SALMON ROE, TUNA.
YOU GET CHEAP DEAL.
UM...I DON'T HAVE... MONEY ...
HEY SIMON! LONG TIME NO SEE!

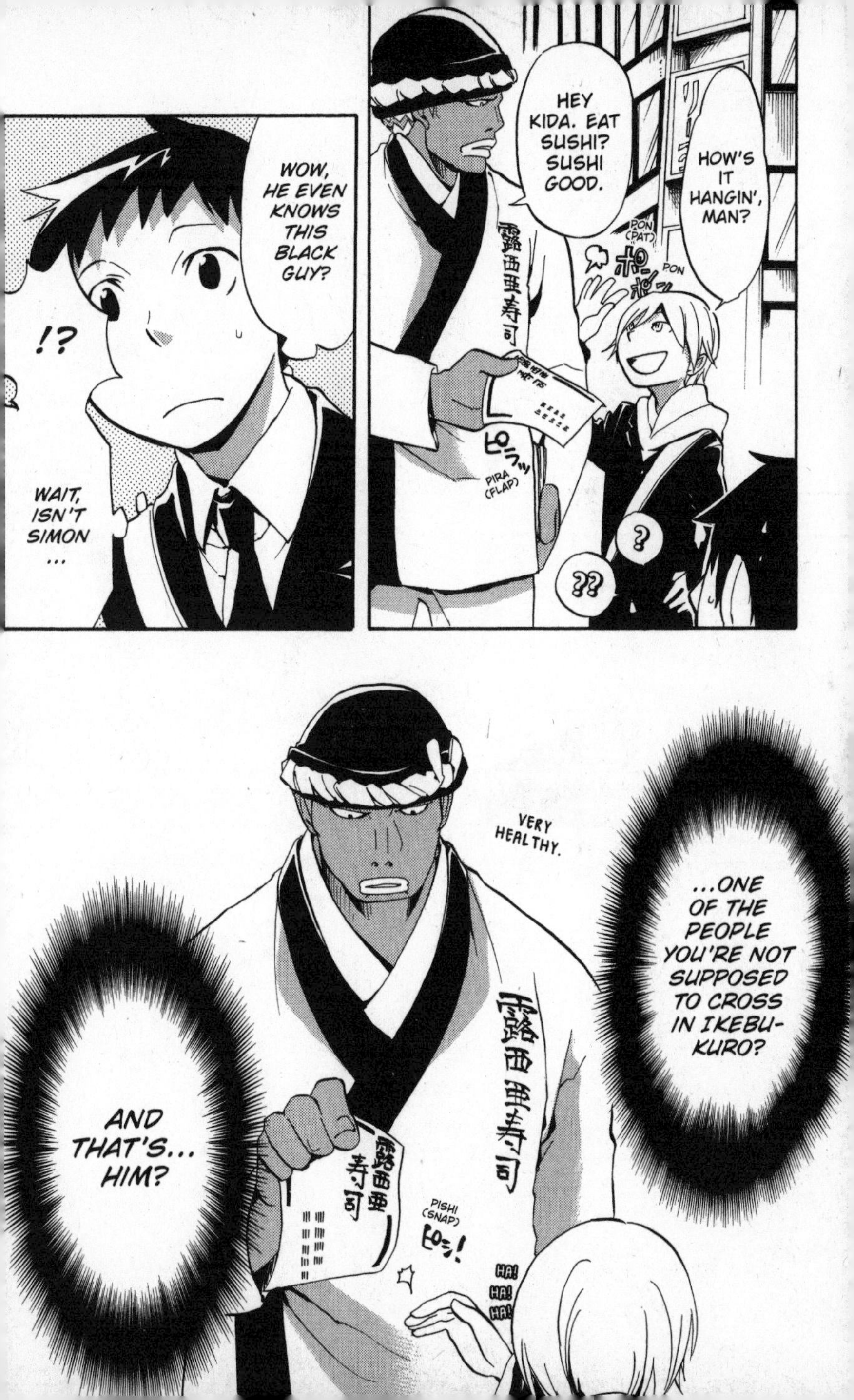
HOW'S IT HANGIN', MAN?
HEY KIDA. EAT SUSHI? SUSHI GOOD.
露西亜寿司
PON (PAT)
ポン
PON
ポン
ピラッ
PIRA (FLAP)
?
??
WOW, HE EVEN KNOWS THIS BLACK GUY?
!?
WAIT, ISN'T SIMON ...
VERY HEALTHY.
...ONE OF THE PEOPLE YOU'RE NOT SUPPOSED TO CROSS IN IKEBU-KURO?
露西亜寿司
AND THAT'S... HIM?
露西亜寿司
PISHI (SNAP)
ピシッ!
HA! HA! HA!

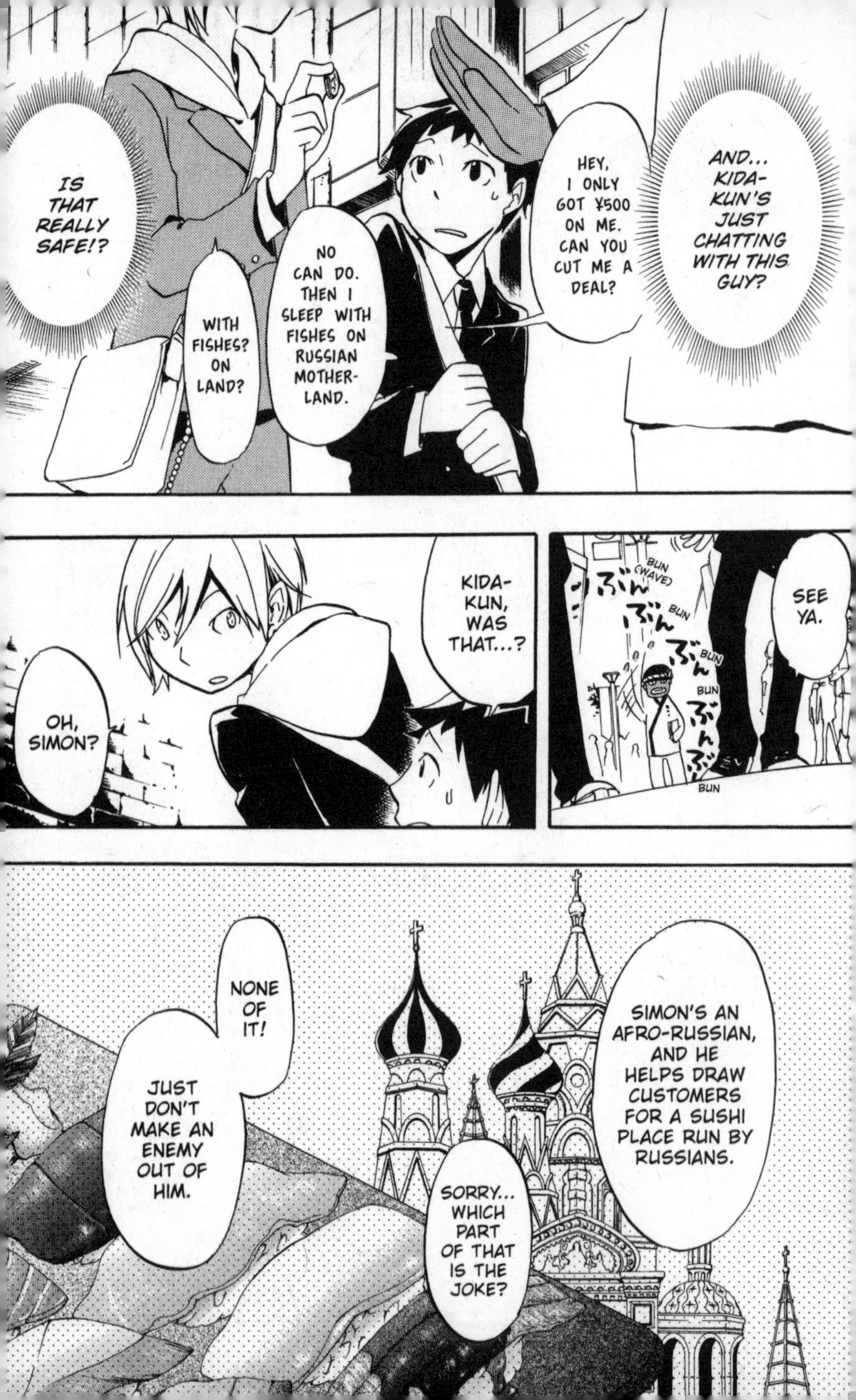
AND... KIDA-KUN'S JUST CHATTING WITH THIS GUY?
HEY, I ONLY GOT ¥500 ON ME. CAN YOU CUT ME A DEAL?
NO CAN DO. THEN I SLEEP WITH FISHES ON RUSSIAN MOTHERLAND.
WITH FISHES? ON LAND?
IS THAT REALLY SAFE!?
SEE YA.
ぶん BUN (WAVE)
ぶん BUN
ぶん BUN
ぶん BUN
ぶ BUN
KIDA-KUN, WAS THAT...?
OH, SIMON?
SIMON'S AN AFRO-RUSSIAN, AND HE HELPS DRAW CUSTOMERS FOR A SUSHI PLACE RUN BY RUSSIANS.
SORRY... WHICH PART OF THAT IS THE JOKE?
NONE OF IT!
JUST DON'T MAKE AN ENEMY OUT OF HIM.

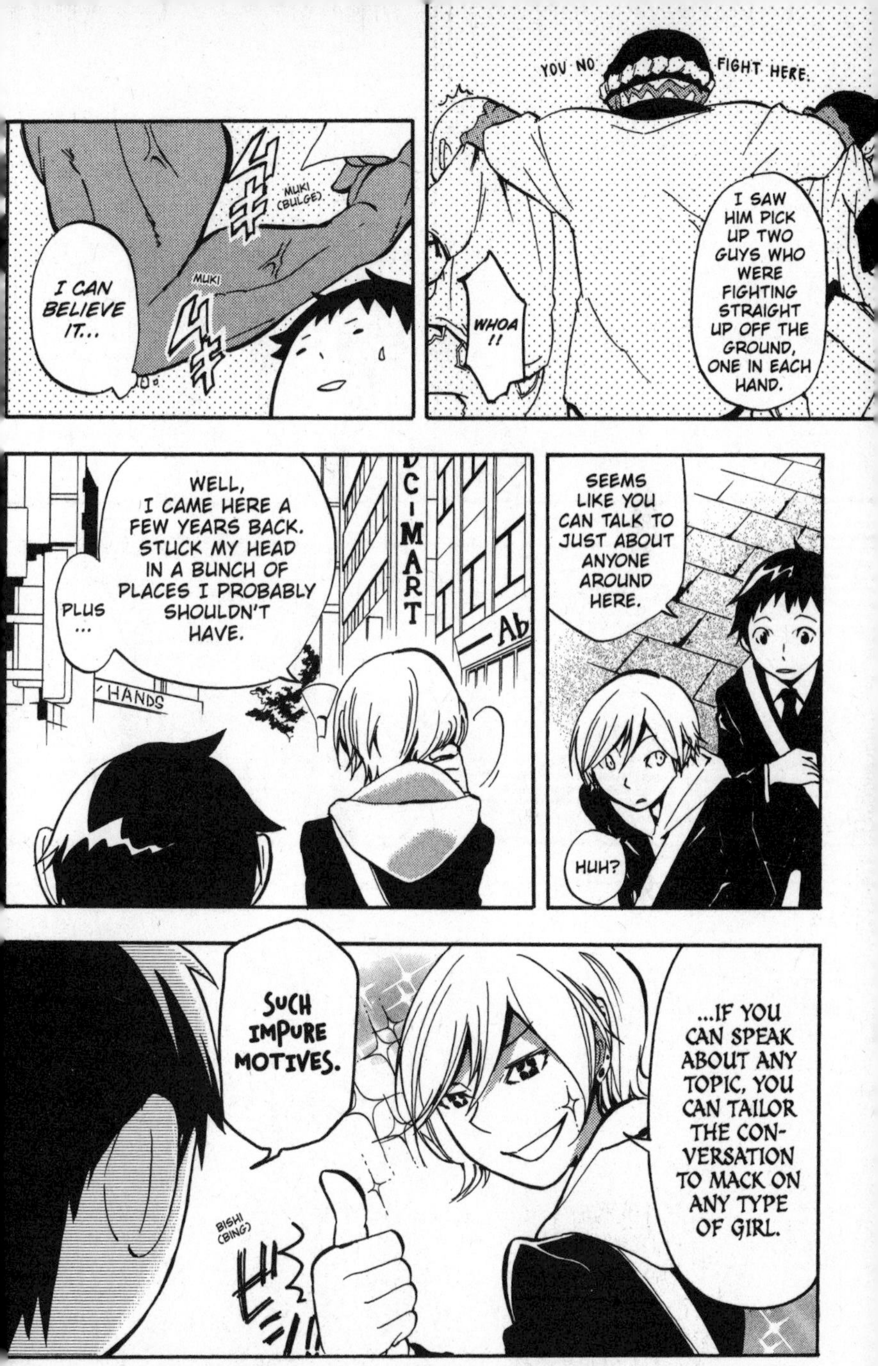
YOU NO FIGHT HERE.
I SAW HIM PICK UP TWO GUYS WHO WERE FIGHTING STRAIGHT UP OFF THE GROUND, ONE IN EACH HAND.
WHOA!!
MUKI (BULGE)
MUKI
I CAN BELIEVE IT...
SEEMS LIKE YOU CAN TALK TO JUST ABOUT ANYONE AROUND HERE.
HUH?
DCI MART
Ab
WELL, I CAME HERE A FEW YEARS BACK. STUCK MY HEAD IN A BUNCH OF PLACES I PROBABLY SHOULDN'T HAVE.
PLUS...
HANDS
...IF YOU CAN SPEAK ABOUT ANY TOPIC, YOU CAN TAILOR THE CONVERSATION TO MACK ON ANY TYPE OF GIRL.
SUCH IMPURE MOTIVES.
BISHI (BING)

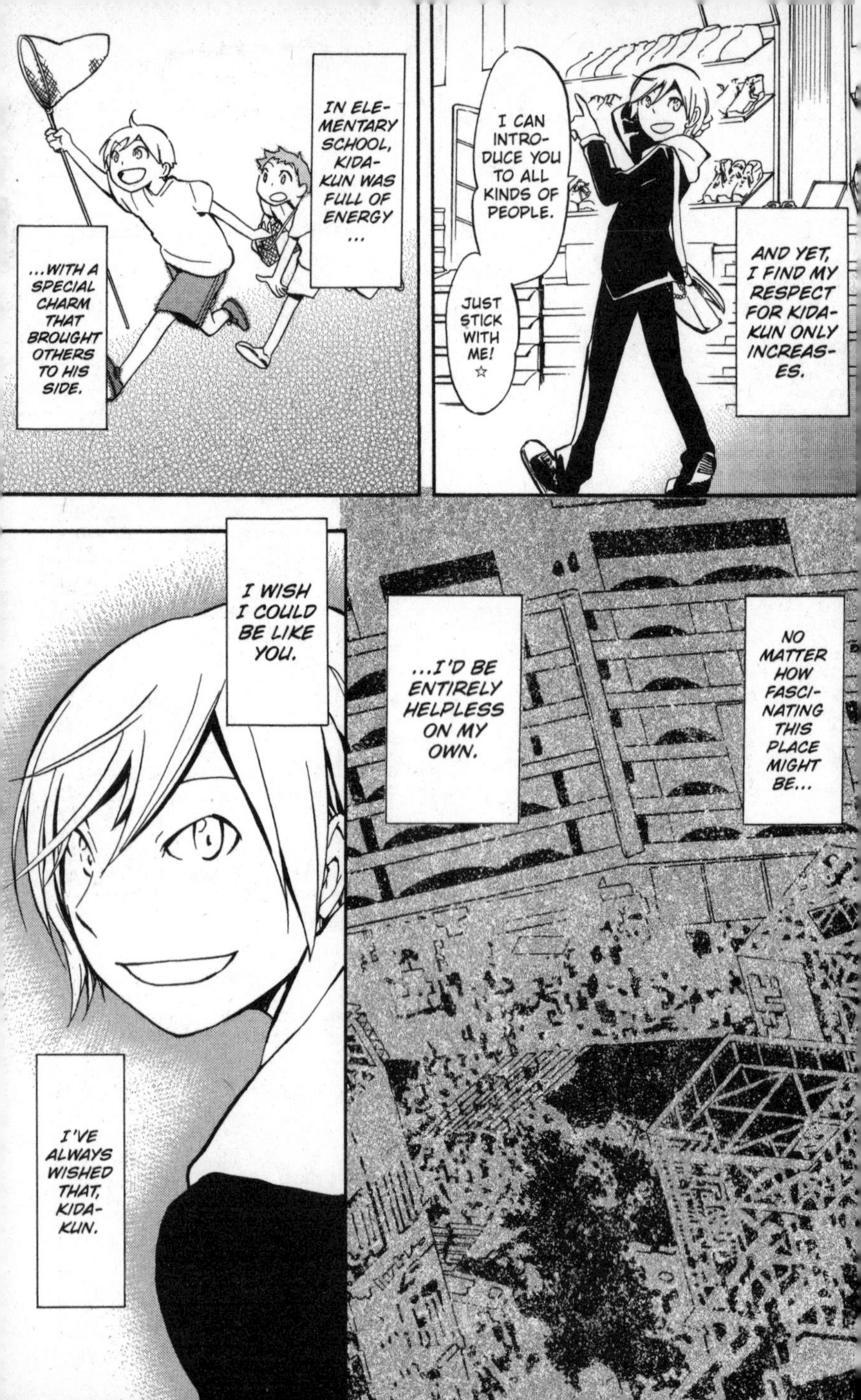
I CAN INTRODUCE YOU TO ALL KINDS OF PEOPLE.
JUST STICK WITH ME! ☆
AND YET, I FIND MY RESPECT FOR KIDA-KUN ONLY INCREASES.
IN ELEMENTARY SCHOOL, KIDA-KUN WAS FULL OF ENERGY...
...WITH A SPECIAL CHARM THAT BROUGHT OTHERS TO HIS SIDE.
NO MATTER HOW FASCINATING THIS PLACE MIGHT BE...
...I'D BE ENTIRELY HELPLESS ON MY OWN.
I WISH I COULD BE LIKE YOU.
I'VE ALWAYS WISHED THAT, KIDA-KUN.

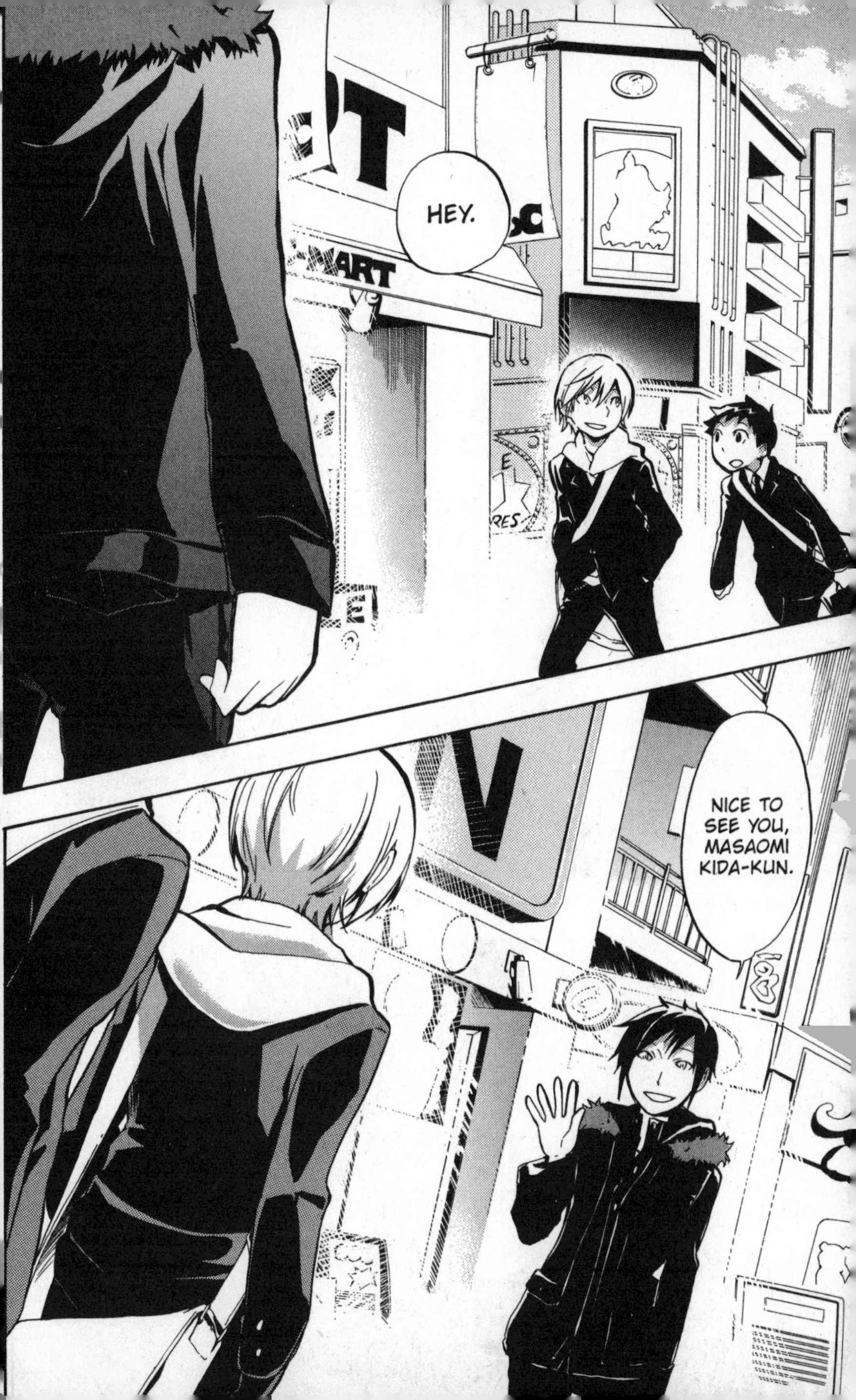
HEY.
NICE TO SEE YOU, MASAOMI KIDA-KUN.

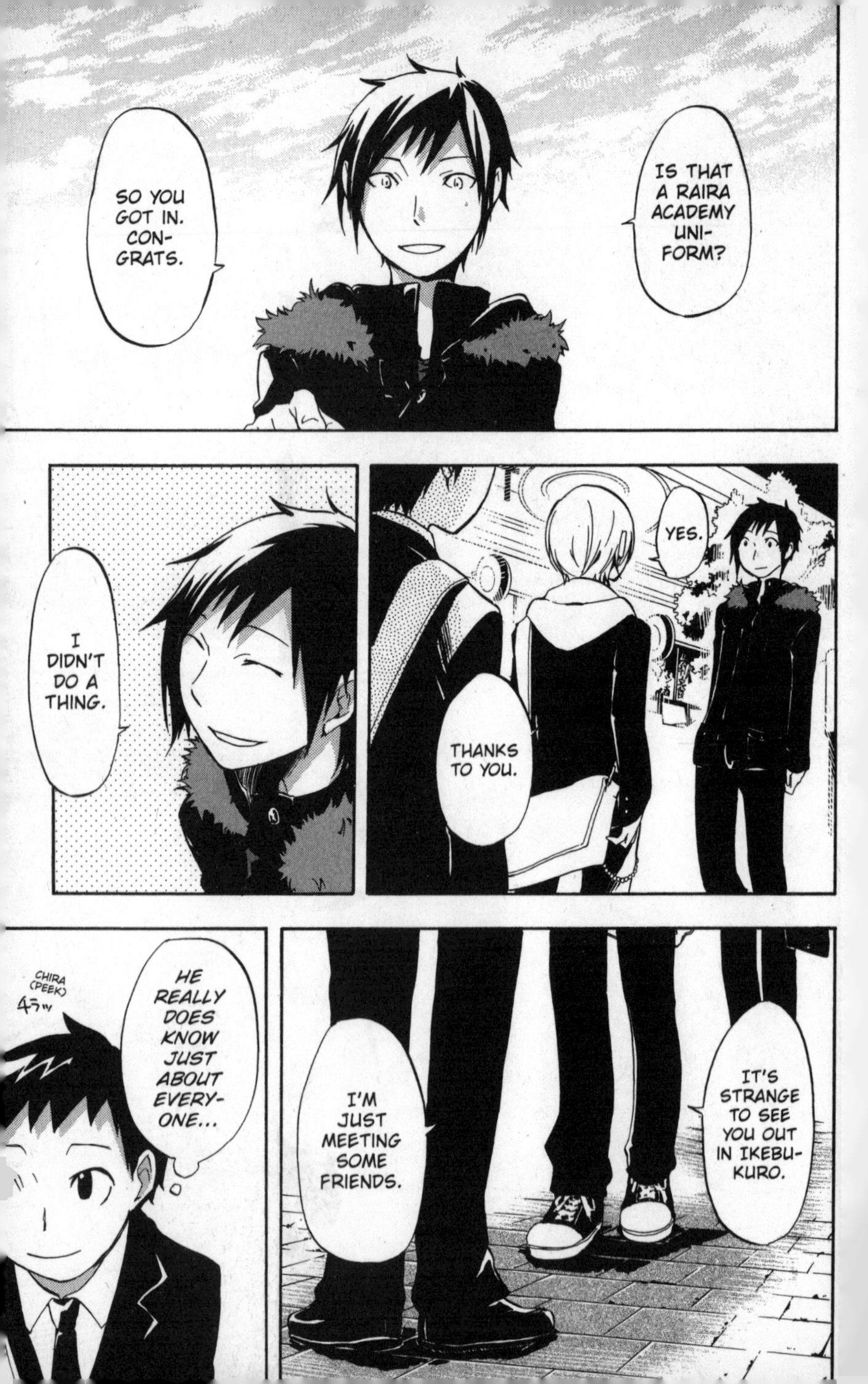
IS THAT A RAIRA ACADEMY UNIFORM?
SO YOU GOT IN. CONGRATS.
YES.
THANKS TO YOU.
I DIDN'T DO A THING.
IT'S STRANGE TO SEE YOU OUT IN IKEBUKURO.
I'M JUST MEETING SOME FRIENDS.
HE REALLY DOES KNOW JUST ABOUT EVERYONE...
CHIRA (PEEK)
チラッ

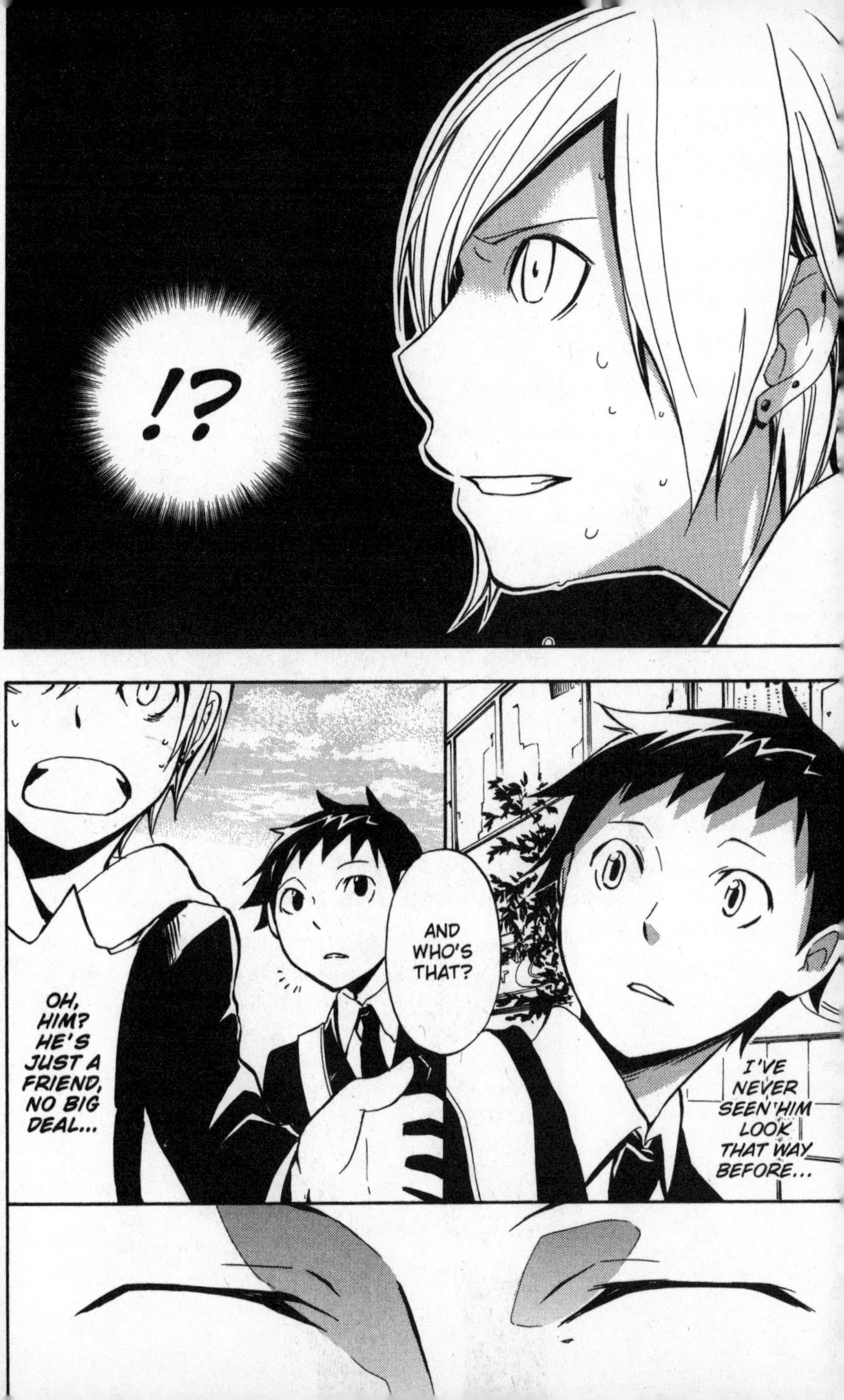
!?
I'VE NEVER SEEN HIM LOOK THAT WAY BEFORE...
AND WHO'S THAT?
OH, HIM? HE'S JUST A FRIEND, NO BIG DEAL...

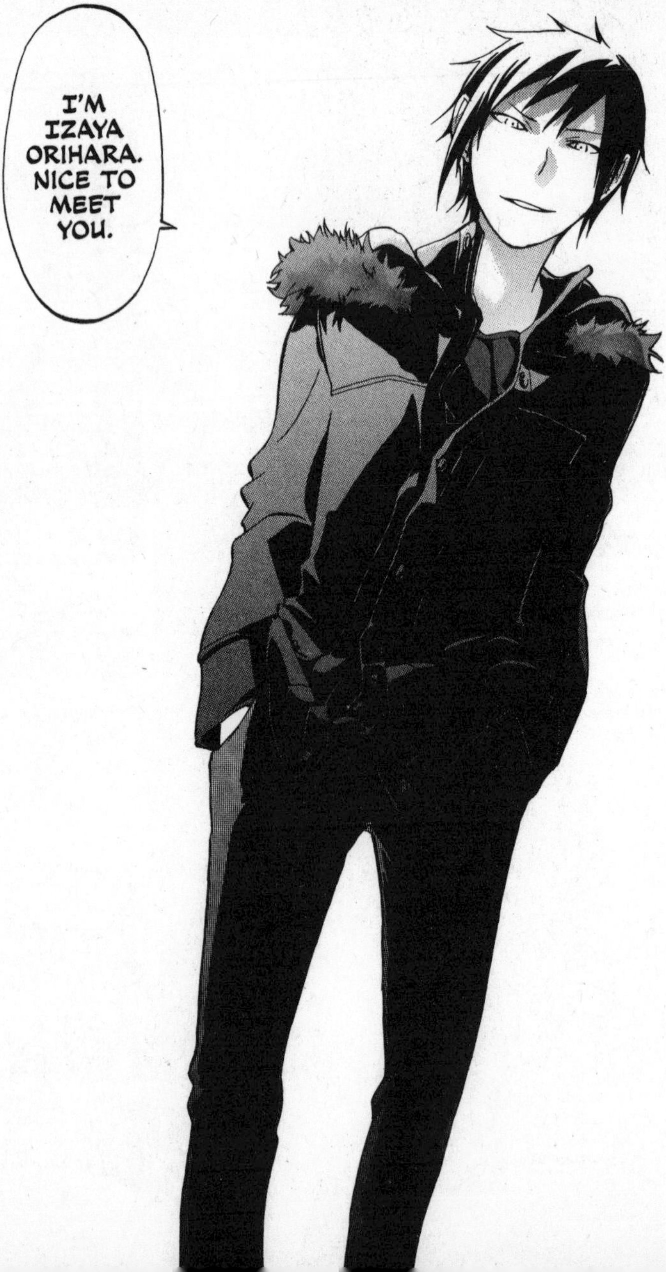
I'M IZAYA ORIHARA. NICE TO MEET YOU.

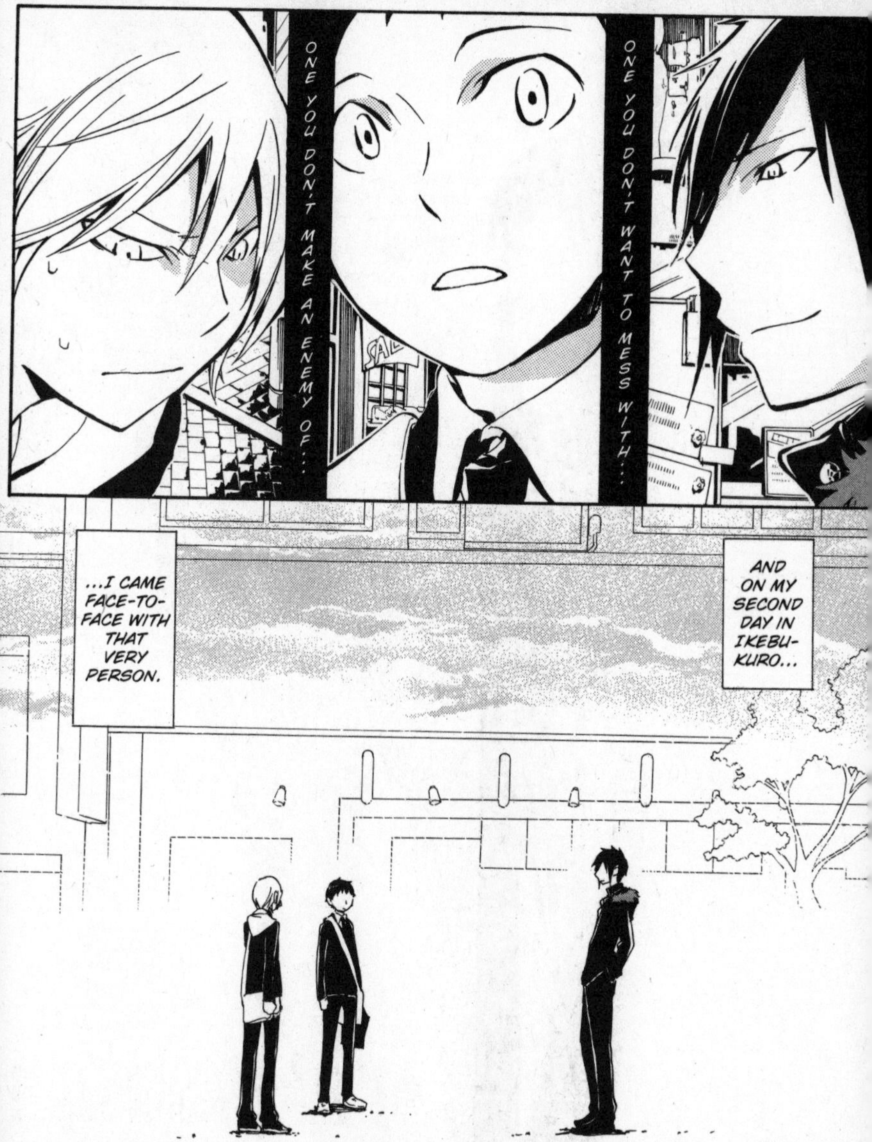
ONE YOU DON'T WANT TO MESS WITH...
ONE YOU DON'T MAKE AN ENEMY OF...
AND ON MY SECOND DAY IN IKEBUKURO...
...I CAME FACE-TO-FACE WITH THAT VERY PERSON.

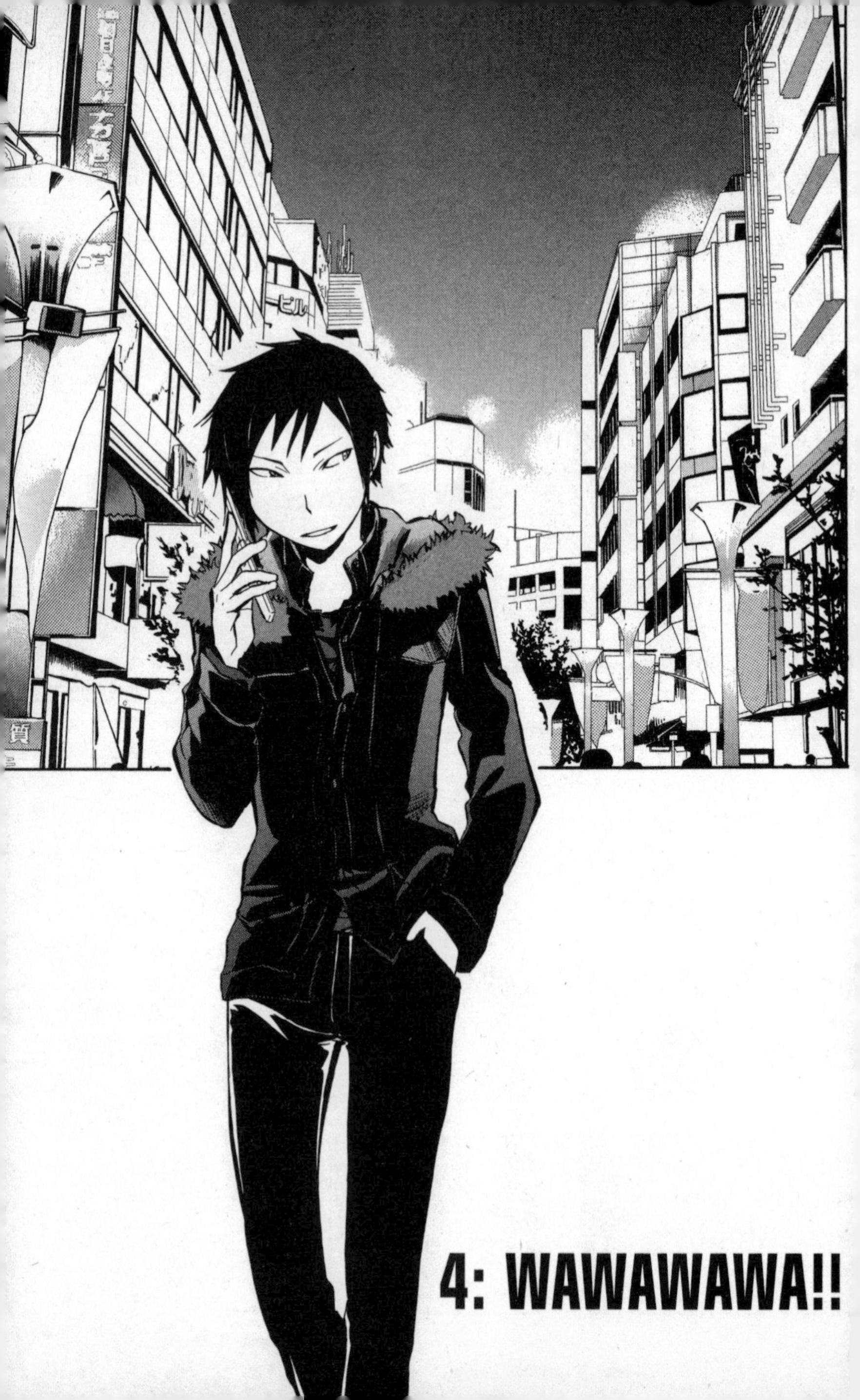
ビル
質

4: WAWAWAWA!!

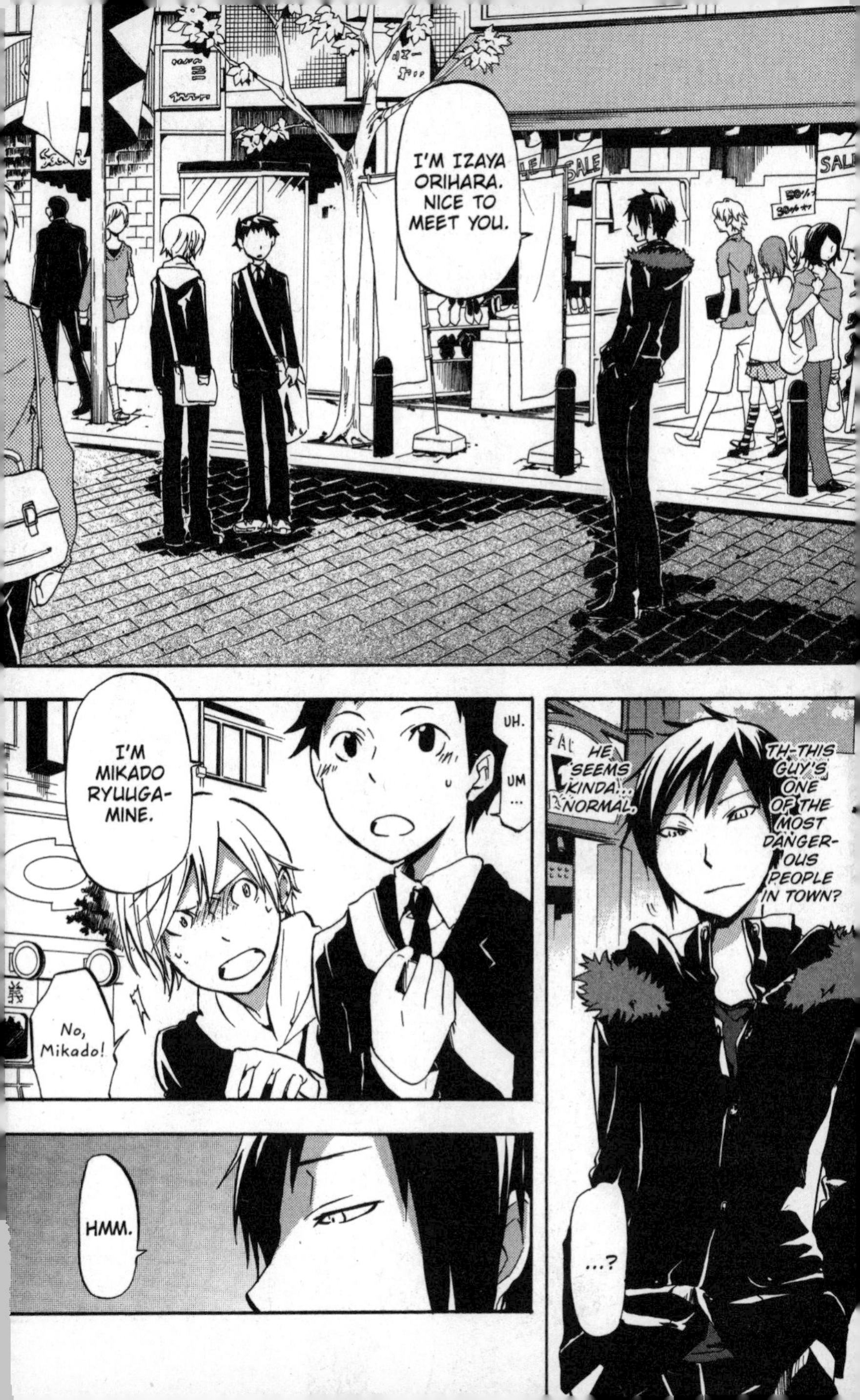

I'M IZAYA ORIHARA. NICE TO MEET YOU.
TH-THIS GUY'S ONE OF THE MOST DANGER-OUS PEOPLE IN TOWN?
HE SEEMS KINDA... NORMAL.
...?
UH. UM ...
I'M MIKADO RYUUGA-MINE.
No, Mikado!
HMM.

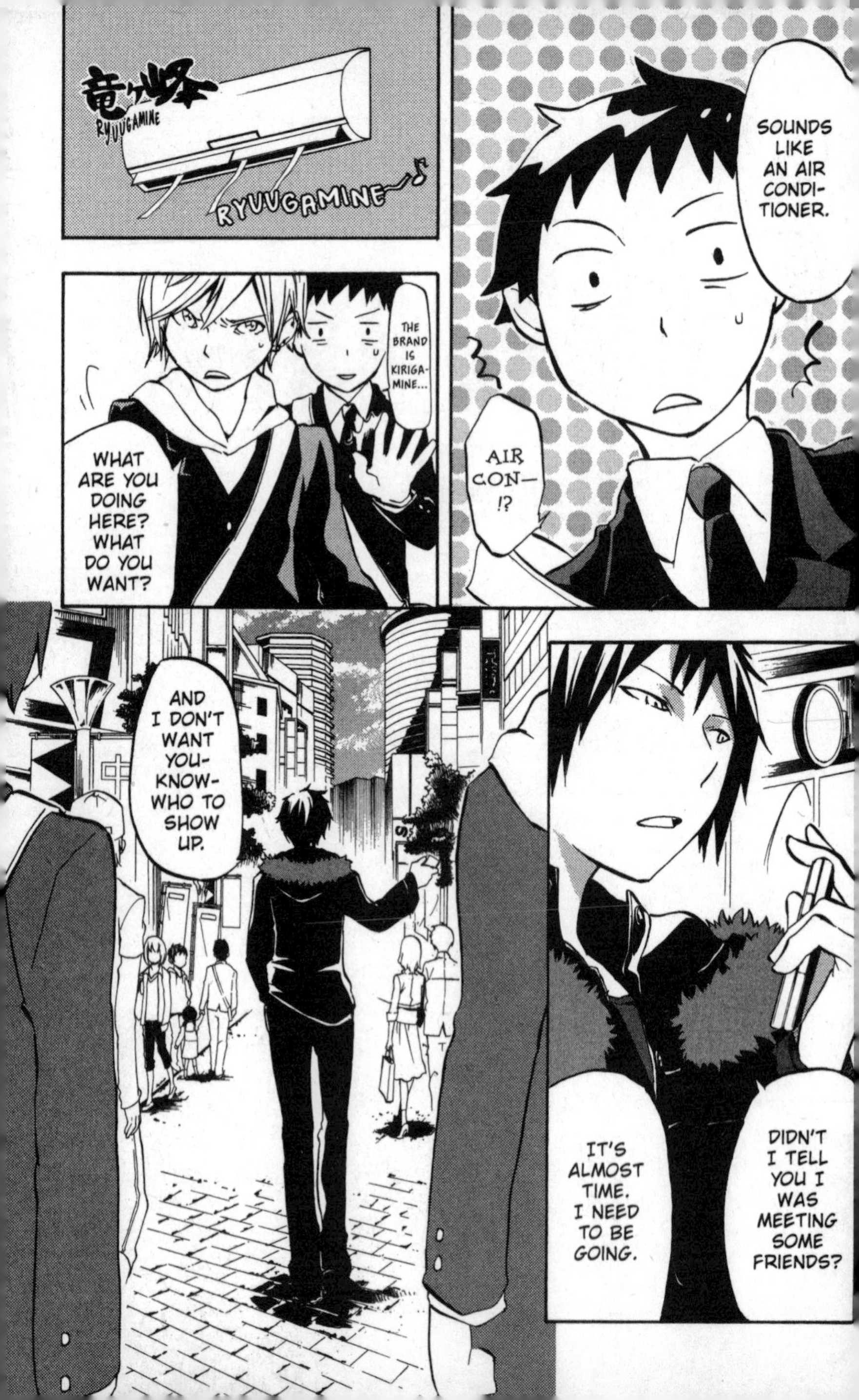
SOUNDS LIKE AN AIR CONDITIONER.
AIR CON—!?
竜ヶ峰
RYUUGAMINE
RYUUGAMINE~♪
THE BRAND IS KIRIGAMINE...
WHAT ARE YOU DOING HERE? WHAT DO YOU WANT?
DIDN'T I TELL YOU I WAS MEETING SOME FRIENDS?
IT'S ALMOST TIME. I NEED TO BE GOING.
AND I DON'T WANT YOU-KNOW-WHO TO SHOW UP.

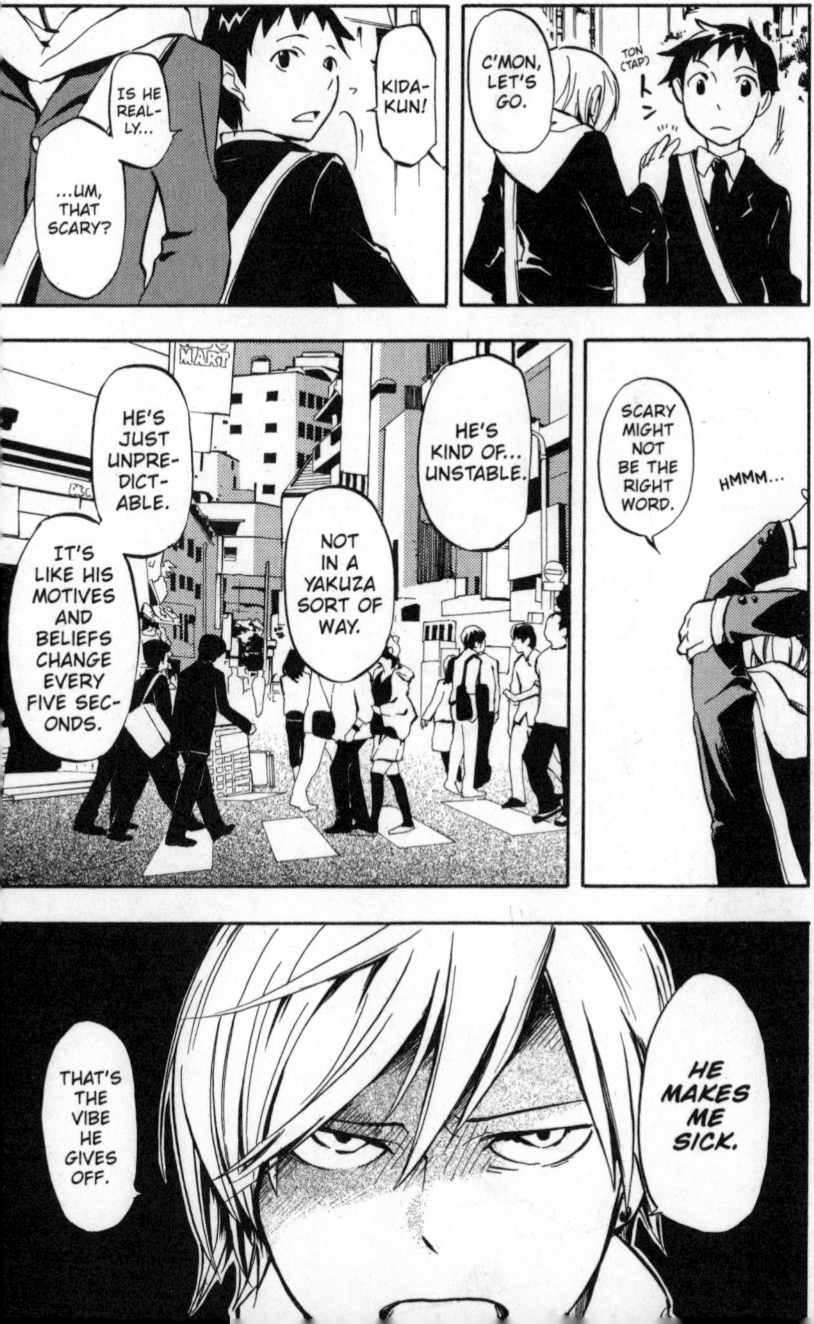
TON (TAP)
C'MON, LET'S GO.
KIDA-KUN!
IS HE REALLY...
...UM, THAT SCARY?
HMMM...
SCARY MIGHT NOT BE THE RIGHT WORD.
HE'S KIND OF... UNSTABLE.
NOT IN A YAKUZA SORT OF WAY.
HE'S JUST UNPREDICTABLE.
IT'S LIKE HIS MOTIVES AND BELIEFS CHANGE EVERY FIVE SECONDS.
THAT'S THE VIBE HE GIVES OFF.
HE MAKES ME SICK.

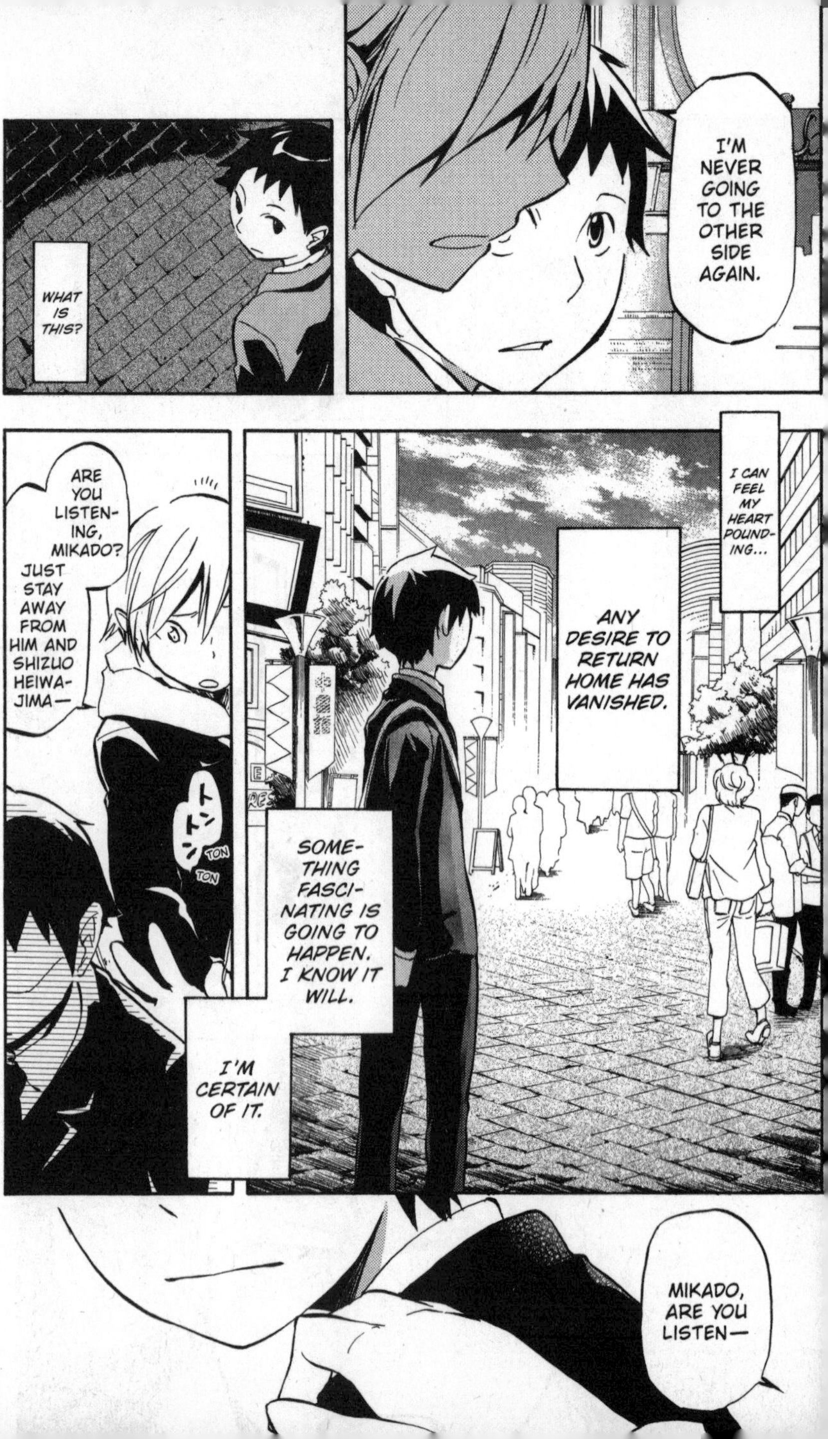
I'M NEVER GOING TO THE OTHER SIDE AGAIN.
WHAT IS THIS?
I CAN FEEL MY HEART POUND-ING...
ANY DESIRE TO RETURN HOME HAS VANISHED.
SOME-THING FASCI-NATING IS GOING TO HAPPEN. I KNOW IT WILL.
I'M CERTAIN OF IT.
ARE YOU LISTEN-ING, MIKADO? JUST STAY AWAY FROM HIM AND SHIZUO HEIWA-JIMA—
トントン
TON TON
MIKADO, ARE YOU LISTEN—

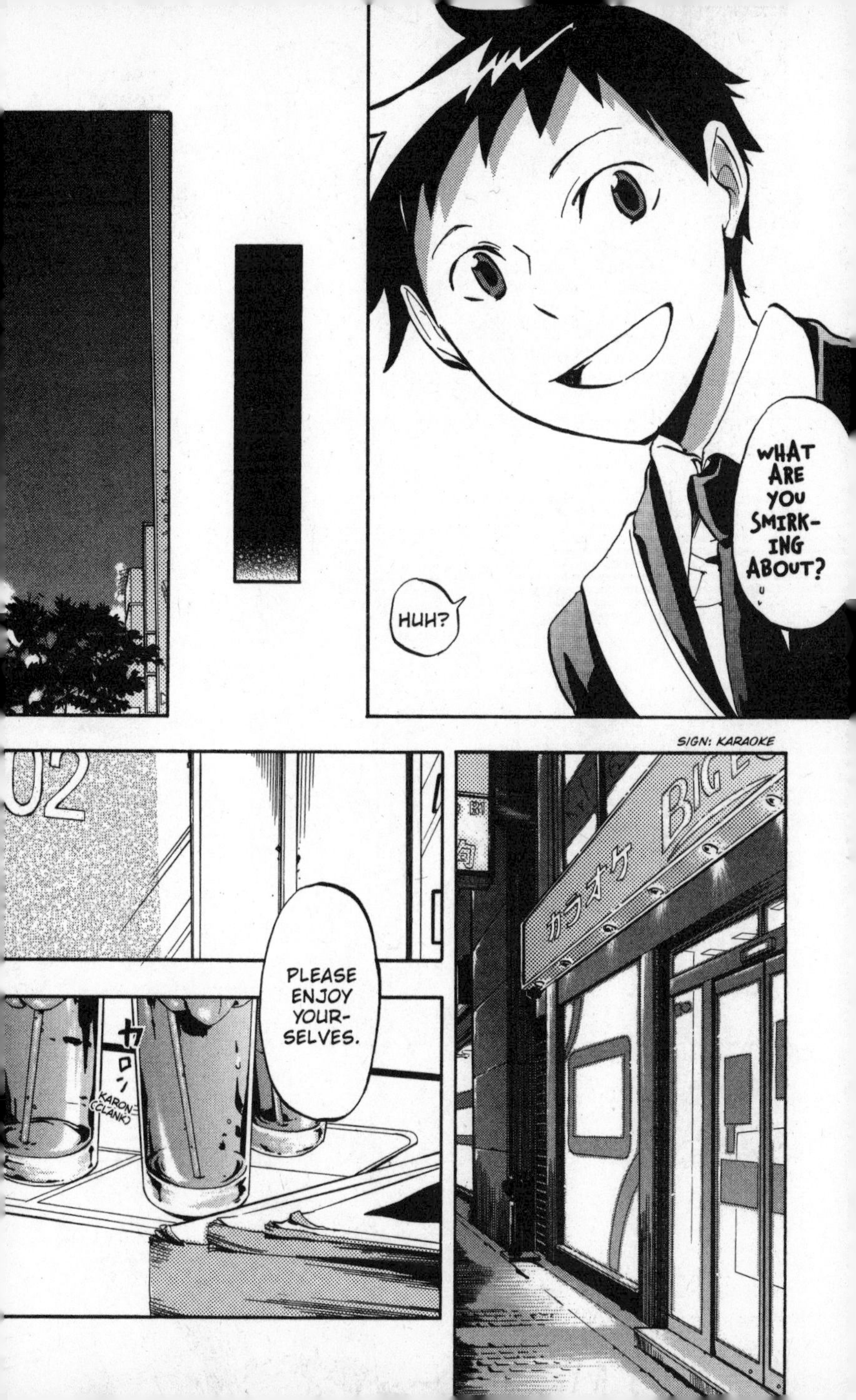
WHAT ARE YOU SMIRKING ABOUT?
HUH?
SIGN: KARAOKE
カラオケ
PLEASE ENJOY YOURSELVES.
KARON (CLANK)

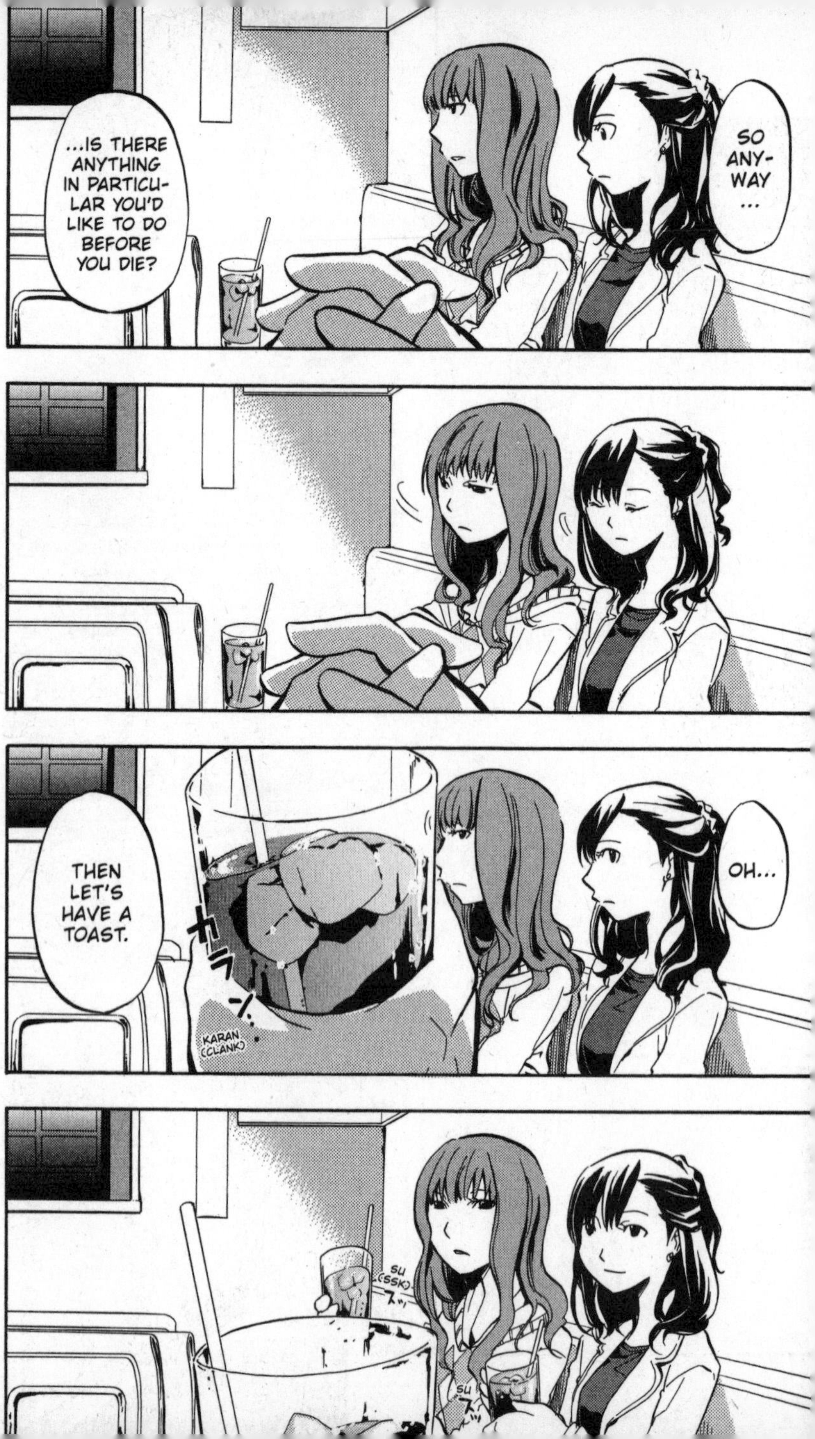
SO ANY-WAY...
...IS THERE ANYTHING IN PARTICULAR YOU'D LIKE TO DO BEFORE YOU DIE?
OH...
THEN LET'S HAVE A TOAST.
KARAN (CLANK)
SU (SSK)
SU

TO OUR FIRST MEETING...

...AND OUR ETERNAL FAREWELL TO THIS WORLD.

JULIET-SAN, BLACKBELLE-SAN, ARE YOU SURE YOU WANT TO DO THIS WITH ME?

THERE ISN'T ANYONE YOU'D RATHER COMMIT SUICIDE WITH?

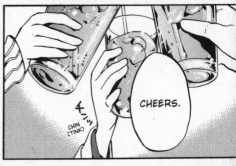

CHIN (TINK)

CHEERS.

114

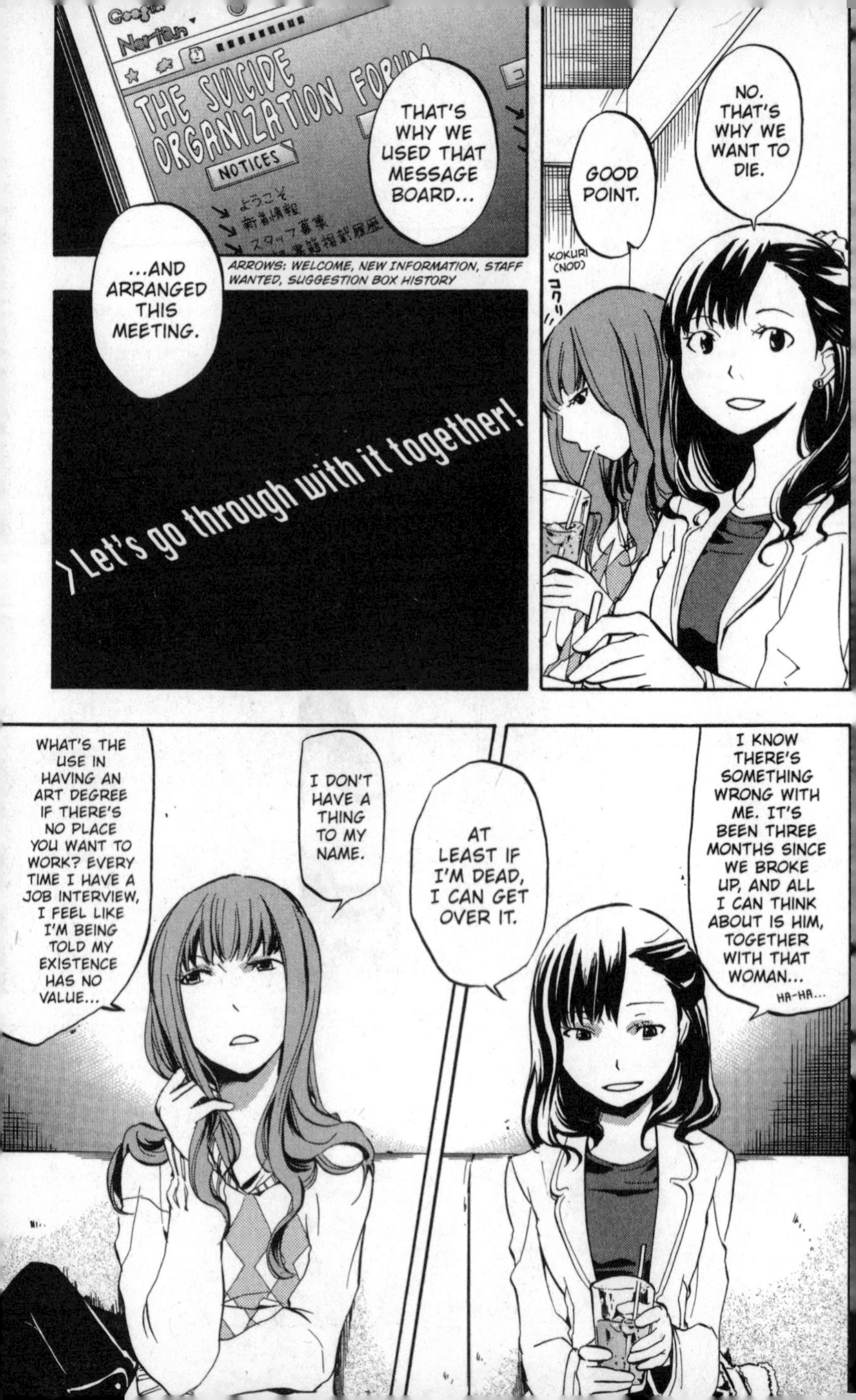
NO. THAT'S WHY WE WANT TO DIE.
GOOD POINT.
KOKURI (NOD)
THE SUICIDE ORGANIZATION FORU
NOTICES
ようこそ
新着情報
スタッフ募集
THAT'S WHY WE USED THAT MESSAGE BOARD...
...AND ARRANGED THIS MEETING.
ARROWS: WELCOME, NEW INFORMATION, STAFF WANTED, SUGGESTION BOX HISTORY
›Let's go through with it together!
I KNOW THERE'S SOMETHING WRONG WITH ME. IT'S BEEN THREE MONTHS SINCE WE BROKE UP, AND ALL I CAN THINK ABOUT IS HIM, TOGETHER WITH THAT WOMAN...
HA-HA...
AT LEAST IF I'M DEAD, I CAN GET OVER IT.
I DON'T HAVE A THING TO MY NAME.
WHAT'S THE USE IN HAVING AN ART DEGREE IF THERE'S NO PLACE YOU WANT TO WORK? EVERY TIME I HAVE A JOB INTERVIEW, I FEEL LIKE I'M BEING TOLD MY EXISTENCE HAS NO VALUE...

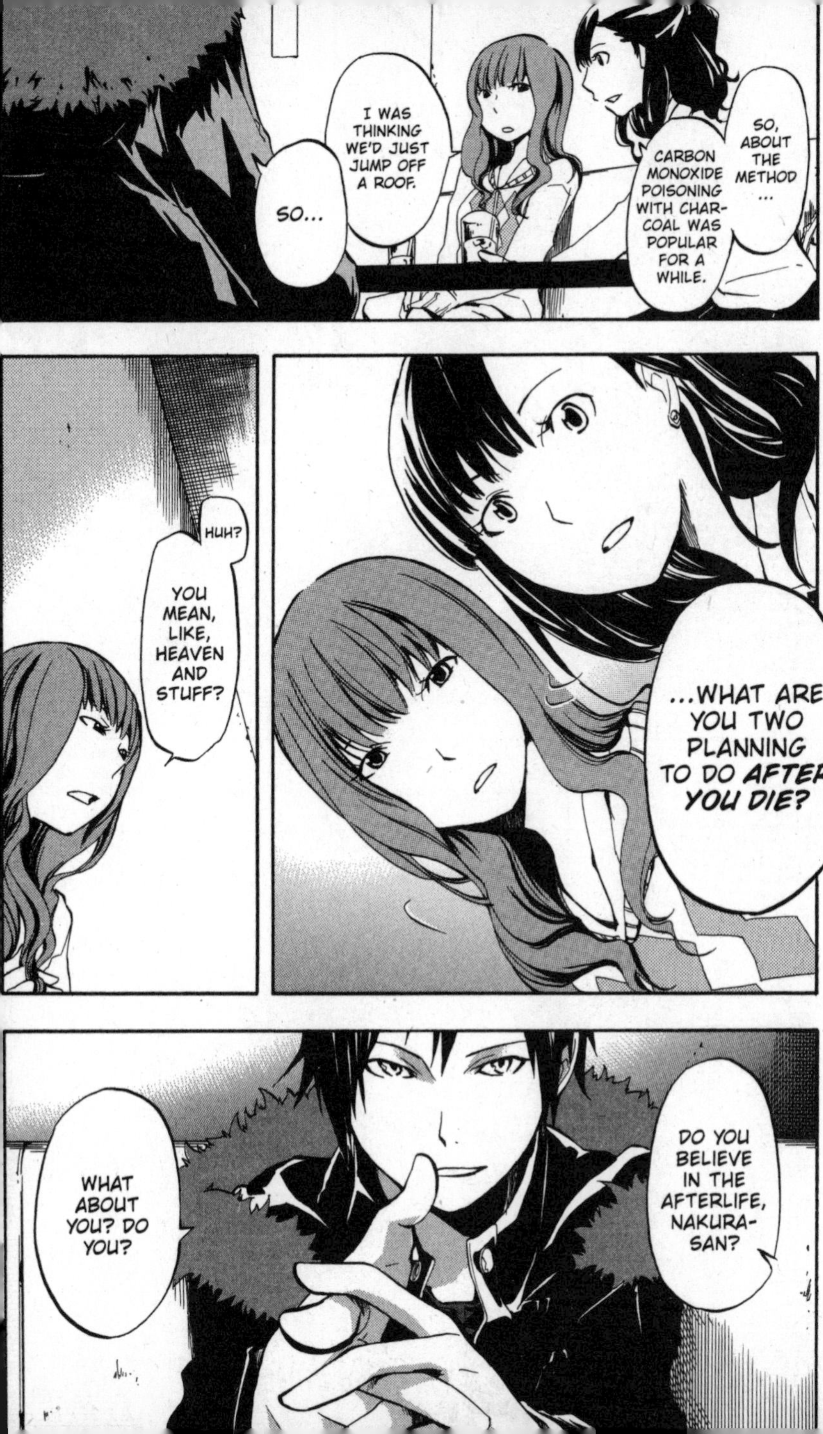
SO, ABOUT THE METHOD...
CARBON MONOXIDE POISONING WITH CHARCOAL WAS POPULAR FOR A WHILE.
I WAS THINKING WE'D JUST JUMP OFF A ROOF.
SO...
...WHAT ARE YOU TWO PLANNING TO DO *AFTER YOU DIE?*
HUH?
YOU MEAN, LIKE, HEAVEN AND STUFF?
DO YOU BELIEVE IN THE AFTERLIFE, NAKURA-SAN?
WHAT ABOUT YOU? DO YOU?

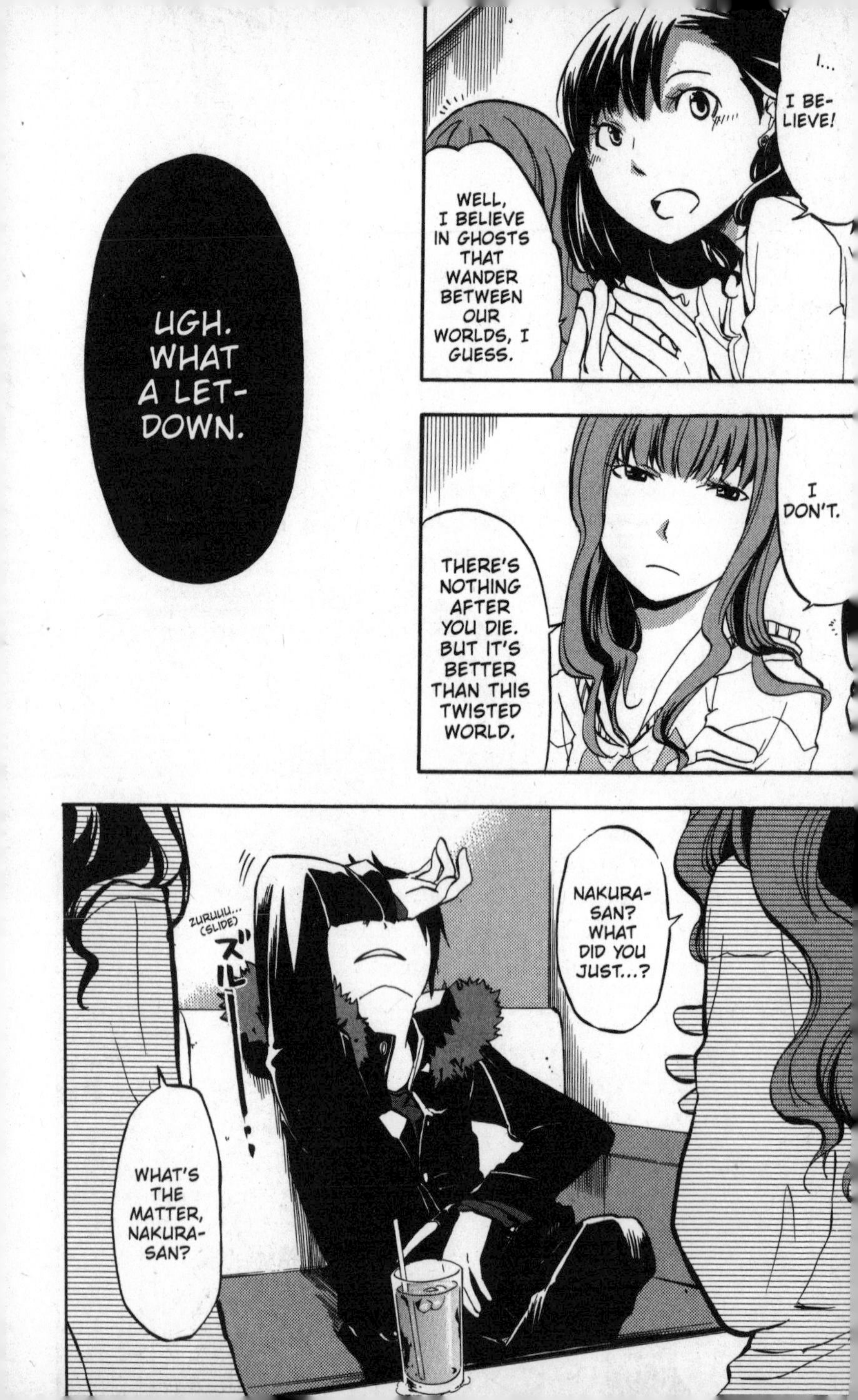
I... I BE-LIEVE!
WELL, I BELIEVE IN GHOSTS THAT WANDER BETWEEN OUR WORLDS, I GUESS.
I DON'T.
THERE'S NOTHING AFTER YOU DIE. BUT IT'S BETTER THAN THIS TWISTED WORLD.
UGH. WHAT A LET-DOWN.
NAKURA-SAN? WHAT DID YOU JUST...?
ZURUUU... (SLIDE)
ズルー
WHAT'S THE MATTER, NAKURA-SAN?

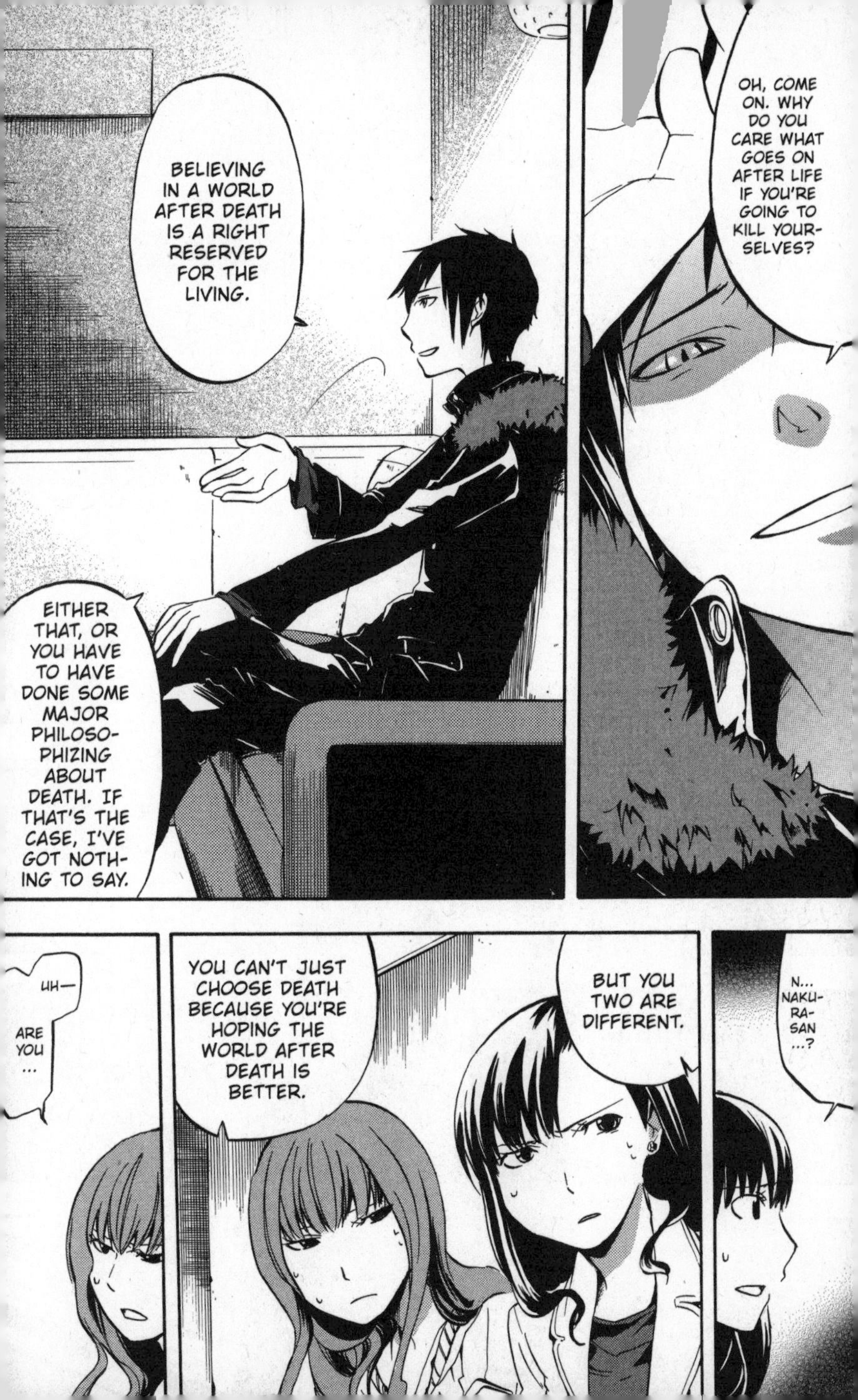
OH, COME ON. WHY DO YOU CARE WHAT GOES ON AFTER LIFE IF YOU'RE GOING TO KILL YOURSELVES?
BELIEVING IN A WORLD AFTER DEATH IS A RIGHT RESERVED FOR THE LIVING.
EITHER THAT, OR YOU HAVE TO HAVE DONE SOME MAJOR PHILOSOPHIZING ABOUT DEATH. IF THAT'S THE CASE, I'VE GOT NOTHING TO SAY.
N... NAKURA-SAN ...?
BUT YOU TWO ARE DIFFERENT.
YOU CAN'T JUST CHOOSE DEATH BECAUSE YOU'RE HOPING THE WORLD AFTER DEATH IS BETTER.
UH— ARE YOU ...

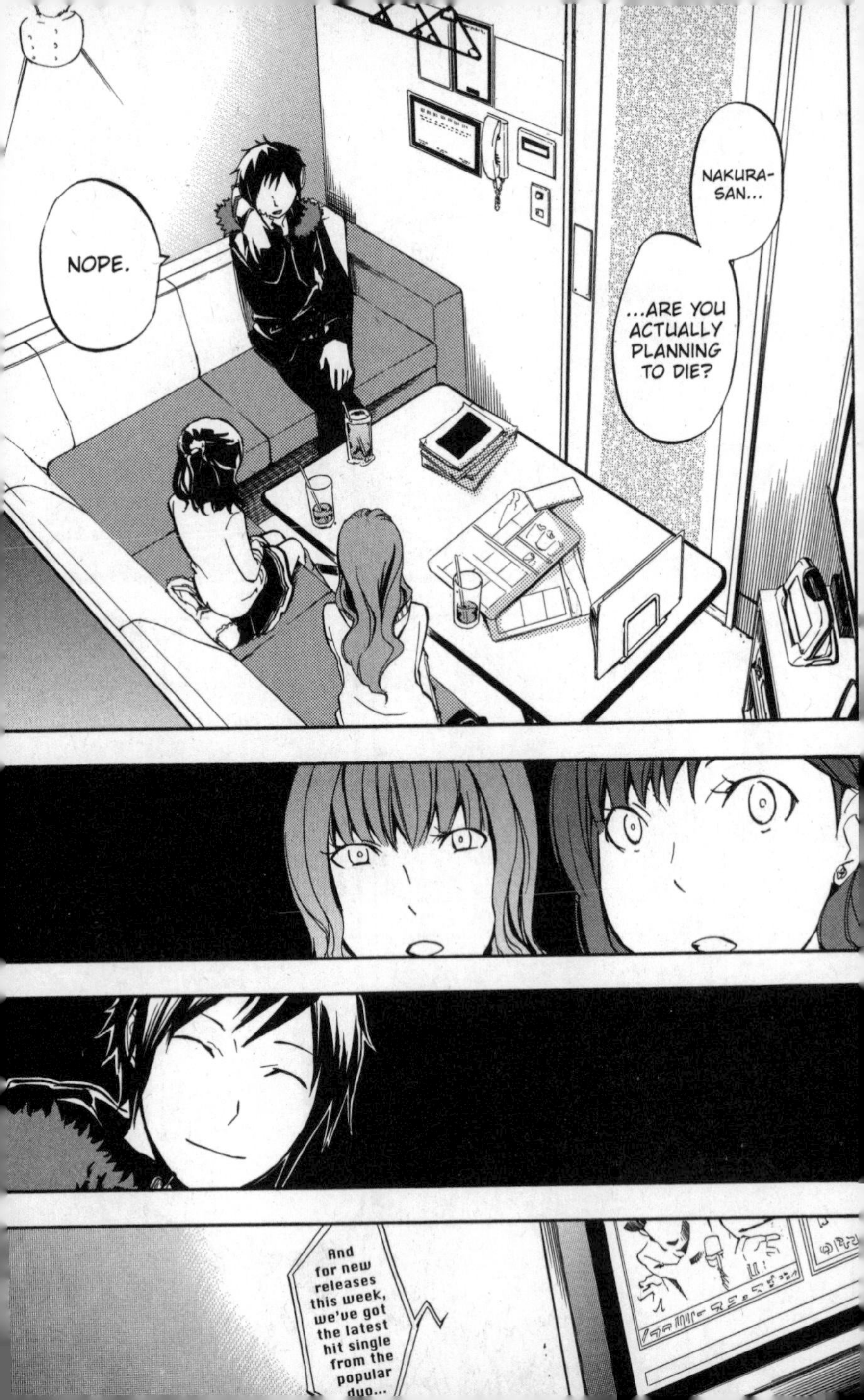
NAKURA-SAN...
...ARE YOU ACTUALLY PLANNING TO DIE?
NOPE.
And for new releases this week, we've got the latest hit single from the popular duo...

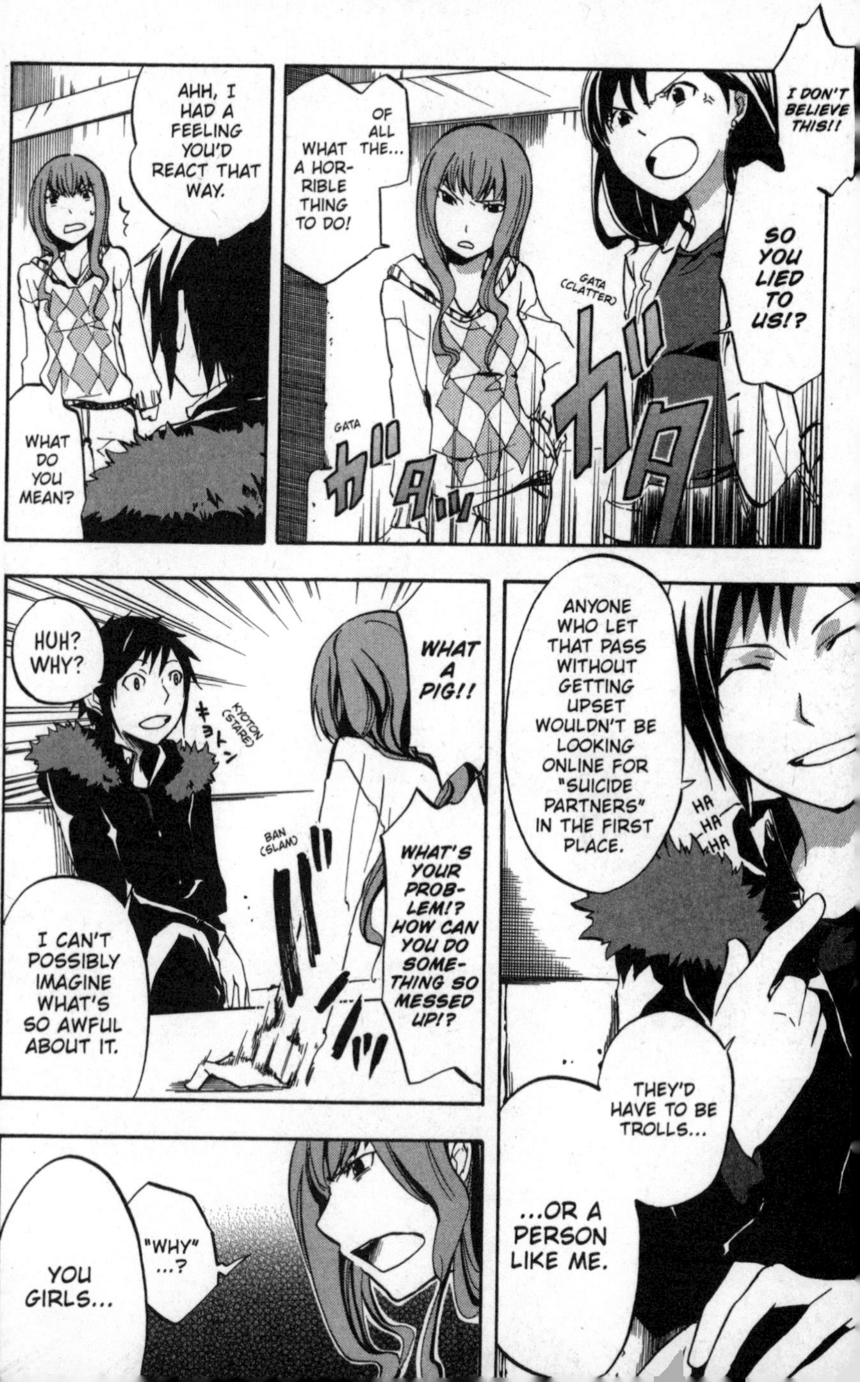
I DON'T BELIEVE THIS!!
SO YOU LIED TO US!?
GATA (CLATTER)
OF ALL THE... WHAT A HOR-RIBLE THING TO DO!
GATA
AHH, I HAD A FEELING YOU'D REACT THAT WAY.
WHAT DO YOU MEAN?
ANYONE WHO LET THAT PASS WITHOUT GETTING UPSET WOULDN'T BE LOOKING ONLINE FOR "SUICIDE PARTNERS" IN THE FIRST PLACE.
HA HA HA
THEY'D HAVE TO BE TROLLS...
...OR A PERSON LIKE ME.
WHAT A PIG!!
HUH? WHY?
KYOTON (STARE)
BAN (SLAM)
WHAT'S YOUR PROB-LEM!? HOW CAN YOU DO SOME-THING SO MESSED UP!?
I CAN'T POSSIBLY IMAGINE WHAT'S SO AWFUL ABOUT IT.
"WHY" ...?
YOU GIRLS...

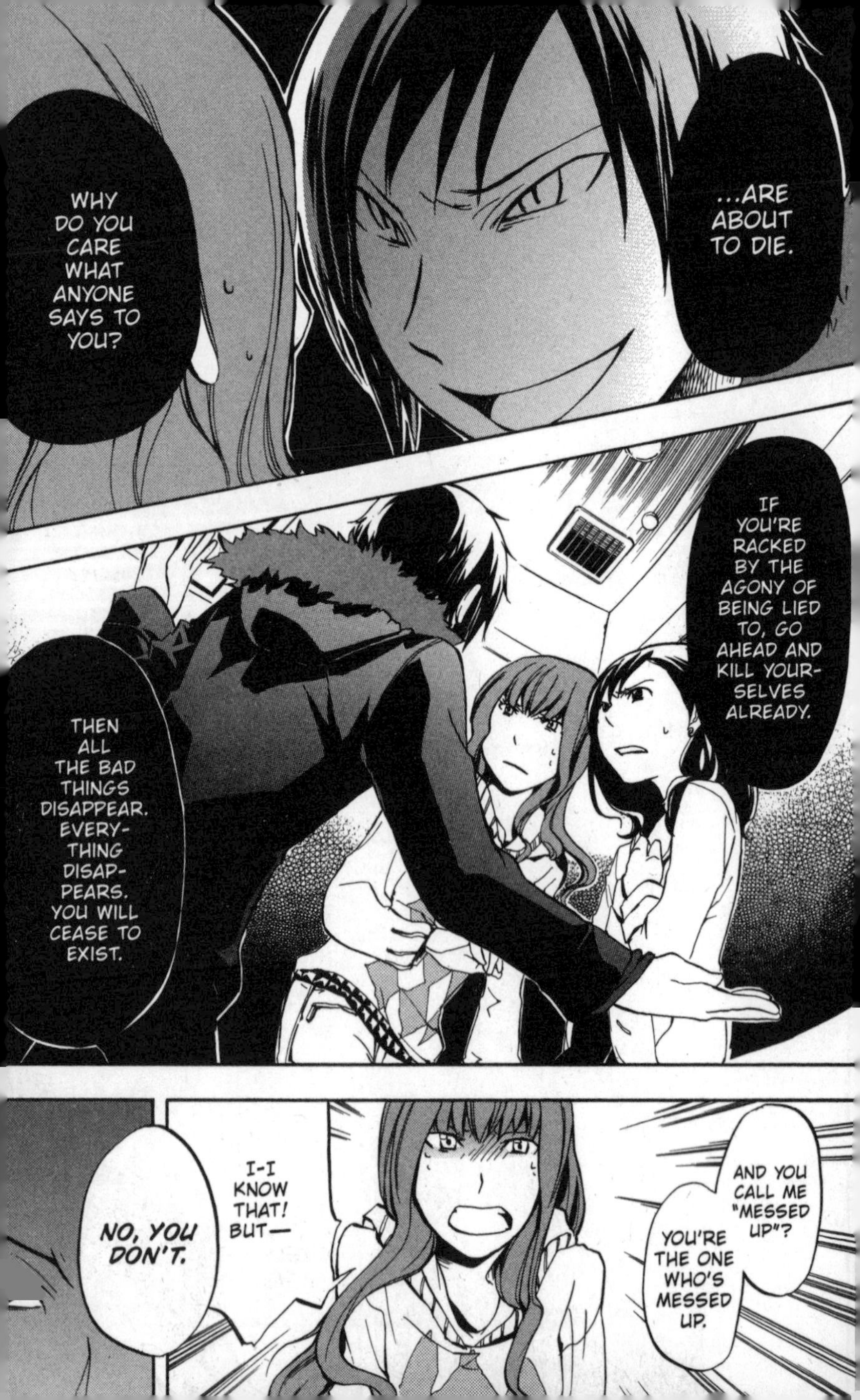
...ARE ABOUT TO DIE.
WHY DO YOU CARE WHAT ANYONE SAYS TO YOU?
IF YOU'RE RACKED BY THE AGONY OF BEING LIED TO, GO AHEAD AND KILL YOURSELVES ALREADY.
THEN ALL THE BAD THINGS DISAPPEAR. EVERYTHING DISAPPEARS. YOU WILL CEASE TO EXIST.
AND YOU CALL ME "MESSED UP"?
YOU'RE THE ONE WHO'S MESSED UP.
I-I KNOW THAT! BUT—
NO, YOU DON'T.

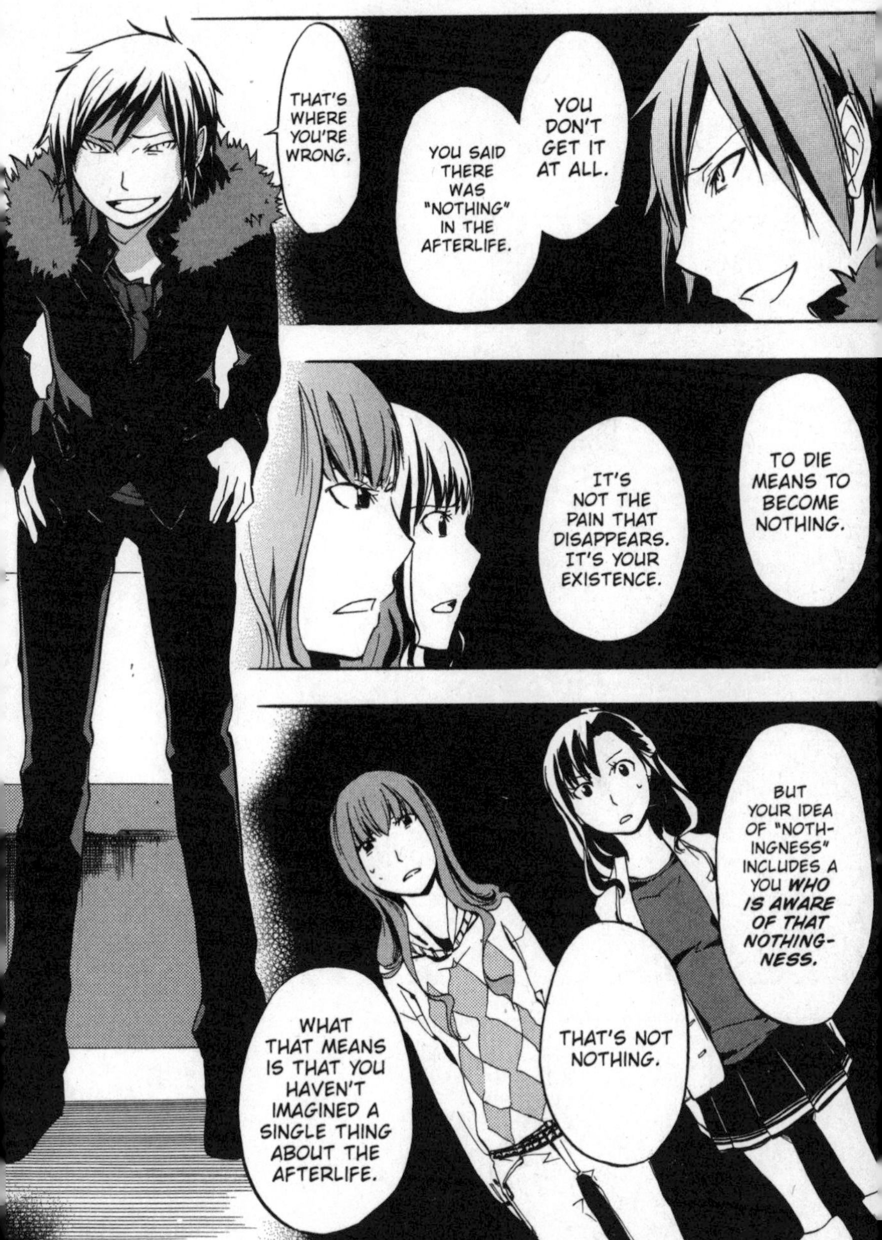
YOU DON'T GET IT AT ALL.
YOU SAID THERE WAS "NOTHING" IN THE AFTERLIFE.
THAT'S WHERE YOU'RE WRONG.
TO DIE MEANS TO BECOME NOTHING.
IT'S NOT THE PAIN THAT DISAPPEARS. IT'S YOUR EXISTENCE.
BUT YOUR IDEA OF "NOTHINGNESS" INCLUDES A YOU *WHO IS AWARE OF THAT NOTHINGNESS.*
THAT'S NOT NOTHING.
WHAT THAT MEANS IS THAT YOU HAVEN'T IMAGINED A SINGLE THING ABOUT THE AFTERLIFE.

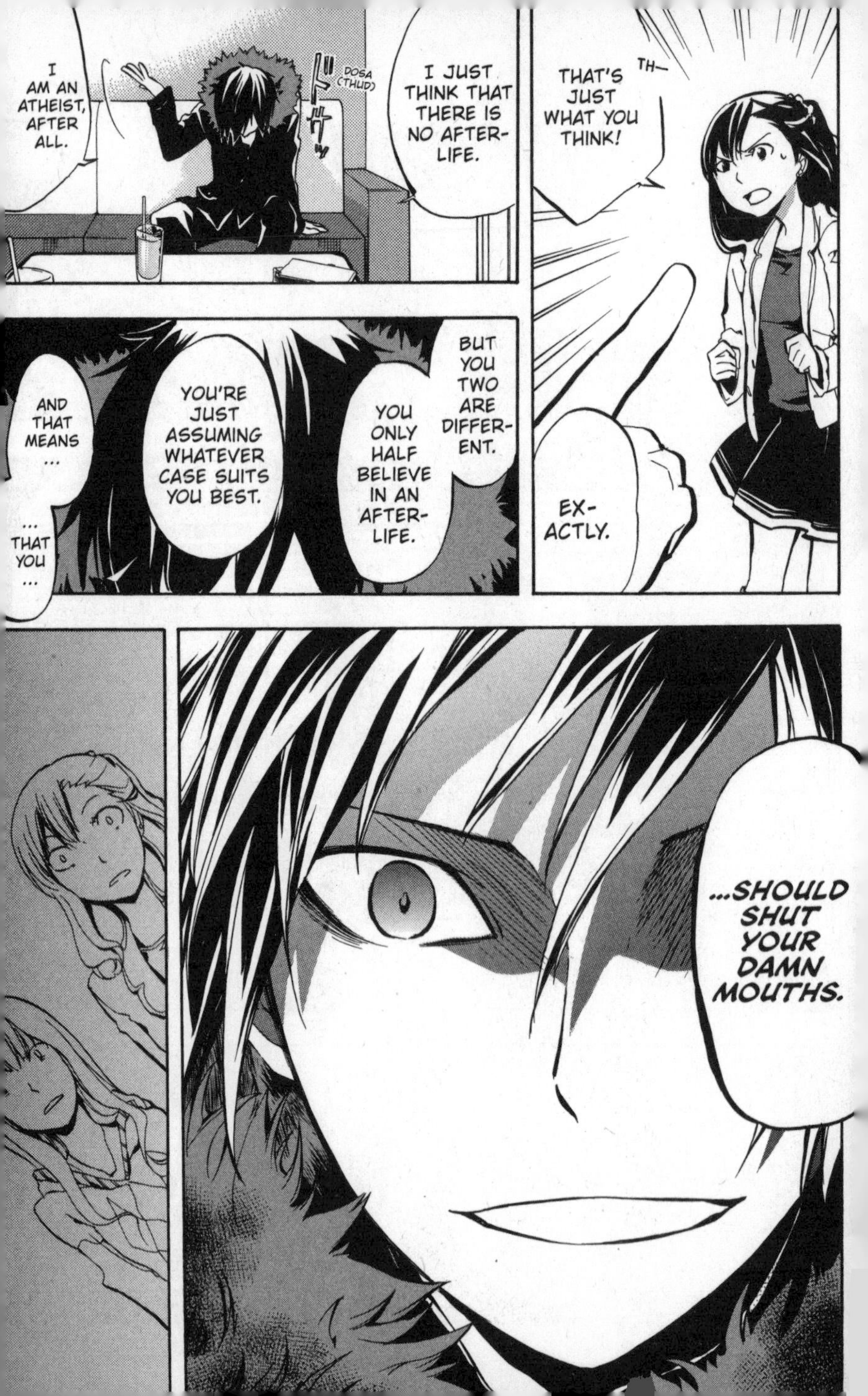
TH—
THAT'S JUST WHAT YOU THINK!
I JUST THINK THAT THERE IS NO AFTER-LIFE.
DOSA (THUD)
I AM AN ATHEIST, AFTER ALL.
EX-ACTLY.
BUT YOU TWO ARE DIFFER-ENT.
YOU ONLY HALF BELIEVE IN AN AFTER-LIFE.
YOU'RE JUST ASSUMING WHATEVER CASE SUITS YOU BEST.
AND THAT MEANS ...
... THAT YOU ...
...SHOULD SHUT YOUR DAMN MOUTHS.

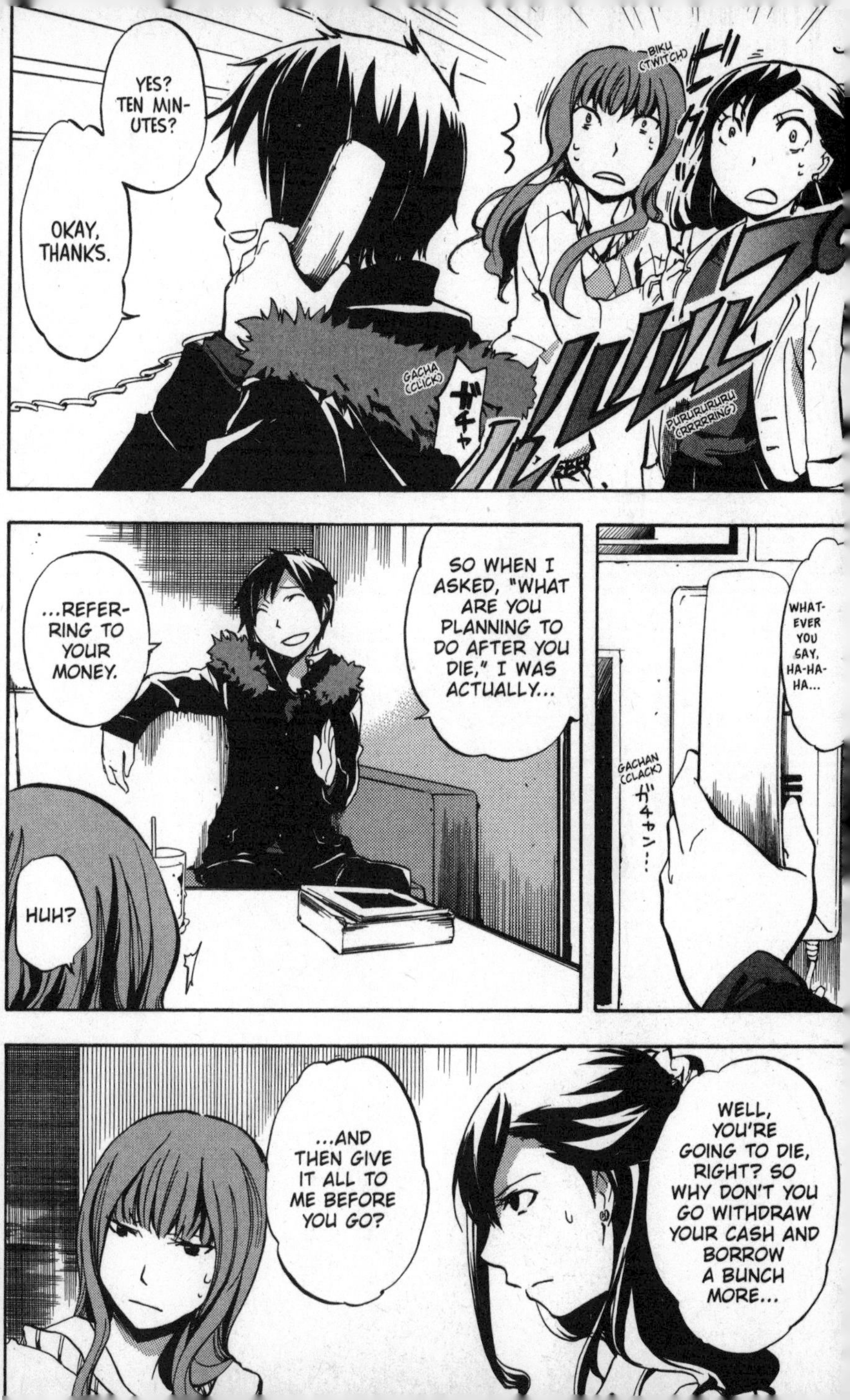
BIKU (TWITCH)
YES? TEN MIN-UTES?
OKAY, THANKS.
PURURURURU (RRRRRING)
GACHA (CLICK)
WHAT-EVER YOU SAY, HA-HA-HA...
GACHAN (CLACK)
SO WHEN I ASKED, "WHAT ARE YOU PLANNING TO DO AFTER YOU DIE," I WAS ACTUALLY...
...REFER-RING TO YOUR MONEY.
HUH?
WELL, YOU'RE GOING TO DIE, RIGHT? SO WHY DON'T YOU GO WITHDRAW YOUR CASH AND BORROW A BUNCH MORE...
...AND THEN GIVE IT ALL TO ME BEFORE YOU GO?

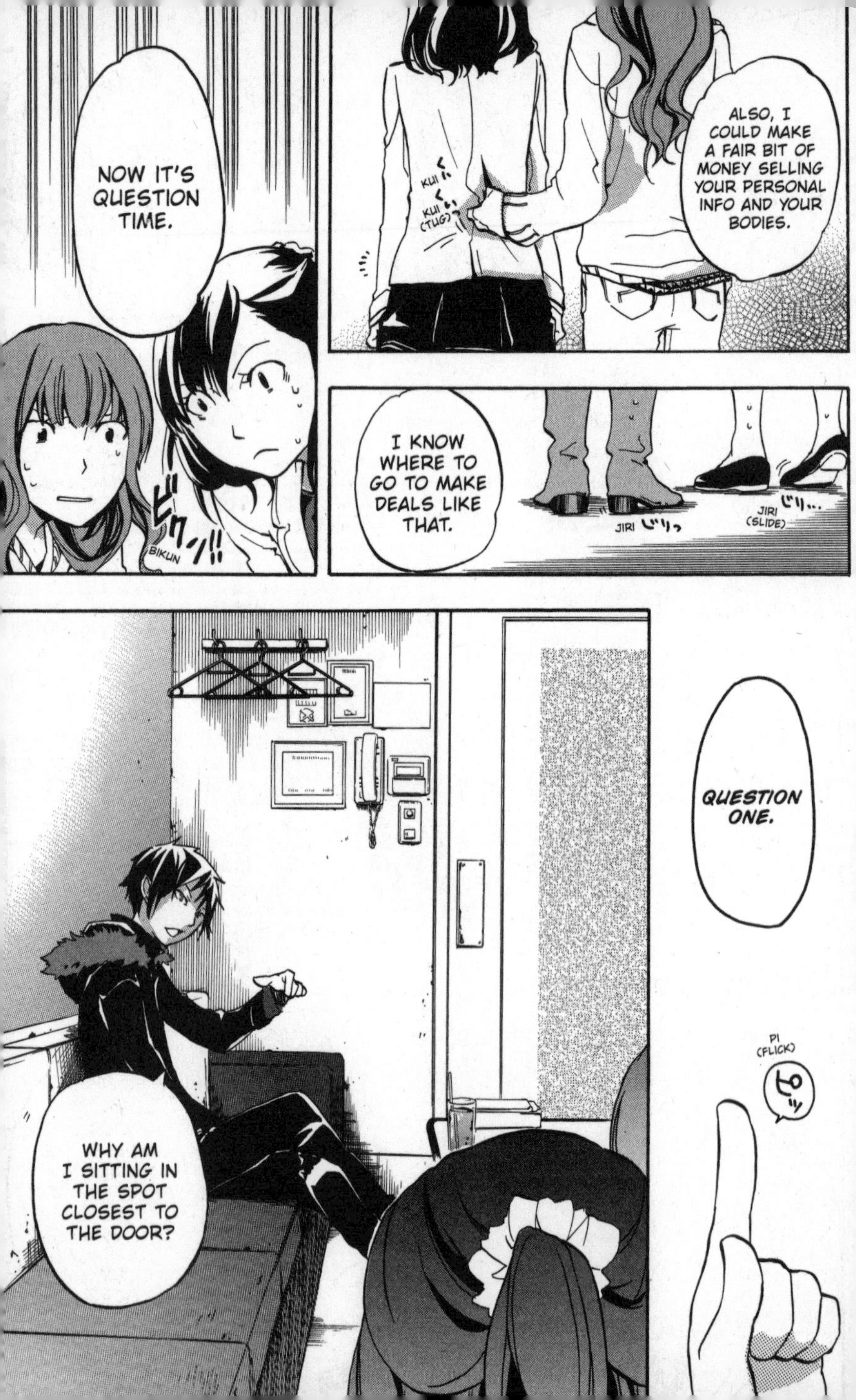
ALSO, I COULD MAKE A FAIR BIT OF MONEY SELLING YOUR PERSONAL INFO AND YOUR BODIES.
KUI KUI (TUG)
I KNOW WHERE TO GO TO MAKE DEALS LIKE THAT.
JIRI (SLIDE)
JIRI
NOW IT'S QUESTION TIME.
BIKUN
QUESTION ONE.
PI (FLICK)
WHY AM I SITTING IN THE SPOT CLOSEST TO THE DOOR?

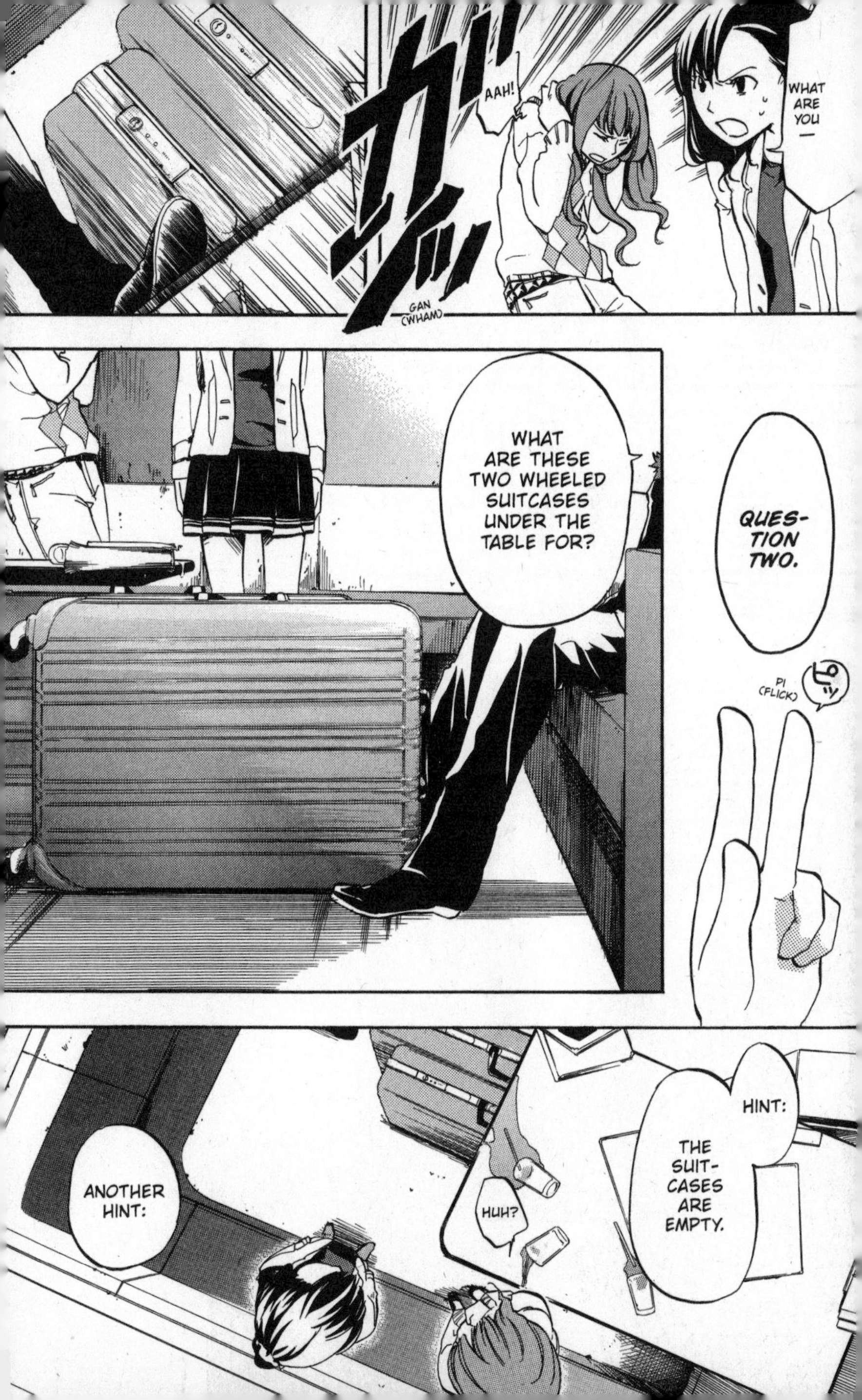
WHAT ARE YOU —
AAH!
GAN (WHAM)
QUES-TION TWO.
PI (FLICK)
WHAT ARE THESE TWO WHEELED SUITCASES UNDER THE TABLE FOR?
HINT:
THE SUIT-CASES ARE EMPTY.
HUH?
ANOTHER HINT:

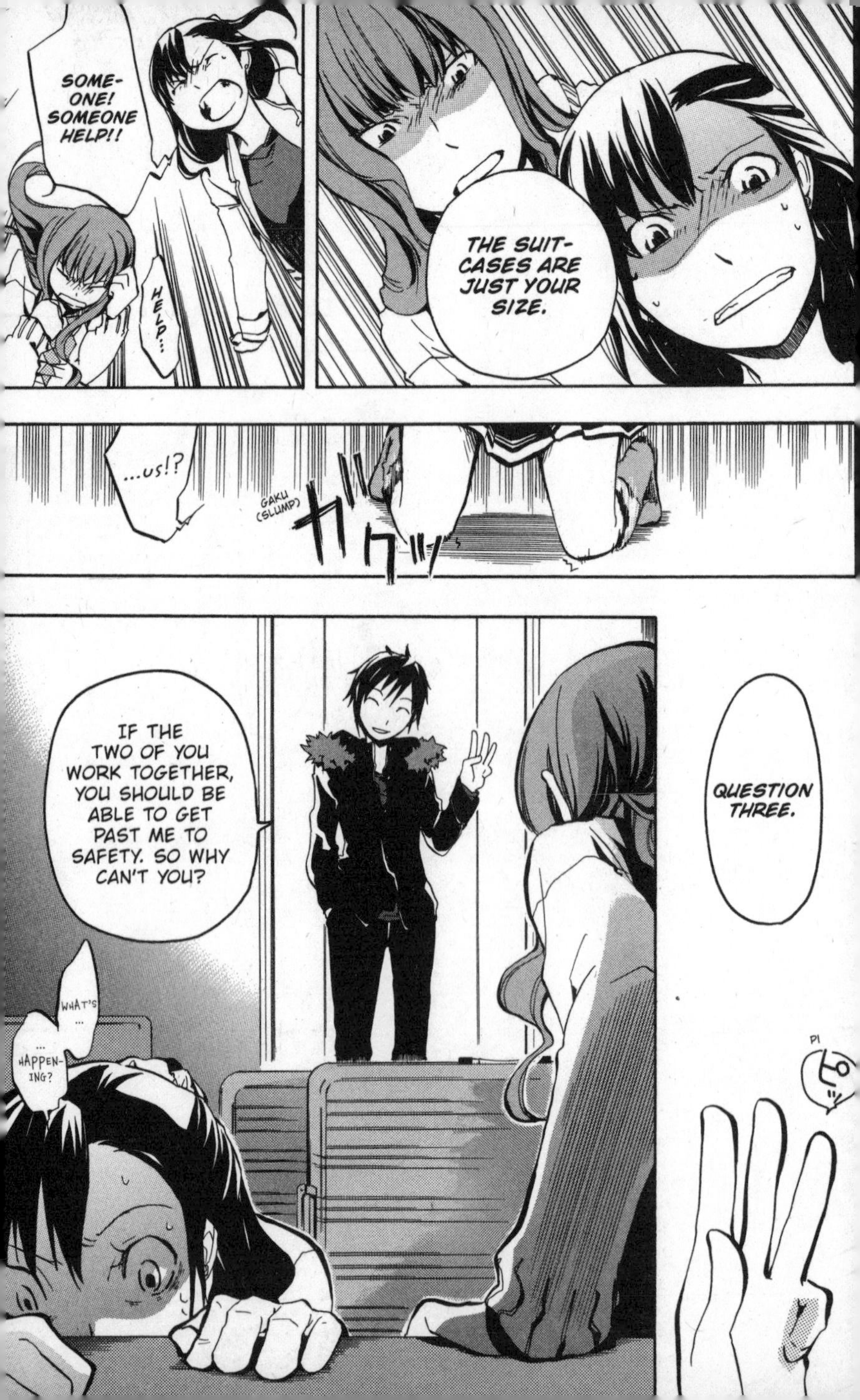
THE SUIT-CASES ARE JUST YOUR SIZE.
SOME-ONE! SOMEONE HELP!!
HELP...
GAKU (SLUMP)
...us!?
QUESTION THREE.
PI
IF THE TWO OF YOU WORK TOGETHER, YOU SHOULD BE ABLE TO GET PAST ME TO SAFETY. SO WHY CAN'T YOU?
WHAT'S ... ... HAPPEN-ING?

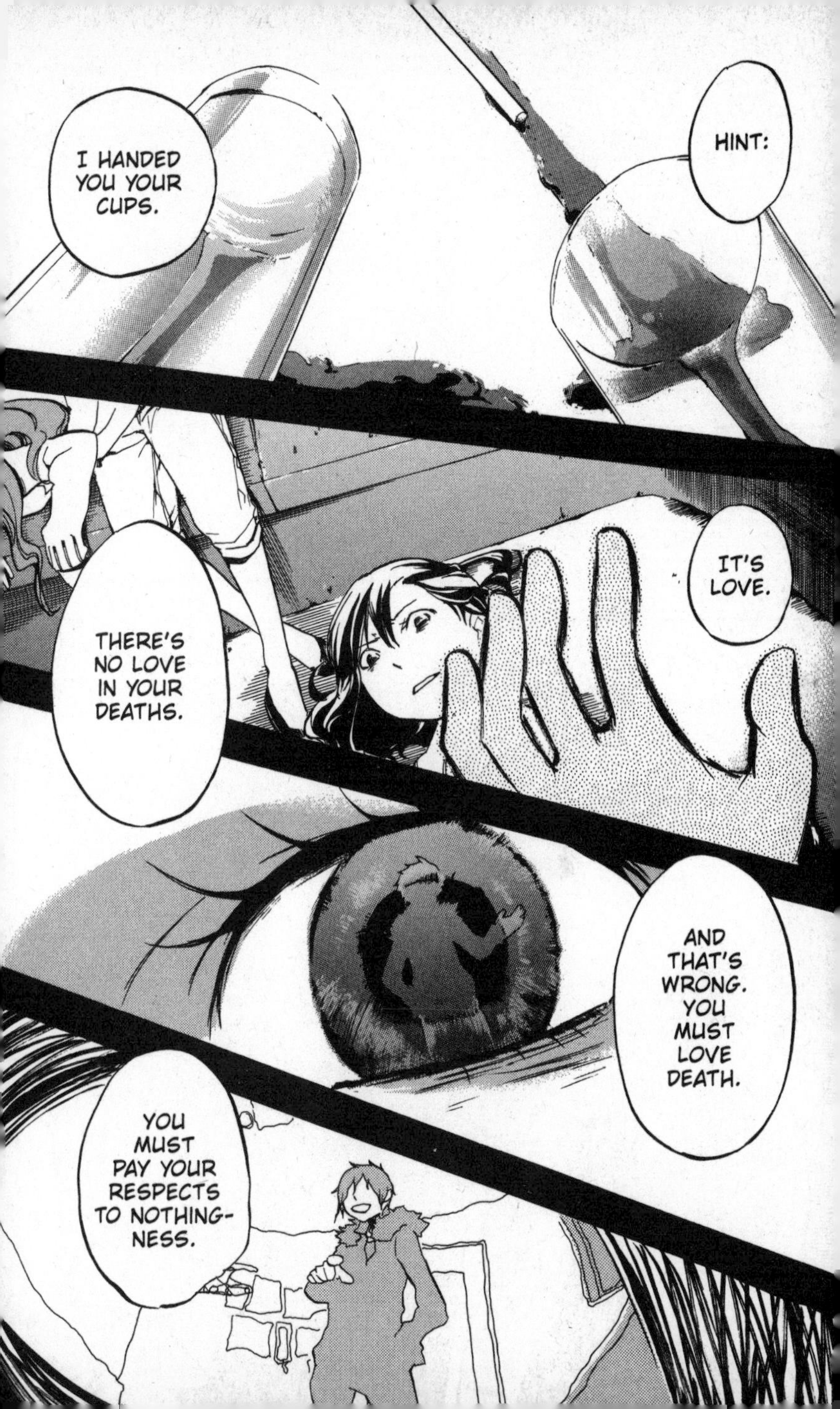
HINT:
I HANDED YOU YOUR CUPS.
IT'S LOVE.
THERE'S NO LOVE IN YOUR DEATHS.
AND THAT'S WRONG. YOU MUST LOVE DEATH.
YOU MUST PAY YOUR RESPECTS TO NOTHING-NESS.

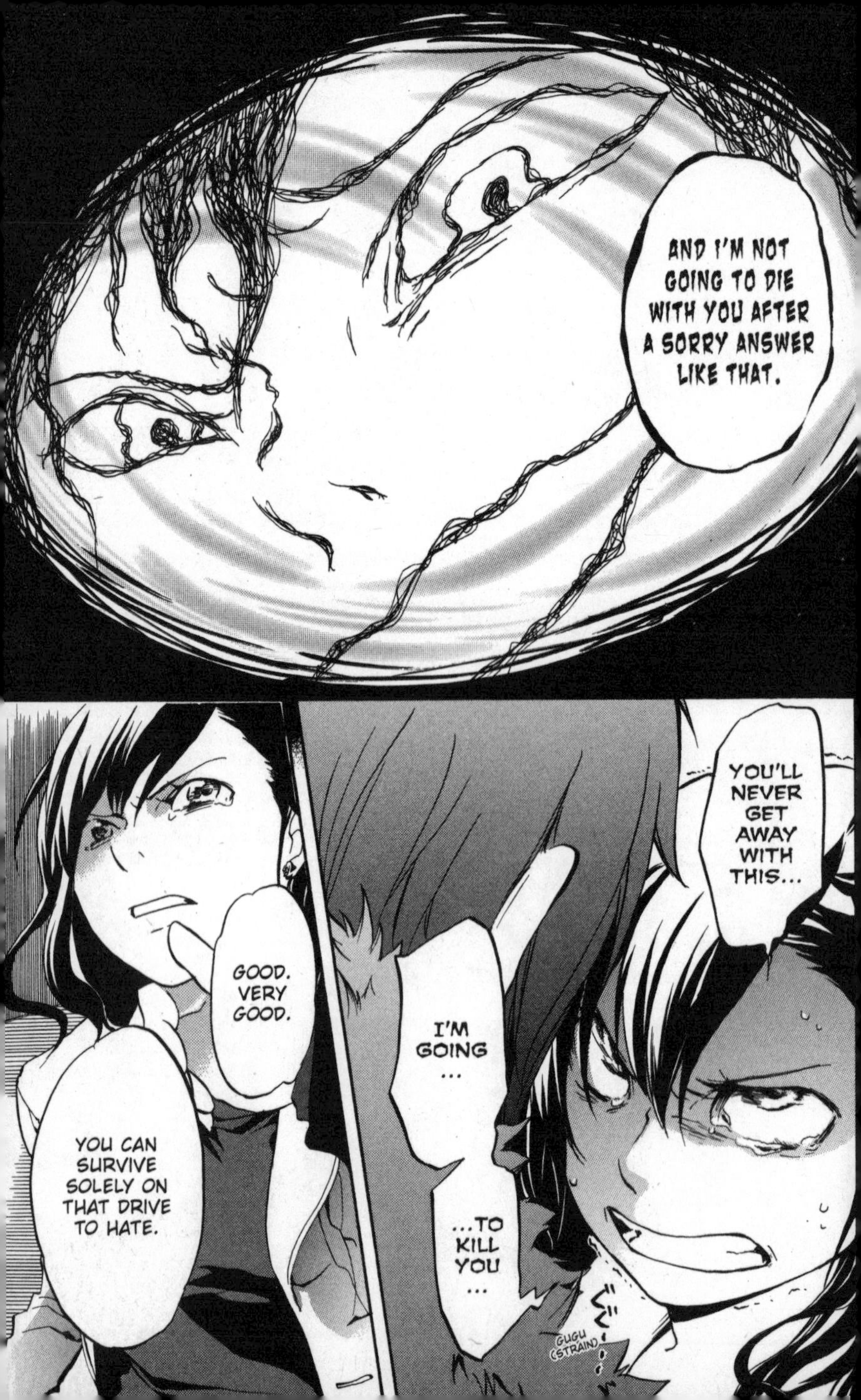
AND I'M NOT GOING TO DIE WITH YOU AFTER A SORRY ANSWER LIKE THAT.
YOU'LL NEVER GET AWAY WITH THIS...
I'M GOING...
...TO KILL YOU...
GUGU (STRAIN)
GOOD. VERY GOOD.
YOU CAN SURVIVE SOLELY ON THAT DRIVE TO HATE.

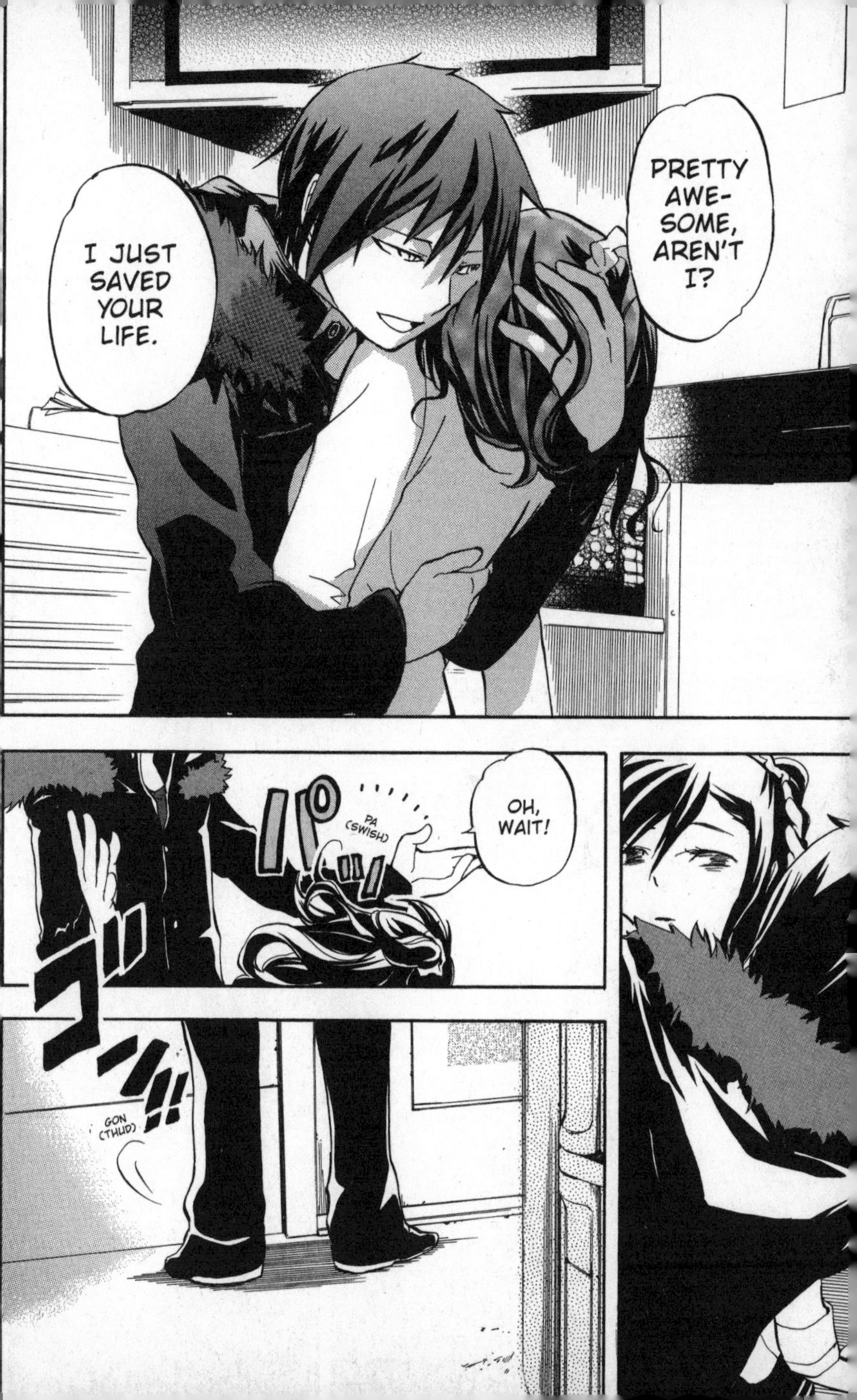
PRETTY AWE-SOME, AREN'T I?
I JUST SAVED YOUR LIFE.
OH, WAIT!
PA (SWISH)
GON (THUD)

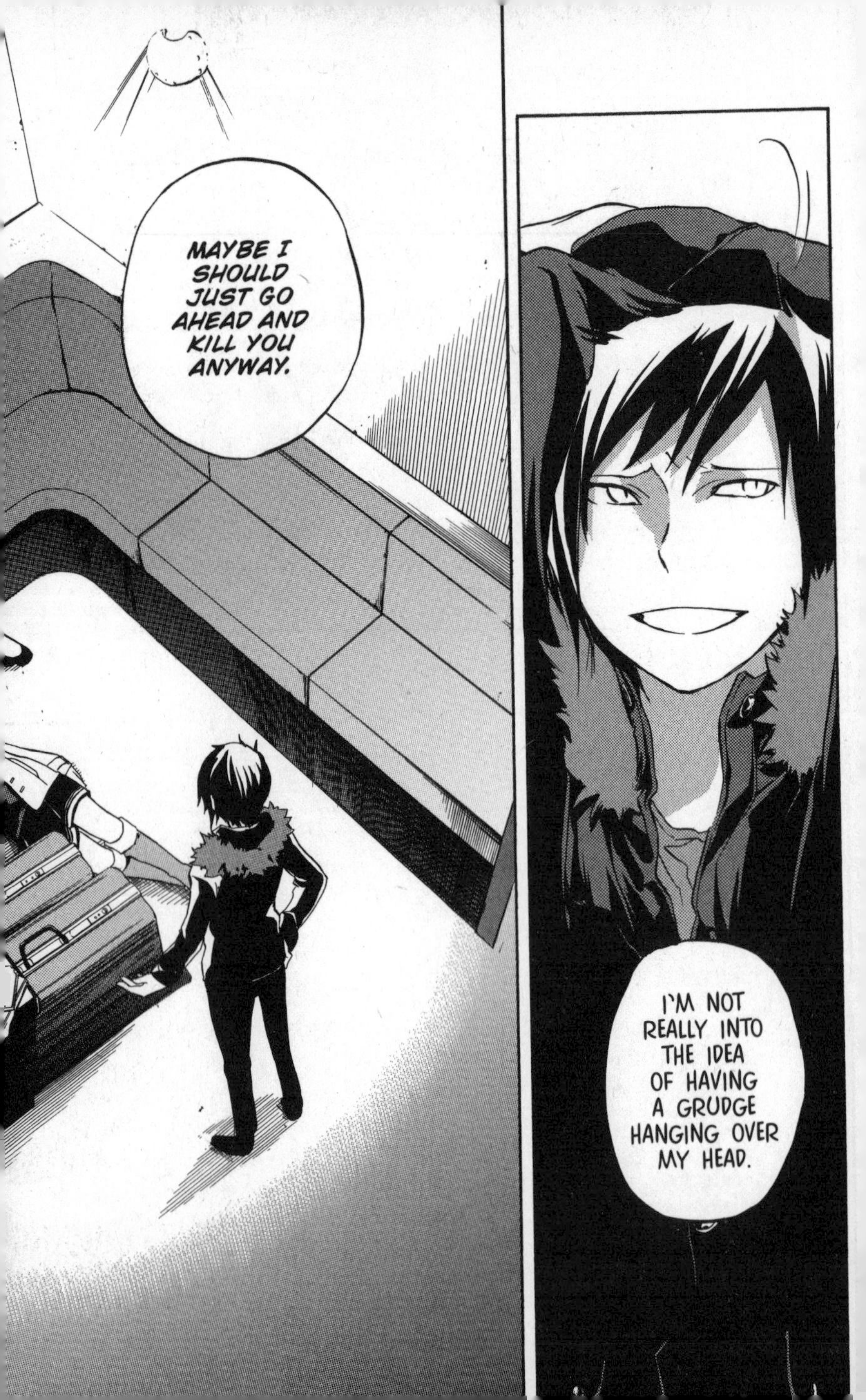
I'M NOT REALLY INTO THE IDEA OF HAVING A GRUDGE HANGING OVER MY HEAD.
MAYBE I SHOULD JUST GO AHEAD AND KILL YOU ANYWAY.

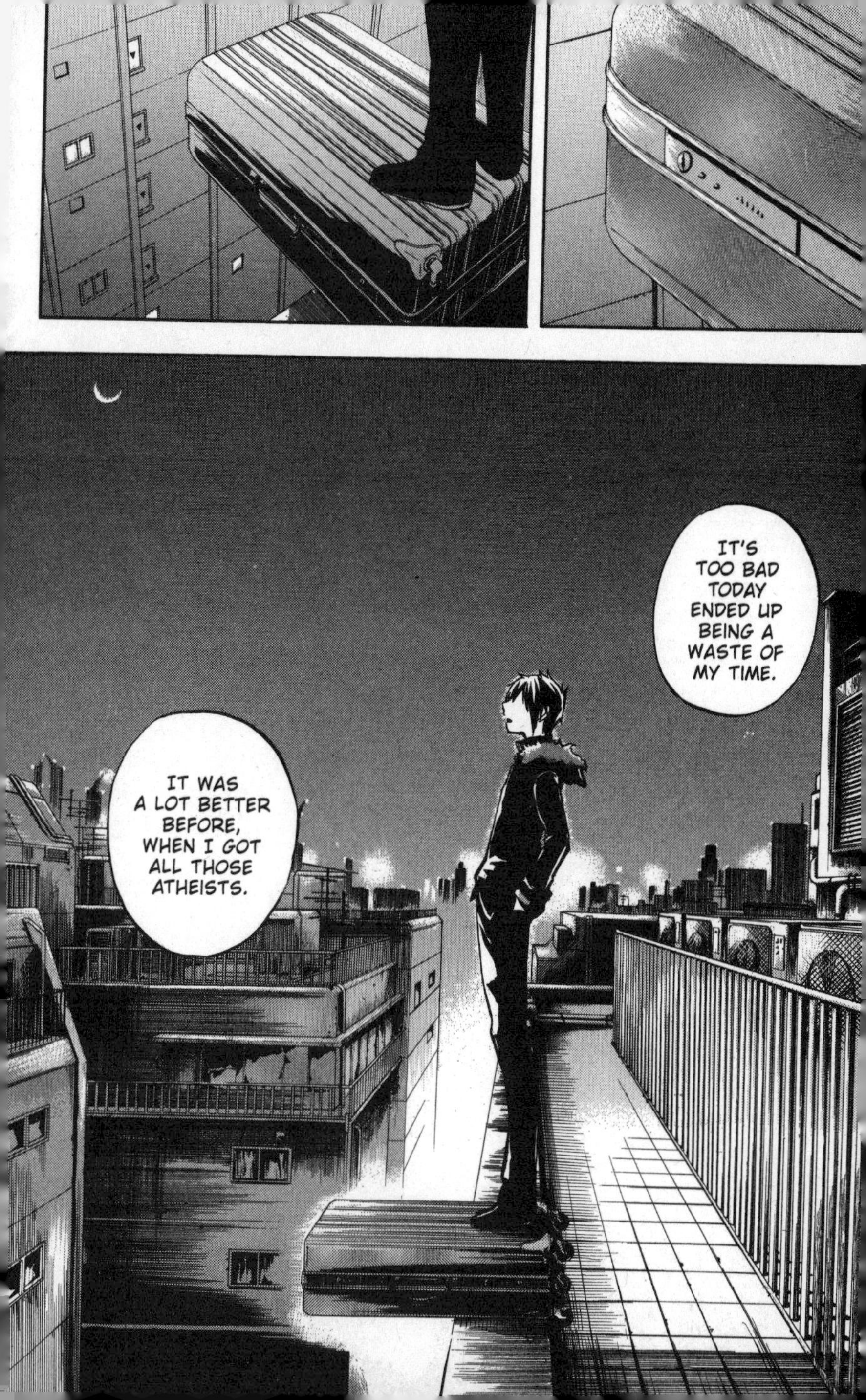
IT'S TOO BAD TODAY ENDED UP BEING A WASTE OF MY TIME.
IT WAS A LOT BETTER BEFORE, WHEN I GOT ALL THOSE ATHEISTS.

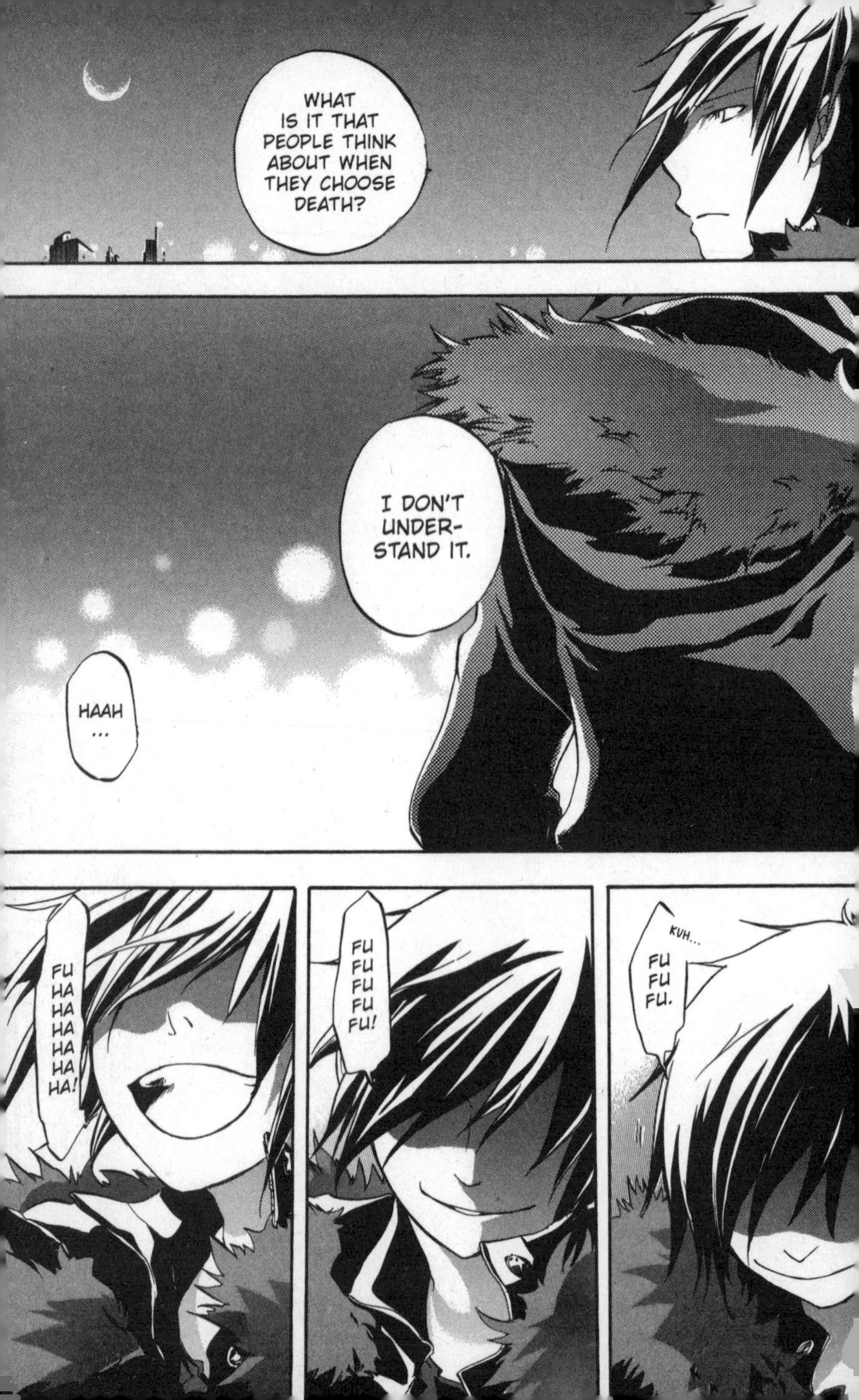
WHAT IS IT THAT PEOPLE THINK ABOUT WHEN THEY CHOOSE DEATH?
I DON'T UNDER-STAND IT.
HAAH ...
KUH...
FU FU FU.
FU FU FU FU FU!
FU HA HA HA HA HA HA!

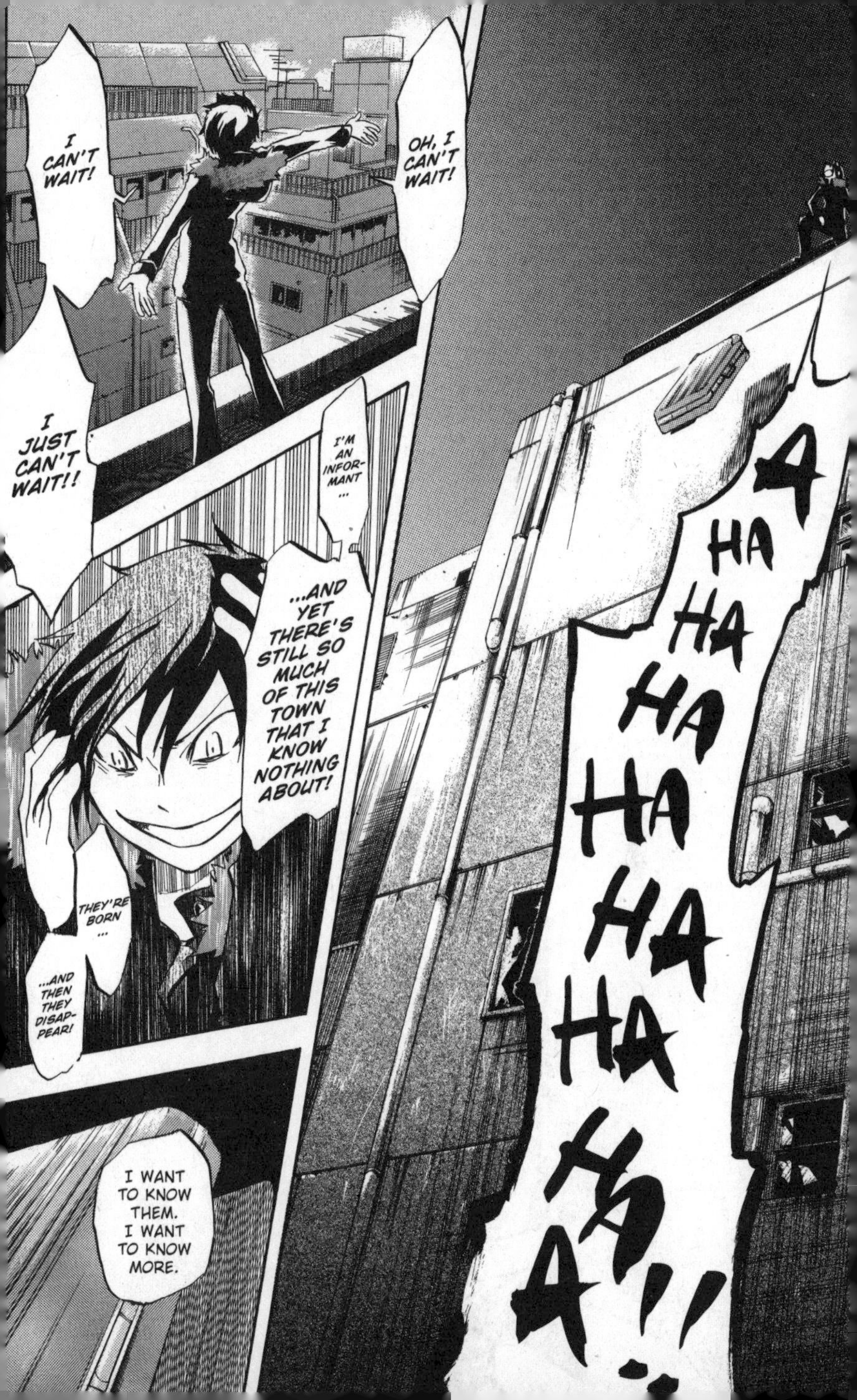
A HA HA HA HA HA HA HA A!!
OH, I CAN'T WAIT!
I CAN'T WAIT!
I JUST CAN'T WAIT!!
I'M AN INFORMANT...
...AND YET THERE'S STILL SO MUCH OF THIS TOWN THAT I KNOW NOTHING ABOUT!
THEY'RE BORN...
...AND THEN THEY DISAPPEAR!
I WANT TO KNOW THEM. I WANT TO KNOW MORE.

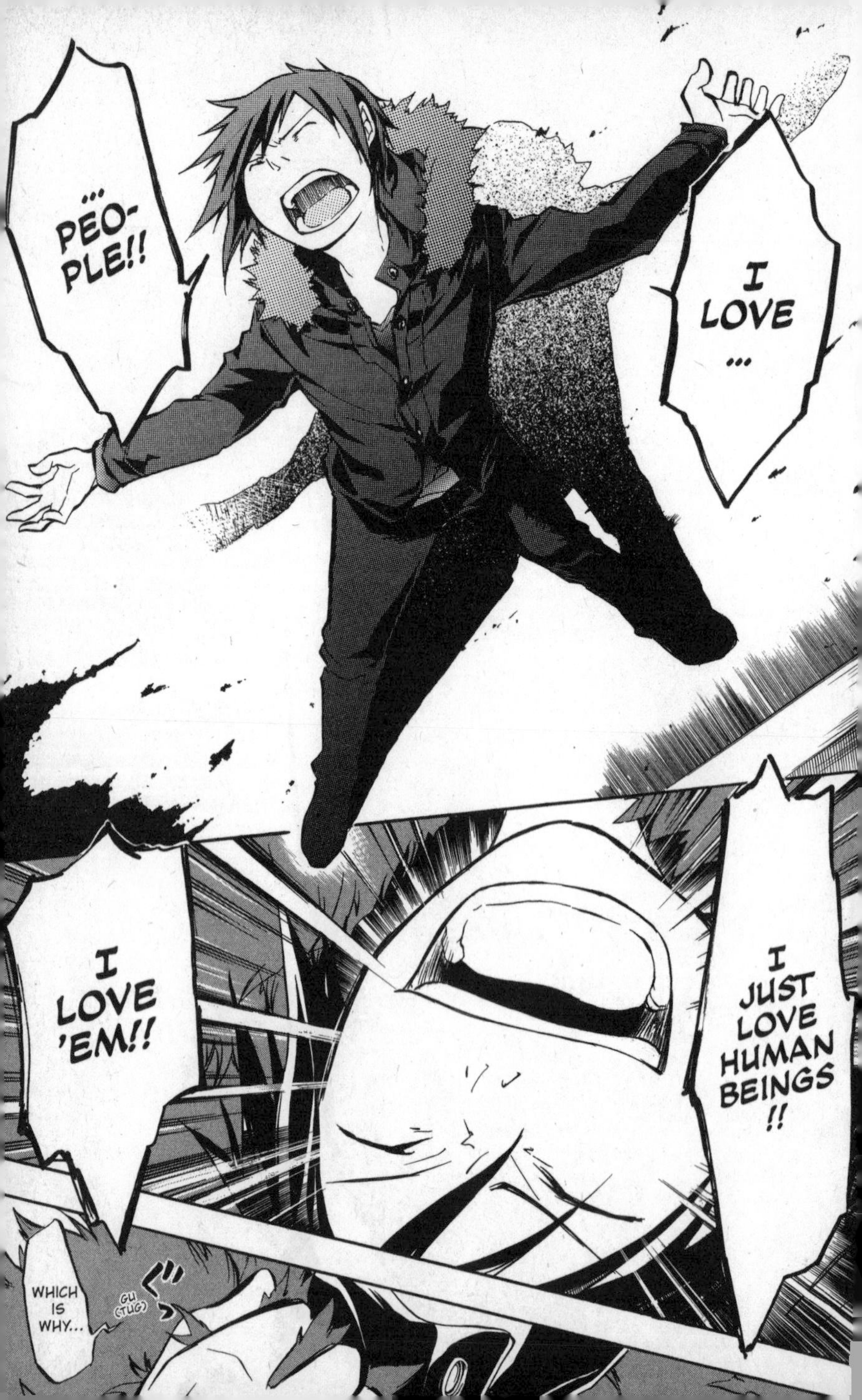
I LOVE ...
... PEO-PLE!!
I JUST LOVE HUMAN BEINGS !!
I LOVE 'EM!!
GU (TUG)
WHICH IS WHY...

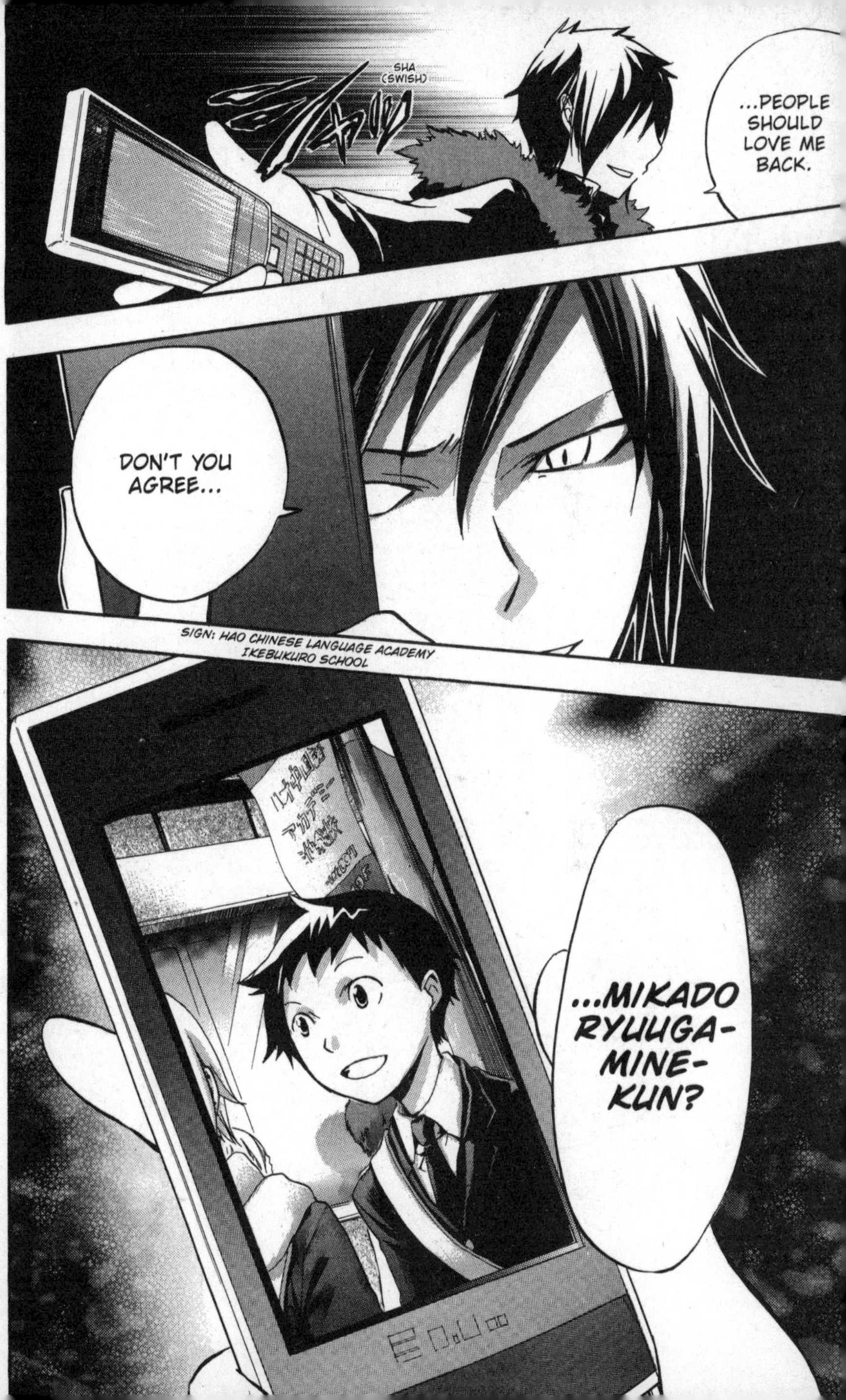
...PEOPLE SHOULD LOVE ME BACK.
SHA (SWISH)
DON'T YOU AGREE...
SIGN: HAO CHINESE LANGUAGE ACADEMY IKEBUKURO SCHOOL
...MIKADO RYUUGA-MINE-KUN?

5: WAWAWAWAWA!!

YESTERDAY WAS AN ABSOLUTE CATASTROPHE.

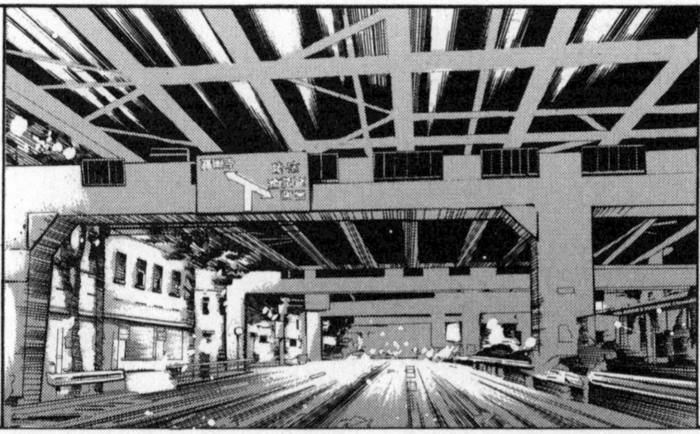

IT WAS SUPPOSED TO BE AN EASY JOB.

THE CLIENT WAS A GROUP OF YOUNG PEOPLE IN IKEBUKURO.

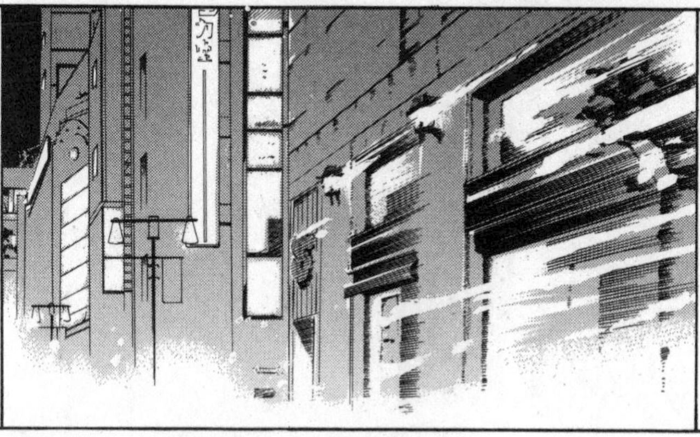

SOME OF THEIR FRIENDS WERE ABDUCTED.

THE KIDNAPPERS WERE SOME COMMON THUGS WAY DOWN THE TOTEM POLE IN A QUITE CORRUPT ORGANIZATION—THE KIND OF PEOPLE WHO TREAT HUMAN BEINGS LIKE PROPERTY.

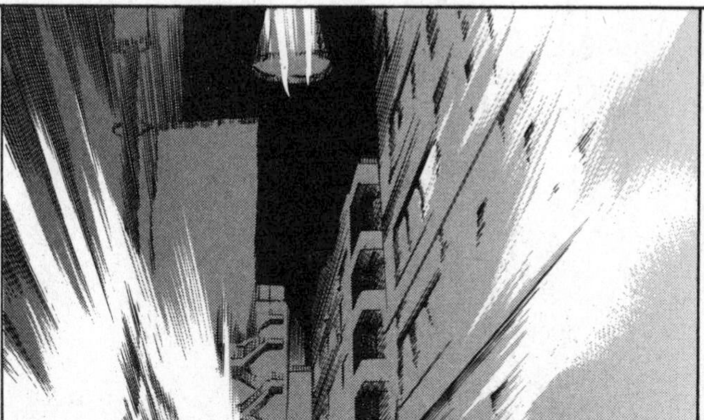

MY JOB WAS SIMPLE: PUT THE HURT ON THE KIDNAPPERS AND SEE THAT THE VICTIMS WERE RETURNED SAFELY.

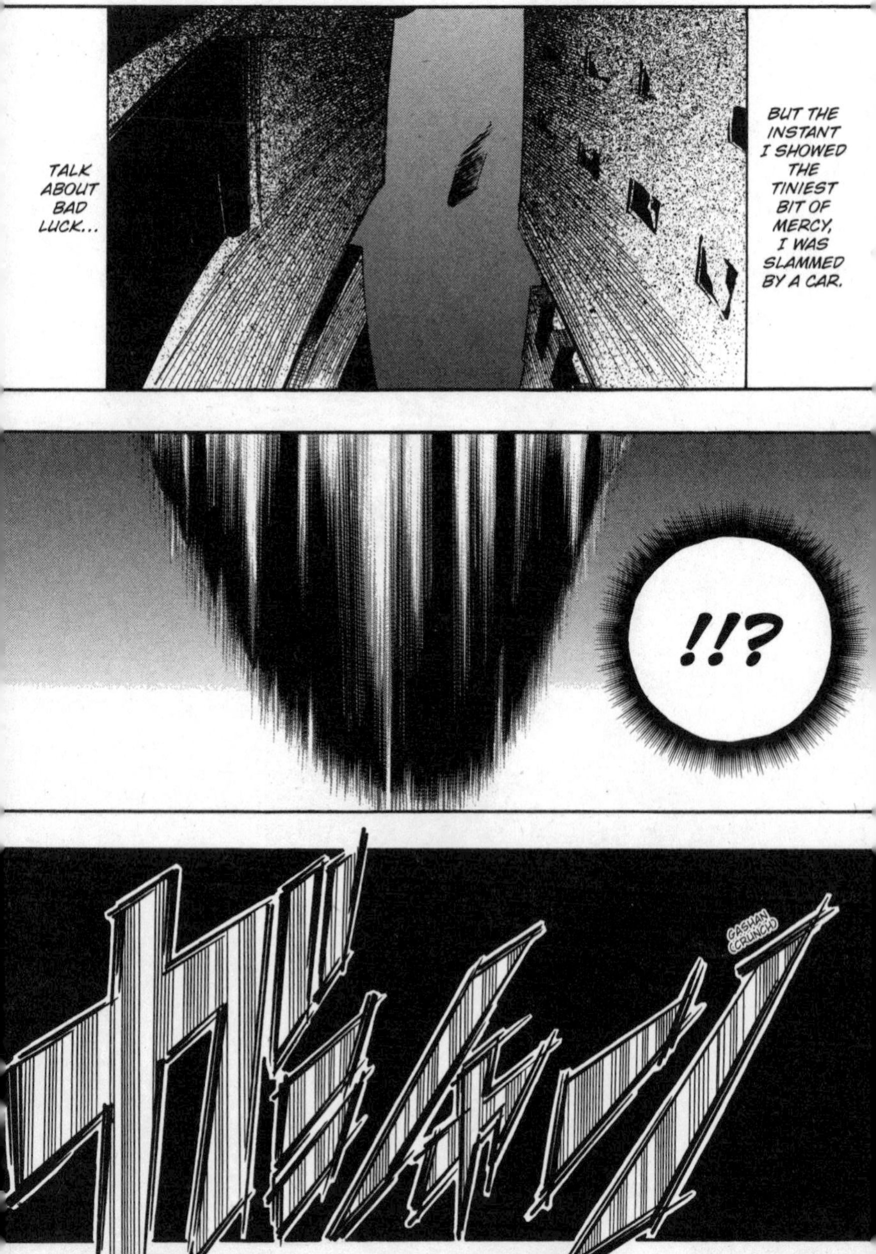
BUT THE INSTANT I SHOWED THE TINIEST BIT OF MERCY, I WAS SLAMMED BY A CAR.
TALK ABOUT BAD LUCK...
!!?
GASHAN (CRUNCH)

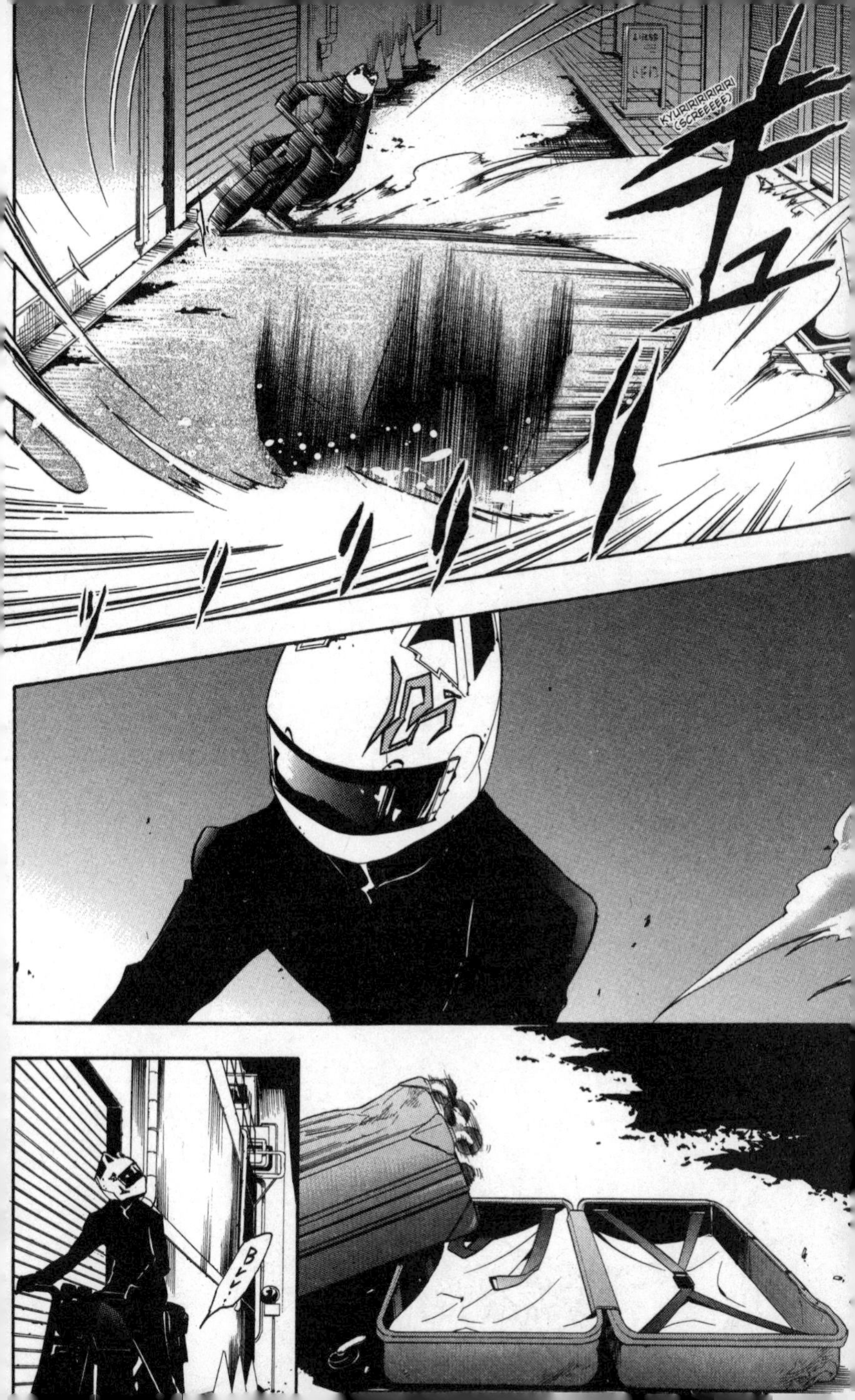
KYURIRIRIRIRI
(SCREEEEE)
BVV...

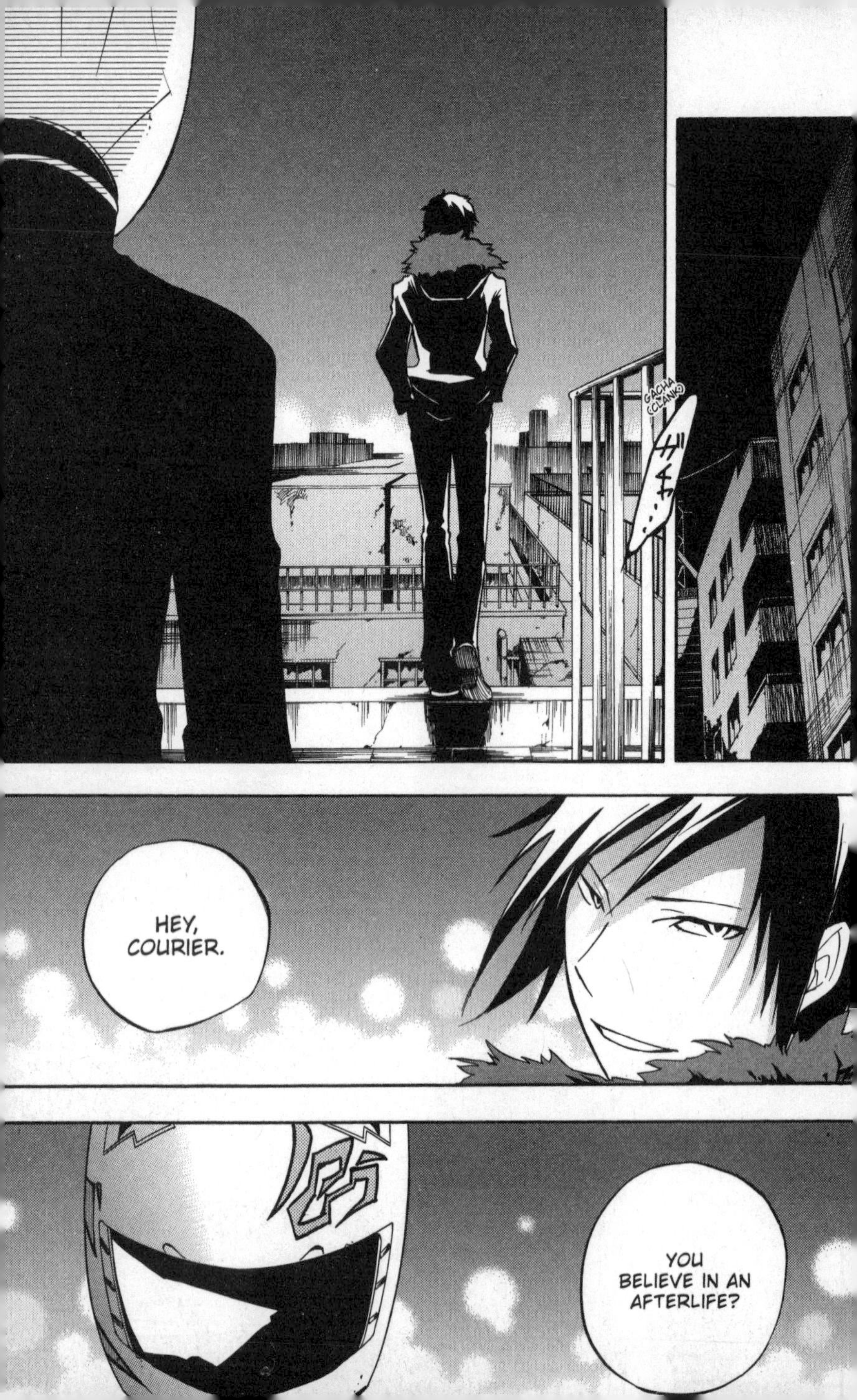
GACHA (CLANK)
ガチャ…
HEY, COURIER.
YOU BELIEVE IN AN AFTERLIFE?

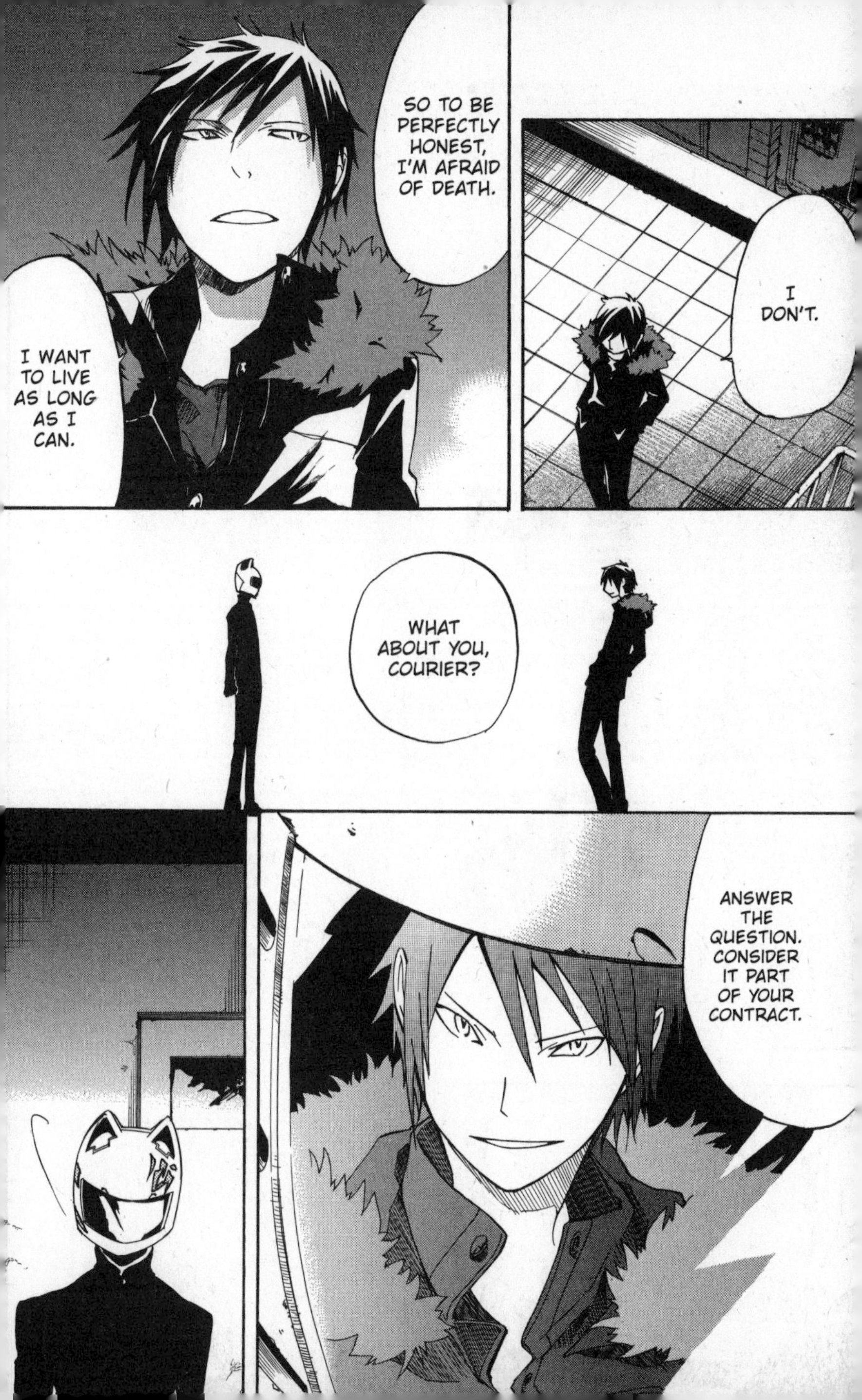
I DON'T.
SO TO BE PERFECTLY HONEST, I'M AFRAID OF DEATH.
I WANT TO LIVE AS LONG AS I CAN.
WHAT ABOUT YOU, COURIER?
ANSWER THE QUESTION. CONSIDER IT PART OF YOUR CONTRACT.

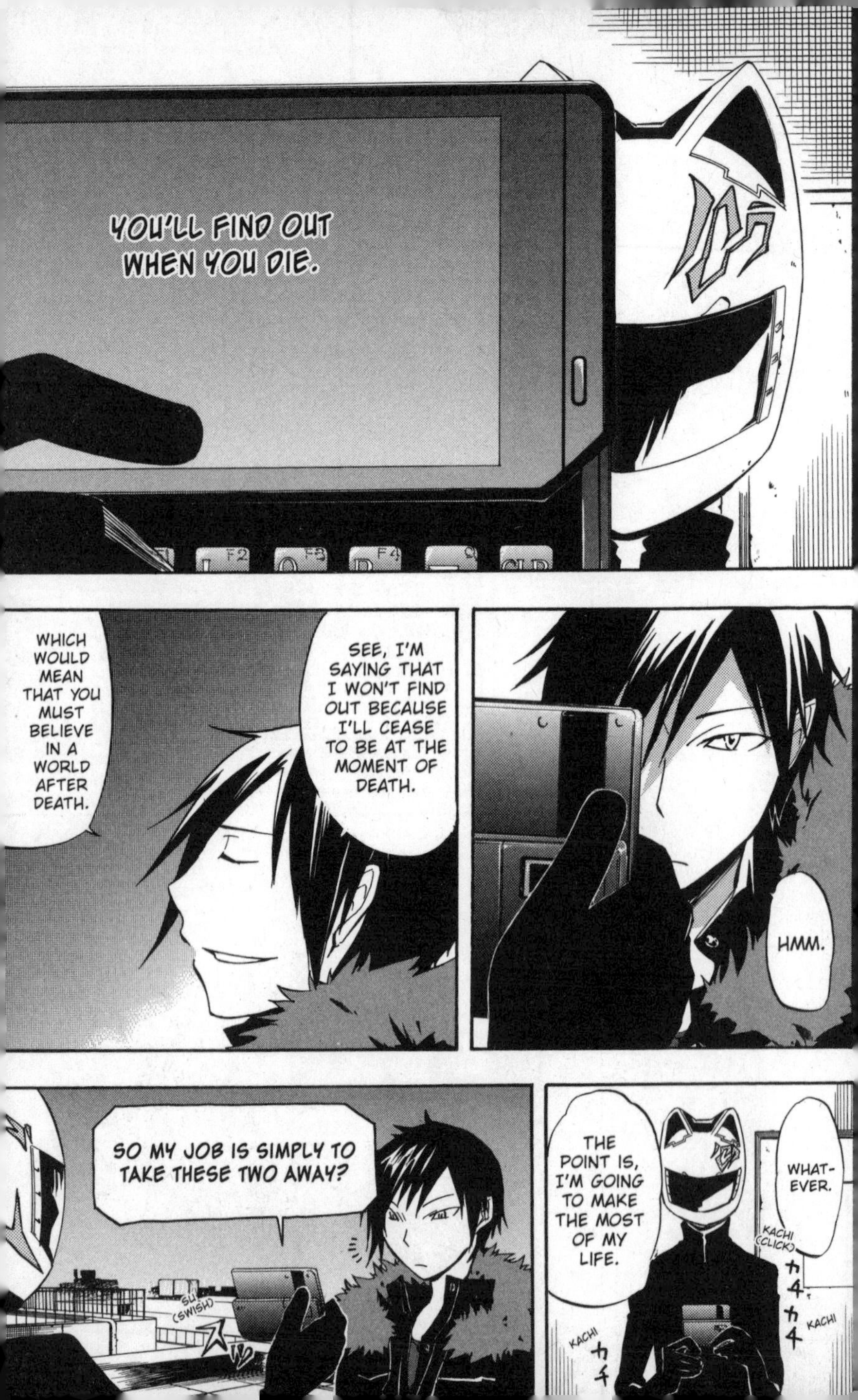
YOU'LL FIND OUT WHEN YOU DIE.
HMM.
SEE, I'M SAYING THAT I WON'T FIND OUT BECAUSE I'LL CEASE TO BE AT THE MOMENT OF DEATH.
WHICH WOULD MEAN THAT YOU MUST BELIEVE IN A WORLD AFTER DEATH.
WHAT-EVER.
KACHI (CLICK)
カチカチ
KACHI
THE POINT IS, I'M GOING TO MAKE THE MOST OF MY LIFE.
KACHI
カチ
SO MY JOB IS SIMPLY TO TAKE THESE TWO AWAY?
SU (SWISH)

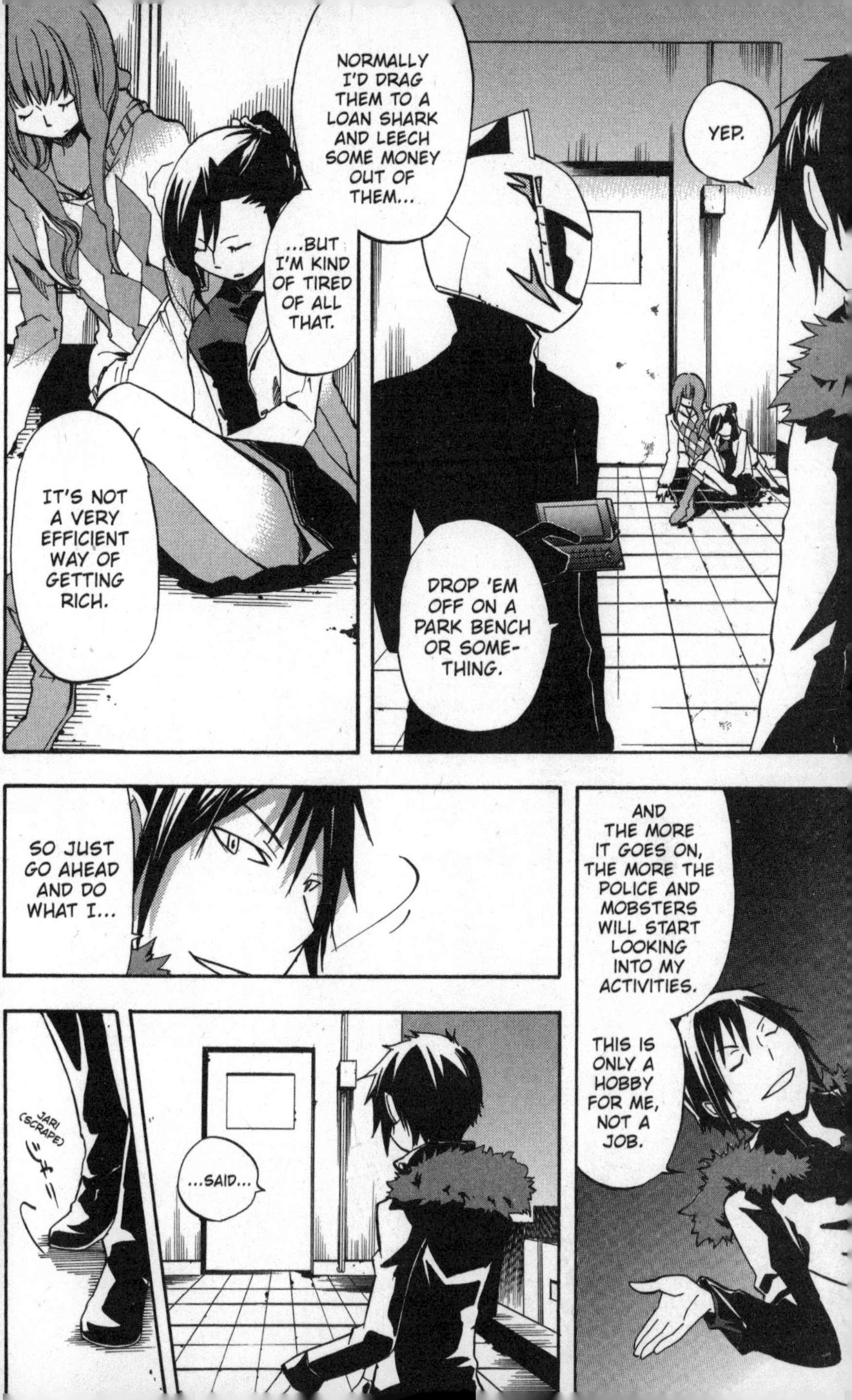
YEP.
NORMALLY I'D DRAG THEM TO A LOAN SHARK AND LEECH SOME MONEY OUT OF THEM...
DROP 'EM OFF ON A PARK BENCH OR SOME-THING.
...BUT I'M KIND OF TIRED OF ALL THAT.
IT'S NOT A VERY EFFICIENT WAY OF GETTING RICH.
AND THE MORE IT GOES ON, THE MORE THE POLICE AND MOBSTERS WILL START LOOKING INTO MY ACTIVITIES.
THIS IS ONLY A HOBBY FOR ME, NOT A JOB.
SO JUST GO AHEAD AND DO WHAT I...
...SAID...
JARI (SCRAPE)

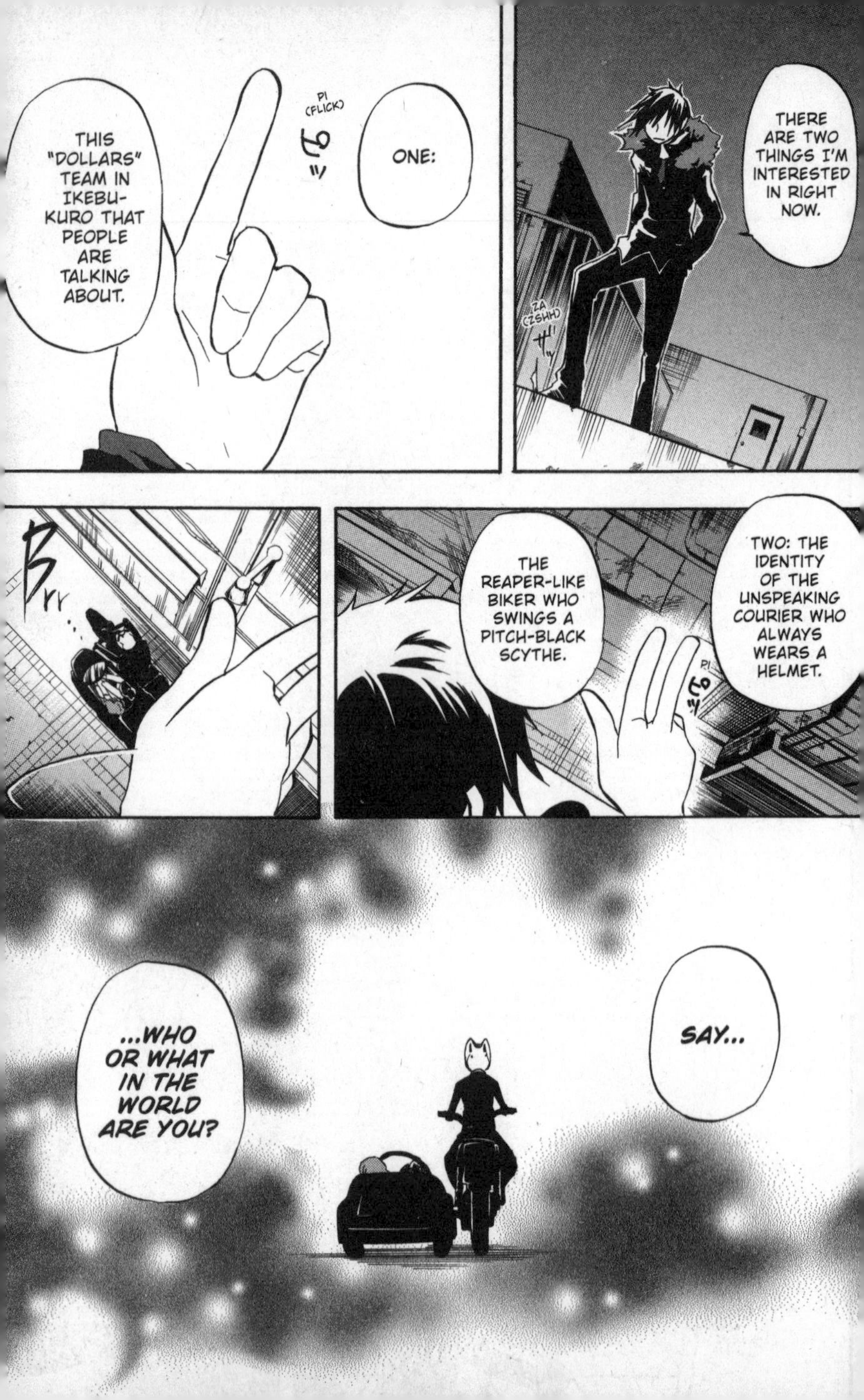
THERE ARE TWO THINGS I'M INTERESTED IN RIGHT NOW.
ZA (ZSHH)
ONE:
PI (FLICK)
THIS "DOLLARS" TEAM IN IKEBUKURO THAT PEOPLE ARE TALKING ABOUT.
TWO: THE IDENTITY OF THE UNSPEAKING COURIER WHO ALWAYS WEARS A HELMET.
PI
THE REAPER-LIKE BIKER WHO SWINGS A PITCH-BLACK SCYTHE.
Brr...
SAY...
...WHO OR WHAT IN THE WORLD ARE YOU?

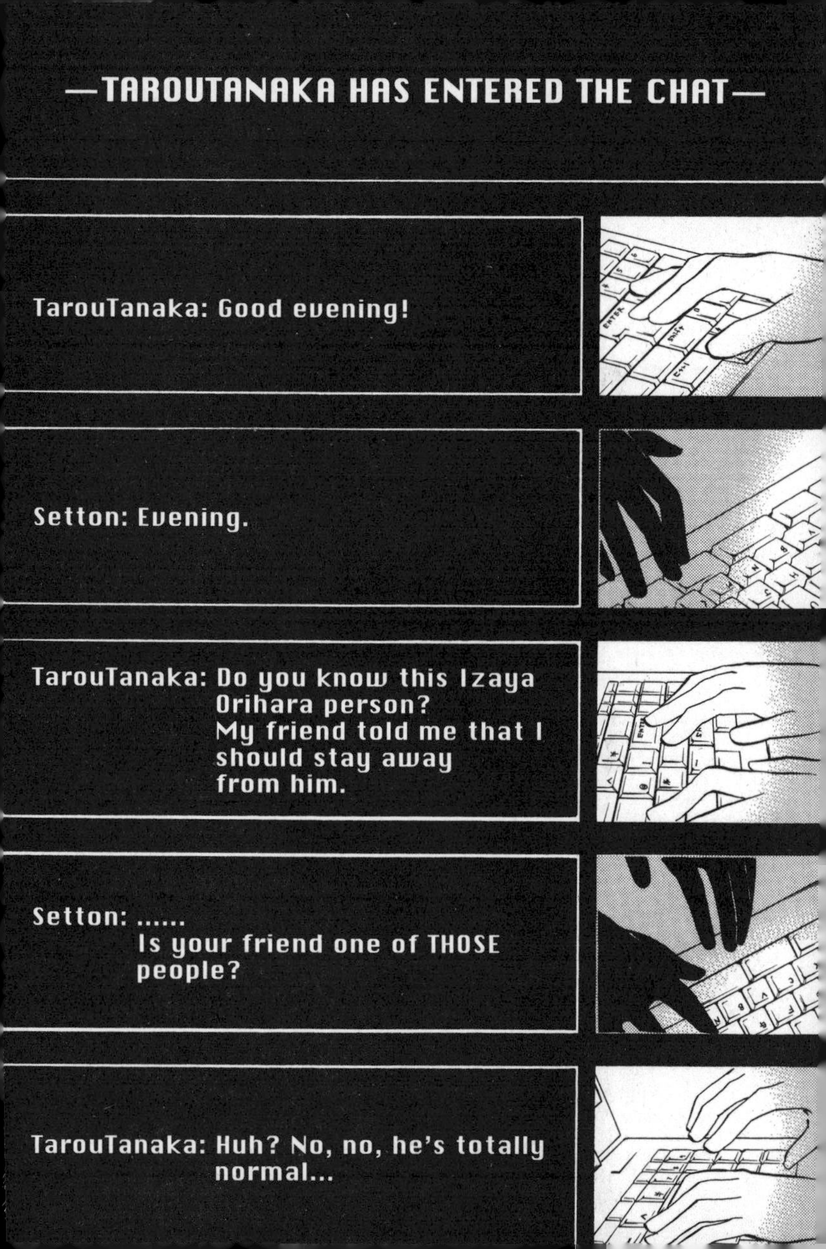
—TAROUTANAKA HAS ENTERED THE CHAT—
TarouTanaka: Good evening!
Setton: Evening.
TarouTanaka: Do you know this Izaya Orihara person? My friend told me that I should stay away from him.
Setton: ...... Is your friend one of THOSE people?
TarouTanaka: Huh? No, no, he's totally normal...

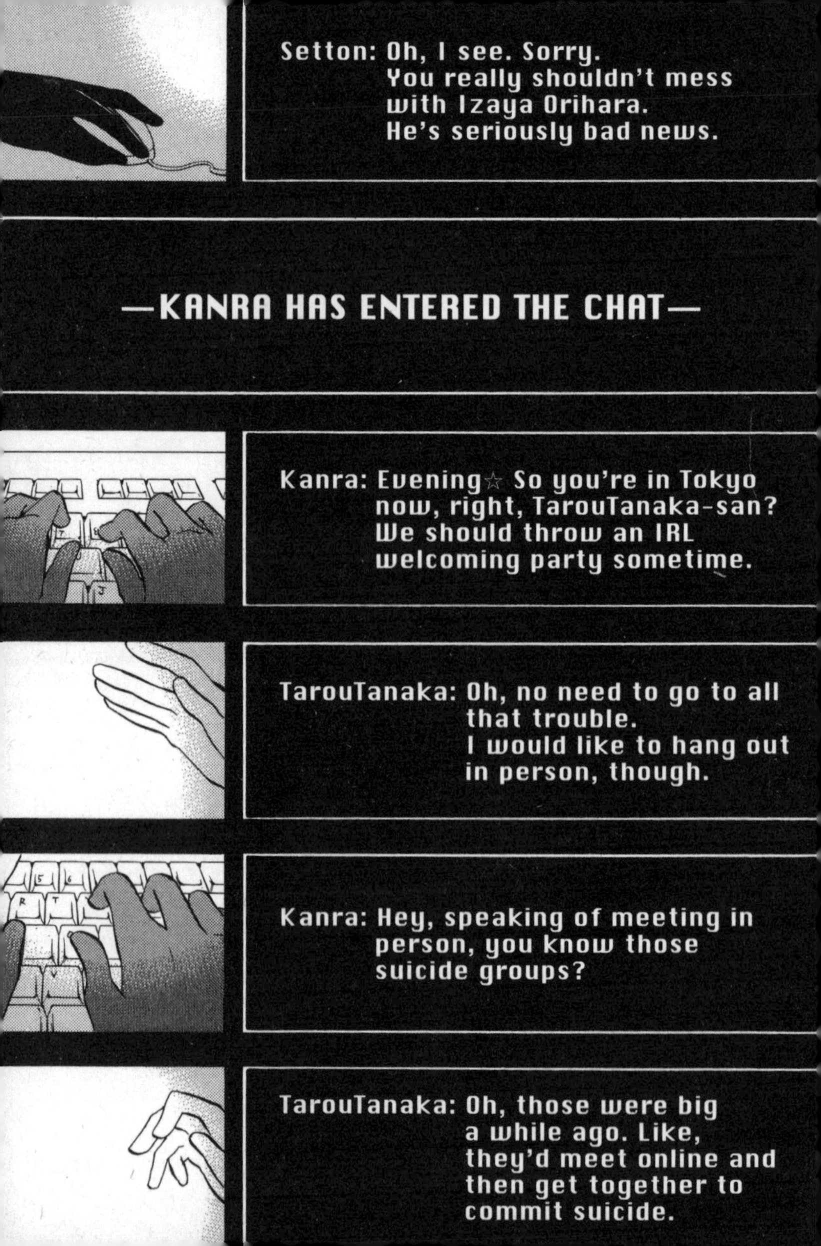

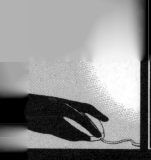

Setton: Oh, I see. Sorry. You really shouldn't mess with Izaya Orihara. He's seriously bad news.
—KANRA HAS ENTERED THE CHAT—
Kanra: Evening☆ So you're in Tokyo now, right, TarouTanaka-san? We should throw an IRL welcoming party sometime.
TarouTanaka: Oh, no need to go to all that trouble. I would like to hang out in person, though.
Kanra: Hey, speaking of meeting in person, you know those suicide groups?
TarouTanaka: Oh, those were big a while ago. Like, they'd meet online and then get together to commit suicide.

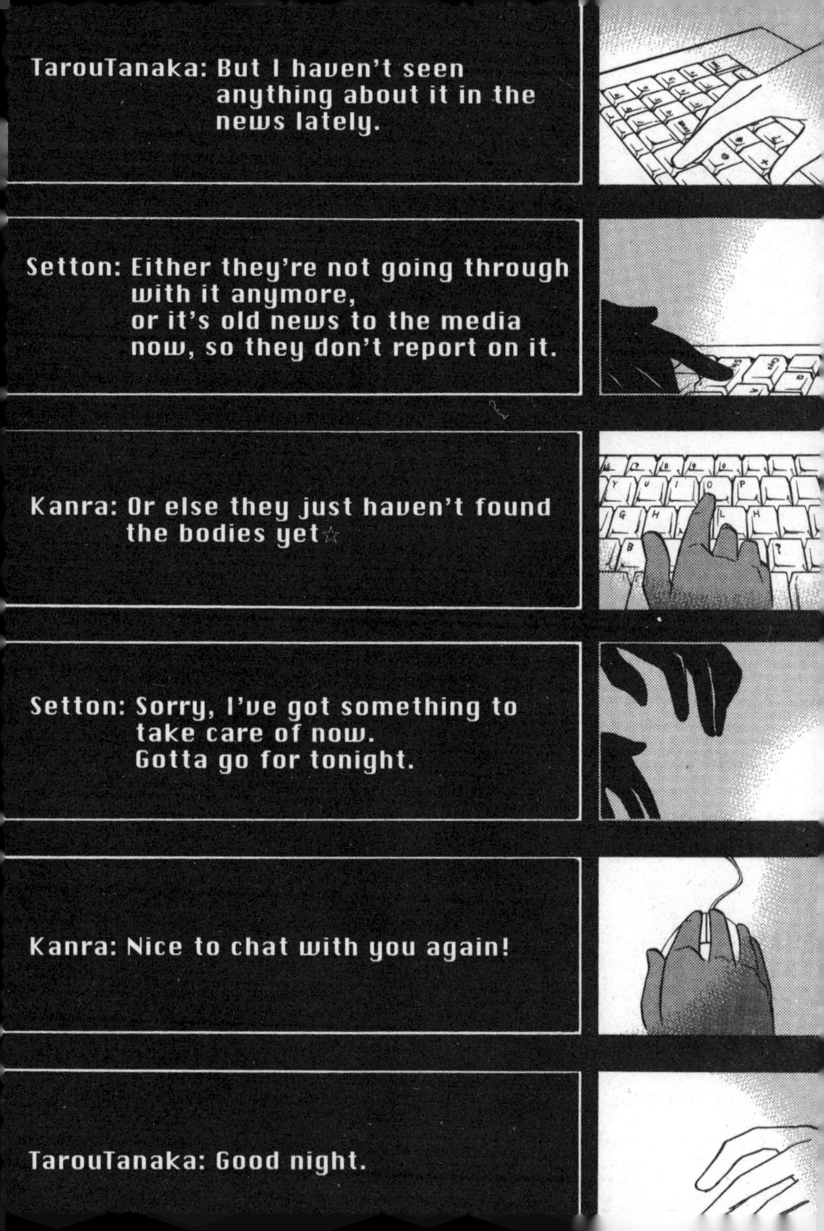
TarouTanaka: But I haven't seen anything about it in the news lately.
Setton: Either they're not going through with it anymore, or it's old news to the media now, so they don't report on it.
Kanra: Or else they just haven't found the bodies yet☆
Setton: Sorry, I've got something to take care of now. Gotta go for tonight.
Kanra: Nice to chat with you again!
TarouTanaka: Good night.

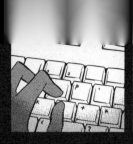

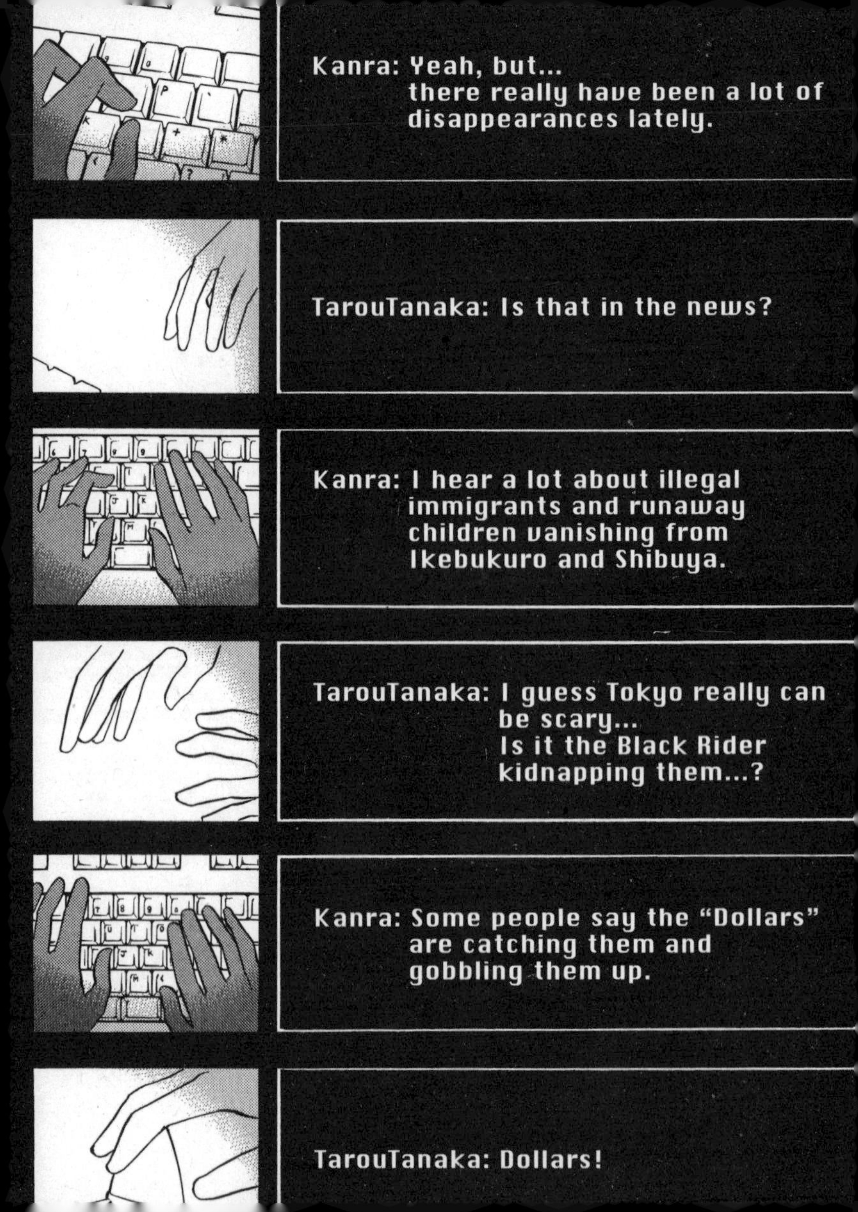
Kanra: Yeah, but... there really have been a lot of disappearances lately.
TarouTanaka: Is that in the news?
Kanra: I hear a lot about illegal immigrants and runaway children vanishing from Ikebukuro and Shibuya.
TarouTanaka: I guess Tokyo really can be scary... Is it the Black Rider kidnapping them...?
Kanra: Some people say the "Dollars" are catching them and gobbling them up.
TarouTanaka: Dollars!

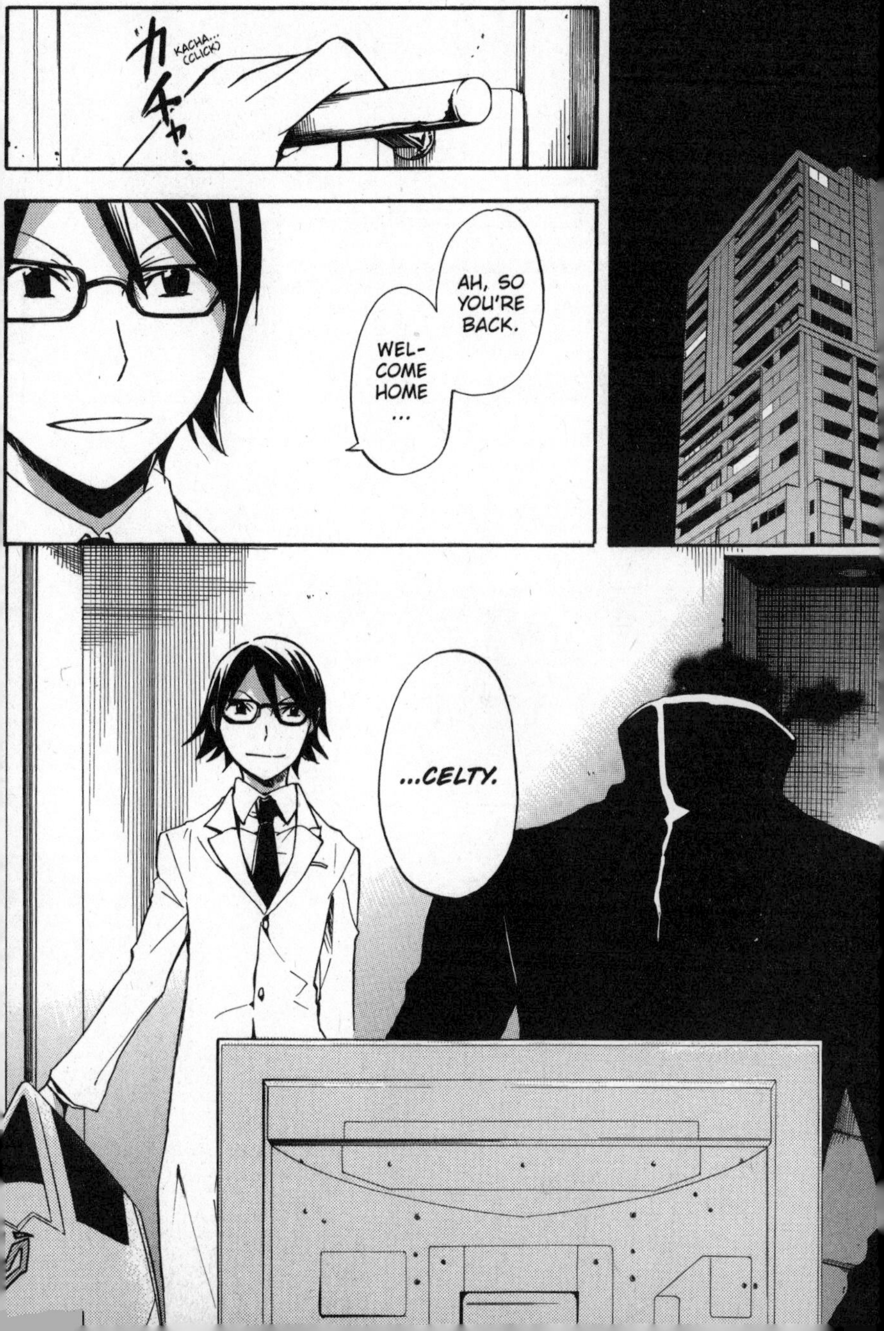
カチャ…
KACHA... (CLICK)
AH, SO YOU'RE BACK.
WEL-COME HOME ...
...CELTY.

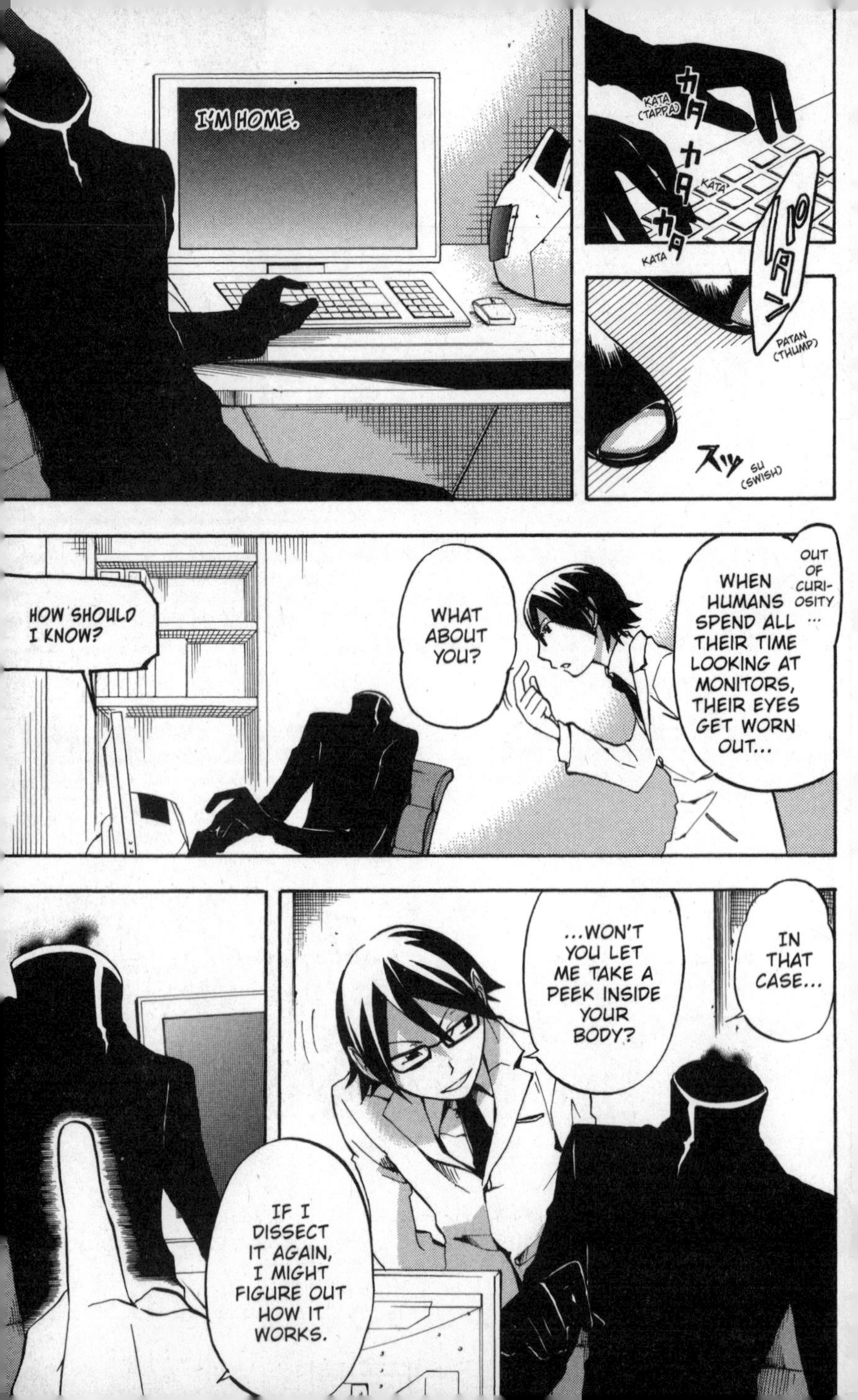

カタ
KATA (TAPPA)
カタ
KATA
カタ
KATA
パタン
PATAN (THUMP)
スッ
SU (SWISH)
I'M HOME.
OUT OF CURIOSITY...
WHEN HUMANS SPEND ALL THEIR TIME LOOKING AT MONITORS, THEIR EYES GET WORN OUT...
WHAT ABOUT YOU?
HOW SHOULD I KNOW?
IN THAT CASE...
...WON'T YOU LET ME TAKE A PEEK INSIDE YOUR BODY?
IF I DISSECT IT AGAIN, I MIGHT FIGURE OUT HOW IT WORKS.

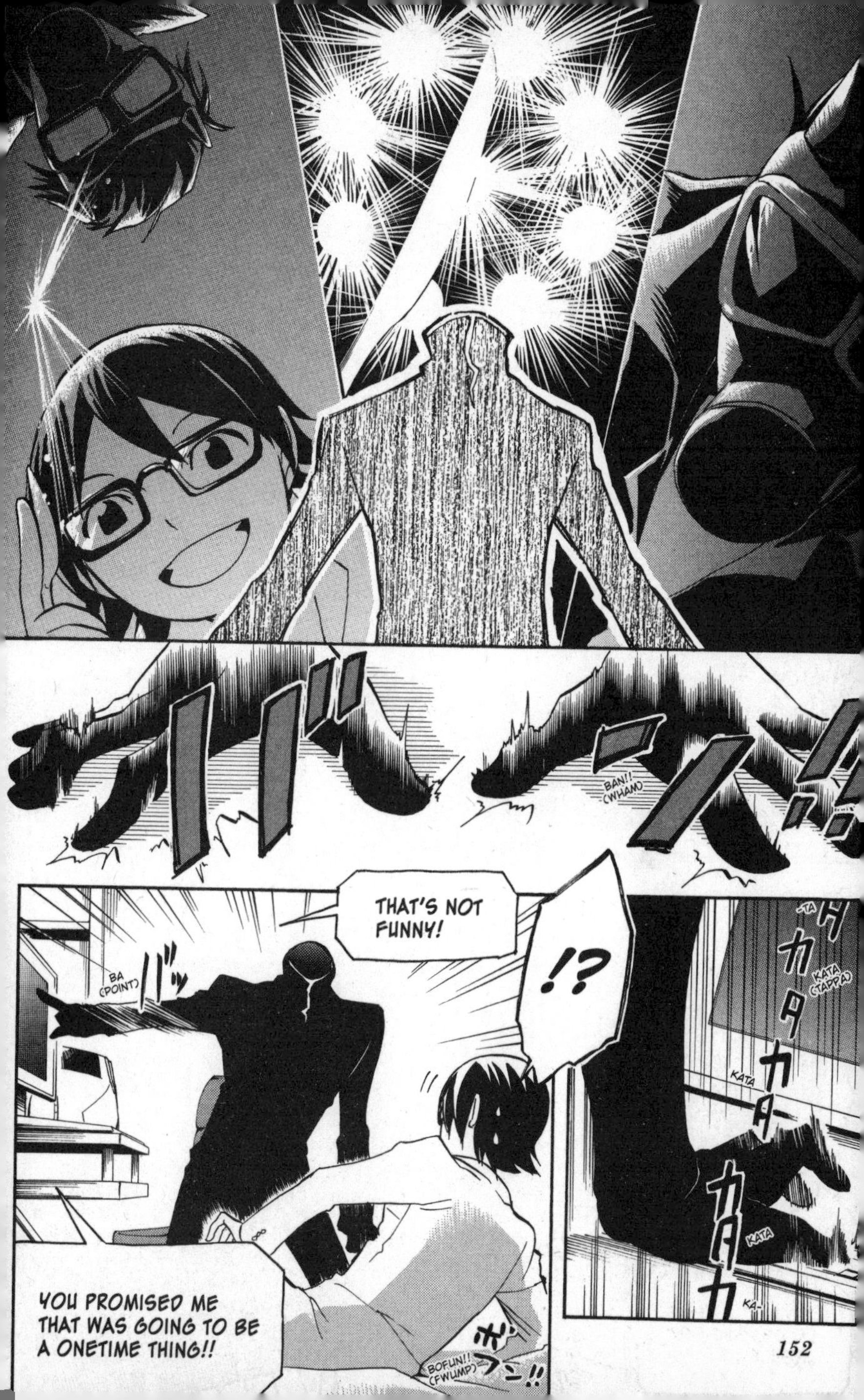
BAN!! (WHAM)
-TA
KATA (TAPPA)
KATA
KATA
KA-
!?
THAT'S NOT FUNNY!
BA (POINT)
YOU PROMISED ME THAT WAS GOING TO BE A ONETIME THING!!
BOFUN!! (FWUMP)

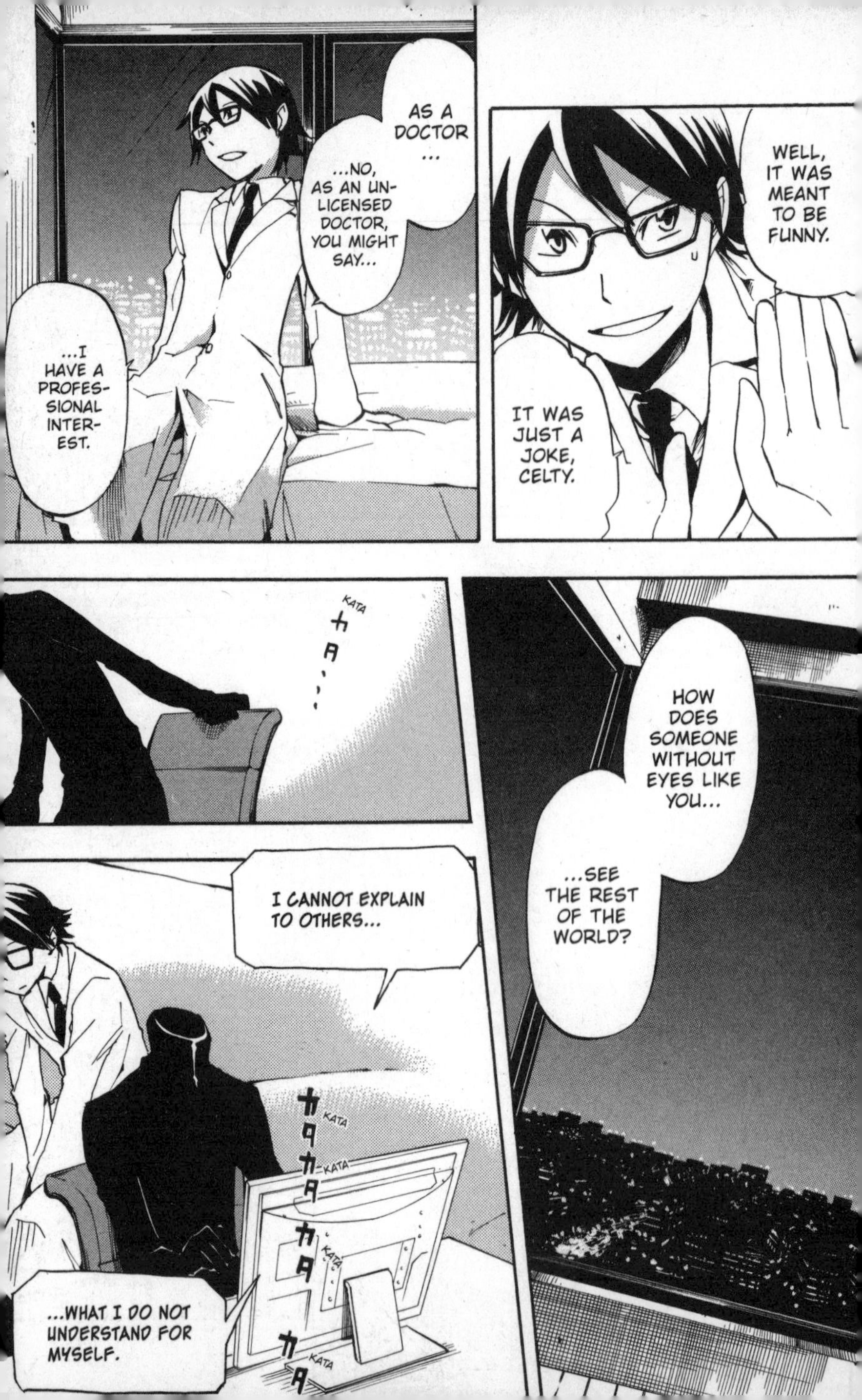
WELL, IT WAS MEANT TO BE FUNNY.
IT WAS JUST A JOKE, CELTY.
AS A DOCTOR...
...NO, AS AN UN-LICENSED DOCTOR, YOU MIGHT SAY...
...I HAVE A PROFES-SIONAL INTER-EST.
HOW DOES SOMEONE WITHOUT EYES LIKE YOU...
...SEE THE REST OF THE WORLD?
カタ...
KATA
I CANNOT EXPLAIN TO OTHERS...
...WHAT I DO NOT UNDERSTAND FOR MYSELF.
カタカタカタカタ
KATA
KATA
KATA
KATA

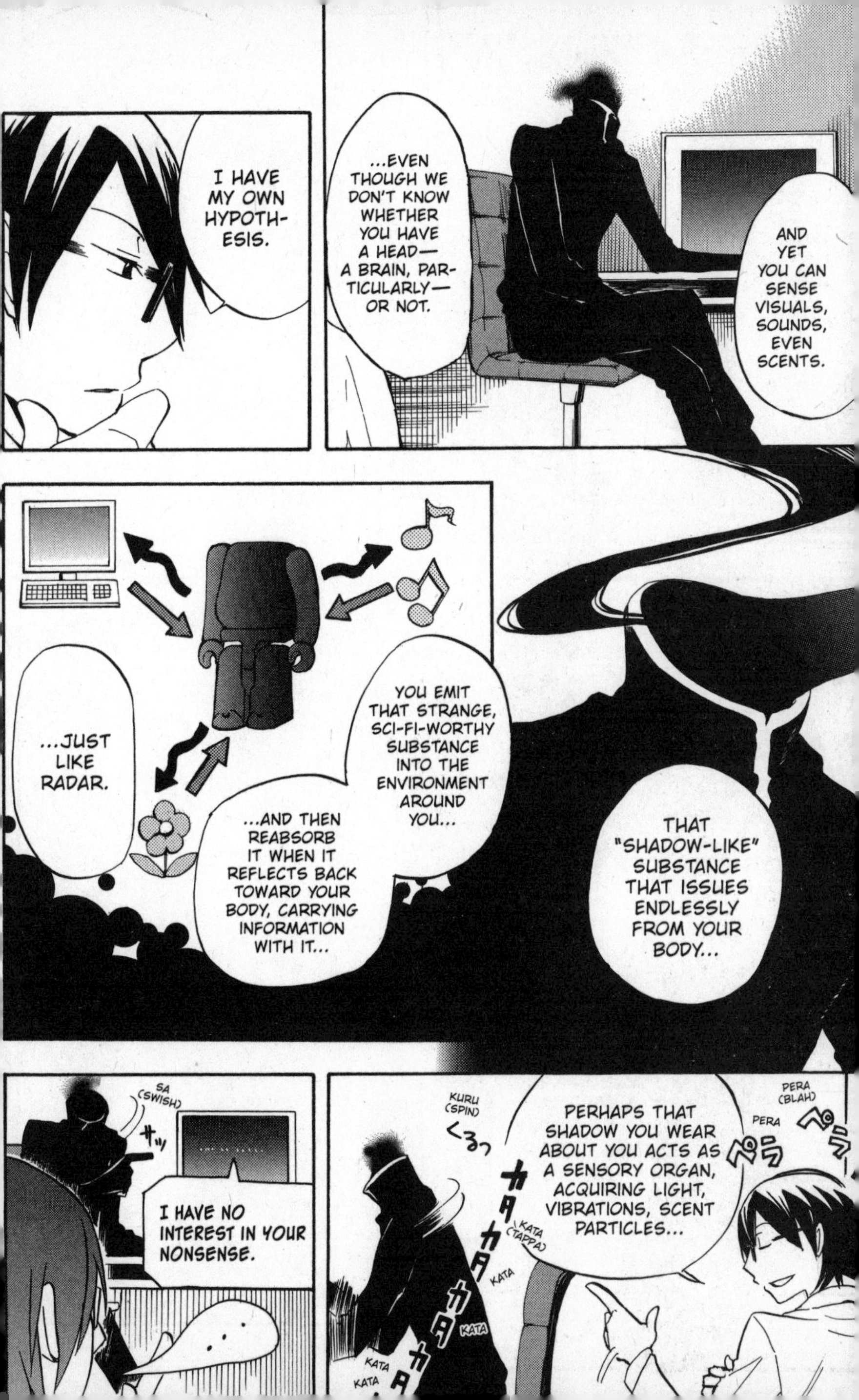
AND YET YOU CAN SENSE VISUALS, SOUNDS, EVEN SCENTS.
...EVEN THOUGH WE DON'T KNOW WHETHER YOU HAVE A HEAD—A BRAIN, PARTICULARLY—OR NOT.
I HAVE MY OWN HYPOTHESIS.
THAT "SHADOW-LIKE" SUBSTANCE THAT ISSUES ENDLESSLY FROM YOUR BODY...
YOU EMIT THAT STRANGE, SCI-FI-WORTHY SUBSTANCE INTO THE ENVIRONMENT AROUND YOU...
...AND THEN REABSORB IT WHEN IT REFLECTS BACK TOWARD YOUR BODY, CARRYING INFORMATION WITH IT...
...JUST LIKE RADAR.
PERA (BLAH)
ペラ
PERA
ペラ
PERHAPS THAT SHADOW YOU WEAR ABOUT YOU ACTS AS A SENSORY ORGAN, ACQUIRING LIGHT, VIBRATIONS, SCENT PARTICLES...
KURU (SPIN)
くるっ
KATA (TAPPA)
KATA
KATA
KATA
KATA
SA (SWISH)
サッ
I HAVE NO INTEREST IN YOUR NONSENSE.

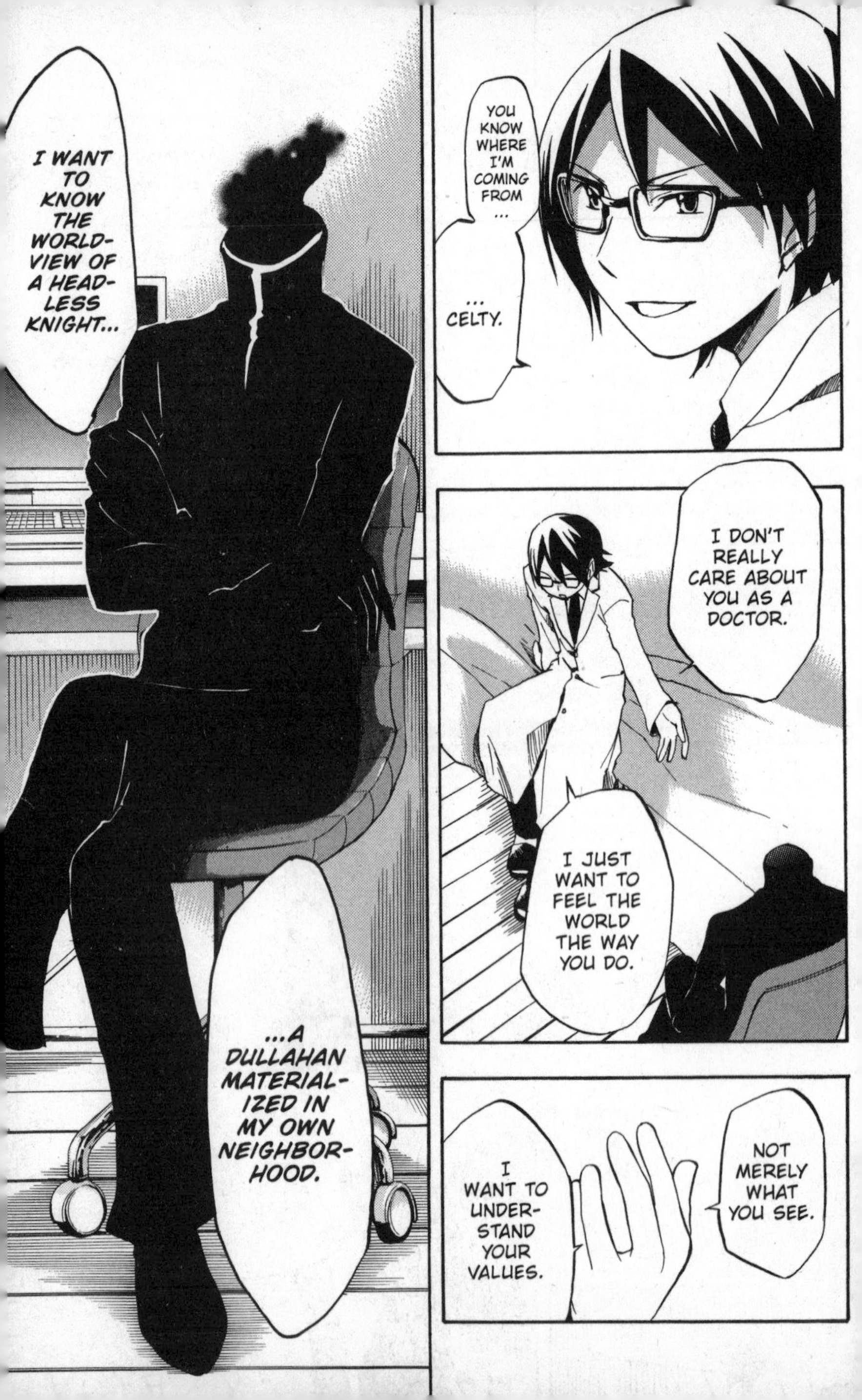
YOU KNOW WHERE I'M COMING FROM ... ... CELTY.
I DON'T REALLY CARE ABOUT YOU AS A DOCTOR.
I JUST WANT TO FEEL THE WORLD THE WAY YOU DO.
NOT MERELY WHAT YOU SEE.
I WANT TO UNDERSTAND YOUR VALUES.
I WANT TO KNOW THE WORLD-VIEW OF A HEADLESS KNIGHT...
...A DULLAHAN MATERIALIZED IN MY OWN NEIGHBORHOOD.

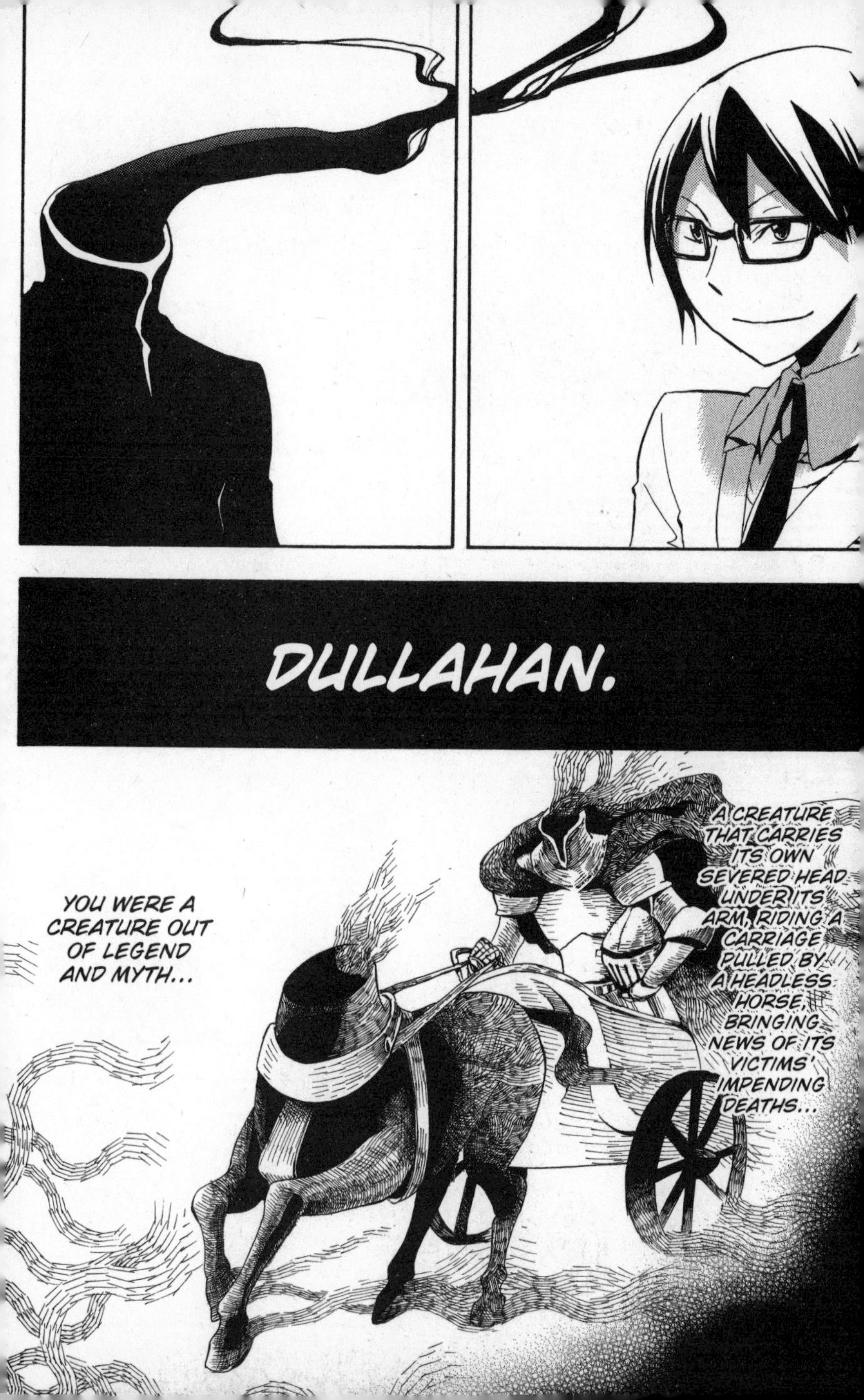
DULLAHAN.
A CREATURE THAT CARRIES ITS OWN SEVERED HEAD UNDER ITS ARM, RIDING A CARRIAGE PULLED BY A HEADLESS HORSE, BRINGING NEWS OF ITS VICTIMS' IMPENDING DEATHS...
YOU WERE A CREATURE OUT OF LEGEND AND MYTH...

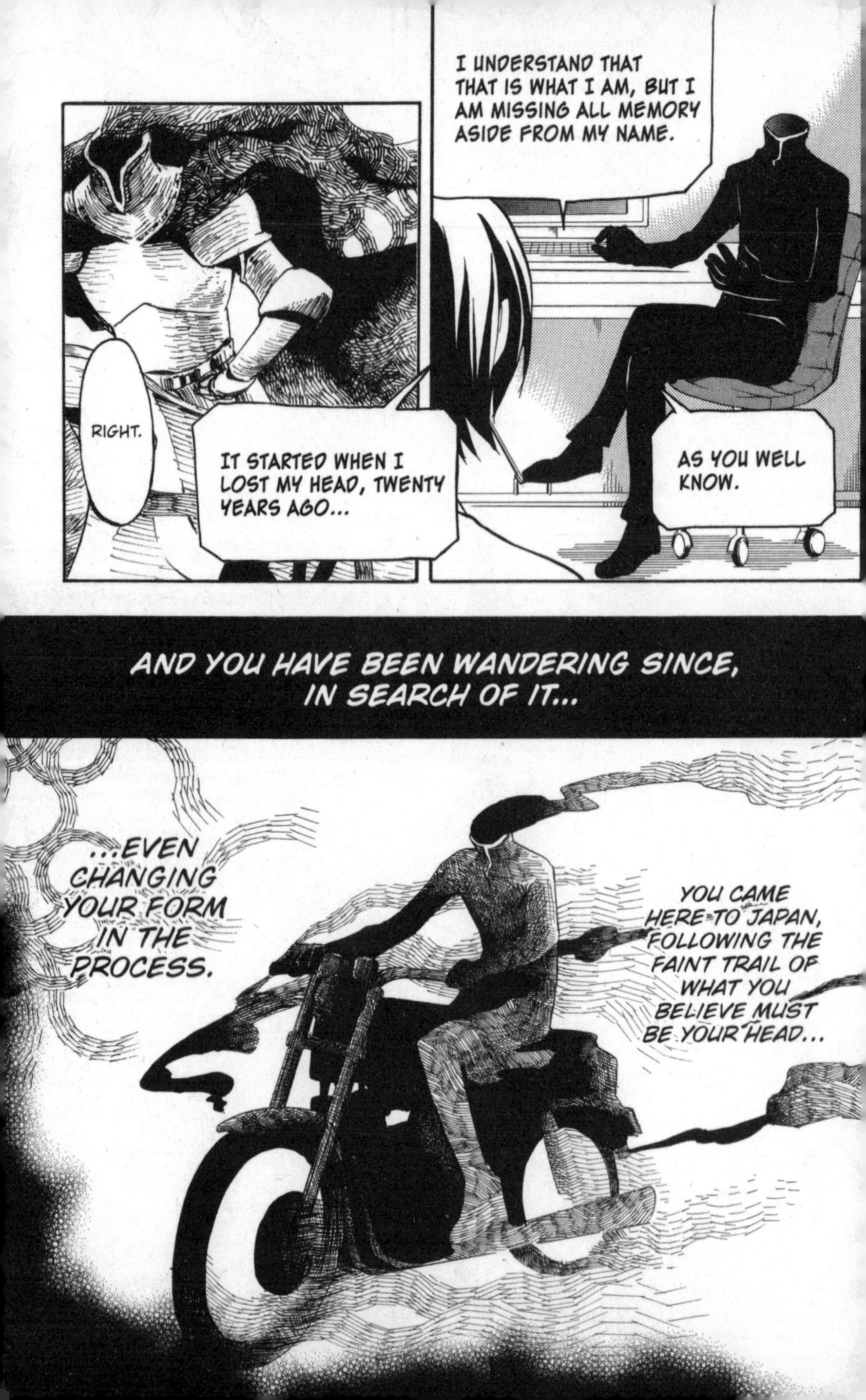
I UNDERSTAND THAT THAT IS WHAT I AM, BUT I AM MISSING ALL MEMORY ASIDE FROM MY NAME.
AS YOU WELL KNOW.
IT STARTED WHEN I LOST MY HEAD, TWENTY YEARS AGO...
RIGHT.
AND YOU HAVE BEEN WANDERING SINCE, IN SEARCH OF IT...
...EVEN CHANGING YOUR FORM IN THE PROCESS.
YOU CAME HERE TO JAPAN, FOLLOWING THE FAINT TRAIL OF WHAT YOU BELIEVE MUST BE YOUR HEAD...

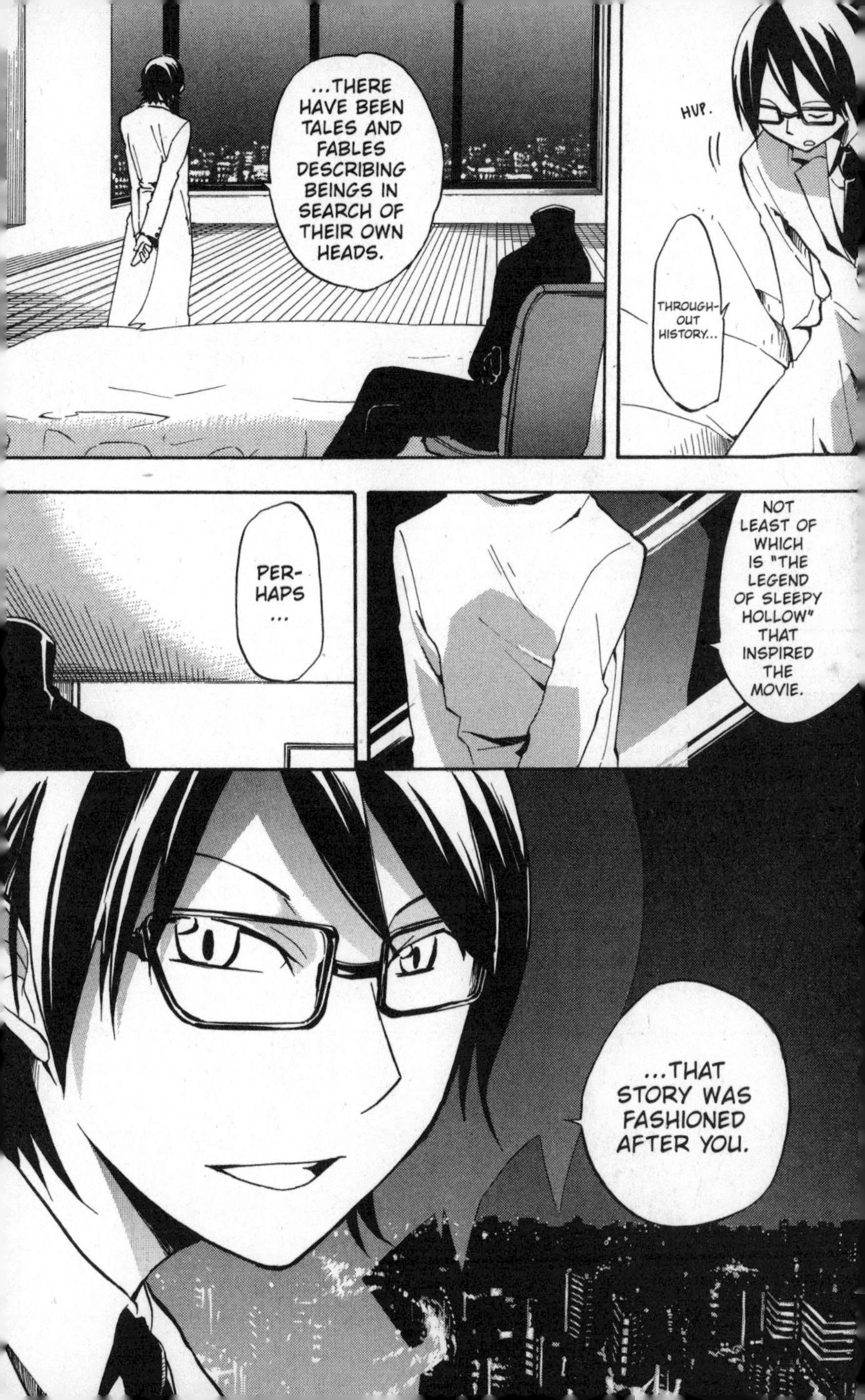
HUP.
THROUGH-OUT HISTORY...
...THERE HAVE BEEN TALES AND FABLES DESCRIBING BEINGS IN SEARCH OF THEIR OWN HEADS.
NOT LEAST OF WHICH IS "THE LEGEND OF SLEEPY HOLLOW" THAT INSPIRED THE MOVIE.
PER-HAPS ...
...THAT STORY WAS FASHIONED AFTER YOU.

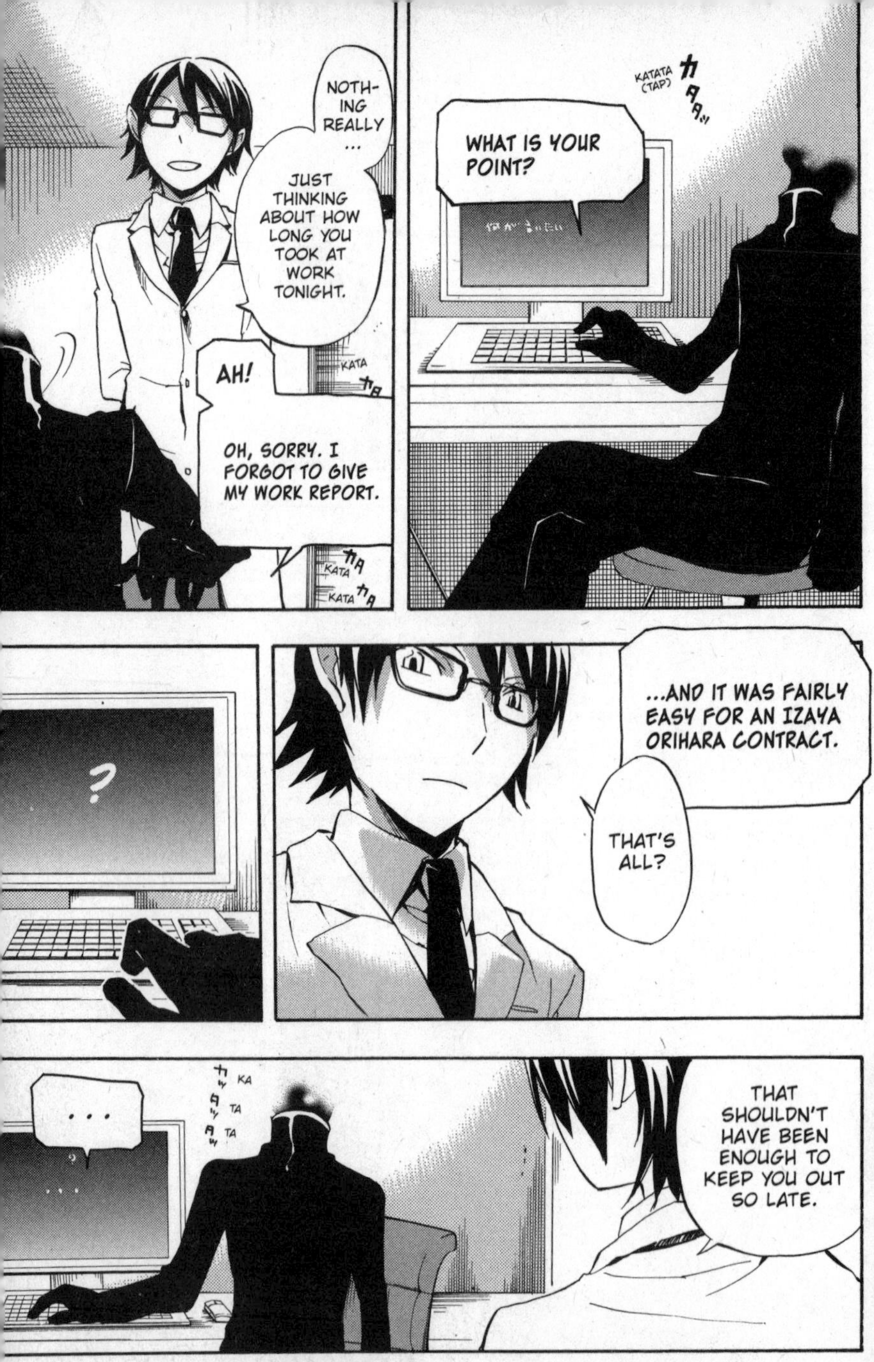
KATATA (TAP)
WHAT IS YOUR POINT?
NOTHING REALLY ...
JUST THINKING ABOUT HOW LONG YOU TOOK AT WORK TONIGHT.
KATA
AH!
OH, SORRY. I FORGOT TO GIVE MY WORK REPORT.
KATA
KATA
...AND IT WAS FAIRLY EASY FOR AN IZAYA ORIHARA CONTRACT.
THAT'S ALL?
?
THAT SHOULDN'T HAVE BEEN ENOUGH TO KEEP YOU OUT SO LATE.
KA
TA
TA
...

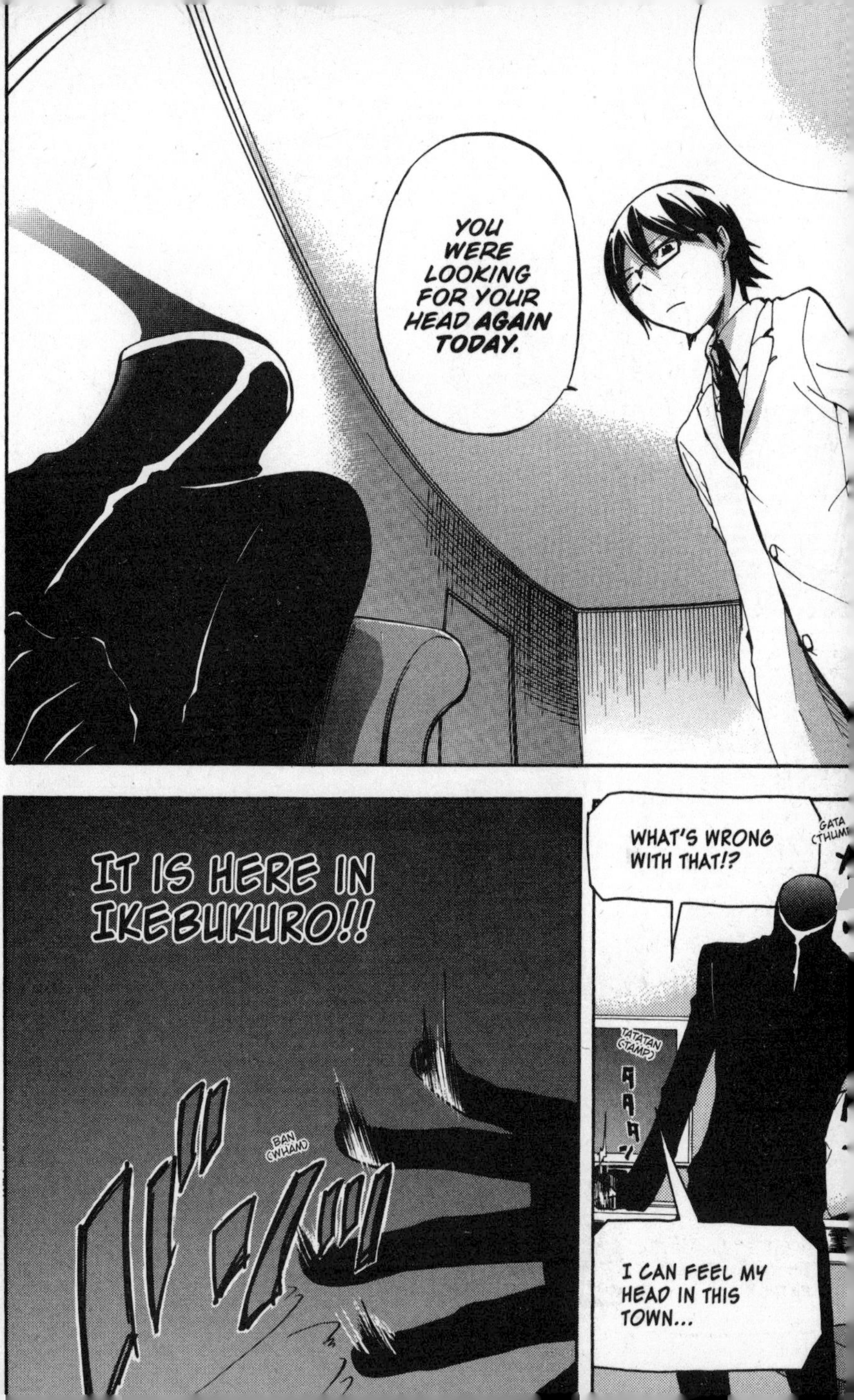
YOU WERE LOOKING FOR YOUR HEAD AGAIN TODAY.
GATA
WHAT'S WRONG WITH THAT!?
TATATAN (TAMP)
I CAN FEEL MY HEAD IN THIS TOWN...
IT IS HERE IN IKEBUKURO!!
BAN (WHAM)

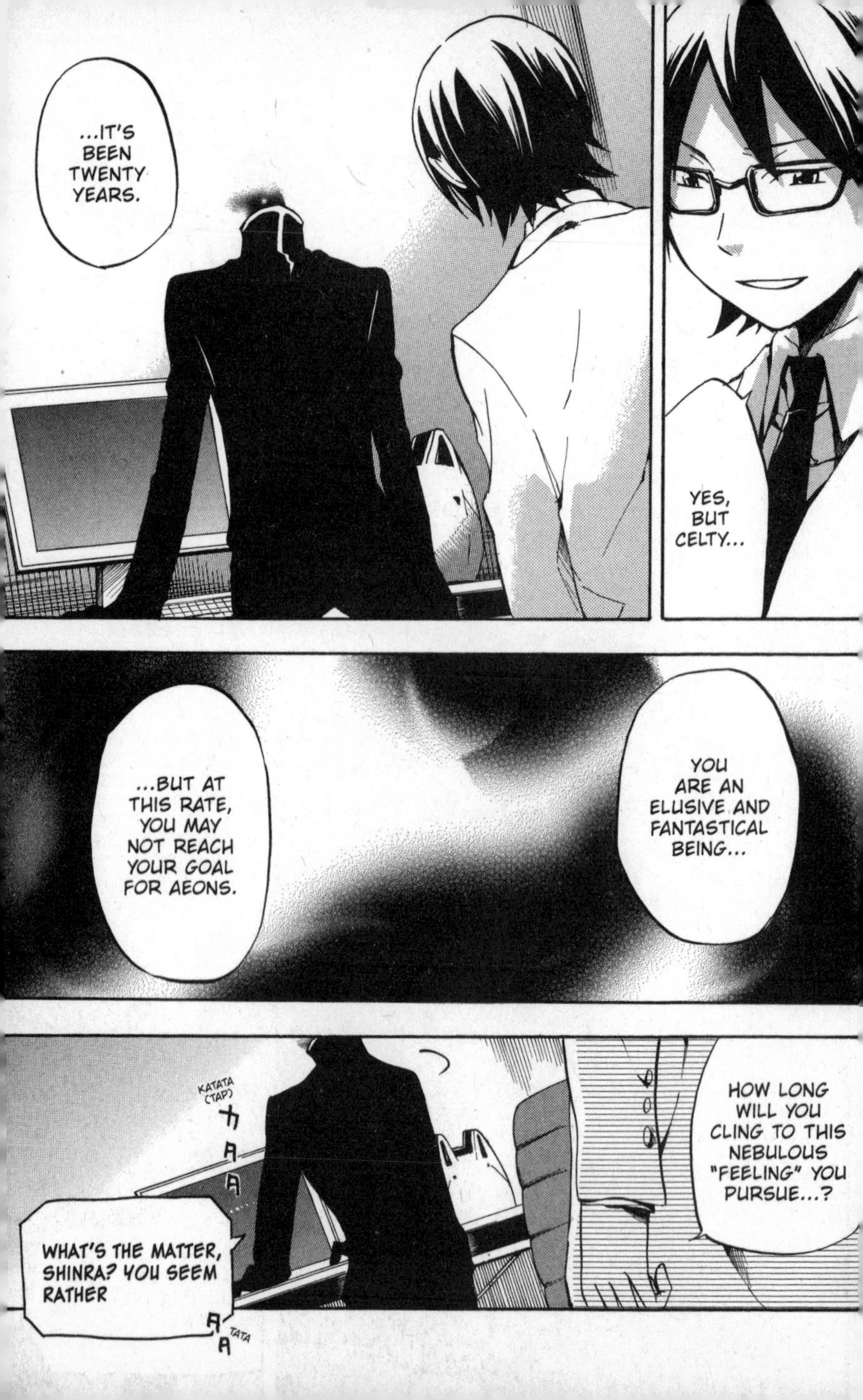
YES, BUT CELTY...
...IT'S BEEN TWENTY YEARS.
YOU ARE AN ELUSIVE AND FANTASTICAL BEING...
...BUT AT THIS RATE, YOU MAY NOT REACH YOUR GOAL FOR AEONS.
HOW LONG WILL YOU CLING TO THIS NEBULOUS "FEELING" YOU PURSUE...?
KATATA (TAP)
WHAT'S THE MATTER, SHINRA? YOU SEEM RATHER
TATA

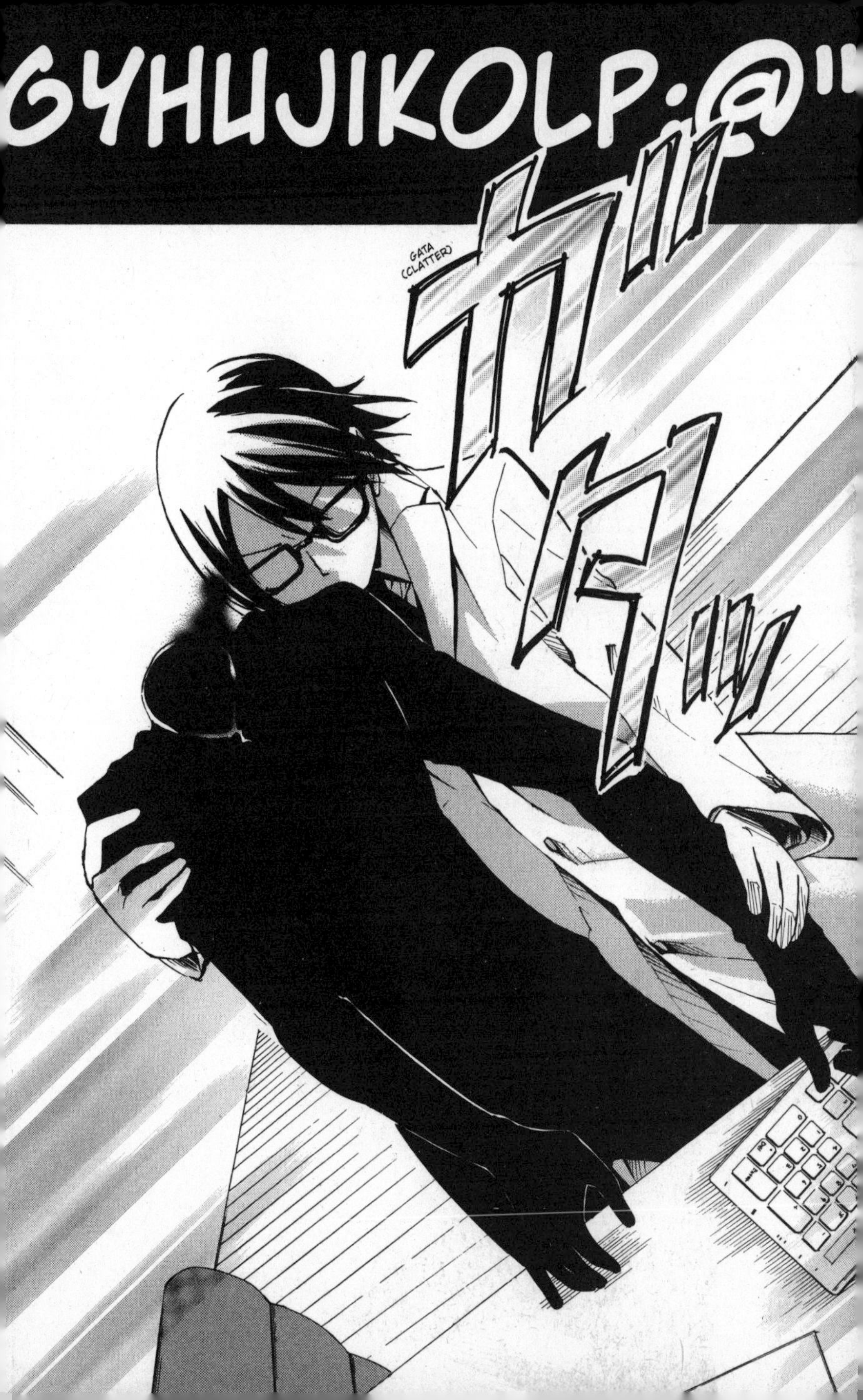
GYHUJIKOLP;@"
GATA
(CLATTER)

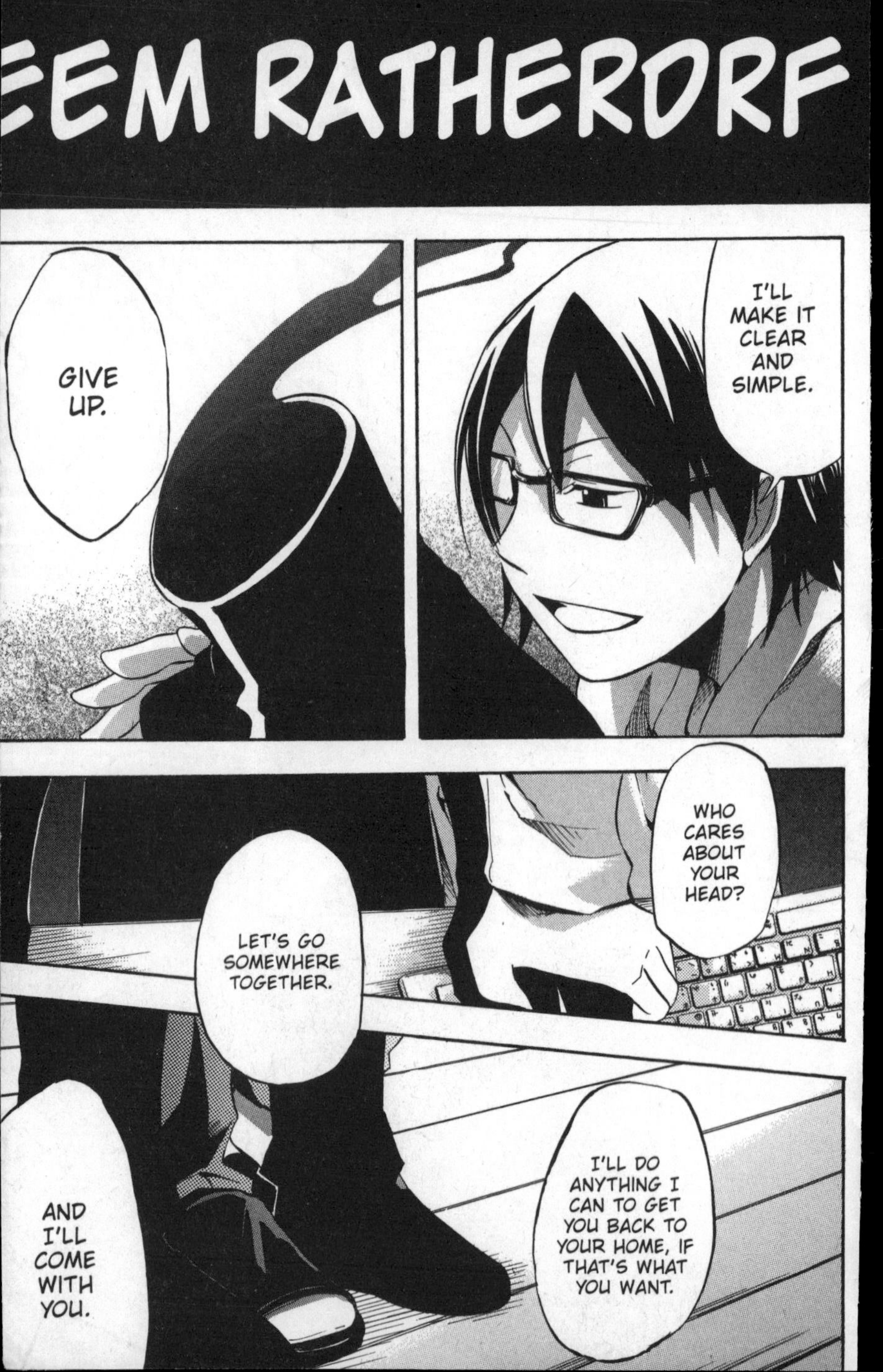
EEM RATHERORF
I'LL MAKE IT CLEAR AND SIMPLE.
GIVE UP.
WHO CARES ABOUT YOUR HEAD?
LET'S GO SOMEWHERE TOGETHER.
I'LL DO ANYTHING I CAN TO GET YOU BACK TO YOUR HOME, IF THAT'S WHAT YOU WANT.
AND I'LL COME WITH YOU.

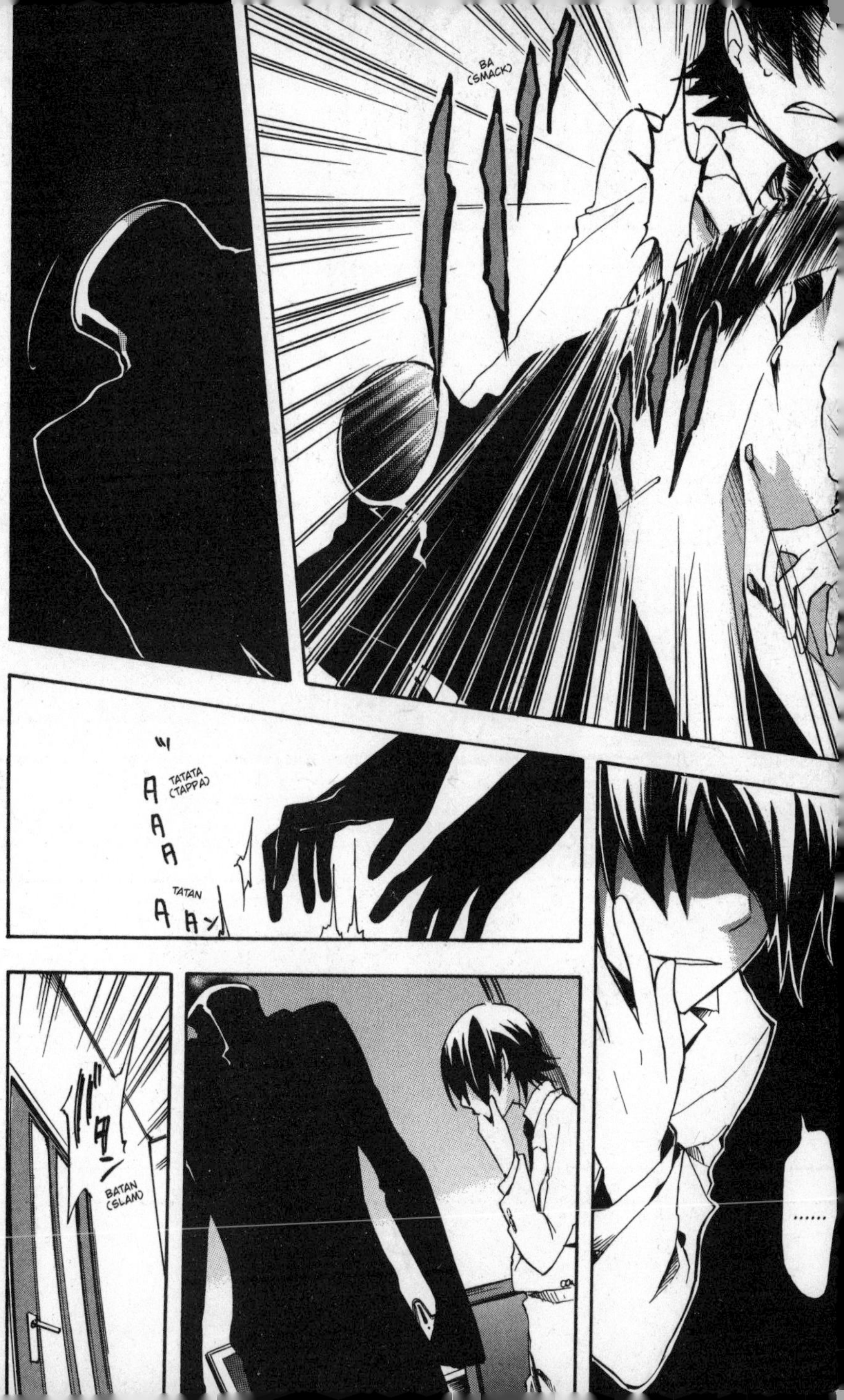
BA
(SMACK)
......
TATATA
(TAPPA)
TATAN
BATAN
(SLAM)

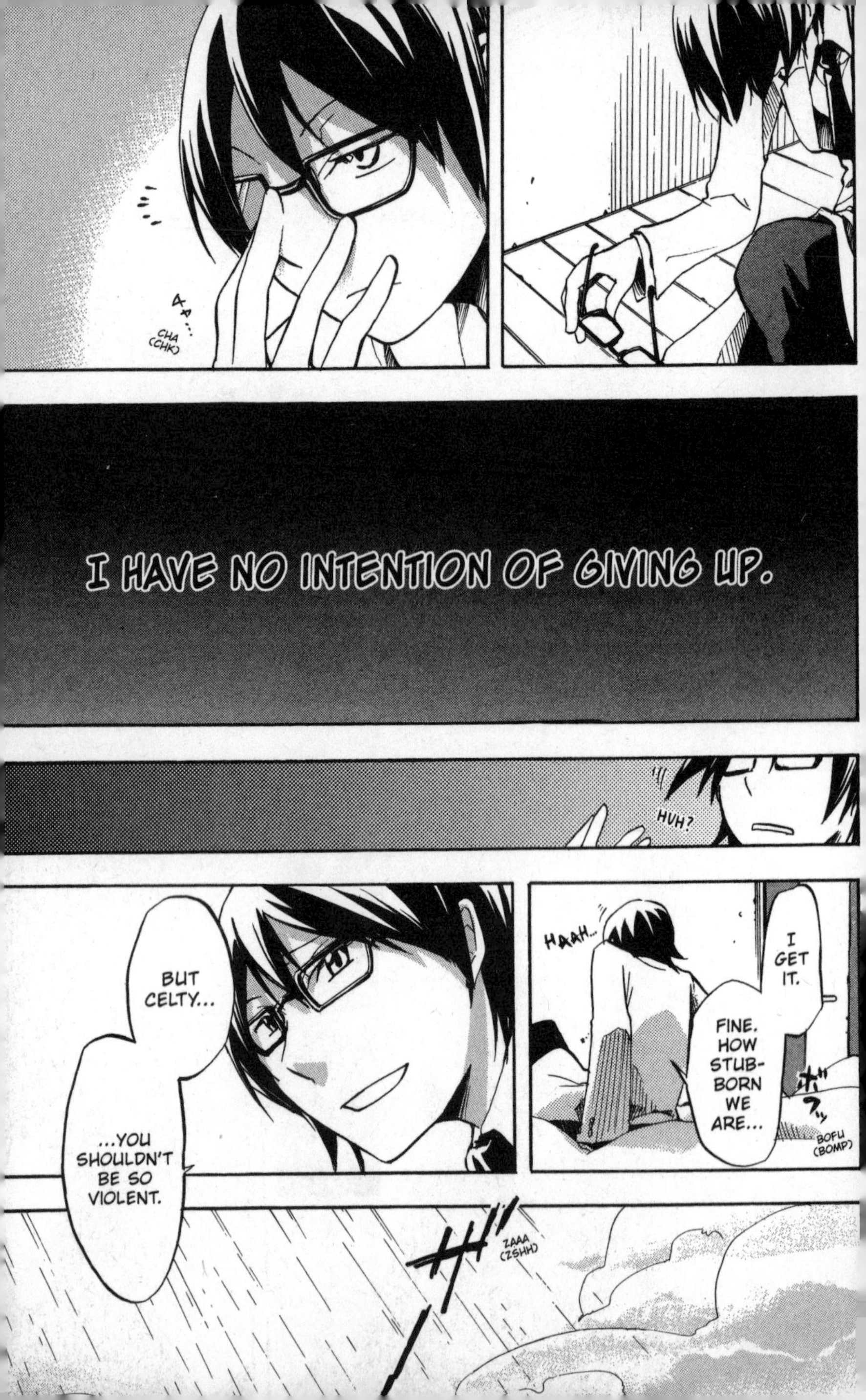
CHA (CHK)
I HAVE NO INTENTION OF GIVING UP.
HUH?
I GET IT.
HAAH...
FINE. HOW STUBBORN WE ARE...
BOFU (BOMP)
BUT CELTY...
...YOU SHOULDN'T BE SO VIOLENT.
ZAAA (ZSHH)

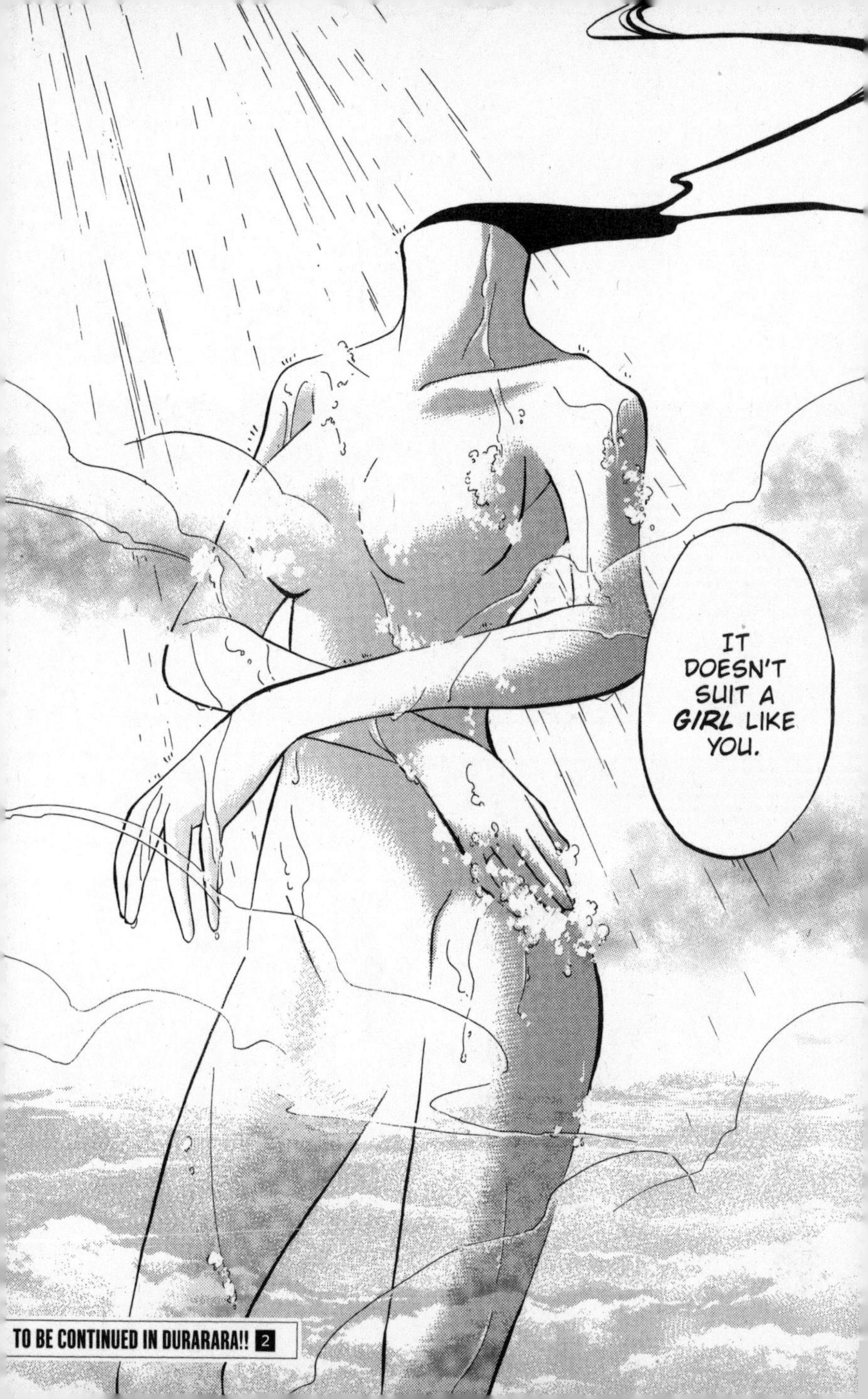
IT DOESN'T SUIT A GIRL LIKE YOU.
TO BE CONTINUED IN DURARARA!! 2

DRRR!!

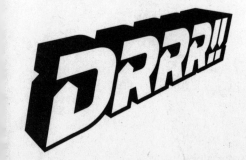

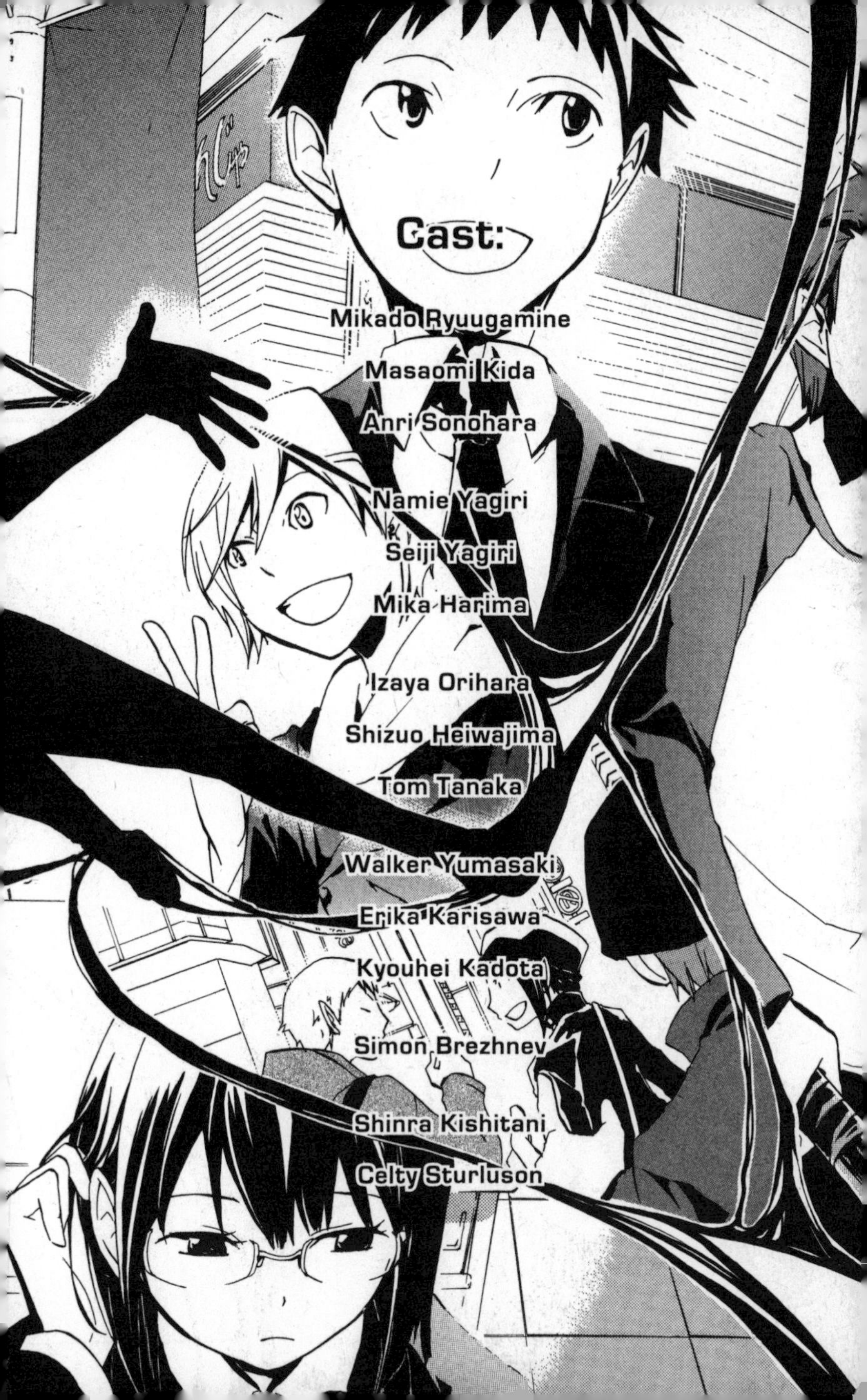
Cast:
Mikado Ryuugamine
Masaomi Kida
Anri Sonohara
Namie Yagiri
Seiji Yagiri
Mika Harima
Izaya Orihara
Shizuo Heiwajima
Tom Tanaka
Walker Yumasaki
Erika Karisawa
Kyouhei Kadota
Simon Brezhnev
Shinra Kishitani
Celty Sturluson

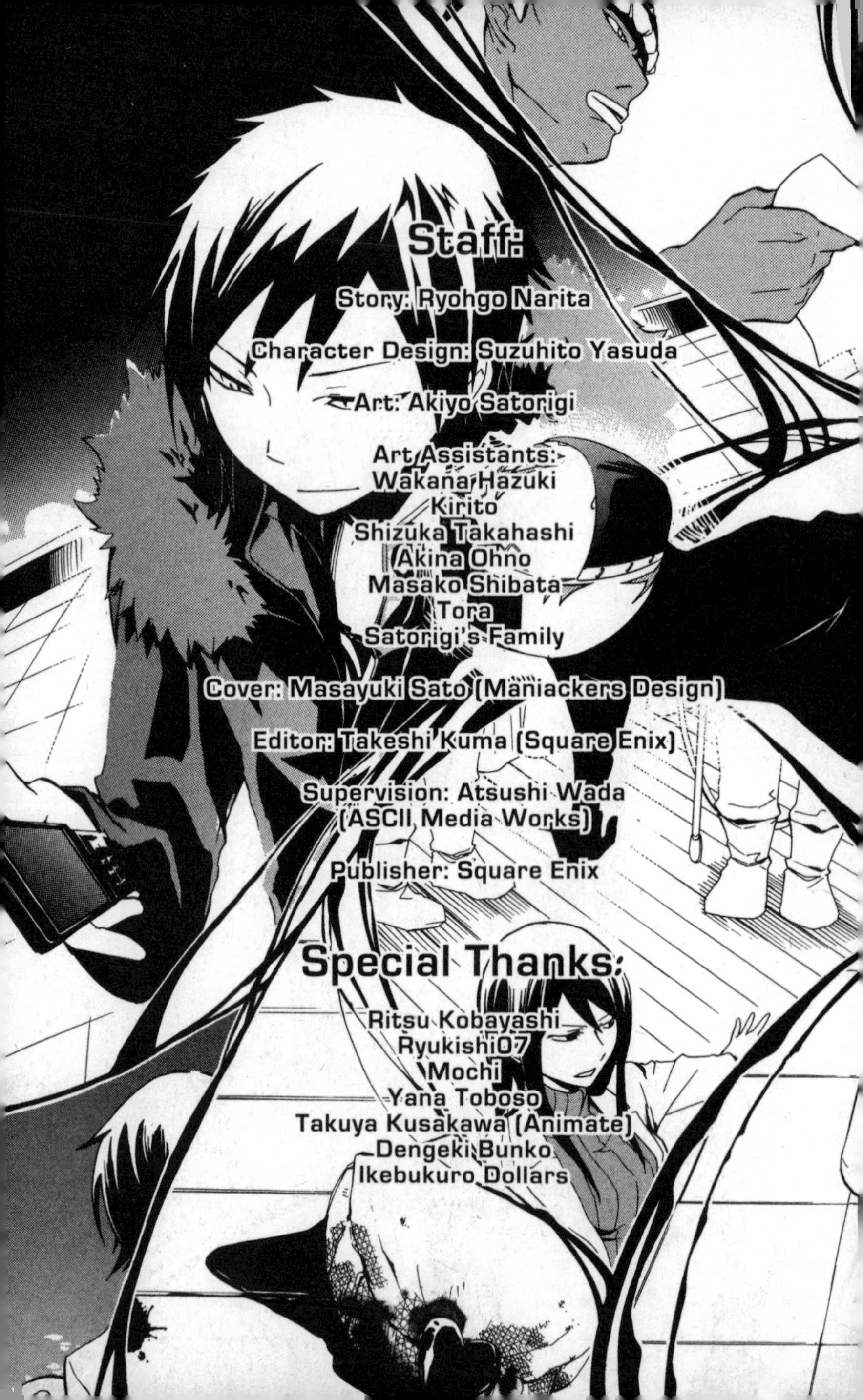

Staff:

Story: Ryohgo Narita

Character Design: Suzuhito Yasuda

Art: Akiyo Satorigi

Art Assistants:
Wakana Hazuki
Kirito
Shizuka Takahashi
Akina Ohno
Masako Shibata
Tora
Satorigi's Family

Cover: Masayuki Sato (Maniackers Design)

Editor: Takeshi Kuma (Square Enix)

Supervision: Atsushi Wada
(ASCII Media Works)

Publisher: Square Enix

Special Thanks:

Ritsu Kobayashi
Ryukishi07
Mochi
Yana Toboso
Takuya Kusakawa (Animate)
Dengeki Bunko
Ikebukuro Dollars

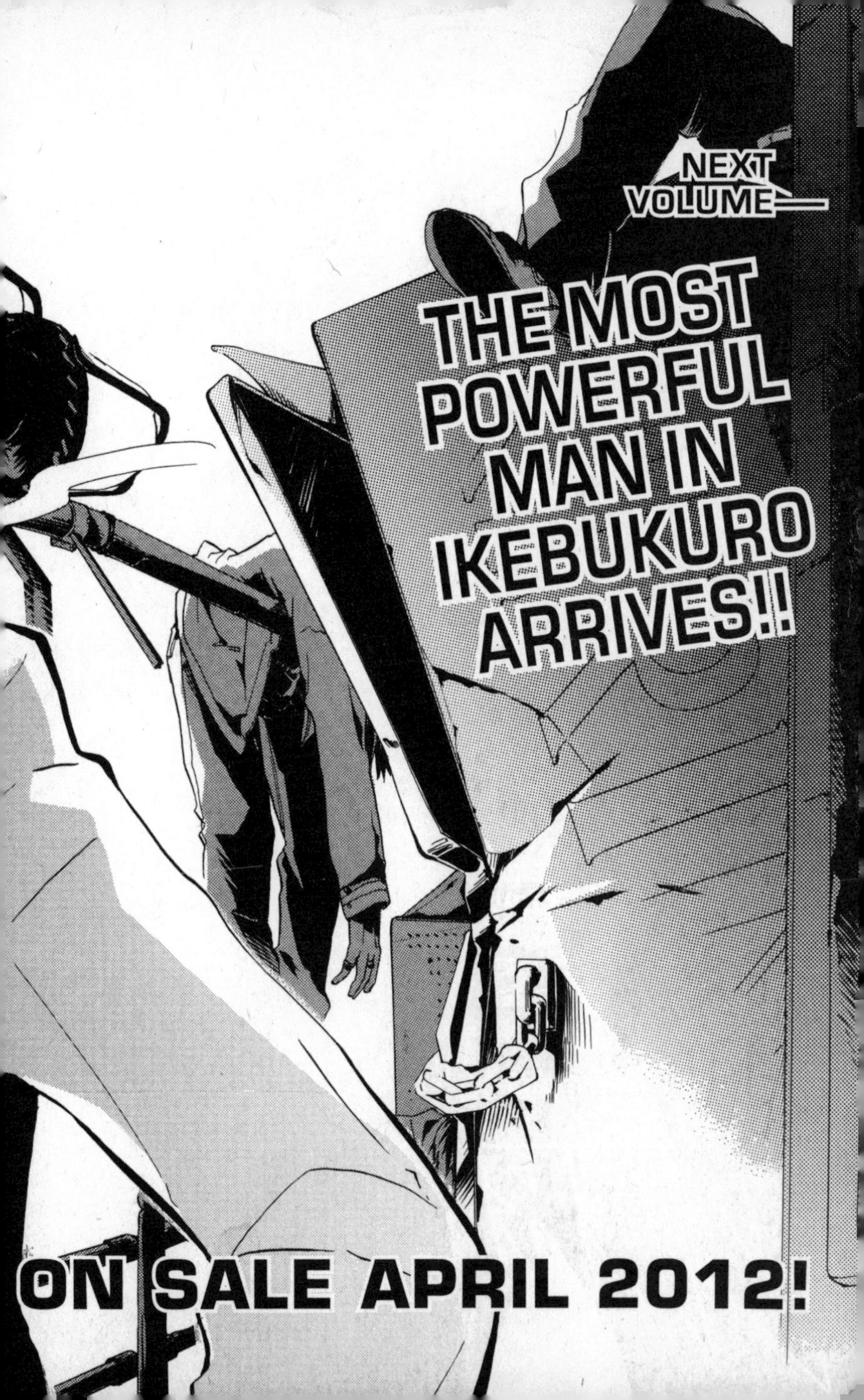
NEXT VOLUME—
THE MOST POWERFUL MAN IN IKEBUKURO ARRIVES!!
ON SALE APRIL 2012!

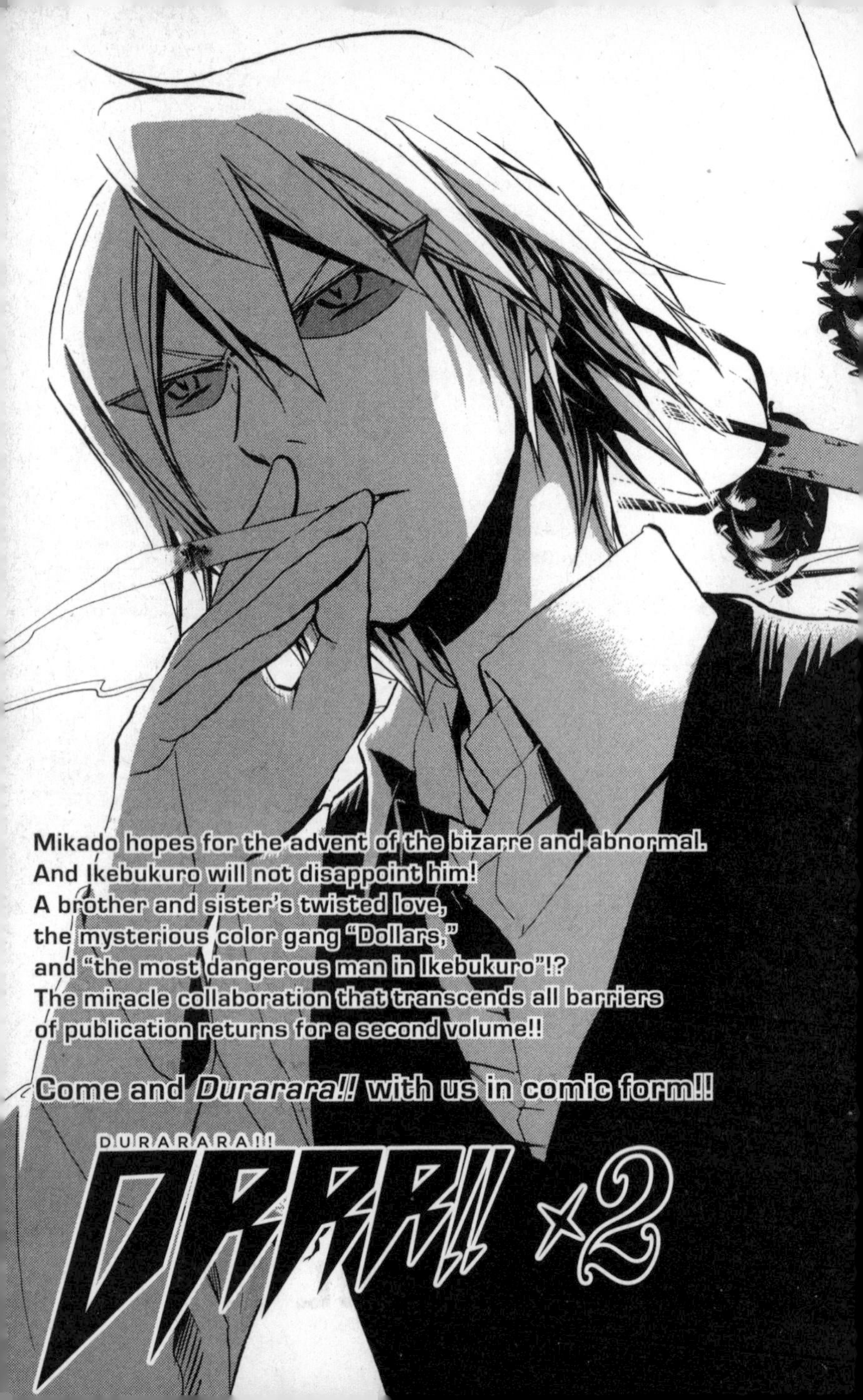
Mikado hopes for the advent of the bizarre and abnormal.
And Ikebukuro will not disappoint him!
A brother and sister's twisted love,
the mysterious color gang "Dollars,"
and "the most dangerous man in Ikebukuro"!?
The miracle collaboration that transcends all barriers
of publication returns for a second volume!!
Come and *Durarara!!* with us in comic form!!
DURARARA!!
DRRR!! ×2

So as you can see, *Durarara!!* continues to develop in many directions thanks to the help and enthusiasm of many different people.

I think that the story we call *Durarara!!* moves forward like a drill: a three-sided machine comprised of manga, anime, and novel that moves in a spiral, each influencing the others, and none considered more or less important than the others. And one of the engines that drives this vehicle forward is the manga version of *Durarara!!* I just can't wait to see how far this story will go, carried on the backs of its faithful readers! So in closing, I hope you continue to enjoy Satorigi-san's manga version of *Durarara!!*

Ryohgo Narita

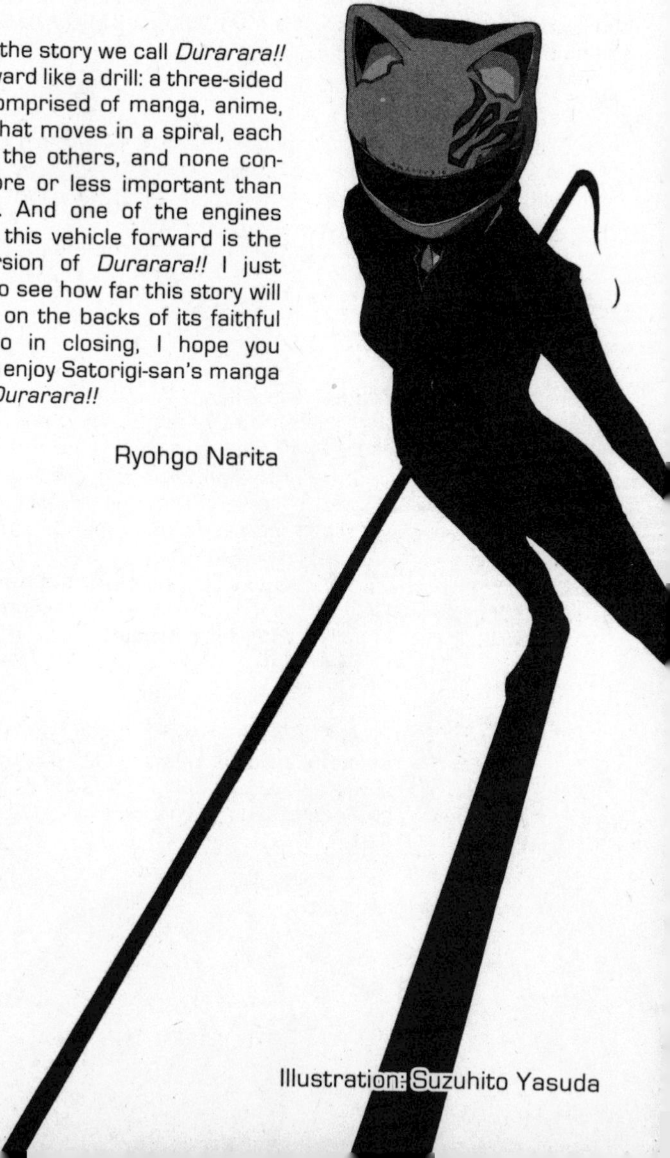

Illustration: Suzuhito Yasuda

Hello, and it's nice to meet those of you I haven't met before! I am Ryohgo Narita, the so-called "creator" of this mixed-media project called *Durarara!!* As a recreational author for the Dengeki Bunko book line, I am an outsider to *GFantasy* readers in two ways: genre and publisher. I hope you don't mind. And for those of you whose interest in this title was piqued after seeing the novel or anime version of *Durarara!!*, I hope you enjoy this adaptation to the manga format. As a unique franchise straddling multiple publishing companies, I think there are many ways to enjoy this story, and I encourage all readers to find their own...!

Anyway, I first had a manga adaptation offer from Square Enix's Kuma-san about four years ago. At the time, I was quite busy with an anime version of another work of mine, *Baccano!*, so it took quite some time for this manga to come to fruition... But fortunately, *Durarara!!* received the same anime treatment, and Kuma-san's enthusiasm for working with me was finally rewarded. Thank you so much for your dedication, Kuma-san!

So Kuma-san says to me, "Heh-heh-heh. About this manga—I've got the perfect artist for the job!" That person turned out to be Akiyo Satorigi, the artist of this very book you hold in your hands. I think Satorigi-san draws spectacular manga. Even from the draft stage, the feeling of movement in the characters was tangible, and my anticipation for the next chapter only increases with time. Of course, I know what happens next in the story, but the way that story is depicted is just as exciting to me as the actual plot. And it's all thanks to Satorigi-san's manga talent. Satorigi-san, thank you for everything! I look forward to the rest of our working relationship!

Also, great thanks must go to Satorigi-san's teacher(?) Yana Toboso-san for her wonderful advertisement for *Dura* in the latest volume of *Black Butler*! She's also written about Shizuo and Izaya many times on her home page. I can't thank her enough!

MESSAGE
from Yana Toboso

Congratulations on getting *Durarara!!* x1 out! I am Yana Toboso, onetime collaborator with Satorigi-sensei on the fold-out illustration in this book. I currently draw *Black Butler* for *Monthly GFantasy*, the magazine that also runs the *Durarara!!* manga.

Our collaboration came to be thanks to the fact that I've known Satorigi-sensei for quite some time and that we share the same editor. When we came together for the illustration, our editor said, "If you're going to do this, it has to be Shizuo and Izaya! Those are my favorite characters!!" So we were forced to do those characters: Izaya-kun for Satorigi-sensei and Shizuo-kun for me. He's a petty tyrant, he is.

Then again, I can't wait to see what they do in Volume 2!

Personally, I just can't get over Celty!!

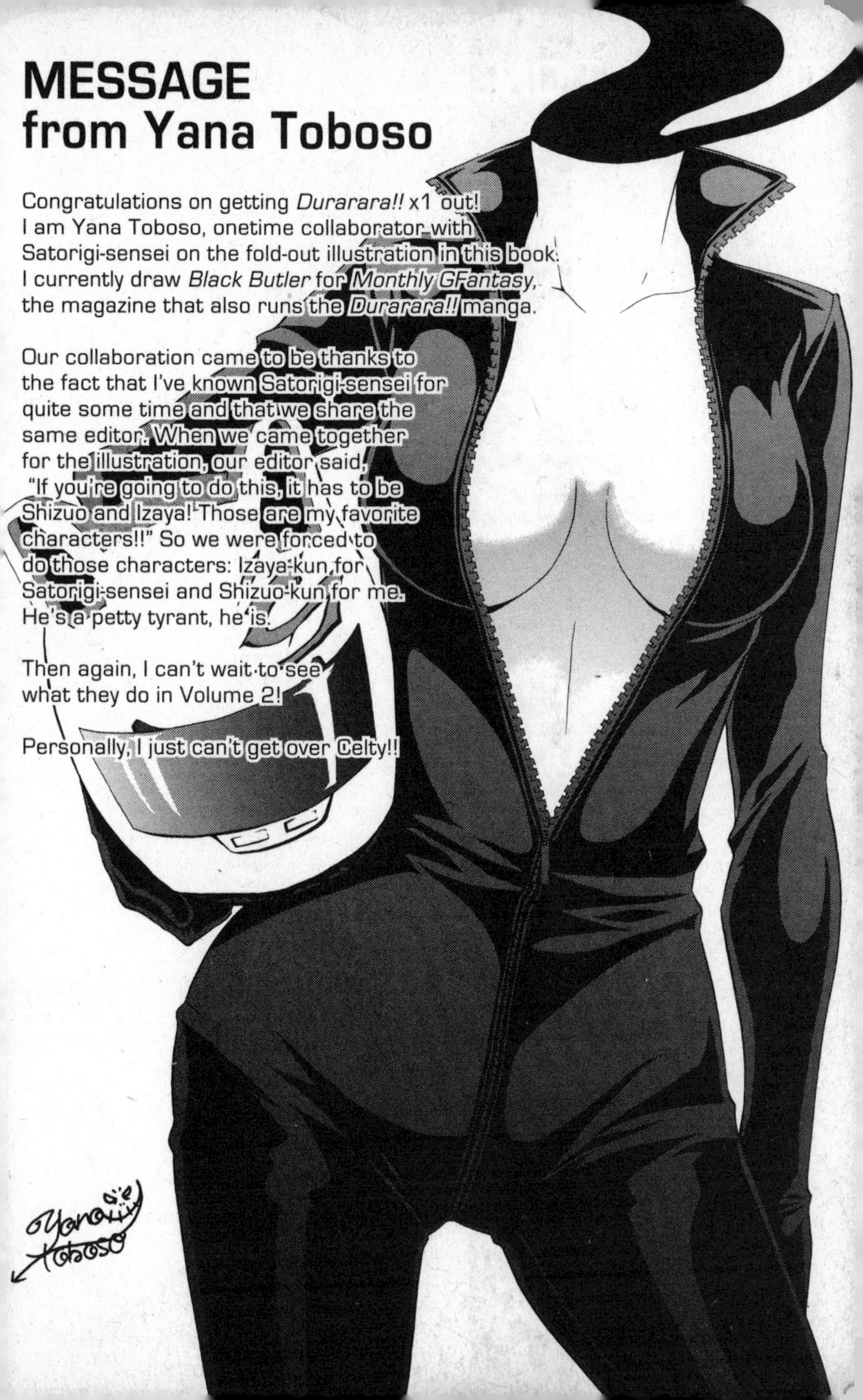
Yana Toboso

TRANSLATION NOTES

COMMON HONORIFICS

No honorific: Indicates familiarity or closeness; if used without permission or reason, addressing someone this way would constitute an insult.

-san: The Japanese equivalent of Mr./Mrs./Miss. If a situation calls for politeness, this is the fail-safe honorific.

-kun: Used most often when referring to boys, this indicates affection or familiarity. Occasionally used by older men among their peers, but it may also be used by anyone referring to a person of lower standing.

PAGE 15

Tobu/Seibu: Tobu and Seibu are two major railway companies in Japan that both have lines running through Ikebukuro Station, which is the second-busiest train station in the world after Shinjuku Station, also in Tokyo. Tobu and Seibu have similar names, literally stemming from East Musashi and West Musashi respectively, where Musashi is an archaic name for the province where most of modern Tokyo is located. The two railways do indeed have platforms at misleading ends of the station (Tobu on the west side, Seibu on the east side) and manage department stores outside of those exits.

PAGE 17

Sunshine City: A little "city within a city" in Ikebukuro, Sunshine City is a tightly constructed series of buildings that forms a shopping/entertainment complex. There are hotels, restaurants, aquariums, museums, and a theme park called Namja Town run by video game developer Namco.

PAGE 26

Magic: The "magic" joke here was originally a reference to "Seal" magic within the universe of the *Shana* (*Shakugan no Shana*) novel/anime series. The *Shana* novels were published in Japan by Dengeki Bunko, the light novel publishing arm of ASCII Media Works and the Japanese publisher of the *Durarara!!* novels.

PAGES 38-39

Lord of the Crimson Realm: A class of ultra-powerful characters in the world of *Shana*. They have special powers over the Crimson Realm, which is the magical world in opposition to the real world.

PAGE 91

Saki: A manga series about the competitive world of high school mah-jongg told through the eyes of teenager Saki Miyanaga. It's published in *Young Gangan* magazine, which is a sister magazine of sorts to *Monthly GFantasy*, the magazine that runs the manga of *Durarara!!* Stealth Momo and the captain of Kazekoshi Girls School are characters in the series.

Toranoana: A manga-oriented store that specializes in retail sales of *doujinshi* (fan-created issues of manga). Due to its heavy presence in Tokyo and prominence within the otaku community, there are often special bonus items such as the kind mentioned here that come with new releases.

PAGE 93

Ushiromiya: The name of an extensive clan of characters in the game/manga/anime series *Umineko no Naku Koro Ni* (*When the Seagulls Cry*), a sequel to the *Higurashi WHEN THEY CRY* series. Though the game is set in the 1980s, the many characters of the Ushiromiya family have archaic and extravagant names, somewhat similar to the way Mikado's name sounds to other Japanese. The family crest is a one-winged eagle. Several manga series have been published based on the original PC game, including at least one from Square Enix, the Japanese publisher of the *Durarara!!* manga.

PAGE 94

Dengeki Bunko: A major publishing line of Japanese light novels, part of the ASCII Media Works company. Dengeki Bunko puts out many novel tie-ins to anime and video game series, as well as producing some highly successful novel lines that have led to media franchises of their own (*Durarara!!*, *Baccano!*, *Kino's Journey*, *Shana*).

PAGE 109

Kirigamine: The name of a brand of air-conditioning units manufactured and sold by Mitsubishi. It is named after a mountain in Japan, meaning "misty peak." Mikado's family name, Ryuugamine, means "dragon peak."

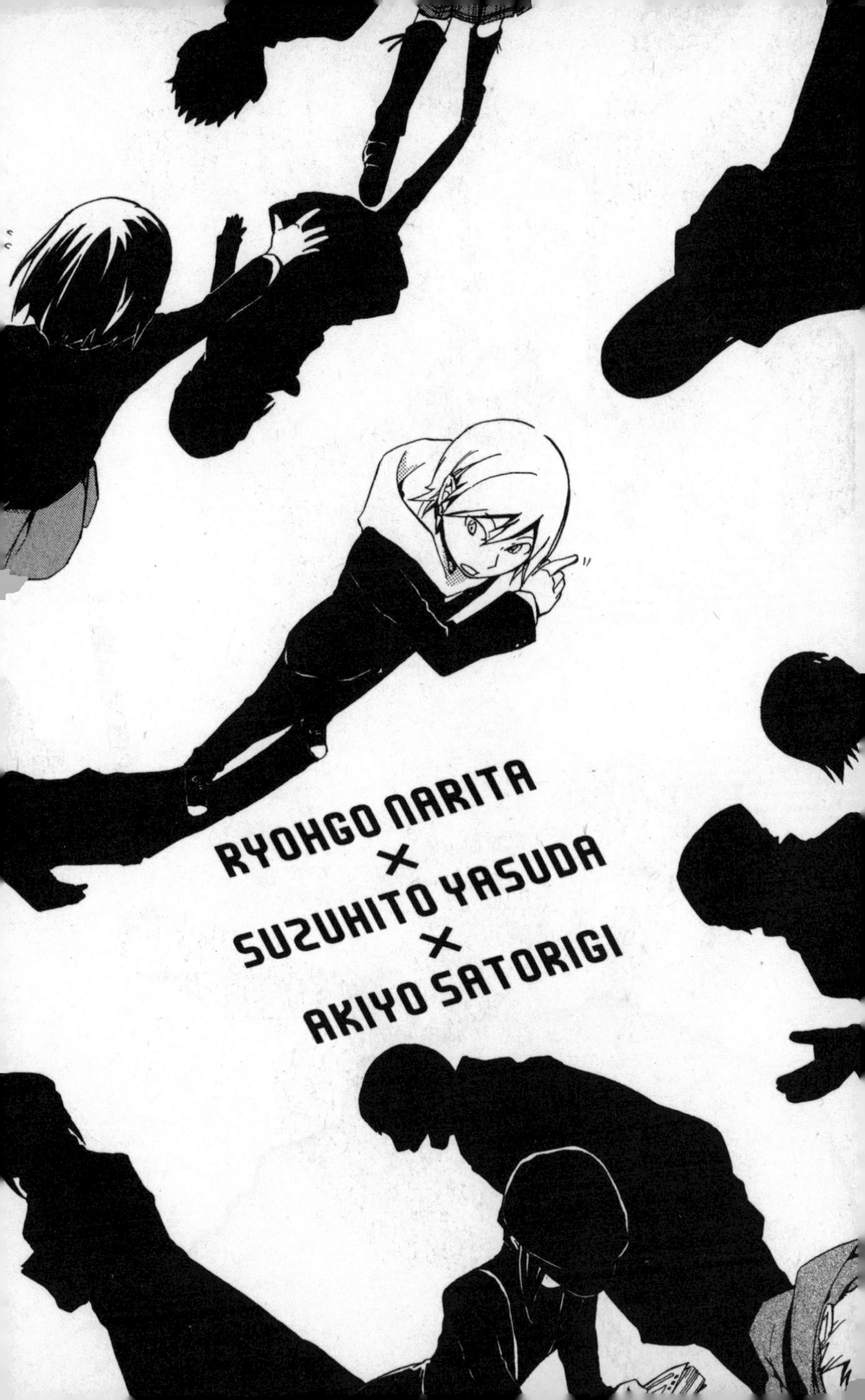
RYOHGO NARITA
×
SUZUHITO YASUDA
×
AKIYO SATORIGI

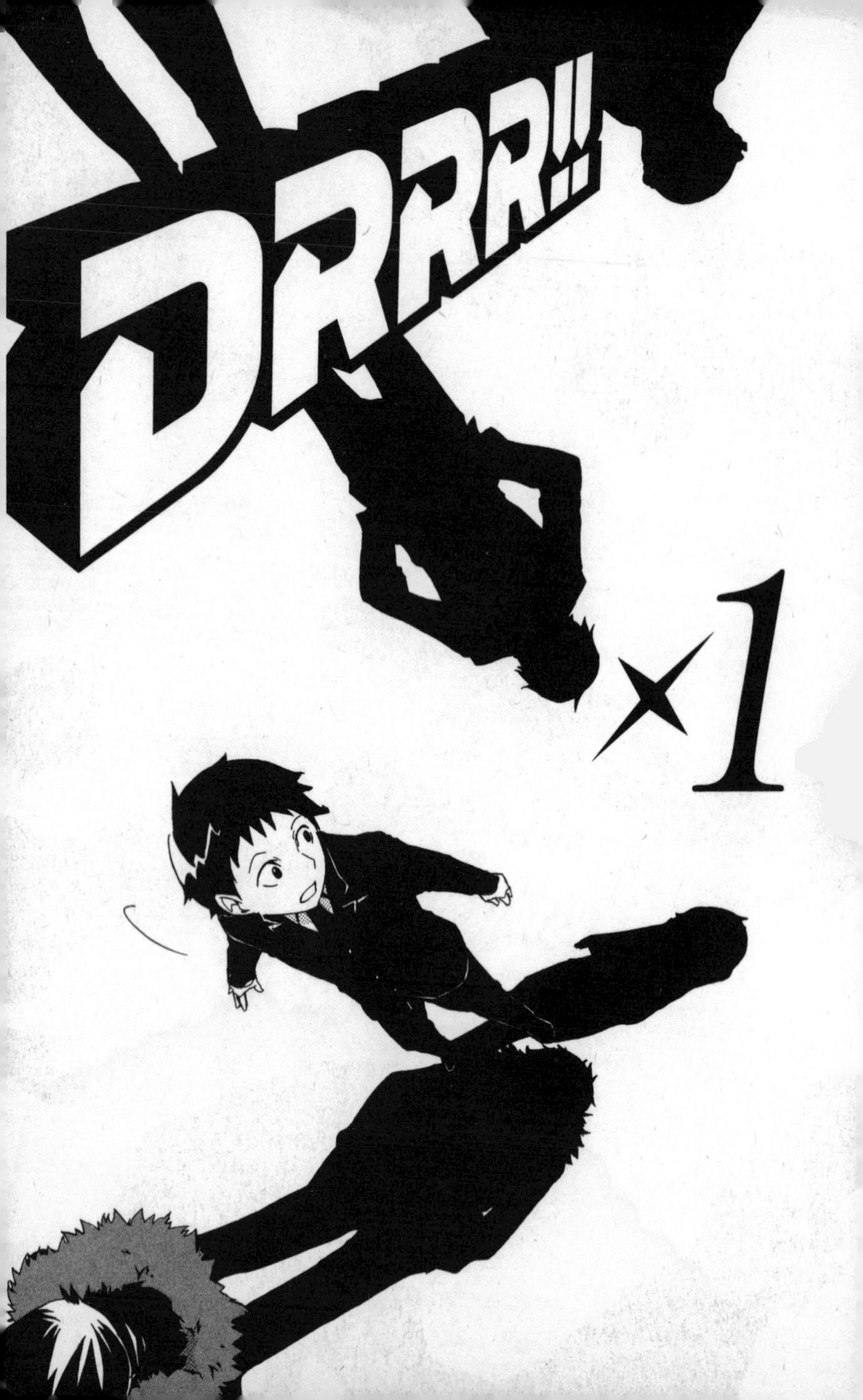
DRRR!!
×1

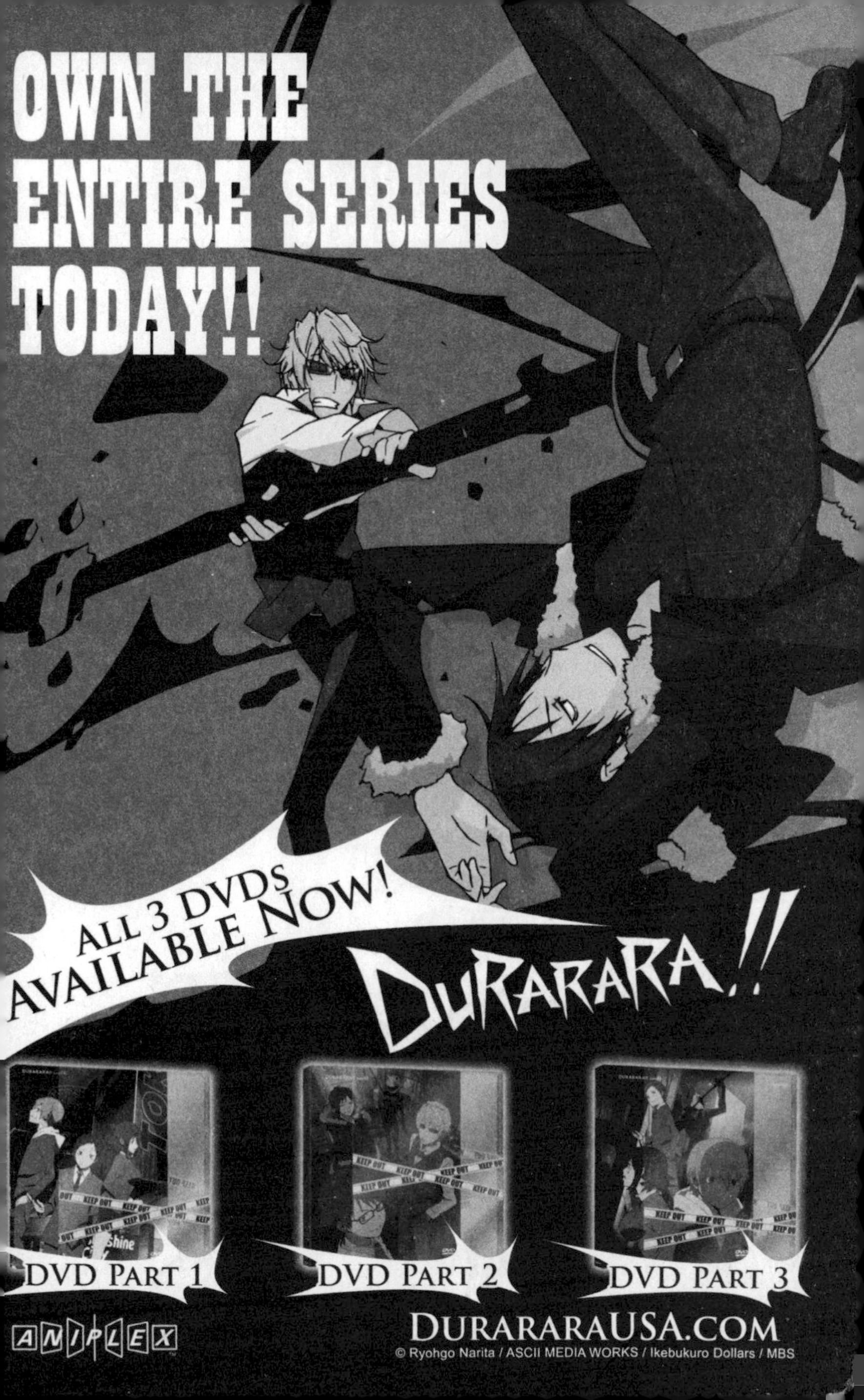
OWN THE ENTIRE SERIES TODAY!!
ALL 3 DVDS AVAILABLE NOW!
DURARARA!!
DVD PART 1
DVD PART 2
DVD PART 3
ANIPLEX
DURARARAUSA.COM
© Ryohgo Narita / ASCII MEDIA WORKS / Ikebukuro Dollars / MBS

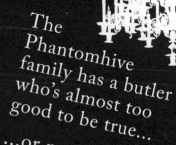

The Phantomhive family has a butler who's almost too good to be true...

...or maybe he's just too good to be human.

Black Butler

YANA TOBOSO

VOLUME 8 IN STORES NOW!

DURARARA!!

RYOHGO NARITA
SUZUHITO YASUDA
AKIYO SATORIGI

Translation: Stephen Paul

Lettering: Lys Blakeslee

This book is a work of fiction. Names, characters, places, and incidents are the product of the author's imagination or are used fictitiously. Any resemblance to actual events, locales, or persons, living or dead, is coincidental.

DURARARA!! Vol. 1 © Ryohgo Narita / ASCII MEDIA WORKS
© 2009 Akiyo Satorigi / SQUARE ENIX CO., LTD. All rights reserved.
First published in Japan in 2009 by SQUARE ENIX CO., LTD. English translation rights arranged with SQUARE ENIX CO., LTD. and Yen Press, LLC through Tuttle-Mori Agency, Inc.

English translation © 2012 by SQUARE ENIX CO., LTD.

Yen Press
1290 Avenue of the Americas
New York, NY 10104

Visit us at yenpress.com
facebook.com/yenpress
twitter.com/yenpress
yenpress.tumblr.com
instagram.com/yenpress

First Yen Press Edition: January 2012

Yen Press is an imprint of Yen Press, LLC.
The Yen Press name and logo are trademarks of Yen Press, LLC.

The publisher is not responsible for websites (or their content) that are not owned by the publisher.

ISBN: 978-0-316-20490-3

20 19 18 17

WOR

Printed in the United States of America